Churches respond to BEM

Official responses to the "Baptism, Eucharist and Ministry" text, Vol. 1

Edited by Max Thurian

Faith and Order Paper 129
World Council of Churches, Geneva

Cover design: Michael Dominguez

ISBN 2-8254-0845-X

© 1986 World Council of Churches, 150 route de Ferney,
1211 Geneva 20, Switzerland

Typeset by Thomson Press (India) Ltd., New Delhi

Printed in Switzerland

CONTENTS

PREFACE

The convergence document on "Baptism, Eucharist and Ministry" (BEM) has received extraordinarily wide attention from the member churches of the World Council of Churches and beyond. Accepted by the Faith and Order Commission of the WCC at its meeting in Lima, Peru, in 1982, this text has stimulated reflection and discussion at all levels of the life of the churches. Through this "reception process" BEM contributes to the renewal of the thinking and life of the churches and to the establishment of new relations and the deepening of existing relations between churches.

The official responses of the churches to BEM are a significant expression of this broader reception process, but they do not mark the conclusion of this process. Rather, they will, in many cases, provide additional encouragement for further reflection and exchange.

A considerable number of official responses to BEM have already been received; we expect to receive more during 1986. It is now the task of the Faith and Order Commission to prepare an overview of the BEM reception process and an evaluation of the responses, both official and non-official. One element in thus working towards a "response to the responses" is to provide also a documentation of the official reactions to BEM. There exists an obvious interest to see how churches of different traditions and living in highly diverse contexts see the significance of BEM, feel its impact and respond to its content.

The present volume begins this task of documentation. It contains a fairly representative selection of the responses from churches belonging to different Christian traditions. Responses from Catholic Bishops' Conferences are not included because these have to be collected by Rome's Secretariat for Promoting Christian Unity, before a common official response from the Roman Catholic Church to BEM is offered. The Faith and Order Commission will continue this documentation of responses, although because of the large number of texts, we may not be able to publish all of them in the present form.

This documentation, prepared by our Faith and Order colleague Frère Max Thurian, who carries special responsibility for the evaluation of the BEM process, will indicate something of the seriousness and ecumenical commitment with which the churches are considering this important ecumenical document. It will witness to the important advances already made on our ecumenical pilgrimage and will remind us of the task which still requires our concentrated efforts.

Geneva, December 1985   Günther Gassmann
                               Director, WCC Faith and Order
                               Secretariat

Introduction

THE LIMA DOCUMENT ON "BAPTISM, EUCHARIST AND MINISTRY": THE EVENT AND ITS CONSEQUENCES

MAX THURIAN

The Lima document on "Baptism, Eucharist and Ministry" is now being studied in the different churches of the World Council of Churches and in the Roman Catholic Church. Whatever the character of their responses and comments may be, the Lima document is already an event unique in the annals of the church since the separations of East and West. For the first time, all the Christian churches have been asked for their considered opinion concerning a doctrinal document which touches their faith at the deepest level. That so demanding a doctrinal text should so swiftly meet with such a widespread welcome shows that this document responds to a deeply felt need in the life of the churches which requires them to reflect on the fundamental faith they share. Despite the predictions that a theological text of this kind could no longer grip the attention of ordinary Christians, the Lima document has become a best-seller.

So far the document has been published in the following languages: English, French, German, Russian, Italian, Spanish (Castilian), Catalan, Dutch, Norwegian, Swedish, Finnish, Danish, Greek, Romanian, Portuguese, Czech, Polish, Korean, Malayalam, Hindi, Malagasy, Icelandic, Hungarian, Arabic, Chinese, Japanese. Versions in Indonesian, Thai and Swahili are in preparation. A great many parish groups are studying the text with considerable interest. A number of study guides have been published in several languages to interpret the document for ordinary Christians.

The interest taken in the Lima document shows, if any demonstration was needed, that ordinary Christians, lay people as well as clergy, remain keenly alert to the problems of their faith and to the way the church answers these problems today. Even if some churches

---

● This text has been translated from the French by the WCC Language Service.

feel obliged to maintain a certain reserve towards it, the Lima document exists as the harvest of a long and patient process of reflection recognized by over a hundred theologians representing all the Christian confessions in Lima in January 1982 as ripe enough for presentation to all the churches. Since that historic day, the Lima document has become a key text for all Christians. In the ecumenical dialogue between Christians it is now no longer possible to discuss baptism, eucharist and ministry without making this document the basis of reflection.

This document shows that when Christians set out together to probe their common faith with the firm resolve to continue probing until they have rediscovered their visible unity, by the grace of the Holy Spirit something happens. This "conciliar" effort to recover our unity in the faith is the price to be paid for the renewal of the Christian life. Ecclesial communities refusing to make this effort and the sacrifices it entails and preferring to rest content with their confessional traditions would certainly be in danger of failing to experience the renewal which is indispensable for their growth.

Each church is expected to answer three important questions about the Lima document:

—To what extent can it recognize in this document the faith of the church through the ages?
—What consequences can it draw from this document for its relations and dialogues with other churches, particularly with those churches which also recognize the document as an expression of the apostolic faith?
—What guidance can it take from this document for its worship, educational, ethical, and spiritual life and witness?

What the churches are invited to experience and undertake, therefore, is an authentic ecumenical conversion, the enrichment of their own spiritual tradition from the patrimony of others, the surrender of all that separates them from the others and is not required by a faithful obedience to the word of God. What we are invited to do is not to judge the Lima document in the light of our distinctive confessional tradition but rather to expose ourselves to the judgment and stimulus of those aspects of the faith of the undivided church of which this document reminds us.

An ecumenical tradition

The Lima document is the fruit of a long history of study and dialogue. Four world conferences (Lausanne 1927, Edinburgh 1937, Lund 1952, Montreal 1963) and ten plenary meetings of the Faith and Order Commission (from Chichester 1949 to Lima 1982, taking in on the way the meetings in Bristol 1967 and Accra 1974 which were important stages in the evolution of the Lima document) signpost the course of this history. As one who has been directly involved in this quest since 1949, I can testify that the representation of the churches in this work has been truly universal, with Orthodox theologians and, after the Second Vatican Council, Roman Catholic theologians also. The history of Faith and Order and of "Baptism, Eucharist, and Ministry" falls naturally into two distinct periods, corresponding to two different styles in the methods employed.

The first period, from Lausanne 1927 to Bristol 1967, falls into two stages: that of doctrinal comparisons between the definitions given by the different churches of their own identity (Lausanne 1927 to Lund 1952), and that of common building on the biblical and Christological foundations (from Lund 1952 to Montreal 1963). With a curtain-raiser at Aarhus in 1964, when the themes of eucharist and ministry were re-examined in the light of Montreal, the second period began in earnest in Bristol in 1967. There the study of the relation between scripture and Tradition was resumed and the systematic study of the eucharist begun. Above all, however, it was realized that there already existed something in the nature of an "ecumenical tradition", developed throughout the successive world conferences and plenary meetings of the Faith and Order Commission. This tradition can be found embedded in the various final reports adopted by the delegates of the different churches. Whereas the first period produced noteworthy individual papers on various themes, in the second period an attempt was made to formulate a consensus on the same themes. Whereas the first period stimulated certain theologians to produce texts which, though ecumenical, carried the hallmark of an individual personality, the second period relied more confidently on group work on the basis of an ecumenical tradition with a genuine doctrinal consensus between the churches as the goal.

The initial drafts which I was asked to produce from 1967 onwards as a basis for this quest for consensus consisted almost entirely of quotations from official reports, arranged in an intelligible theological pattern. The text on the eucharist came first (1967), then the text on baptism (1968) and finally the one on the ministry (1972).[1] In the successive meetings devoted to these three themes, a great many theologians joined in the work of correcting and completing the embryonic Lima document, under the guidance of Dr Lukas Vischer, the then director of the Faith and Order secretariat. After Accra 1974, the document was sent to the churches for their comments. When these responses and proposed changes were evaluated (a hundred and fifty letters were received by the Geneva secretariat), it was possible for a smaller group (the Steering Group) to start putting the final touches to the text on "Baptism, Eucharist and Ministry" (from 1977 onwards).[2]

The ecclesiological conviction underlying this production of the Lima document is that the churches are no less churches when they are brought together by the World Council of Churches in the persons of their representatives than when they meet separately to make a decision. We even dared to believe that when a church is officially represented at an authorized ecumenical meeting, its tradition and witness are enriched by the contribution of the other churches. It is through the sharing of the truth in love that the deepest identity of a church becomes clear and manifest.

This ecclesiological conviction rests on faith in the Holy Spirit who inspires the ecumenical movement. None of the advances made in the dialogue between the churches would ever have been possible without the work of the Holy Spirit who wills and effects the unity of all in the one church of Christ to the glory of God the Father. This ecumenical work of the Holy Spirit in the churches has left clear traces in what can rightly be called an "ecumenical tradition".

This ecumenical tradition, which we believe to be guided by the Holy Spirit, is the fruit of a common "reading" of holy scripture and of the great Tradition interpretative of the word of God, by the churches, in the hope of recovering the visible unity which is the will of Christ. In a sense, it is the application of the ecclesial principle of conciliarity to theological research. It is listening together to what the Spirit is saying to the churches concerning their unity in the fundamental faith. We must emphasize again here that the Roman Catholic Church is involved in this work. While it is not a member of the World Council of Churches, it participates officially in the theological work of the Faith and Order Commission, in which there are twelve Catholic theologians as well as a number of Catholic consultants. Nowhere, therefore, is there a more comprehensive or more ecumenical quest for unity in the faith.

Scripture, Tradition and the church

The Lima document on "Baptism, Eucharist and Ministry" is founded on the word of God; that is certainly its deepest intention. It quotes scripture frequently and the theological argument is controlled by the Bible even where such citations seem absent. The principle of the sovereign authority of holy scripture, vigorously recalled by the Reformation of the sixteenth century, is applied consciously and manifestly in the Lima document. There is no question, however, of a simplistic biblicism treating scripture as if it were an untouchable law. The Lima document takes the word of God as its basis; it reads and interprets scripture within the communion of the whole church and not according to a purely confessional tradition or a particular theological school.

This is where the Tradition (with a capital T) comes in and performs its role as the act whereby the word of God is handed on by the church, as the universal interpretation of holy scripture and as the "sound deposit" of the doctrine (teaching of the truth) which is to be "safeguarded" (pastoral Epistles). The Lima document takes its stand on the word of God contained in holy scripture as sovereign authority in matters of belief; but this submission to the authority of scripture is that of the whole church; it is achieved in the fellowship of all the churches throughout time and space; it is alert to hear what the Spirit is saying to the churches when they live by the word of God, when they read scripture in communion with the fathers in the faith, in the community of all the saints. The Lima document is attentive to the great Tradition of the church, in accord with what the world conference in Montreal (1963) affirmed concerning the relationships between scripture and Tradition.[3] The *sola scriptura* principle was then judged to be an illusion if taken to mean that it was possible to read scripture without any theological presuppositions, without any conditioning confessional tradition, as if the Bible·came to us like a meteor from the sky and was so crystal clear as to have no need of the church to interpret it in the light of the Holy Spirit. The *sola scriptura* principle was wisely reduced to its true proportions: scripture is a sovereign authority in matters of faith but only in the church, i.e. within the authentic and universal Tradition of the word of God, can it be fully understood. As the Montreal report put it:

> Thus we can say that we exist as Christians by the Tradition of the Gospel (the *paradosis* of the *kerygma*) testified in Scripture, transmitted in and by the Church through the power of the Holy Spirit. Tradition taken in this sense is actualized in the preaching of the Word, in the administration of the Sacraments and worship, in Christian teaching and theology, and in mission and witness to Christ by the lives of the members of the Church.[4]

A colloquium of Faith and Order and the Vatican Secretariat for Unity, meeting in Venice in June 1978, summed up this ecumenical view of the relationships between scripture and Tradition by making the most illuminating distinction between the normative apostolic period and the building period of the church, the latter being the period of the church fathers, the creeds, the first liturgies and the main ecumenical councils:

The essential elements of the Christian mystery are known to us through the witness of the apostolic community, transmitted in the Scriptures. These are the fruit of the Gospel and of the action of the Spirit in the primitive Church. On the one hand, they bear witness of the apostolic Church's understanding of the mystery of Christ. On the other hand, however, the truth they transmit could be fully grasped only in the context of the life of that early community faithful to the teaching of the apostles, to the fellowship of the brethren, to the breaking of bread and to prayer (cf. Acts 2.42).... After the normative apostolic period, the Church, bearer of the Spirit but engaged in history, saw itself led to make more explicit the faith it had received from the apostles. What it lived in its liturgy and bore witness to, sometimes to the point of martyrdom, it had to express in terms which would allow it to safeguard its unity and give an account of its hope... This building period is that of the Fathers, of the creeds, of the birth of the great liturgies, of the great councils. [5]

Clearly, therefore, how the Lima document is understood and welcomed by the different churches greatly depends on the ecclesiological doctrine of each of them. The way the study of the Lima document is approached and the assessment made of its theological content will be conditioned by the view taken of the nature of the church. Is the church part of the revelation of God and of the faith of Christians, or is it only the human and social consequence of the gospel message which alone is of decisive importance? Are the foundations of the church's structure given in an apostolic institution issuing from Christ's own words, or does this structure depend solely on the decisions taken by the Christian community living in a given cultural context? Were the fundamental ministries given to the apostolic church with a view to their transmission in a succession faithful to Christ's initial purpose, or has the church the right and the duty to invent these ministries in the light of given circumstances? Does the unity of the church mean visible reconciliation in the fundamental faith, in the sacraments and in the ministries of this faith, or does it mean a brotherly coexistence of believers with divergent views whose dialectic is thought to be essential if the gospel is to be proclaimed in its totality?

Clearly these alternatives represent different ecclesiologies. They could be summed up as follows: Is the church the sign of God's presence, the body of Christ and the temple of the Holy Spirit, or is it merely the gathering of believers who obey the gospel and furnish themselves with ways and means of living, witnessing and praying together? The ecclesiology presupposed by the Lima document and thought of as that of the New Testament (which does not rule out institutional diversity), is definitely a "sacramental" ecclesiology.

The church is the sign of God's presence and the instrument of God's work in the world; it is the body of Christ which unites believers by the word and sacraments; it is the temple of the Holy Spirit in which Christians are sanctified by faith and prayer.

The ecclesiology of the Lima document

A careful reading of the Lima document will disclose the main lines of an ecumenical ecclesiology.

1. The church is the community of the New Covenant which *God* has established between God and God's people (B1, E17); it is a community of faith and life, composed of believers in Christ who have been baptized in the name of the Father, the Son and the Holy Spirit (B12). The church is the body of Christ in which those who follow the Lord are united, liberated and renewed by the Holy Spirit (E19, M1 and 3). The church is communion with God through Jesus Christ in the Holy Spirit (M1). The church is a proclamation and prefiguration of God's kingdom by its announcement of the gospel to the world and its life as the body of Christ; it offers the world a foretaste of the joy and glory of the kingdom (M4), which it receives from the Holy Spirit in the eucharist (E18); it receives the life of the new creation in order to show to the world the image of a new humanity (M18). The church can be described as a priesthood serving the whole of humanity by the proclamation of the gospel, their prayers of intercession and their service (M17). The apostles prefigure the whole church and those entrusted with authority and a specific responsibility in the church (M10). The church is one, holy, catholic and apostolic; it lives in continuity with the apostles and their proclamation (B6, M34). The primary manifestation of the apostolic succession is found in the apostolic tradition of the whole church. The orderly transmission of the ordained ministry is a powerful statement of the continuity of the church (M35). The Spirit keeps the church in the apostolic tradition (M34). The church of all the ages and all places, the church of the saints and martyrs, the catholic church, is manifested in the local church, above all in the celebration of the eucharist (E19). The ministry, and in particular that of the *episkopē*, relates the local church to the universal church (M25).

2. *Christ* is the source of the church's mission and the foundation of its unity (M12). The life of the church is based upon Christ's victory (M2). The saving words and acts of Jesus Christ constitute the life of the church. As witnesses of the life and resurrection of Christ and as his envoys, the apostles are at the origin of the transmission of the gospel. This apostolic tradition connects the church with its origins in Christ and in the college of the apostles (M34). Christ gathers, teaches

and feeds the church (E29, M14). In a variety of ways Christ fulfills his promise to be with his own always, even to the world's end; but the manner of Christ's presence in the eucharist is uniqu: (E13). It is Christ who confers authority on the ordained ministry; it is the Risen Lord who is the true celebrant of ordination and who bestows the gift of the ministry (M15, 39).

3. *The Holy Spirit* unites in a single body those who follow Jesus Christ and sends them as witnesses into the world (M1). The Spirit keeps the church in the truth and guides it in spite of the frailty of its members (M3). The Holy Spirit gives the church diverse and complementary gifts (M5). The church is constituted body of Christ and God's eschatological people by the Holy Spirit through a diversity of gifts and ministries (M23). By the eucharist, the Holy Spirit gives a foretaste of the kingdom of God; the church receives the life of the new creation and the assurance of the Lord's return (E18).

4. The church is continually being built up by the good news of *the gospel* and by the gift of *the sacraments* (M1). The proclaimed *word* is the *anamnesis* of Christ. The celebration of the eucharist normally implies the preaching of the word. The proclamation and teaching of the word of God is part of the specific function of the ministry in the church (M13) whereby the gospel is to be spread and the community built up in love (M6).

Baptism is the sacrament by which believers are incorporated in the body of Christ, filled with the Holy Spirit and united with each individual Christian, with the church of all times and all places (E19, B6). The baptismal unity achieved in the one, holy, catholic and apostolic church bears witness to the love of God which heals and reconciles (B6).

The eucharist, the memorial and sacrament of Christ's unique sacrifice, is the thanksgiving and intercession which the church offers to the Father, in union with the Son, its High Priest and Intercessor who ever lives to make intercession on our behalf (E8, M17). Through the eucharist, a sacrifice of praise, the church speaks on behalf of the whole creation; the eucharist reveals to the world what the world is to become: an offering and act of praise to the Creator, a universal communion in the body of Christ, a kingdom of justice, love and peace in the Holy Spirit (E4). By the eucharist, by communion in the body and blood of Christ really present, the church grows as the body of Christ (E19).

Response and reception

On the basis of the great number of responses and reports received from study groups, individual theologians, or from churches giving their official response, it can be said that on the whole the Lima document is positively welcomed, even if clarifications are called for on specific points. In the light of the questions raised in various quarters, an attempt can be made to define more precisely the significance of the Lima document. As more and more of the official responses come in, other aspects will emerge. Once the evaluation of official responses is completed, it will be possible to indicate the main points of theological convergence, on the one hand and, on the other hand, which themes still require to be probed more deeply with a view to visible unity and real consensus.

The real significance of the "reception" of the Lima document has perhaps not been sufficiently explained. There is no question of "receiving" it in the same way that decisions of the ecumenical councils have formerly been received in the churches, i.e. as texts recognized as authoritative explanations of the word of God. The churches are asked to say whether they recognize in the Lima document "the faith of the church through the ages", whether they are prepared to use it as a basis or framework in their ecumenical dialogues and to embody these texts in their theological and catechetical instruction, their liturgical reforms, and in the spiritual life of communities, parishes, mixed households, ecumenical groups, youth groups, etc....

The decisive underlying purpose of this invitation to the churches to receive the Lima document is a concern for the renewal of all Christians in faith, prayer and a responsible life in this world. It is not a question of establishing uniformity in the life of the churches nor of trying to turn the clock back towards a supposed model of the ideal church. It is a question of discovering whether, in all the diversity of our legitimate and enriching confessional traditions, yet confessing the same fundamental faith of our common creed, we are able and willing to work together for the renewal and unity of the churches. The basis of this work is our one baptism. It demands a common view of the eucharist and a mutual recognition of the ministry, with the hope that we may find ourselves one day at the same table of the Lord who imparts to us his word and his body and blood. This broad process of reception will continue even after our churches have formulated their responses.

The purpose of the Lima document is to encourage our growth in faith with the help of all baptized Christians who long for one and the same eucharist celebrated by communities and ministries reconciled in the church of Christ, visibly gathering all Christians together for a common life and a common witness and service in the world.

The following pages are meant to assist in a better understanding of the Lima document during the process of reception which will still be pursued after the official responses are in.

Baptism: sacrament of the new birth and ecclesial unity of Christians
For the Lima document, baptism is quite evidently a sacrament; in other words an effective liturgical sign, a sign which really effects what it signifies in image or symbol.

> Since the earliest days, baptism has been understood as the sacrament by which believers are incorporated into the body of Christ and are endowed with the Holy Spirit (E19 Commentary).

The document does not contain any explicit definition of the sacrament, but the context clearly implies some such definition as the one just given: the sacrament is a liturgical sign which effectively produces in reality that which it signifies in image or symbol. The term "sign" occurs a number of times in the text, as does the term "seal", which adds the idea that the sacrament marks the person with a spiritual imprint:

> Baptism is the sign of new life through Jesus Christ (B2).... God bestows upon all baptized persons the anointing of the promised Holy Spirit, marks them with a seal and implants in their hearts the first instalment of their inheritance as sons and daughters of God (B5).... Baptism is a sign and seal of our common discipleship (B6).

The sacrament consists of images and symbols which enrich the significance of the sign.

As used in the Lima document, the term "sign" should be understood in the emphatic sense of "effective sign". This is equivalent to the term "sacrament". It does not minimize the reality which is present and at work; it is intended to affirm this reality as efficacious in God's sight, in a mysterious way and not according to the flesh or as an act of magic. The document strongly affirms the spiritual reality which is the fruit of the sacrament, of the effective sign: baptism *is* our incorporation into Christ, our entry into the new covenant, a gift of God. "It unites the one baptized with Christ and with his people" (B2). For the baptized person, whether adult or infant, an event takes place; this is not simply a symbolic act making explicit individual conversion, the divine pardon and inner cleansing owed to the faith of the believer. As we shall see, there is indeed a close connection between faith and baptism; but it is not primarily a question of the believer signifying his faith by baptism but rather that baptism, divine action, effects the participation of the baptized person in Christ's death and resurrection, converts, pardons and cleanses, gives the Spirit, incorporates into the body of Christ, anticipates the life of the kingdom of God in the personal life of each believer. We have just recalled the five main meanings of baptism indicated in the Lima document which correspond to five aspects of the spiritual reality conveyed by the sacrament of baptism: the baptized are:

> fully identified with the death of Christ... are buried with him and are raised here and now to a new life... those baptized are pardoned, cleansed and sanctified by Christ.... God bestows on all baptized persons the anointing of the promised Holy Spirit... Through baptism, Christians are brought into union with Christ, with each other and with the Church of every time and place... Baptism... is a sign of the Kingdom of God and of the life of the world to come... (B3–7).

What the sacrament of baptism proclaims, therefore, is the initiative of God in the gift of the new life; this new life is not the fruit of our efforts nor even of our confession of faith but of the Holy Spirit who converts the heart. Baptism emphasizes the prevenience of the grace bestowed over the faith confessed; it affirms the justification by faith which precedes the obedience of works.

The Lima document has already been criticized as being "too sacramental". It will certainly be necessary to go further into the concept of sacrament as presented in the document so as to demonstrate that there is no great gulf here between the catholic churches and those of the Reformation but that the sacramental reality of the Christian life, far from being a form of natural religion with tendencies towards magical and mechanistic ideas, is, on the contrary, the liturgical form of faith in God's sovereignty and grace.

While affirming quite clearly the efficacy of the sacrament of baptism, the Lima document also insists just as clearly on the necessity of faith as fruit and fulfilment of the sacrament:

> The necessity of faith for the reception of the salvation embodied and set forth in baptism is acknowledged by all churches. Personal commitment is necessary for responsible membership in the body of Christ (B8).

Baptism is related not just to one particular moment at the start of the Christian life but also to "life-long growth into Christ" (B9). The faith which necessarily accompanies the baptism of infants is the faith of the Christian community with its responsibility of supervising the development of the personal faith of the baptized person. In the case of the baptism of an adult where the latter confesses his faith personally, the Christian community is likewise deeply implicated in this commitment and in the responsibility it entails.

The Lima text expresses the hope that churches will recognize adult baptism and infant baptism as "equivalent alternatives" (B12, Commentary) according to the historical, cultural and religious situations. It recognizes here the legitimacy of a practice hallowed by the Tradition even if "baptism upon personal profession of faith is the most clearly attested pattern in the New Testament documents" (B11). Baptism always takes place "in the Church as the community of faith" (B12). When it is an adult who is baptized, the latter will confess his faith personally; when it is an infant, the personal response will be made later on in the baptized person's life. In both cases the baptized person will have to grow in understanding of the faith. In both cases, the Christian community pledges itself "to provide an environment of witness and service" (B12).

Finally, the Lima document deals with the role of the Holy Spirit in the sacrament of baptism. "All agree that Christian baptism is in water and the Holy Spirit" (B14). The Easter mystery (Christ's death and resurrection) is inseparable from the pentecostal gift of the Spirit.

The sign of the gift of the Spirit is understood in a variety of ways: the water rite itself, anointing, imposition of hands, confirmation... For all the churches, the problem of the sequence of the acts of Christian initiation arises: water baptism, chrismation and first communion. The Lima document stresses the importance of re-discovering the symbolic dimensions of the baptismal mystery: the act of immersion can express more vividly the believer's dying and rising again with Christ (B18), the imposition of hands or chrismation brings out more forcefully the gift of the Spirit, the sign of the cross on the forehead recalls more vividly "the Holy Spirit who is the instalment and pledge of what is yet to come when God has fully redeemed those whom he has made his own" (B19).

The Lima document highlights the unity of faith in the sacrament of baptism and stresses that "our one baptism into Christ constitutes a call to the churches to overcome their divisions and visibly manifest their fellowship" (B6). It ties in here with the teaching of the Second Vatican Council for which baptism is a sacrament of Christian unity. Since baptism incorporates all Christians into the body of Christ, they all form part of the one church of God and are under obligation to manifest this unity visibly. Their divisions contradict the one baptism which has established fellowship between them and they must do everything in their power to show once again their visible unity, especially in the celebration of the eucharist and the reconciliation of their ministries. The need for the churches to recover their eucharistic unity on the basis of their baptismal unity is at the very core of all ecumenical work.

The eucharist: trinitarian mystery at the heart of the church's life
The celebration of the eucharist is the central act of the church's
worship and always includes both the proclamation of the word and
the celebration of the sacrament (E1,3). When the Lima document
speaks of the eucharist, therefore, it always has in view the
sacramental meal of proclamation and celebration instituted by
Jesus. It cannot be justly accused, as it has been more than once, of
emphasizing the sacrament at the expense of the word; there is no
celebration of the eucharist without a proclamation of the word in
one form or another. The eucharist, word *and* sacrament, is not just a
family meal nor just a fellowship meeting. It is a liturgical and
sacramental meal instituted by Jesus following the Jewish tradition of
the passover meal. There is also continuity between the eucharist and
the meals in which Jesus shared during his earthly ministry and which
were signs heralding the kingdom of God (for example, the feeding of
the multitude) as well as with the meals in which Jesus shared after his
resurrection, when the Lord made himself known to his disciples in the
breaking of the bread.

> The eucharist is essentially the sacrament of the gift which God makes to
> us in Christ through the power of the Holy Spirit (E2).

This gift of salvation is received through communion in Christ's body
and blood under the signs of bread and wine: every member of the
church, the body of Christ, is renewed by this communion in which he
or she is given the assurance of the forgiveness of sins (Matt. 26:28)
and the pledge of eternal life (John 6:51–58). The church as
community is likewise renewed by the eucharist: God himself is at
work here giving life to the body of Christ.

Having first shown the origins of the institution of the eucharist
by Jesus and pointed out its deep significance as sacrament of Christ's
body and blood, the Lima document unfolds the main significations
of the eucharist and to do so adopts a trinitarian pattern: thanksgiving
to the Father, the memorial of Christ, and the invocation of the Spirit. It
then brings out the ecclesiological dimension and eschatological
horizon of the eucharist and concludes with some liturgical reflections
concerning its celebration.

The eucharist is a sacrifice or an offering of thanksgiving and praise
to God the Father. Firstly, thanksgiving or benediction (the *berakah*
of the Old Covenant), "by which the Church expresses its thankfulness for all God's benefits" (E3).

It is common knowledge that the word "eucharist" means
"thanksgiving". It is thus the primary significance of eucharist which
furnishes the sacrament with its most beautiful name. The eucharist is

also a sacrifice of praise (the *todah* of the Old Testament) in which the church hymns God's glory on behalf of the whole creation. In every eucharist the created and reconciled world is present "in the bread and wine, in the persons of the faithful, and in the prayers they offer for themselves and for all people" (E4). The words of the offertory are recalled: the bread and wine are the fruits of the earth and of the labour of men and women; they are presented to the Father in faith and thanksgiving. Only through Christ, with him and in him, is this sacrifice of praise possible for Christians: Christ unites them to himself, to his own praise and intercession, so that the sacrifice of praise to the Father is offered by Christ.

> The eucharist thus signifies what the world is to become: an offering and hymn of praise to the Creator, a universal communion in the body of Christ, a kingdom of justice, love and peace in the Holy Spirit (E4).

This aspect of the eucharist, as offering or sacrifice of thanksgiving and praise, is not self-evident for all the churches. It goes back to the biblical tradition and to the first great liturgies of the church. It makes it possible for the order of creation to be united with the order of redemption. Yet the Reformation, probably because of abuses, reacted against this sacrificial aspect and placed the primary emphasis on the eucharist as gift of God and the presence of Christ.

> The eucharist is the memorial of the crucified and risen Christ, i.e. the living and effective sign of his sacrifice, accomplished once and for all on the cross and still operative on behalf of all humankind. The biblical idea of memorial as applied to the eucharist refers to this present efficacy of God's work when it is celebrated by God's people in a liturgy (E5).

This paragraph sums up very clearly the doctrine of the memorial, which is a most important element in the Lima document and a key to the understanding of the whole chapter on the eucharist. The memorial (or *anamnesis*) is not a simple recollection on the part of the human memory, nor is it simply a recalling of events in the earthly life of Christ and in particular of his sacrifice on the cross, nor a reminder of their significance for today. It is "the Church's effective proclamation of God's mighty acts and promises" (E7); it is the actualization of the sacrifice on the cross whereby we are made contemporaries of that sacrifice. In union with the Son, our High Priest and Intercessor (Rom. 8:34; Heb. 7:25), the church presents to the Father the memorial of the sacrifice of Jesus the Christ as its prayer that "the benefits of these acts" may be given "to every human being" (E8). The Lima document enunciates this doctrine of the memorial in two important sentences:

> The eucharist is the sacrament of the unique sacrifice of Christ who ever lives to make intercession for us... In the memorial of the eucharist... the Church offers its intercession in communion with Christ, our great High Priest (E8).

The commentary on this paragraph seeks to understand the Roman Catholic doctrine of the propitiatory sacrifice and expresses the hope that, in the light of the biblical conception of memorial, all churches might want to review the old controversies about the eucharistic sacrifice.

At this point the Lima document tackles the theme of Christ's real presence in the eucharist, since this theme is at one and the same time connected with the argument about the memorial of Christ and with that about the invocation of the Spirit.

> The eucharistic meal is the sacrament of the body and blood of Christ, the sacrament of his real presence... But Christ's mode of presence in the eucharist is unique... The Church confesses Christ's real, living and active presence in the eucharist (E13).

The commentary on this paragraph 13, as well as that on paragraph 15, lists the various ways of interpreting this real presence of Christ. Are these different ways complementary? That will be for the churches to judge in their responses. It is clear, however, that the Lima document offers a realistic view of this real presence.

> What Christ declared is true, and this truth is fulfilled every time the eucharist is celebrated... (E13).

> Many churches believe that by the words of Jesus and by the power of the Holy Spirit, the bread and wine of the eucharist become, in a real though mysterious manner, the body and blood of the risen Christ, i.e. of the living Christ present in all his fullness (E13 Commentary).

This real presence of Christ is the fruit of the words of Jesus, the fulfilment of a promise, and the fruit of the action of the Holy Spirit, an effective power.

> The Spirit makes the crucified and risen Christ really present to us in the eucharistic meal, fulfilling the promise contained in the words of institution.... The Holy Spirit... makes the historical words of Jesus present and alive (E14).

Jesus' words of institution and the invocation of the Holy Spirit are intimately related in the eucharist:

> It is in virtue of the living word of Christ and by the power of the Holy Spirit that the bread and wine become the sacramental signs of Christ's body and blood. They remain so for the purpose of communion (E15).

The so-called Lima Liturgy, which was prepared in order to provide an illustration of the teaching of the Lima document, expresses, therefore, the relationship between the Spirit and Christ, between the *epiklesis* and the institution, as follows:

O God, Lord of the universe,
You are holy and Your glory is beyond measure.
Upon Your eucharist send the life-giving Spirit,
Who spoke by Moses and the prophets,
Who overshadowed the Virgin Mary with grace,
Who descended upon Jesus in the river Jordan
and upon the Apostles on the day of Pentecost.
May the outpouring of this Spirit of Fire
transfigure this thanksgiving meal
that this bread and wine may become for us
the body and blood of Christ...
May this Creator Spirit accomplish the words
of Your beloved son,
Who, in the night in which He was betrayed...

In the paragraphs on the ecclesiological dimension of the eucharist, it is emphasized that communion in the body and blood of Christ is at the same time communion in the body of Christ, the church. The eucharist makes the faithful one with all communicants at all times and in all places. The celebration of the eucharist is always related to the whole church and thus implies a liturgical, ministerial and ethical discipline which takes the sister churches into account. One important paragraph, which in its original form was proposed by an Orthodox, shows the ethical consequences of the eucharist, which embraces every aspect of human life:

All kinds of injustice, racism, separation and lack of freedom are radically challenged when we share in the body and blood of Christ (E20).

There is an eschatological dimension to the eucharist; it is a foretaste of the kingdom of God, which is often symbolized as a meal; it is a foretaste of the final renewal of the creation. The eucharist is the festival in which the church thanks God for the signs of renewal already present in the world "wherever the grace of God is manifest and human beings work for justice, love and peace" (E22).

Finally, the Lima document examines a number of liturgical problems. It suggests a pattern for the eucharistic liturgy, one which has been adopted in the Lima Liturgy, an experimental liturgy; it nevertheless rejects any attempt to impose liturgical uniformity, since "a certain liturgical diversity compatible with our common eucharistic faith is recognized as a healthy and enriching fact" (E27, 28).

In most churches, the presidency at the eucharistic celebration is entrusted to an ordained minister who is a sign of Christ presiding— Christ who is the "shepherd who leads the people of God, the prophet who announces the Word of God, the priest who celebrates the mystery of God" (E29). The minister who presides at the eucharist "represents the divine initiative and expresses the connection of the local community with other local communities in the universal Church" (E29).

The Lima document urges frequent celebration of the eucharist and frequent communion, at least every Sunday. It then comes to the delicate problem of the reservation of the consecrated elements. It expresses the hope that mutual respect will be the rule between churches which follow different practices here; at the same time, it insists that in any case respect be shown for the bread and wine consecrated in the eucharist, i.e. by consuming them or using them for the communion of the sick (E32). The chapter ends with the hope that "the increased mutual understanding" expressed in the Lima document may "allow some churches to attain a greater measure of eucharistic communion among themselves and so bring closer the day when Christ's divided people will be visibly reunited around the Lord's Table" (E33).

The ministry: service of Christ in the church

1. The calling of the whole people of God
God our Creator and Father summons all humankind to become his people in the midst of a broken world. The call of God which constitutes the church is universal: no human being is excluded from it. Right from the beginning of this chapter on the ministry, the people of God is viewed in its widest extent; it can gather in one the whole of humanity. God's call and the church's ministry, therefore, are addressed to all human beings; their object is the whole world in all its dividedness. The church is not apart from the world; it is in the world and the world is in the church. The church's ministry concerns the whole cosmos.

In order to summon all human beings to become God's people, God chose first of all Israel, a typical nation, symbol of what the whole of humanity was to become, a first sacrament of the word and presence of God, the womb from which would come the Messiah, the Christ, in whom the Father will speak in a unique and decisive way. Jesus the Christ, Son of God, identifies himself with humanity and gives himself as a sacrifice for the whole of humanity. His life, his ministry, his death and his resurrection are the foundation of the church, a new community constantly constructed by the gospel and the sacraments. The Holy Spirit unites Christ's faithful together and sends them into the world as witnesses. The ministry of the whole church, therefore, continuous with that of Israel, is in communion with that of Christ. Its basic purpose is the mission in all the world, preaching the word of God and celebrating the sacraments of God's presence and God's work (M1).

The church's life and ministry spring from the victory of the crucified and risen Christ over the powers of evil and death. Having won this victory by the resurrection, Christ offers forgiveness to all human beings, calls them to repentance, delivers them from destruction.

Because of the resurrection of Christ, all can repent and devote themselves to the praise of God and the service of the neighbour. The victory of Christ's resurrection is the source of a new life in freedom, reconciliation and love. The risen Christ leads believers to look forward in eager hope to the kingdom of God in which everything in this world will be made new. The purpose of God is through the church's ministry to enable all human beings to share these blessings in the fellowship of the body of Christ (M2).

The Holy Spirit given to those who believe in the risen Christ unites them in a single body, the church, and empowers them to live by his renewing and liberating power. By the Spirit, human beings are called to faith, believers are sanctified and have the gifts of the Spirit showered on them, the baptized are consecrated for witness to the gospel and the service of their brothers and sisters of the whole human family. The Holy Spirit "keeps the Church in the truth and guides it despite the frailty of its members" (M3).

The church proclaims the coming of the kingdom of God by announcing the good news of the word to the world; by its very existence as the body of Christ, it prefigures this kingdom of justice and peace. The church's ministry is thus accomplished by the word of God which it proclaims and by the life of the Risen Lord which shines through it. All the members of the church, the body of Christ, confess their faith by giving account of the hope that is in them, by showing a love imbued with compassion, by sharing the joys and sorrows of their fellow human beings. They struggle for freedom and dignity for all alongside the oppressed. By this mission and this ministry in the various political, social and cultural contexts of this world, the members of the body of Christ convey to all human beings a foretaste of the kingdom of God and are radiant with its joy and its glory (M4).

For the accomplishment of this ministry of the whole people of God, the Holy Spirit bestows a variety of complementary gifts on the church: "gifts of communicating the Gospel in word and deed, gifts of healing, gifts of praying, gifts of teaching and learning, gifts of serving, gifts of guiding and following, gifts of inspiration and vision" (M5). Every member of the body of Christ is summoned to discover with the aid of the church the gifts he or she has received and has a duty to use these gifts to build up the ecclesial community and to serve the world to which the church is sent on its mission (M5).

The starting point for reflection on the various ordained ministries in the church, therefore, must be the calling of the whole people of God. To achieve the reconciliation and unity of these ministries, therefore, we must seek to discover how, in accordance with the will of God, the institution of Christ our Saviour and the guidance of the Holy Spirit, the life and ministry of the church are to be understood and ordered so that the gospel may be proclaimed and furthered and the Christian community built up as a living sign of the love of God (M6).

2. The church and the ordained ministry

If the church as the people of God and body of Christ is to accomplish its universal mission and global ministry, it needs people who have received a calling and gift of the Holy Spirit. These people have the public, permanent and continuing responsibility of fulfilling on behalf of Christ and of the church, that part of the ministry common to the whole people of God which is necessary if the royal and prophetic priesthood of all the members of the body of Christ is to be alerted, guarded and edified. By their ministry, these people show that the Christian community depends in a fundamental way on Christ the High Priest and Sovereign Pastor. These people represent the Servant Christ in the servant church so that all the faithful may become servants of one another and servants of their sisters and brothers in the entire human family. The ministry of these people is a sort of focal point unifying all the various gifts and services received and exercised by all the members of the body of Christ. Without the ministry of these particular people, the church could not live nor accomplish its mission and ministry. The ministry of the church cannot be exercised globally by the whole company of believers; it must have organs by which to express itself; it needs people to proclaim the word, to preside at the celebration of the sacraments and of the eucharist in particular, to lead the Christian community in its life and witness. The ministry of such persons, who receive ordination, is "constitutive for the life and witness of the Church"; without this ministry of ordained persons, the people of God or body of Christ cannot exist visibly as church nor make the witness of the gospel heard (M8).

The church has never been without the ministry of responsible persons vested with a special authority in accordance with the gift of the Holy Spirit they have received. Jesus chose and sent disciples (Matt. 10:1–18). The primitive church recognized the twelve as having a special role, that of witnesses to the life and resurrection of Christ (Acts 1:21–26); they are the community's guides in the teaching, in brotherly communion, in the breaking of bread, in prayer (Acts 2:42–47;6:2–6). The twelve and the other apostles show that from the very beginning of the church's life, in accordance with the will and institution of Christ, there were always particular persons within the Christian community who were called and appointed by the Lord to perform roles of a distinctive kind compared with the people of God as a whole.

Called by Jesus, the twelve represent the twelve tribes of Israel (Luke 22:30), the renewed Israel in all its fullness and completeness, the whole church; they represent the entire people of God, but they perform a particular personal ministry within this people. At one and the same time the apostles represent the whole church at its beginnings and are persons entrusted with a particular ministry within this church. The apostles are witnesses of the resurrection: in this respect, their role is unique and non-transferable. But they also prefigure those who will subsequently be invested with a specific authority and responsibility in the church; in this respect, as foreshadowing the personal ministries, their role is typical and transferable. The church as a whole can therefore be said to be founded on the apostles and the particular personal ministries can also be said to be founded on those of the apostles, as the first to proclaim the gospel, first to guide the church in the doctrine of the word of God, in the celebration of the eucharist, in the life of prayer and in the brotherly fellowship of sharing and service (Acts 2: 42–47). The whole church therefore succeeds to the apostles, insofar as the latter represent the new Israel, and the particular ministries of the word, the sacraments and the unity of the Christian community, also succeed to the apostles, insofar as the latter performed specific ministries within the primitive Christian community.

Christ chose, called and sent the apostles at the beginning of the church's life; he continued and continues, by the Holy Spirit, to choose, call and send individuals whom the church ordains to particular ministries (M11). Primarily, therefore, the apostolic succession is a succession in the choosing, calling and mission of Christians ordained by the church in the power of the Holy Spirit to assume responsibility for the gospel, the sacraments and ecclesial unity, as successors of the apostles of Christ.

It is precisely here that the Lima document suggests a first definition of the ordained ministry as distinct from the witness and service of every Christian.

Ordained ministers, the Lima document says, are heralds and ambassadors. In military terminology, the herald is a middle-ranking officer whose function is to carry messages, make solemn announcements and organize ceremonies. Ordained ministers are therefore heralds who carry and proclaim in the church and to the world the message of reconciliation from and on behalf of their Lord. Ordained ministers are also described as ambassadors. This image has been given us by St Paul: "We are ambassadors for Christ, as if God exhorted you by us" (2 Cor. 5:18–20). Ordained ministers are the Lord's envoys who represent him and speak in his name.

Ordained ministers are also leaders and teachers who have the responsibility of summoning the Christian community to be obedient to the word of God and to the authority of Christ at the bidding of the Holy Spirit.

Finally, they are pastors or shepherds under the authority of the Supreme Shepherd, Christ himself, with the task of uniting and leading the people of God and encouraging it to expectant hope of the coming kingdom of God.

Although Christ chooses, calls and sends particular persons to be ordained to the ministry in the church, he does not separate them from the believing community. All the ordained ministers and the other believers are closely inter-related (M12). The Christian conception of ministry excludes clericalism. The community needs the ordained ministry set before it, reminding it that the word of God which is proclaimed is the source of its mission, that the celebration of the eucharist of Christ is the place where its unity is renewed, that it depends on its obedience to the authority of the Holy Spirit. On the other hand, the ordained ministry cannot exist without the ecclesial community. There is no ordination in isolation whereby ministers would be instituted outside the community. Ordained ministers exist only in relation to the church whose servants they are. It is in and for the community that the ordained ministers fulfill their calling; they need the recognition, support and encouragement of the community.

The basic and specific function of the ordained ministers is to unite and build up the body of Christ. They perform this function by way of three fundamental responsibilities which fall to them:
1) the proclamation and teaching of the word of God;
2) the celebration of the sacraments;
3) the leadership of the life of the community in its liturgy, in its mission, and in its service.

This paragraph (M13), which defines the specific function of the ordained ministry has undergone very little change in the history of the Lima document. The first draft of 1972 stated:

> The ordained ministry (a) unites and builds up the community for its mission in the world, (b) proclaims in word and deed the good news of God's reconciliation in Christ, and (c) presides over the liturgical and sacramental life of the eucharistic community.

Agreement between the churches here, therefore, is broad and deep.

This specific function of the ordained minister is included in the joint responsibility shared with all the members of the ecclesial community. Every gift of the Spirit serves to unite and build up the body of Christ. Every member of the body can participate in the proclamation of the word of God and in the teaching of that word, can contribute to the sacramental life of the body. Ordained ministers exercise this specific function in a representative way, i.e. they represent Christ in dialogue with his church and the church in its responsibility in face of the world. The ordained ministry is a focus of unity where the life and witness of the ecclesial community are sustained. This specific function of the ordained ministry which rallies and builds up the church as the body of Christ in unity and for its mission to the world is manifested in a quite special way in the eucharistic celebration: "In the celebration of the eucharist, Christ gathers, teaches and nourishes the Church. It is Christ who invites to the meal and who presides at it" (M14).

Christ uses the ordained minister as a sign and instrument to represent his own presiding over the eucharistic celebration, to gather his church in unity and prayer, to proclaim and teach his word, to nourish the members of his body with the bread of life and wine of the eternal kingdom.

3. The forms of the ordained ministry

In the view of the Lima document, the New Testament does not describe the church and the ministry as having one unique form. In primitive Christianity there is a diversity of ecclesiologies and conceptions of the ministry. This diversity originates in the plurality of places and cultures in which the Christian faith has been implanted. We must recognize, however, that under the guidance of the Holy Spirit the church has developed certain elements of this primitive variety. In the Pastoral Epistles (to Timothy and Titus) we already find the ministries of the episkopos (entrusted with the responsibility of supervision), the presbyter (the one who has pastoral experience), the deacon (the one who is at the service of the poor of every sort) becoming fixed. These ministries were to become the threefold ministry of bishop, presbyter and deacon, which would spread everywhere in the church in the second and third centuries. St Ignatius of Antioch, who suffered martyrdom in Rome, was already familiar with this threefold pattern at the beginning of the second century. It was a Christian church organized according to this threefold pattern of ministry which would gradually recognize the list of books composing the New Testament which are authoritative for all, without seeing any contradiction between this episcopal ministerial pattern which it had adopted as its own, on the one hand, and the various descriptions of the church and the ministry contained in the New Testament, on the other. In other words, from the standpoint of the Lima document, this first Tradition of the church, this first interpretation on the part of the first Christians, is in harmony with the word of God contained in the New Testament. In the succeeding centuries, the threefold ministry of bishop, presbyter and deacon underwent many formal changes yet the substance of this pattern persisted.

At the Reformation, when the Bible was read with fresh insight, certain rediscoveries focused attention on the variety of ministries, though without any radical challenge to the ancient Tradition of the church. The oldest attestations of the threefold ministry, in St Ignatius of Antioch, for example, see it as the diversified form of the ordained ministry in the local eucharistic community. It is impossible to speak of bishops without at the same time speaking of the presbyters or pastors who surround them and of the deacons who assist them in their work. From the beginning, the ministry is thought of as at one and the same time personal, collegial and communal. The bishop is the president of the local church, a Christian community which in general covers a city. The bishop is responsible for proclaiming the word of God, leading the celebration of the eucharist of Christ, and safeguarding the unity of the ministries and of the community in the Holy Spirit. The bishop is surrounded by a college of presbyters or pastors who assist in these various tasks, who share in celebrating the eucharist around the same altar, and who can be delegates and envoys for functions at which it is impossible for the bishop to be present in person. Deacons also share in this common ministry of the bishop and the presbyters, by carrying out a whole number of diaconal services. This threefold ordained ministry would be further developed as the local church grew. Like the apostles and then their co-workers such as Timothy and Titus, the local bishops would find themselves exercising their ministry of encouragement and oversight over areas far more extensive than that of a single city; they would gradually become responsible for several local communities in which presbyters themselves would be entrusted with the pastoral ministry in communion with the regional bishop. The deacons, too, still inseparable from the bishop, would come to have a much broader field of activity. Originally a local pastor surrounded by a college of presbyters, the bishop thus becomes a regional pastor responsible for several communities and the various ministers who activate them locally. Their regional episcopal ministry, which tends to expand, comes more and more to resemble that of the apostles whose responsibility embraced a number of local churches and that of the apostles' co-workers such as Timothy and Titus, whose function of supervising a particular region is described for us in the Pastoral Epistles.

There is more, of course, to the diversity of spiritual gifts and ministries in the church than this threefold form of ordained ministry. Many other forms of ministry are revealed to us in the New Testament; the Holy Spirit has guided the church to adapt its ministries to changing historical contexts and has blessed with his gifts new ministries called into existence by him for the building up of the body of Christ. The valuable ministry of elders in the Reformed tradition can be cited as one example.

Yet this threefold ministry of episcopate, presbyterate and diaconate which we find emerging so early in the Tradition and spreading so rapidly to the universal church, seems well-suited to serve as an expression of the visible unity of the churches and as a means of achieving that unity. The threefold ministry was the generally accepted form of ministry in the church of the first centuries; at the Reformation it was recognized as a pattern inherited from the ancient church even if it was not always applied; it is preserved today by many churches; it finds its balance in the synodal structure. As the Lima document declares:

> In the fulfilment of their mission and service, the churches need people who in different ways express and perform the tasks of the ordained ministry in its diaconal, presbyteral and episcopal aspects and functions (M22).

The threefold form of ordained ministry addresses questions to all the churches. Is the personal responsibility of ministry really safeguarded? Is the collegial exercise of ministry really assured? Does the diaconal ministry really exist in all the churches? It is vital that the ministry should be exercised in a personal, collegial and communal manner in the church at all levels. The pastorate of Christ in his church can best be displayed by a responsible individual, whether at the local level (the pastor or presbyter) or at the regional level (the bishop). But this responsible individual acts in communion and collaboration with a college of ministers who share the responsibilities and cares of the common ministry of the local or regional church. Finally, the ordained ministry always exists within a company of believers, in solidarity with it and sharing with it the responsibility for the church's mission in the world. Bishops have an individual ministry of unity within a region, but they do not perform it in isolation; they accomplish this ministry of unity at the centre of a college of various ministers, with the pastors and deacons of the region; the bishops exist in the community of the whole people of God whose problems and joys they share. The synodal structure emphasizes this communal dimension of ministry; it guards against an authoritarian exercise of this responsibility based on a conception of power which is hierarchical in the wrong sense.

Bishops are in communion with the other bishops of the church and related to them. They are a bond between the particular or local church in their charge and the other churches which make up the universal church. They relate the regional church with the universal church and are a sign and a witness of the universal church within the regional church and its constituent communities.

In communion with the other ministers and the whole ecclesial community, the bishop is responsible for the continuity of ministry and its orderly transmission in the church.

Bishops have responsibility for the various ministries: for the calling to and training for the ministry and ordination to the ministry. They have to ensure the continuity of the apostolic ministry in the church.

According to the Lima document, ordination is a sacramental sign. The laying-on of hands is a sign of the gift of the Spirit; it is an action, accomplished by God and by the church, in which the persons ordained receive the gifts and the power of the Holy Spirit for the fulfilment of their specific task, for their ministry as deacon, their ministry as presbyter (or pastor), their ministry as bishop. The Lima document gives the following definition of the act of ordination by the laying-on of hands of those who have this special responsibility:

1) it is an invocation of the Holy Spirit (an *epiklesis*), praying that new ministers may receive the gifts and strength for their own ministry;

2) it is a sacramental sign of the granting of this prayer, this invocation of the Holy Spirit, by the Lord who gives the gifts and strength of ministry;

3) it is an acknowledgment by the church of the gifts of the Spirit in the one ordained;
4) it is a mutual commitment of the church and the new minister in their new relationship; the new minister also enters into a collegial relationship with other ordained ministers.

The Lima document concludes by expressing the hope that the churches will achieve a mutual recognition of their ordained ministries which will be the sign of their reconciliation in visible unity.

This hope of the mutual recognition of ordained ministries and the reconciliation of the churches in visible unity is the spur to our ecumenical journey. In order to advance towards this goal, we must do everything possible to reach a fuller understanding of the other churches at the deepest level of their faith and true intention. The requisite for this is a genuine conversion of the heart of the kind to which the Second Vatican Council invites us. We must cease to cherish within ourselves an attitude of suspicion towards a sister church; we must learn to trust one another, to have full confidence in each other. By the one baptism, by the one holy scripture, source of the fundamental common faith, Christians are all members of the body of Christ; they can already make this reality the basis of their common life in the assurance that their present unity is stronger than anything which would still keep them apart.

Notes

1. These first papers are published in "Ecumenical Perspectives on Baptism, Eucharist and Ministry", *Faith and Order Paper No. 116*, Geneva, WCC, 1983.
2. The membership of the Steering Group was as follows: Vitaly Borovoy (Orthodox), Nils Ehrenström (Lutheran), Bert Hoedemaker (Reformed), Anton Houtepen (Roman Catholic), Max Thurian (Reformed), Emilianos Timiadis (Orthodox), Lukas Vischer (Reformed), Geoffrey Wainwright (Methodist). Among the experts who were also involved in the work of the Steering Group were Nikos Nissiotis and Jean Zizioulas (Orthodox), Emmanuel Lanne and Jean Tillard (Catholic), Günther Gassmann and Harding Meyer (Lutheran) and Günther Wagner (Baptist).
3. The third and fourth Plenary Commission meetings of Faith and Order had already tackled the problem of "Tradition and Traditions" at New Haven (USA) in 1957 and St Andrews (Scotland) in 1960. The work of Montreal was pursued further at Bristol in 1967. All this hermeneutical research and research on the role of the fathers of the church and the Councils had a considerable influence on the document on "Baptism, Eucharist and Ministry".
4. It should be remembered that while Montreal was correcting the *sola scriptura* principle, the Second Vatican Council was working on the Constitution *Dei Verbum* which presented a balanced doctrine of the relationship between scripture and Tradition and rendered the theory of the "two sources of revelation" obsolete. This was certainly more than just a coincidence.
5. "Towards a Confession of the Common Faith", *Faith and Order Paper 100*, Geneva, WCC, 1980. The notion of the supreme authority of scripture within a

Tradition of interpretation by the church is in keeping with the main convictions of the Reformation, especially Calvin who always showed great respect for the Tradition of the first centuries of the church, the tradition of the fathers and the first four ecumenical councils (cf. for example, Chapter IV of Book IV of the *Institutes*, where Calvin indicates general agreement with the Tradition of the church of the early centuries).

LUTHERAN CHURCH IN AMERICA

Preface

In January 1982 the plenary meeting of the Commission on Faith and Order of the World Council of Churches transmitted a document entitled "Baptism, Eucharist and Ministry" to the churches. The product of 55 years of theological work by Faith and Order, "Baptism, Eucharist and Ministry" is intended to assist the churches to grow together on these important topics and thus to aid the churches to move towards visible unity.

The churches have been asked by the Faith and Order Commission to study and review the document in the light of specific questions asked by the Commission. Churches were requested to make a formal, official response to the document by December 31, 1984, a deadline which has since been extended to December 31, 1985. "Response," a relatively short-term process of review and study, is really the first phase of a longer-term process of "reception." "Reception" includes all the phases and aspects of a process by which a church makes the results of an ecumenical dialogue or statement part of its faith and life. It is a process which involves all believers, and all parts of the church. It may take years and occurs only as Christ graciously accomplishes it by his Spirit.

The Lutheran Church in America has endeavored to take the request of the Commission on Faith and Order seriously. In the summer and fall of 1983 a process of response was developed which involved as many areas of this church as possible. A random sampling of congregations was selected to study the document and offer a narrative response to a set of specific questions and all

---

• 3,051,417 members, 6,157 parishes, 8,724 pastors.

congregations were offered the opportunity to study and respond as well. Synod bishops, seminary and college faculties, and churchwide agency staff were all asked to respond. Based on the results of these study groups, a preliminary draft response was presented to the Twelfth Biennial Convention in Toronto in July 1984. The final text was approved by the Convention and transmitted to the Faith and Order Commission of the World Council of Churches shortly thereafter as the official response of the Lutheran Church in America.

What follows is the final text of that response. It is shared here so that it will be readily available to a growing audience of persons interested in the process of study and reception of "Baptism, Eucharist and Ministry."

William G. Rusch
Director for Ecumenical Relations

The response
The By-laws of the World Council of Churches state, "The Faith and Order Commission is to proclaim the oneness of the Church of Jesus Christ and to call the churches to a goal of visible unity in one faith and one eucharistic fellowship expressed in worship and common life in Christ in order that the world might believe." In 1978 the meeting of the Faith and Order Commission identified three elements needed for a united Church: 1. a common understanding of the apostolic faith; 2. full mutual recognition of baptism, the eucharist and the ministry; and 3. agreement on common ways of teaching and decision-making.

"Baptism, Eucharist and Ministry" must be seen in this context. This document is a product of over 55 years of the ecumenical movement in its conciliar form. Its history can be traced from the first World Conference on Faith and Order at Lausanne in 1927 until the meeting of the Faith and Order Commission in Lima in January, 1982 when the following motion passed unanimously without negative votes or abstentions:

> The commission considers the revised text on "Baptism, Eucharist and Ministry" to have been brought to such a stage of maturity that it is now ready for transmission to the churches in accordance with the Mandate given at the Fifth Assembly of the World Council of Churches, Nairobi 1975 and re-affirmed by the Central Committee, Dresden, 1981.

● This response was adopted by the 1984 convention of the Lutheran Church in America.

"Baptism, Eucharist and Ministry" does not claim to fulfill the second element listed above, but it does claim a remarkable degree of agreement. Because of this contention, the Faith and Order Commission has asked the churches to prepare an official response at the highest level of authority. The churches are requested to reply to the question whether or not they find in "Baptism, Eucharist and Ministry" "the faith of the church throughout the ages." For the Lutheran Church in America, this means a response from the national convention of the church. This is the first time that this church has been asked in this way to respond officially to an ecumenical document of this type. The request itself is a sign of the maturity of the ecumenical movement. An official reply to "Baptism, Eucharist and Ministry" by this church is appropriate for two reasons:

First, *Ecumenism: A Lutheran Commitment* states:

> The Lutheran Church in America declares that the ecumenical commitment to the unity of the church is among its highest priorities under the proclamation of the Gospel (1982 LCAM, p. 287) and,

> The Lutheran Church in America, through its appropriate structures commits itself to receive and act with promptness on:

>> a) Reports, documents, and recommendations which affect external relationships, from ecumenical organizations in which it holds membership or takes part, ... (1982 LCAM, p. 287) and,

> This church acknowledges the vision of fuller unity such as has been presented by the World Council of Churches and its Faith and Order Commission ... Nevertheless, it realizes that it (this church) may have to proceed step by step toward unity. (1982 LCAM, p. 286)

Second, after a hesitating start, the Lutheran Church in America and its predecessor bodies have had a long involvement and commitment to the Faith and Order Movement. North American Lutherans were ably represented at the First World Conference at Lausanne in 1927, at the Second World Conference on Faith and Order at Edinburgh in 1937, at the Third World Conference on Faith and Order at Lund in 1952, and the first North American Conference at Oberlin in 1957 and at the Fourth World Conference at Montreal in 1963, and by active participation in the continuing work of the Faith and Order Commission. By history and commitment the Lutheran Church in America is called upon to take with utmost seriousness the invitation:

> As concrete evidence of their ecumenical commitment the churches are being asked to enable the widest possible involvement of the whole people of God at all levels of church life in the spiritual process of reviewing this text.

The Faith and Order Commission now respectfully invites all churches to prepare an official response to this text at the highest appropriate level of authority, whether it be a council, synod, conference, assembly or other body. ("Baptism, Eucharist and Ministry", Preface)

The request of the Faith and Order Commission to the churches is twofold. The first involves a process of receiving, *reception*. It includes all the phases and aspects of a process by which a church makes the results of an ecumenical dialogue or statement a part of its faith and life. Reception thus is a process involving all parts of the church, all believers. It may take years and it only occurs as Christ graciously accomplishes it by his spirit. This convention is not being asked to "receive" "Baptism, Eucharist and Ministry" in this sense of the term "reception."

The second fold of the Commission's request involves an official response. This is what this convention is being asked to do. Such a response may be seen as part of the process leading to reception, but it is not to be identified with reception. The response offered here assumes that "Baptism, Eucharist and Ministry" is a unique document. It is the product of over 50 years of ecumenical work transmitted to the churches for common study and official response by over one hundred theologians representing virtually all the major church traditions: Eastern Orthodox, Oriental Orthodox, Roman Catholic, Old Catholic, Lutheran, Anglican, Reformed, Methodist, United, Disciples, Baptist, Adventist, and Pentecostal. "Baptism, Eucharist and Ministry" is a document of a remarkable convergence. It shows how in spite of much diversity in theological expression the churches are coming together in a common understanding of essential elements of the Christian Tradition. The text does not represent consensus, which means that experience of life and articulation of faith necessary to realize and maintain the church's visible unity. Full consensus is only to be acknowledged after the churches reach the point of living and acting together in unity.

In offering a response, the Lutheran Church in America recognizes that it shares a common problem with other churches today, viz. how to teach authoritatively. It acknowledges that the invitation of the Faith and Order Commission places this question before it with a new urgency. Simply to repeat the words of Scripture or of the Lutheran Confessions will not suffice in the present ecumenical situation.

This reply is not intended to be juridical in character; it is rather to be a Lutheran witness and contribution to the Church Catholic presented in the conviction that in this response Lutherans may both teach and be taught.

The Lutheran Church in America in making this response is

drawing on a number of resources available to it. In recent years, quite apart from "Baptism, Eucharist and Ministry," this church has experienced a renewed appreciation of the sacraments as a means of grace. The Commission for a New Lutheran Church has stimulated reflection and discussion about ordination and the office of oversight. In the development of this response, a detailed and extensive study process of "Baptism, Eucharist and Ministry" was conducted by congregations, seminary and college faculties, churchwide agencies, synodical bishops and others. While the response was somewhat limited, it was enthusiastic and informative about the views of the wider church on "Baptism, Eucharist and Ministry."

Deserving of special mention is the 450th Anniversary of the Augsburg Confession. This event, with the accompanying attention of many Christians, aided Lutherans and others to recover the ecumenical nature of the Lutheran Confessions and especially the ecumenical commitment of Article VII with its *satis est*. This confessional recovery is conspicuous in *Ecumenism: A Lutheran Commitment* (1982 LCAM, p. 281).

> 5. The primary Lutheran confessional document, the Augsburg Confession of 1530, claims to be a fully catholic as well evangelical expression of Christian faith. It states that nothing here departs from Scripture or the Catholic Church. The confessors at Augsburg asked only for freedom to preach and worship in accordance with the Gospel, and were willing, provided this freedom was granted, to remain in fellowship with those who did not share their theological formulations or reforming practices. It is in this historical context that the *satis est* of Article VII is to be understood: "For the true unity of the church it is enough (*satis est*) to agree concerning the teaching of the Gospel and the administration of the sacraments." What was asked for as a condition of church unity was the recognition of the Lutheran reforms as legitimately Christian rather than the adoption of these reforms by others.
>
> The historical situation is now different. The question is no longer that of preserving the existing church unity, but that of reestablishing a communion which has been broken. Yet Article VII of the Augsburg Confession continues to be ecumenically liberating because of its insistence that agreement in the Gospel suffices for Christian unity. This interpretation of Article VII frees Lutherans, as they seek to promote the proclamation of the message of God's saving action in Jesus Christ, to enter into church fellowship without insisting on doctrinal or ecclesiastical uniformity. Lutherans still place considerable emphasis on formulation and expression of theological consensus. Yet they recognize from this article that, where there is consensus on the Gospel, there is room for a living and experiencing of fellowship within the context of seeking larger theological agreement.

Guidance is also available for the Lutheran Church in America from a number of its earlier documents: *The Communion Practices Statement* of 1978; the *Statement of Ministry*, 1980; *Ecumenism: A Lutheran Commitment*, 1982; and the *Lutheran-Episcopal Agreement*, 1982. In addition there are the rich and varied results of multilateral dialogues and bilateral dialogues, published in numerous volumes of theological papers and common statements, coming from the work of the Faith and Order Commission and from the Lutheran-Roman Catholic dialogue, the Lutheran-Episcopalian dialogue, the Lutheran-Reformed dialogue, the Lutheran-Methodist dialogue, and the Lutheran-Baptist dialogue.

Cognizant of its history and commitments, the Lutheran Church in America, after a careful study of "Baptism, Eucharist and Ministry" by means of the resources enumerated here, rejoices over the convergence in the text with its promise of the realization of greater visible unity of the Church. This church wishes to express its appreciation to the Faith and Order Commission of the World Council of Churches for the achievement of "Baptism, Eucharist and Ministry".

With this word of appreciation and rejoicing, this church notes certain questions opened by "Baptism, Eucharist and Ministry" in which Lutherans will wish to stress certain aspects of the Christian faith as their contribution. It also recognizes that reception ultimately will not be a matter of documents, but a renewed people under the Spirit expressing their unity in Christ. Nevertheless, every recognition of the convergence of Christians around the Triune God, in spite of the difficulty of formal recognition of each other, and in spite of the present inability to commune together, is cause for rejoicing and thanksgiving. Such convergence indeed affects our common witness in a divided world and brings us closer to the visible unity we seek.

The Faith and Order Commission has addressed four questions to the churches. In answering these questions, the Lutheran Church in America wishes to make some preliminary observations.

Effective steps toward the visible unity of all Christians will require a foundation in the evangelical, catholic and ecumenical tradition. All three aspects of the Tradition are reflected in "Baptism, Eucharist and Ministry". Questions, however, must be addressed as to whether or not the document adequately holds all three in tension or whether there is some imbalance which slights the evangelical.

The language of the text seeks to create a new theological vocabulary. This is clearly to be approved. At critical points the language of the documents is open to a number of possible interpretations. This must be viewed as both a contribution and a problem.

"Baptism, Eucharist and Ministry" asks to be judged as to whether or not it is a reflection of the Apostolic Faith. The Apostolic Faith is described by, and limited by, "Baptism, Eucharist and Ministry". Lutherans are able to approve the document as a witness to the Apostolic Faith, while also stating that there is more of the Tradition than is set forth in "Baptism, Eucharist and Ministry".

The strong commitment to the Bible, the ecumenical creeds and the concerns of the Lutheran Confessions is evident in "Baptism, Eucharist and Ministry". The major items of the text do recognize that all Christian teaching is grounded in Christ. Lutherans would welcome the consideration of the following four motifs in the discussion of "Baptism, Eucharist and Ministry", especially in light of the Lutheran understanding of the Gospel as justification by grace through faith which they regard as their witness to the Church catholic.

1. *A stronger articulation of the Word and what this means for an understanding of baptism, eucharist and ministry.* Such articulation could lead to a clearer understanding of what is constitutive for the sacraments, to a more precise location of the living voice (*viva vox*) of the Gospel, and to a more complete theology of ministry.

2. *A clearer expression of the dynamic of sin and grace and what this means for baptism, eucharist and ministry.* A stress is needed on the sinfulness of humankind and how this condition of humanity is related to the sacraments. The concept of *simul justus et peccator* could strengthen the document. It is not necessary that the actual words associated with the concept be in the text.

3. *The priority of a certain period of history as normative for the faith.* While Lutherans affirm their sixteenth century confessions and ecumenical creeds, they place primary emphasis on the Gospel as witnessed to in Scripture. The Gospel is the foundation of the faith in every age, including the biblical period, the apostolic age or the second, third and sixteenth centuries. The concept of "*ecclesia semper reformanda est*" is still valid and should be maintained.

4. *A wider perspective on ministry.*
a)　"Baptism, Eucharist and Ministry" affirms that the universal priesthood of all the baptized is the proper context for a discussion of the ordained ministry. But it does not stress adequately the active role of the universal priesthood in the proclamation of the Gospel. Thus the discussion of ministry is too narrowly construed. The Gospel creates a people of women and men who are all called to serve.

b)   "Baptism, Eucharist and Ministry" does acknowledge that there is no one pattern of ministry in the New Testament. "Baptism, Eucharist and Ministry" affirms a public office of ordained ministry. We recognize that some churches have adopted the three-fold pattern of bishop-presbyter-deacon, although with varying patterns of *episcopé*, and of the office of deacon. There is no Lutheran consensus on these matters. We do affirm that "Baptism, Eucharist and Ministry" grounds the ordained ministry in the Gospel.

c)   The pastoral sense of the ordained ministry, which the Lutheran tradition has always stressed, is insufficiently in focus in "Baptism, Eucharist and Ministry".

d)   In all ecumenical discussions of ministry the Lutheran Church in America feels compelled to witness to the enrichment that has come to us by the ordination of women as pastors in our church. Our commitment to the ordination of women is an integral part of our obedience to the Gospel.

e)   Problems are posed by the statement (in "Ministry" par. 12) that, within the interrelatedness of ordained and lay members of the believing community, the presence of ordained ministers "reminds the community of the divine initiative, and of the dependence of the Church on Jesus Christ" and that "in them the Church sees an example of holiness and loving concern" (cf. "Eucharist," par. 29, "The minister of the eucharist is the ambassador who represents the divine initiative...").

The four questions regarding "Baptism, Eucharist and Ministry" posed by the Faith and Order Commission and the Lutheran Church in America responses are as follows:

Question 1 : The extent to which your church can recognize in this text the faith of the Church throughout the ages.

We are able to affirm that they see the Apostolic faith in "Baptism, Eucharist and Ministry". But this positive response must be conditioned by the four motifs described above. Lutherans will always wish to share with the Church Catholic their understanding of the Gospel as justification by grace through faith, although they will insist neither on that vocabulary nor on that formulation in ecumenical documents. Besides the basic approval of the document as a whole there are many specific points in the text that are to be applauded, e.g.:

—The concept of apostolicity, Ministry, Section 34. (this and subsequent references to Baptism, Eucharist and Ministry are to the

text of the Faith and Order document and not to the commentary).
—The placement of the universal priesthood at the beginning of the Ministry section. Ministry, Section 1, p. 20.
—The recognition that the advocacy of the Tradition does not require adherence to specific forms of the Tradition. Ministry, Section 38.
—The affirmation of the real presence in the Eucharist. Eucharist, Section 13, p. 12.

Question 2: The consequences your church can draw from this text for its relations and dialogues with other churches, particularly with those churches which also recognize the text as an expression of apostolic faith.

"Baptism, Eucharist and Ministry" is a resource in differing ways for Lutherans in their dialogues with the Anglican, Orthodox, Reformed and Roman Catholic traditions. It gives Lutherans all the more reason to be involved in multilateral dialogues and bilateral dialogues, showing how both belong together. The document aids Lutherans by reminding them of the nature of their tradition. In a Church Catholic, Lutherans want to say the Gospel. In a Church Evangelical they want to say a word catholic. It is in making both of these affirmations together that Lutherans are ecumenical.

Question 3: The guidance your church can take from this text for its worship, educational, ethical, and spiritual life and witness:

The document offers a spirituality rooted in baptism and nourished by Word and sacrament. A particular concern is "renewal of the eucharist itself" (par. 28). It supports "affirmation of a common eucharistic faith," without implying "uniformity in either liturgy or practice" (par. 28), and thus unity within the entire Christian family without the unfortunate competitiveness of the past. Thus, "Baptism, Eucharist and Ministry" reminds Lutherans that their reflection and actions on such matters must always be in a context of a church that is larger than the Lutheran church, yet with many emphases that Lutherans welcome. "Baptism, Eucharist and Ministry" is a pastoral and prophetic call to Lutherans to celebrate the eucharist "frequently" and to receive it "frequently." The emphasis on deepening of faith (par. 30) must not be overlooked. As for celebration "at least every Sunday," some Lutheran congregations have this practice, and many do not. Attention needs to be given to the rationale for frequency of communion, along with other forms of being nourished by the Word.

Lutherans in this church particularly welcome the accent ("Eucharist," par. 20) on the ethical imperatives for justice in "social, economic and political life," for in the eucharist, as with other forms of the Word, we are placed under judgement and confronted with the reconciling presence of God.

Lutheran worship forms have also been affected by the ecumenical concerns of "Baptism, Eucharist and Ministry". Thus Lutherans have been active participants in projects of common translation of the Bible and of liturgical and credal texts, and in the development of a common lectionary and church year. *The Lutheran Book of worship* is a concrete example of this ecumenical commitment. *Ecumenism: A Lutheran Commitment* supports the need for education about ecumenism and commits this church to this task. Several churchwide agencies are giving increased attention to the interpretation of ecumenism. The process of the study and response of "Baptism, Eucharist and Ministry" in the Lutheran Church in America is evidence of this.

"Baptism, Eucharist and Ministry" provides ethical guidance in its discussion of baptism and Christian witness and in its sensitivity to new church-dividing issues. It reminds Lutherans that they must listen to other churches as they together are one community, one people created by God, mutually responsible and accountable.

Question 4: The suggestions your church can make for the ongoing work of Faith and Order as it relates the material of this text on "Baptism, Eucharist and Ministry" to its long-range research project "Towards the Common Expression of the Apostolic Faith Today."

As we affirm the achievement of "Baptism, Eucharist and Ministry" we also affirm the importance of Faith and Order's work on the other two elements needed for a united church. As a contribution to "a common understanding of the apostolic faith," we believe that the motifs we have stressed above as somewhat lacking, namely motifs 1 and 2, will need to be taken into serious consideration. As a contribution to "agreement on common ways of teaching and decision-making," we maintain in the spirit of the Augsburg Confession, especially Article VII, that questions of decision-making are open to much variation within the search for Christian unity.

It was VOTED: That the Lutheran Church in America in the light of the official request of the World Council of Churches' Commission on Faith and Order:

a. Express its appreciation to the Faith and Order Commission of the World Council of Churches for the achievement of "Baptism, Eucharist and Ministry";

b. Approve this response by the Lutheran Church in America to the document "Baptism, Eucharist and Ministry" of the World Council of Churches as a contribution to the Commission's continuing efforts to call the churches to the goal of visible unity in one faith and one eucharistic fellowship, expressed in worship, and common life in Christ, that the world might believe;

c. Encourage the Commission on Faith and Order to proceed with its studies on a common understanding of the apostolic faith and agreement on common ways of teaching and decision-making;

d. Continue to use "Baptism, Eucharist and Ministry" together with this response, as a resource and occasion to carry out the commitment of this church as expressed in *Ecumenism: A Lutheran Commitment*. Whenever possible our congregations should work with this document with ecumenical partners and use these conversations as foundations for greater cooperative service. This church should also be encouraged and informed by this document in its ecumenical dialogues; and

e. Continue the ongoing process of the reception of "Baptism, Eucharist and Ministry" within this church.

NORTH ELBIAN EVANGELICAL LUTHERAN CHURCH

Introduction

The adoption of the convergence statements on "Baptism, Eucharist and Ministry" by the Faith and Order Commission of the World Council of Churches and their transmission to the member churches has initiated a reception process which is welcomed by the North Elbian Evangelical Lutheran Church. Our Church participates in this process because it recognizes it as an important step towards the achievement of greater visible unity among the churches. In virtue of its doctrinal confession and its constitution, our Church considers itself in duty bound to engage in this reception process since it proclaims Jesus Christ, the Crucified and Risen One, as "the Lord of the one, holy, catholic and apostolic church", acknowledges itself "called to the constant renewal of its life" and heeds "the views of Christians both of its own and other confessions" (preamble to the Constitution of the North Elbian Evangelical Lutheran Church).

We recognize with gratitude the new possibilities opened up by these convergence statements since, as others, we too are pained by the divisions in the church. With other churches, we realize that these divisions have been detrimental to us all and that we all need the mutual help which the ecumenical fellowship affords.

We not only endorse the direction taken but also approve in principle the main affirmations made in these texts. This endorsement is given despite certain objections and questions in respect of detail; in the case of the statement on ministry, these objections and questions are more substantial than in the case of the statements on baptism and eucharist.

• 2,877,637 members, 671 parishes, 3 dioceses, 3 bishops, 1,312 pastors.

This basic endorsement of the convergence statements is accorded because we have already found our church life much enriched by their study in the reception process so far in our church. We are confident that this growing enrichment and renewal will continue in the coming years.

We also approve these texts in principle because in their fundamental affirmation we clearly recognize not only the scriptural basis which our Reformation approach to doctrinal statements requires but also the tradition of the apostolic faith through the ages as formulated in the ancient church creeds and adhered to in our confession of faith.

Maintaining as we do, in accordance with holy scripture and our confession of faith, that for the true unity of the church it is sufficient that the gospel be purely preached and the sacraments celebrated in obedience to God's word, we are able to exercise considerable freedom in recognizing among ourselves and in respect of others different ways of ordering the life of the church.

Not that we gloss over or minimize the existence and the importance of divergences. But if other churches can recognize our positions and we theirs as not divisive of the church, then we are able to enter into and practise church fellowship despite our differences.

In presenting this official response, we set forth with faith, love and hope on the common road to greater unity, a unity which we understand to be both a gift and a task.

In this response we concentrate mainly on the first and second of the italicized questions in the preface to the convergence statements. As for the third question, we shall simply indicate the direction of our thinking by noting the themes and questions on which we shall concentrate in the next stage of the reception process. In respect of the fourth question, we shall mention in conclusion some of the objectives which we regard as important for the future course of this project.

BAPTISM

The faith of the Church through the ages (Question 1)

In this section on baptism we recognize the apostolic faith of the church as maintained and a living reality in our church and other churches through the ages in accordance with holy scripture.

Explanation: The convergence statement on baptism brings out sufficiently clearly the significance of baptism as participation in the death of Christ for our sins and in his resurrection; namely, as participation in salvation through Christ, the forgiveness of sins, and blessedness.

We further agree that by baptism we have been incorporated into the "one, holy, catholic (i.e. universal) and apostolic church" as the one body of Christ and at the same time become members of a church.

We emphasize that this "one baptism... constitutes a call to the churches to overcome their divisions and visibly manifest their fellowship" (§6). We also affirm that our baptism forbids us to allow "differences of sex, race, or social status to divide the body of Christ" (§6 Commentary). We affirm that baptism, by its very nature, has "ethical implications" (§10) and, in virtue of our Lutheran tradition, emphasize in particular that "baptism is related... to a lifelong growth into Christ" (§9). We confirm that the elements of the baptismal liturgy listed in §20 correspond to our own baptismal practice.

Our objections to a few statements in this section on baptism are not of sufficient moment to undermine our basic agreement here.

Explanation: One criticism is that the *institution* of baptism, to which we attach great importance, is not specifically dealt with here. The Christological basis of baptism, on the contrary, is stated sufficiently clearly in our view, and the command instituting baptism (Matt. 28: 18–20) quoted verbatim, moreover, so that in substance, Christ's institution of baptism is made sufficiently plain (§1).

In the teaching of our church, baptism is inseparably connected with the gift of the *Holy Spirit*. Though this is not stated in the text as clearly as we should wish (§5), we recognize a reference to it in the statement that "baptism gives participation in the community of the Holy Spirit" (§7) and "in its full meaning, signifies and effects" both "participation in Christ's death and resurrection" and "the receiving of the Holy Spirit" (§14; cf. also 19).

We affirm "the *necessity of faith* for the reception of salvation" in baptism but we can only accept the statement that baptism is "both God's gift and our human response to that gift" (§8) with the proviso that faith is itself a gift of God and that only as such is it our "human response". In general, baptism is presented far too unilaterally as a "rite of commitment to the Lord" (§1) rather than as a sacramental act of God ("means of grace"), thus giving the impression that it is only a person's faith, understood as his or her personal decision, which enables that person to receive the "full fruit" of God's gift in baptism (§12 Commentary).

We certainly recognize in this context a considerable convergence taking shape in respect of the traditional controversy within Protestantism over "infant baptism" and "believers' baptism". The churches not only agree in teaching that baptism is "unrepeatable" but are also, correspondingly, in their baptismal practice, beginning to recognize each other's "sacramental integrity" (§13 and Commentary). In every baptism we confess God's prevenient grace (*gratia praeveniens*). We affirm and we practise the baptism of young people and adults as being equal in status and validity to infant baptism, but we continue to practise the latter because we are not willing to refuse children the full offer of God's grace. Precisely this, however, would not be offered in the practice of "a presentation and blessing in infancy" (§12 Commentary).

Consequences for our relations with other churches (Question 2)

We recognize as valid every baptism performed in the name of the Triune God and with water. A baptism of this kind is unrepeatable.

In our view, the convergence statement on baptism offers a new opportunity for intensive discussions with those churches which have traditionally recognized only "believers' baptism" as valid. The object of these discussions would be the complete mutual recognition of our respective baptisms, since church fellowship with churches do not recognize the validity of our baptism is for us impossible.

Consequences for our own Church (Question 3)

Since we in our church practise and value *infant baptism*, we agree that we for our part must "take more seriously" our "responsibility for the nurture of baptized children to mature commitment to Christ". In other words, we must perform the catechetical task arising from baptism with far greater determination and efficacy (§16).

As practised and understood in our church, *confirmation* is not a "completion" of baptism but rather its verification or endorsement; it is not a sacrament in which the Spirit is imparted but an act of confession and blessing (§14). Nor does the widespread practice of admitting only confirmed persons to the Lord's Supper enjoy any dogmatic status in our church. In some congregations, children can take part in the congregation's celebration of the Lord's Supper even when they are under instruction for confirmation or even prior to such instruction. We very readily accept, therefore, what is said (§14 Commentary) about the inherent connection between baptism and the eucharist. We think that *children's communion*, with prior introduction and responsible adult accompaniment, should be encouraged, and, above all, the practice whereby confirmands are admitted to communion while still under instruction for confirmation. As far as our own church is concerned, there can be no question of infants communicating at baptism.

Our *baptismal services* are always public services. We accept the suggestion, however, that baptism should also be celebrated at the main Sunday service or at special baptismal services on feast days (e.g. at Easter).

EUCHARIST

The faith of the church through the ages (Question 1)

In this section on the eucharist we recognize the apostolic faith of the church as maintained and a living reality in our church and other churches through the ages in accordance with holy scripture.

Explanation: Taken quite literally and set within the whole ministry of Jesus in the context of the history of salvation and against the background of the Old Testament, the *words of institution* provide the chief ground for the celebration of the Lord's Supper, whose sacramental character is aptly defined in the description: "a sacramental meal which by visible signs communicates to us God's love in Jesus Christ" (§1).

We acknowledge with gratitude that in the liturgical *tradition of the Orthodox Church* we are offered a comprehensive framework for efforts to achieve a common mind by coming to grips with and getting to the bottom of the centuries-old conflicts between the western churches on eucharistic doctrine. For our Lutheran Church, new horizons then become visible which go further than our traditional interpretation of the Lord's Supper as a concrete embodiment of the offer of the personal forgiveness of sins and can broaden and strengthen our eucharistic theory and practice without eliminating anything we hold vital in doctrine or cherish as familiar in our spirituality:

—praise and thanksgiving to God the Father for all creation and for the history of salvation—the origin of the term "eucharist"[1] as the name of the whole celebration of the Lord's Supper (§§3–4);

—the thankful reverent memorial (*anamnesis*) of Christ's whole work of salvation (§§5–13);

---

[1]Though willing to use this term "eucharist" in the ecumenical dialogue, in our own church we shall continue to speak of the *Abendmahl* or *Herrenmahl* (the Supper or the Lord's Supper).

— the thankful reverent invocation of the Holy Spirit (*epiklesis*), the prayer for his presence making Christ's work of salvation a present reality in his church (§§14–18);

— the thankful reverent experience of the solidarity of the eucharistic congregation with the whole church of God's people of all times and places (§§19–21);

— the thankful reverent experience of the present operation of the eschatological future of God's kingdom (§§22–26).

Faith in the Triune God thus plays a definitive role both in the celebration of the Lord's Supper and in its theology (cf.§14).

The intrinsic unity of *word and sacrament*, of the proclamation of Christ and the celebration of his personal presence (§13;12; cf.27) is in accord with the doctrine of our church. The convergence statement affirms the real presence of Christ the crucified and risen Lord with sufficient clarity, since it asserts this real presence not only in the whole celebration of the Supper but also in the bread and wine (§13;15; cf.19), while leaving open any more detailed account of how this contemporary presence takes place (§13 Commentary). We also welcome particularly the affirmation that bread and wine remain the sacramental signs of Christ's body and blood "for the purpose of communion" only (§15).

The statement that sharing the one bread and the one cup demonstrates and effects "*the oneness of the sharers with Christ* and with their fellow sharers in all times and places", so that "eucharistic celebrations always have to do with the whole church and the whole church is involved in each local eucharistic celebration" (§19) is a central biblical concept (1 Cor. 10:16f.). It is, at the same time, an important theme in Luther's doctrine of the Lord's Supper, though one which has largely been lost sight of in our church and which it is our intention, with gratitude, to reappropriate.

The same applies to the recovery of the note of eschatological jubilation, of festal thanksgiving and joy, in our celebration of the Lord's Supper, as well as to the solid bond between eucharistic experience and intercession (§4).

We also regard this solid bond between eucharist and the *prayer for the Holy Spirit* as demonstrating that God has established an indissoluble bond between His Spirit and word and sacraments as his means of grace. In the *epiklesis*, the church stresses its dependence on the church's Lord. It does not "control" the gifts of the Spirit; only as it first receives them itself can it pass them on.

This aspect, it seems to us, is also a valuable pointer to finding our way out of the labyrinth of theological and philosophical speculations concerning *the nature of our Lord's presence*. The prayer for the Holy Spirit affirms at one and the same time that we may confidently expect this presence under the forms of bread and wine (*Confessio Augustana* 10) and also that we cannot command this presence but only ever receive it as a new gift.

We also endorse in principle and welcome as an enrichment the inclusion of the whole creation both theologically and liturgically (§4) and of the whole world with all its needs and problems (§§20–22;25) in the celebration of the eucharist.

In their totality, the further critical questions which, despite our general agreement with and readiness to accept the convergence statement on the eucharist, we are unable and unwilling to suppress, are not of sufficient weight, however, to cancel our endorsement of the statement.

Explanation · Despite the strong emphasis in the text on the indissoluble unity of word and sacrament, the convergence statement fails to make sufficiently clear the importance of holy scripture and the contemporary proclamation of the gospel in the context of the celebration of the Lord's Supper. A central role is played in our church by the Augustinian and Reformation idea that the Holy Supper is an embodiment of the word of God (*verbum visibile*) because the Christ who is present in bread and wine is himself the incarnate word of God (John 1:14) However much we agree that faith in Christ is "deepened by the celebration of the Lord's Supper" and not only by sermons and that the Lord's Supper should therefore be celebrated frequently (§30), and however true it may also be that the goal to be sought in the further development of our liturgical life is the recovery of the celebration of word and sacrament as the richest and most appropriate form of the main Sunday service, we cannot endorse the one-sided assertion that the celebration of the Lord's Supper as such is "the central act of the Church's worship" (§1). For us, the preaching service, the baptismal service, the prayer service and the service of meditation are all valid forms of the church's worship.

We hail the Commission's achievement in uniting representatives of all the churches in affirming the "real, living and active presence" of Christ in the eucharistic celebration and the fulfilment of the promise of his words of institution in every celebration of the Lord's Supper (§13); and however firmly we maintain that this interpretation is sufficient for fellowship at the Lord's Table (as shown by the Leuenberg Agreement between the Lutheran and Reformed Churches of Europe), we must also affirm equally emphatically that the miracle of the eucharist, the *presence of Christ's body and blood,* is celebrated "in, with and under" bread and wine.

Nowhere in the entire section on the eucharist do we find an adequate account of the central *significance of faith* in the context of the Lord's Supper. It is not enough simply to say that "to discern the body and blood of Christ, faith is required" (§13). Savingly to receive the sacrament of the Lord's Supper, Christ's words: "This is my body—this is my blood" must be accepted with the total saving confidence of the justified sinner in God's saving power and grace. Faith is indispensable for the reception of the sacrament just as the sacrament serves to reinforce faith.

We gratefully endorse the passages where it is affirmed that "it is Christ who invites to the meal and who presides at it". We, too, also consider it important that the ordained minister "expresses the connection of the local community with other local communities in the universal Church" (§29). We also welcome the clear statement that the events of Christ's saving work are "unique and can neither be repeated nor prolonged" (§8); and the statement that the sacrifice of Christ is in no way repeated, therefore, in the celebration of the Lord's Supper by the action of the priest but becomes a present reality in the celebration of the Supper by Christ's action (§§6, 29) as the unique *once-for-all perfect sacrifice on the cross on our behalf*. It is essential, however, that all this should not be jeopardized by the leader of the eucharistic celebration's coming between Christ and the congregation, as happens when the ordained minister is understood as representing Christ at the Lord's Supper (§14).

It is the rule in our church that the celebration of the eucharist is presided at by an ordained minister. To us, however, this is a matter of human order; we see to it that it is kept, but do not regard it as a divine order.

We also welcome the limpid statement that "there is *only one expiation*, that of the unique *sacrifice of the cross*, made actual in the eucharist", which largely takes the heat out of the centuries-old controversy over the Roman Catholic doctrine of the sacrifice of the mass. It is also acceptable to us to say that this sacrifice is "presented before the Father in the intercession of Christ" (§8 Commentary). In our view, however, this cannot mean that the church in any sense offers Christ's sacrifice to God but simply that, in celebrating the Lord's Supper, on the basis of Christ's sacrifice, the church prays to the Father on behalf of the whole world and commits its intercessions to the intercession of its ascended and exalted Lord (Rom.8:34).

That through participation in the Lord's Supper we receive "forgiveness of sins, life and salvation" (Luther) is brought out clearly in §2. But in the basic section on "The Institution of the Eucharist" (§1) and what follows, the treatment of the *forgiveness of sins*, which is the heart of Jesus' proclamation of the kingdom of God and the most important of the saving benefits of his death on the cross, is hardly adequate. This theme of the received forgiveness of sins should also be emphasized more strongly in §20 which deals with the eucharistic challenge and obligation to practise reconciliation and fellowship with all our sisters and brothers, and, on this basis, the challenge and obligation to seek to establish corresponding relationships in social, economic and political life. Although we set great store by this challenge and obligation, we have serious misgivings about the (to us rather obscure) statement about "participating in this ongoing restoration of the world's situation and the human condition" (§20), which could suggest a gradual realization of the kingdom of God in this world.

Consequences for our relations with other churches (Question 2)

If the convergence statement on the eucharist were to be endorsed by other churches as well as ours, this would in our view provide a new basis and promising possibilities for further detailed discussion with these other churches with a view to agreeing on at least an occasional mutual hospitality at eucharistic celebrations, without abandoning the Leuenberg consensus basis. It would also be necessary, therefore, to re-examine passages in our confessional documents in which there is a repudiation of these other churches.

Consequences for our own church (Question 3)

We note in the statement persuasive promptings to encourage our congregations to celebrate the Lord's Supper more frequently (§30) and our church members to participate in the Lord's Supper more frequently (§31). We shall accept gratefully and joyfully the theological and liturgical suggestions for broadening and enriching the significance of the Lord's Supper with the elements of praise and thanksgiving, by the inclusion in it of the whole creation, our responsibility for the world, the commemoration of the entire history of salvation, the invocation of the Holy Spirit, fellowship with one another and with the whole church. We do not, however, regard the summary in §27 as the only binding form for the eucharistic liturgy.

MINISTRY

The faith of the church through the ages (Question 1)

We recognize that the section on ministry brings out essential aspects of the apostolic faith. Here, however, in contrast to the sections on baptism and eucharist, we find ourselves at certain basic points confronted with difficult problems which are not—or not yet—solved in a manner satisfactory to us. We nevertheless attach more importance to the area of agreement and, above all, to the movement of convergence and its claim upon us, than to the remaining differences.

Explanation: We emphatically endorse the choice of "*the calling of the whole people of God*" as the point of departure (§§1–6). We regard the "priesthood of all believers" as exceptionally important (and in the Lutheran doctrinal tradition this priesthood is rooted in baptism) because it is not only the basis of the obligation of all Christians to witness to and answer for their faith but also the basis of the lay ministry of church elders and synod members to whom, alongside the ordained ministry, our church entrusts the responsibility of church government. We welcome the fact that the biblical doctrine of the one Spirit and the rich diversity of spiritual gifts is understood as the basis of all the different forms in which the priesthood of believers is practised (§5).

We agree that the original apostolic ministry of assembling the congregation by word and sacrament and assuming central responsibility for its continuance on the one foundation of the gospel is "constitutive for the life and witness of the Church" (§8). This office has been *instituted by God* (*Confessio Augustana* 5); the bearer of this office is, in ordination, called by Christ himself (§11; cf. *CA* 14). By their "public" proclamation of the word and administration of the sacraments in this sense, the persons thus ordained are called to perform the ministry entrusted to the whole church. We can therefore accept the description of this ministry as one of *proclamation, leadership, teaching and pastoral care* (§§11,13). For, according to Lutheran teaching, only those two fundamental functions (sc. the proclamation of the word and the administration of the sacraments) are "necessary for true unity", whereas all other functions are human arrangements which need not necessarily "be everywhere alike" (*CA* 7). We are also in basic accord with the description of *ordination* (§§15; 39–50) and of the authority of the ordained minister (§§15f.). For this authority is clearly differentiated from that of Christ, and ministers are not only subject to the judgment of their congregation but also, at the same time, independent of it (§16 Commentary).

The *threefold ministry* is certainly a considerable challenge to us. At the same time, it includes certain elements which are not practicable in our church. Yet we cannot ignore the fact that all three ministries (or rather, their functions) have existed in the church from the very beginning. We are ready, therefore, to examine the various suggestions made in the description of them (§§19–30), provided the complete adoption of the threefold ministry is not raised to a *status confessionis*. In our view, questions of this kind are not of the essence of the church (*esse ecclesiae*) or of its ministries; they are to be settled responsibly and reasonably, and in a common ecumenical spirit, in the best interests of the church (*bene esse ecclesiae*).

We warmly welcome, in particular, the guidelines for the exercise of the ordained ministry, namely, "in a *personal, collegial and communal way*" (§§ 26–27), since we attach great importance to the "effective participation of the community" and to mutual "interdependence and cooperation" (§§12; 13 Commentary; 15 and 16).

In virtue of our Lutheran tradition, we attach great importance to the "*apostolic succession*" (§§34–38), in the sense that not only the entire faith and life of the church but also its entire ministry are based on the gospel and must be measured against the gospel proclaimed and taught by the apostles and attested in holy scripture (as *norma normans*). In this sense, our Lutheran Church is "apostolic". In our view, however, the church's ordained ministry is not of necessity bound to a historically unbroken chain of bishops and their successors and, as a church of the Lutheran confession, we feel deeply affronted when the "full" apostolic legitimacy of our ministry is denied in virtue of the absence of such an unbroken chain of succession (cf. §§38, 53). In the freedom of the gospel, however, we are able to accept the succession of our pastors and bishops "as *a sign* of the apostolicity of the life of the whole Church" (§38).

The following are the main further questions and objections

In our reading of it, the text on ministry equates the ordained ministry too directly with *the ministry* of the church. But alongside the ordained ministry there are *many other ministries* which in our view are most important for the church, even if people are not in practice ordained to them. We realize, of course, that the text restricts itself deliberately to the ordained ministry. In our view, however, this is to take into account only one partial aspect of the ministry and its embodiment in ministries (services). It seems to us necessary, therefore, that we and other churches should examine the relationship and interconnections between the ordained ministry and other ministries of the church.

Since it is by word and sacrament that the church (as *creatura verbi*) is created, developed and united, it is certainly permissible to speak of the members of the "ordained ministry" as "a focus of its (sc. the church's) unity" (§8). The same can also be said of the eucharist (§14), since, according to 1 Corinthians 10:16f., the shared communion "demonstrates and effects", in special measure, the unity of the church (cf. Eucharist §19). When it is said, however, that the ordained minister in his own person, when leading the celebration (§14), represents Christ, this seems to us to jeopardize the uniquely decisive personal *action of Christ in the eucharist* as the "Lord's Supper". Since Lutheran doctrine differentiates very carefully and concretely between the authority of the Lord who is himself present in the Supper and the authority of the ordained minister whom he authorizes to act, we cannot possibly make the validity of a celebration of the Lord's Supper depend on its being conducted by an ordained minister, even though, in practice, in the interests of "due" order, we take great care to ensure that this is the case. Moreover, though we have no objection to describing the ordained minister as a "priest"—where the underlying idea here is the act of intercession (§17 with Commentary)—we do have misgivings about bestowing this title—to which, strictly speaking, only Christ the Crucified is entitled—on the ordained minister.

Although we find it possible to envisage acceptance of the *threefold ministry* as "an expression of the unity we seek", we could certainly not do so in terms of "a means for achieving" this unity (§22, cf.25). The view that the ordering of the ministry—apart from the special commission of the ordained ministry to preach the gospel publicly and to administer the sacraments—forms part of the free and responsible jurisdiction of the church is written into our church's confession (*CA* 7). The lay ministry of the church elder and the synod member has been developed in our church as a key office of church leadership and we therefore consider it essential in any future reform of church ministry to relate these lay ministries to the threefold ministry.

In our church, the bishops are pastors with a special mission: that of spiritual oversight (*episkopé*) of the whole church, concern for the unity of the church and responsibility for the ordination of pastors. While we are able broadly to endorse the description of the tasks of the bishop, the pastor ("presbyter") and the deacon, given in §§29–31, we would have to reject unambiguously any interpretation of the inter-relationship of the three ministries in a hierarchical sense. Although such an interpretation is carefully avoided in the terminology employed, the layout of the whole section nevertheless gives the impression of a gradation of ministries in a hierarchical sense. At a point which is most important for the relationship of the churches to one another, therefore, the text betrays a fuzziness which does nothing to dispel the anxiety that what we have here is not an expression of convergence but rather a concealment of real differences. In our judgment, convergence will only have been achieved when a hierarchy is explicitly excluded.

By *ordination* we understand an act of calling, sending, authorizing and blessing in the name of Christ himself and with the invocation of the Holy Spirit. The biblical gesture of the imposition of hands and the lifelong validity and unrepeatability of ordination are signs of this. But we do not regard ordination as a sacrament (in the sense of the definition in Eucharist §1) nor its lifelong validity as irrevocable. Only in this sense can we endorse §§39–50 and we have hesitations about accepting §43 at all.

Consequences for our relations with other churches (Question 2)

On the basis of its confession of faith (*CA* 7), our church has no grounds for refusing to recognize the *ordained ministry of other churches* where this ministry clearly serves the pure proclamation of the gospel and the administration of the sacraments in accordance with Christ's institution. But if the way to church fellowship is not to be blocked, our church, too, is bound to require from other churches a full recognition of its ordained ministry, which in its case is exercised by both men and women. We hope, therefore, that the endorsement of the proposals in §§51–55 by all the churches will permit us to achieve a mutual recognition of ministries even with those of our neighbour churches with whom no such relationship of mutual confidence as yet exists.

Consequences for our own church (Question 3)

The text on the ministry is a powerful challenge to our church to examine our forms of ministry. We are prepared, as requested, to renew our theory and practice of ministry (§51). But we can only do so by reflecting anew, at the same time, on the inter-relationship between all ministries in the church. In such a reflection, the reform of the diaconate and its coordination with other ministries, in our view, has a specially important place.

FUTURE WORK

1. Towards unity: The North Elbian Evangelical Lutheran Church requests the Faith and Order Commission to accept this official response as our contribution to its next meeting, to interpret our endorsements as a partial consensus on the way towards a broader consensus, and to throw more ecumenical light on our misgivings and objections.

Our church requests the Commission to analyze the convergence process and, in the light of this analysis, to provide practical help of various kinds for the next stage on the way towards the mutual recognition for which our church is in principle prepared.

2. *Towards renewal*: The consultation and decision-making process in our own church clearly showed that the question which attracted most interest and was taken as a challenge to renewal was the third main question concerning guidance for our worship, educational, ethical and spiritual life. The answers given to this question in our official responses to the statements on "Baptism, Eucharist and Ministry" simply point out the direction we consider necessary and to which we consider ourselves committed in our future work.

3. In order to make the suggestions of the convergence statements fruitful in the work of the congregations and to pursue on a broader basis the questions and practical steps towards greater church fellowship, it is our intention to prepare and distribute an ecumenical manual.

4. *Towards the common expression of the apostolic faith today:* We have not yet sufficiently discussed the fourth main question concerning the common expression of the apostolic faith today and have therefore refrained from dealing with it in the various sections of our official response. The three ancient church creeds constitute part of the basic stock for our liturgies and confessional documents. Beyond that, we are of the opinion that agreement on one or more of these ancient creeds would not, in itself, be an adequate response to the challenge to achieve a common expression of the apostolic faith today. It is axiomatic for us that every confession of faith requires its *casus confessionis*, i.e. its necessary occasion. In our view this occasion exists today, above all, in virtue of the divisions and differences between the churches. Two elements must therefore be included in a contemporary common confession: firstly, the mutual confession of guilt for the fragmentation of the church and all the painful consequences this entails, matched by a corresponding offer of reconciliation and mutual recognition; secondly, the affirmation of our unity, as described for example in the Lutheran World Federation's 1984 declaration on "The Unity We Seek".

On the recommendation of working group 4, the following statement was adopted by the 7th Assembly of the Lutheran World Federation in Budapest, Hungary, in 1984:

"The true unity of the church, which is the unity of the body of Christ and participates in the unity of the Father, Son, and Holy Spirit, is given in and through proclamation of the gospel in word and sacrament. This unity is expressed as a communion in the common and, at the same time, multiform confession of one and the same apostolic faith. It is a communion in holy baptism and in the eucharistic meal, a communion in which the ministries exercised are recognized by all as expressions of the ministry instituted by Christ in his church. It is a communion where diversities contribute to fullness and are no longer barriers to unity. It is a committed fellowship, able to make common decisions and to act in common.

"The diversity present in this communion rises out of the differing cultural and ethnic contexts in which the one church of Christ lives out its mission and out of the number of church traditions in which the apostolic faith has been maintained, transmitted, and lived throughout the centuries. In recognizing these diversities as expressions of the one apostolic faith and the one catholic church, traditions are changed, antagonisms overcome, and mutual condemnations lifted. The diversities are reconciled and transformed into a legitimate and indispensable multiformity within the one body of Christ.

"This communion lives out its unity in confessing the one apostolic faith. It assembles in worship and in intercession for all people. It is active in common witness to Jesus Christ; in advocacy for the weak, poor, and oppressed; and in striving for peace, justice, and freedom. It is ordered in all its components in conciliar structures and actions. It is in need of constant renewal and is, at the same time, a foretaste of that communion which the Lord will at the end of times bring about in his kingdom."

Kiel, 12 February 1985
The Synod
Dräger, President

The Church Council, for the Chairman: Dr Wilckens, Bishop

Bishop for Holstein-Lübeck, Dr Wilckens
Bishop for Schleswig, D. Stoll
Bishop for Hamburg, D. Krusche

ANGLICAN CHURCH
OF THE SOUTHERN CONE

Clarification

For reasons of space, we have tended to concentrate our observations on those points which appear to be weak. There are some
paragraphs which we consider excellent, such as Ml-M6, e.g. "In
particular, there are differences concerning the place and forms of the
ordained ministry. As they engage in the effort to overcome these
differences, the churches need to work from the perspective of the
calling of the whole people of God", and we must appreciate the
clarity of expression achieved in this last chapter which has been of
use to us in drafting our reply to some questions put to us by the
Provincial Executive Committee. Also, we are glad to see the frank
recognition of areas where it has been impossible to reach agreement
between the churches (e.g. M22, 24 on the differing forms taken by
the threefold ministry and the relationship between the various
orders; E13 Commentary on the real presence).

Doubts about multilateral conversations

1. The possibility of multiple interpretations

In bilateral conversations there is a risk that the representatives of
the two parties end up forging their own theology which, although it
has its beginning in the positions of the two churches, ends up as
something new, be it an advance or a retreat. However, the whole
dynamic of multilateral conversations is different and the main
danger would seem to be that each participant interprets the
documents from his own perspective without reaching a substantial
agreement. Even if they were to reach agreement, the same thing
would happen once the document was released to a wider public. One

● Dioceses of Argentina, Northern Argentina, Chile, Bolivia, Paraguay, Peru: 35,550
members, 222 parishes, 6 bishops. No emphases in quotations are found in the
original: all italics have been done in this drafting to indicate the key words.

member of the commission wrote: "It is such a cleverly written document that.... I feel there is a danger that every church can read into it what it likes", and: "It seems to me that this apparent general consensus has been reached because of the new approach and new language used in the document—and sometimes because of what is *not* said (e.g. only mentioning the word sacrament in connection with baptism in the final paragraph of B23)."

2. The contemporary difficulty of dogmatic definitions

Running the risks inherent in any generalization, one can say that, in spite of divergences, for the space of some eighteen centuries there existed an adequate common conceptual framework to allow the formulation of general dogmatic definitions. However, in recent decades philosophical pluralism and cultural diversification have undermined this framework. New discoveries in the fields of semantics, linguistics and the sociology of knowledge have raised doubts as to the possibility of drafting doctrinal statements akin to the Chalcedonian definition which came to be accepted as the authoritative solution to the Christological problems posed in the fourth century. We believe that it is still possible provided that one realizes that there will be serious problems with the exegesis of the document and its application in a given situation. Furthermore, such statements will not have the same impact on the life of the church today since they will tend to fulfil a more pedagogic role than they did in the past. Unfortunately, it appears that out-of-date techniques are still being used in interconfessional negotiations and conversations without taking into consideration the new range of problems facing thinkers today.

3. Realism in assessing their true importance

The document asks a question about "the extent to which your church can recognize in this text the faith of the church throughout the ages". The real object of faith has never been a doctrinal definition but rather Jesus Christ himself and although Augustine and Luther believed in the same Saviour, it is not clear that they had the same understanding of this faith. We therefore ask if one can speak of "the faith of the church throughout the ages" without making a series of clarifications which are not found in the document.

Concerns about methodology

1. The two starting points

In the search for Christian unity one can start from either of two presuppositions: (1) We are Christian, the truth will be found in our union; or (2) Christians ought to unite on the basis of the truth. The first of these can degenerate into the facile assumption that the truth is basically the sum of the different emphases dear to each group, while the second can end as an unhealthy preoccupation with details of minor importance. While not maintaining that these are strictly contradictory, we believe that the second cannot be left out of consideration and would have liked to see more concern for the "church which has to renew herself continually", particularly in the sections on baptism and eucharist, since we do not accept that a consensus based largely on the status quo is always right.

Some years ago the distinction was made between "descriptive metaphysics" and "prescriptive metaphysics". In the former, one tries to determine how people *are* thinking; in the latter, how they *ought* to think. Theologians face a similar situation which requires that they define their objectives. The present document does not contain a section on authority but it seems that it aims to be largely descriptive trusting that the tradition of the church is sound, or in the terms used in a previous document—scripture, Tradition and traditions—her traditions are reliable (in spite of M33, v. M34; M34 Commentary).

2. Hermeneutical considerations

Doubt was expressed about the hermeneutic implicit in the use of scriptural references in the document. One example must suffice for the moment: the Pauline epistles are very largely "occasional theology", that is products of a specific situation, written to solve it. Is it legitimate to use just them as the sources for a generalized theology? For example, in B2 the Pauline references to baptism are used to suggest what is the significance of baptism; however, Paul was writing to mature adults who were still making an open confession of faith. Can one apply the conclusions drawn by Paul to everyone who has been baptized, even if they have lapsed afterwards, or only to adults who have remained faithful to their baptismal vows (e.g. the more wide-reaching concepts of covenant and grace)? We suggest that the principles behind the use made of biblical quotations in this type of document deserve more study than they have received up till now and that in this specific case one ought not ignore Romans 2: 28–29 where Paul clearly puts circumcision, the sacramental rite of the Old Testament, on a lower plane than the reality it intended to signify.

3. Unresolved tensions

We have the impression that at times statements from different schools of thought have been laid side by side without achieving a real synthesis, e.g. in the first two sentences of B2: "Baptism is the *sign* of new life... It *unites* the one baptized with Christ and with his people." How does a sign effect the union presupposed in the second sentence?

4. Idealistic language

The document seems to use language in an optimistic way as if the ideal is always achieved. This is particularly so at times when using the copula "is" which in any case lends itself to a variety of interpretations.

The chapter on baptism

1. The copula "is"

Should we deduce from B2, "Baptism is participation in Christ's death and resurrection", an *ex opere operato* doctrine? —above all in the light of B8, "Personal commitment is necessary for *responsible* membership in the Body of Christ" (cf. B12 Commentary 2nd par). If a qualifying clause similar to the Anglican article 27 "whereby, as by an instrument, they that receive Baptism rightly are grafted into the Church; the promises of forgiveness of sin... are visibly signed and sealed..." had been included beforehand, there would not be much room for doubt. Without it, there is.

In spite of the possible safeguards in sections III, Baptism and Faith, and IV, Baptismal Practice, e.g. "The necessity of faith for the reception of the salvation embodied and set forth in baptism is acknowledged by all churches" (B8), "Baptism in its full meaning *signifies* and effects both" (B12), the net result is a theology which seems to us to be inadequate, above all when one takes into account the popular understanding of religion and the practice of the majority in Latin America.

2. Challenging comments

In the commentary on B14, the document comments that the churches which do not admit baptized children to the holy communion without some further rite "may wish to ponder whether they have fully appreciated and accepted the consequences of baptism". We believe that this is a question which the Province should study.

In B13 one finds the definitive statement that "baptism is an unrepeatable act". It is not so regarded by many non-Roman Catholic churches in this continent* and the matter deserves further exam-

---

* Practices vary from church to church: some do not recognize the validity of Roman Catholic baptism, others practise believer's baptism, some "re-baptize" adults coming from other Protestant groups. Given the total numbers involved, this problem cannot be dismissed as concerning a small fringe group.

ination, particularly in those dioceses of the Province where there is pressure to conform to "popular Protestant practice". We ought to think seriously about current practices in our churches with the aim of formulating a well-founded theology to regulate what is happening.

3. Lack of a unifying principle

Neither in this chapter nor in the following one on the eucharist is there a key-concept which underlies the whole and gives it coherence. There is one candidate for this role: *covenant* and we regret that the opportunity has been missed.

The chapter on the eucharist

We shall limit ourselves to some key issues.

1. At the end of El it is said that the eucharist "has acquired many names: for example, the Lord's Supper, the breaking of bread, the holy communion..., the mass". Some members of the commission questioned the underlying assumption: i.e. the different names denote the same underlying reality. In practice, each term has acquired a different doctrinal emphasis and it was felt that the divergences are too great to be usefully subsumed under one label (compare the use of the term "socialist" in "Union of Soviet Socialist Republics" and "Christian socialist").

2. Section II, The Meaning of the Eucharist, has as its aim the study of the significance of the eucharist under five heads which apparently are all equally important. It would seem that the biblical account gives a special priority to one of these and that the idea of *anamnesis* ought to serve as the key concept within the general setting of the covenant.

3. We cannot agree that one should to translate *anamnesis* by "memorial". "Remembrance" is used in the quotation of 1 Corinthians 11: 23–25 but from then on one only finds the term "memorial". Although it has become a semi-technical term when used in this context and it could be argued that as such it has the same meaning as "remembrance", we object to the practice on the grounds that while "memorial" is not a dynamic equivalent of the Greek *anamnesis* there is a perfectly good English word "commemoration" which is and this latter should therefore be used in technical works even if the less recondite "remembrance" is retained for popular use. As it stands, "memorial" leaves the document open to serious misunderstanding, especially in the light of past debates.

The words of institution contain three key indicators: *anamnesis*, "covenant" and the emphasis on the death of Jesus "for the remission of sins"; the section which deals with the significance of the eucharist (E2–26) seems to diverge widely from these guidelines; for example the offertory of bread and wine expresses the offering of the fruits of human labours to the Father (E4). While not wishing to deny that in other settings this would be wholesome and right, it was pointed out that in this context the offertory is considered by some to be bad symbolism since the elements which will become the sacrament of the body and blood of Christ should symbolize consistently the divine initiative in redemption rather than play two contradictory roles in a short space of time.

4. In general terms we would criticize this chapter as containing too much description of current practices and insufficient application of the biblical guidelines.

5. We should not allow to pass unnoticed the fact that in paragraph 32 the document implies that, being secondary, the reservation of the sacrament is acceptable and all churches should respect the custom of those which practise it. Although welcoming as a great advance the emphases at the end of the paragraph on the use of the host for sick-communion and its being consumed during the service, we consider that this is not adequate and that despite its deep roots in the Latin culture, reservation for the purpose of adoration is not negotiable practice but a mistaken one.

The chapter on ministry

This is in general excellent; above all the frame of reference which is set up at the beginning about the people of God and commentary 11 which recognizes the complicated factors involved in the evolution of the ordained ministry and the need to avoid considering the particular form adopted by one's own church, to be the form instituted by Christ. We would like to see a clearer recognition of the social and cultural factors which conditioned the process (M19) and as a result a greater willingness to scrutinize afresh the traditional concepts involved in it such as the indelibility of holy orders (nb M40 Commentary) so as to see if they can be adequately understood within our present conceptual framework.

We doubt whether the mention of prophetic and charismatic ministries in M33 is sufficient to balance up the confidence shown in tradition and the apostolic succession (M33, 34)—the church not composed of soldiers who can be drilled into discipline but of sheep who are continually straying. The reference to the need for "an ordained minister" at the level of the local eucharistic community (M27) is an unjustified assumption in the context and would disqualify some Protestant denominations if taken strictly.

It would be useful to clarify at a future date the fundamental concept of "holy order"; nevertheless, the document provides plenty of food for thought and interconfessional conversation and we would specifically mention the need to develop in all its fullness the threefold ministry with the restoration of the diaconate to its proper status. We hope that the last section about mutual recognition of ministries receives the attention it deserves.

Conclusion
While the document as a whole represents an impressive advance, there remains plenty of ground to cover still. In our opinion this includes further revision in order that it may serve as the basis for a theology which will revitalize the church in the last years of this century.

Santiago, January 1985   John Cobb
                                                       Andrew Couch
                                                        David Evans

CHURCH OF IRELAND
(ANGLICAN)

To put Lima in perspective, we need to look both backwards and forwards. In the first instance, it will be seen as representing the fruit of over fifty years of patient ecumenical study, beginning from the first Faith and Order conference held in Lausanne in 1927. But this statement is not the terminus to which interchurch dialogue has been striving. Baptism, eucharist and ministry are not simply matters of doctrinal concern; they touch deeply on the whole life, worship and witness of the church. Lima therefore represents a stage—an important stage—in via towards the final goal when all the churches will not only have achieved doctrinal agreement but will have reached the point of living and acting in visible unity. It must help us to look deeply at the doctrine and practice of our own church as the condition of contributing positively in an ecumenical dimension.

Although it describes itself as an agreed statement, Lima is not intended to be a formula of agreement, to which all the parties involved can fully subscribe. In this respect it differs from bilateral statements such as the Arcic (Anglican-Roman Catholic International Commission) report. As the preface admits, and as any church member will immediately realize, total consensus is not yet possible between all the participating bodies. The WCC consists of some three hundred members, representing a wide range of confessional traditions. The Faith and Order Commission also includes theologians of the Roman Catholic and other churches which do not belong to the WCC itself.

The purpose of Lima may therefore be regarded primarily as *descriptive*, i.e. it sets out side by side the differing convictions and

---

● 376,000 members, 520 parishes, 527 pastors.

practices of the churches in regard to baptism, eucharist and ministry. It aims also to draw out the considerable degree of theological convergence which has emerged, and it underlines the fact that the churches, even where there is a wide diversity of practice, have already reached "a large measure of theological agreement".

> That theologians of such widely different traditions should be able to speak so harmoniously about baptism, eucharist and ministry is unprecedented in the modern ecumenical movement (p.ix).

The text of the document indicates the major areas of convergence; it appeals for them to be recognized and developed as a means of growing together into the deeper experience of Christian unity.

> These convergences give assurance that despite much diversity in theological expression the churches have much in common in their understanding of the faith. The resultant text aims to become part of a faithful and sufficient reflection of the common Christian Tradition on essential elements of Christian communion. In the process of growing together in mutual trust, the churches must develop these doctrinal convergences step by step, until they are finally able to declare together that they are living in communion with one another in continuity with the apostles and the teachings of the universal Church.

This Lima text represents the significant theological convergence which Faith and Order has discerned and formulated.

Lima, however, is realistic enough to recognize that many differences in belief and practice still need to be resolved. These differences are indicated chiefly in the *commentaries* that are added alongside the text. This raises an important question for a church in formulating an official response. What is the status of the commentaries? Are they an integral part of the total document? Do they carry an equal weight with the text itself?

For example, some Anglicans may find difficulty with the commentary on the eucharist (E8):

> It is in the light of the significance of the eucharist as intercession that references to the eucharist in Catholic theology as "propitiatory sacrifice" may be understood. The understanding is that there is only one expiation, that of the unique sacrifice of the cross, made actual in the eucharist and presented before the Father in the intercession of Christ and of the Church for all humanity.
>
> In the light of the biblical conception of memorial, all churches might want to review the old controversies about "sacrifice" and deepen their understanding of the reasons why other traditions than their own have either used or rejected this term.

This committee itself finds no objection to this viewpoint; indeed it welcomes the attempt to find rapprochement between Catholic and Protestant understandings of the eucharist. But while drawing attention to such a statement on the grounds that it might not find unanimous approval, we would again point out that it belongs not to the text itself, but is one of the commentaries.

As to the text itself, because it is largely descriptive in character and concerned with theological convergence, there is little or nothing in it with which we should want positively to disagree. Such reservations as we have would centre round details of emphasis. For example, "Baptism", Section 1, dealing with the institution of baptism in the New Testament records, concludes with the sentence: "The churches today continue this practice as a rite of commitment to the Lord who bestows his grace upon his people." We would not disagree with this statement but we would see the primary emphasis of baptism in the New Testament as representing our Lord's commitment to his church rather than our commitment. But the chapter as a whole represents a balanced theology of baptism, and all that we wish to infer here is that there are certain statements with which we would not be entirely happy, if taken out of context.

We have begun this report by indicating that certain reservations arise in our mind, but we would wish to stress that these are of a minor character. We find Lima a very positive document, admirable in its comprehensiveness, its honesty of approach, and its economy of style. As an effort in reconciliation, it deserves our serious consideration. It does not attempt to cover over differences, nor is it superficial in searching for areas of agreement. Lima claims that the basis for all joint examination of differences in "the tradition of the gospel testified in scripture, transmitted in and by the Church through the power of the Holy Spirit" (p.ix). This is the stance of the preamble to our own constitution which says that our doctrinal criteria are primarily scripture and the profession of faith of the primitive church. It is also worth noting that the ARCIC dialogue is "founded in the scriptures and on the ancient common traditions" (Common Declaration of Pope Paul VI and Archbishop Ramsey of Canterbury). Thus there is established the basic pattern of belief and practice, and it is on this basis that convergence between differing theological viewpoints begins to appear. Much of the strength of Lima seems to us to lie in its summaries of the New Testament evidence. These provide a concise conspectus of New Testament theology, that should prove valuable to clergy, students, teachers and others.

One other feature in Lima's methodology is noteworthy. It

recognizes that the controversies between the churches on baptism, eucharist and ministry are deep-rooted in history; they were formulated in the language and categories of the past. Lima believes that many of our historical controversies are susceptible to reconciliation through the changes in the atmosphere of Christian life in the twentieth century. As the churches seek to carry out the task of mission and renewal in the world, they are asking how their patterns of baptism, eucharist and ministry are fitted to meet this task. Further, with the notable development of biblical and patristic studies, liturgical renewal, and not least with ecumenical progress, many of our former controversies are being seen in a new light.

In other words what Lima appears to say to the churches is that as we live in a time of change, it is also a time of ecumenical opportunity. Hence the urgency for our church to recognize the importance of this document and respond to it not only in an official written statement but at the deeper levels of the church's life.

Baptism
The attitude to Lima we have indicated in general terms applies to the chapter on baptism. We consider it to be balanced and comprehensive. In certain respects it might be seen as a salutory corrective to aspects of our own teaching and practice. But there are points where we would like to see a more definite emphasis or clearer definition.

In the doctrinal section, Anglicans will find little reference to baptism as the sacrament of regeneration. The "new birth" (John 3) is included in the list of New Testament images (B2), but regeneration is not explicitly mentioned again. Some of us would regard it as being covered in the section as a whole while others would detect a confusion between regeneration and conversion. Anglicans familiar with Article 27 will also miss any reference to baptism as "grafting", and any distinct emphasis on the concept of "adoption to sonship".

Lima deals with the relation of baptism and faith with a clarity that should be helpful to the confused. It views faith as man's response to God's gift, so that faith is necessary "to receive the salvation embodied and set forth in baptism" (B8). It follows then that faith as response to God's gift is not simply momentary, but a continuing and growing experience. Further, personal commitment is necessary for responsible membership in the body of Christ.

Lima is particularly strong on the aspect of the church as the community of faith, in which baptism is administered. It lays stress on the baptismal responsibility which devolves on all local congregations.

> At every baptism the whole congregation reaffirms its faith in God and pledges itself to provide an environment of witness and service. Baptism should, therefore, always be celebrated and developed in the setting of the Christian community (B12).

In this context Lima warns those who practise infant baptism of the dangers of indiscriminate baptism. We consider that the Church of Ireland—and Anglicans in general—might well take this aspect of Lima seriously to heart.

Some of us considered Lima to be weak in its defence of infant baptism. Others saw it as an interesting attempt to show that infant baptism and believers' baptism are not theologically opposed but might coexist as pointing to different aspects of the fullness of truth. Here it is important to note that Lima emphatically asserts the act of baptism to be unrepeatable: "Any practice which might be interpreted as 're-baptism' must be avoided" (B13).

Commentary (b) on paragraph 14 deals with confirmation.

> Those churches which baptize children but refuse them a share in the eucharist before such a rite may wish to ponder whether they have fully appreciated and accepted the consequence of baptism.

Insofar as this may be aimed at Anglican practice, we should regard it as based on a misunderstanding of our situation.

In general we found this chapter on baptism interesting and in some respects stimulating. At the same time we were left with a feeling of uneasiness as to where the main thrust of its teaching lies. (Perhaps this is inevitable in a document of ecumenical origin.) In this connection we should like to submit two comments:

1. We felt that there was need of a preliminary section on sacraments and their place in the church. The sacraments are described as "signs", but whether they are mere symbols or effective signs (instruments) does not explicitly emerge (cf. Articles of Religion XXV Book of Common Prayer).
2. It would also have been helpful if a baptismal liturgy had been provided. This might have given life to the text and revealed more clearly the direction of its teaching.

Eucharist

In this chapter the eucharist is expounded in a manner that is characteristic in contemporary theological and liturgical circles. Drawing its inspiration from recent biblical, patristic and liturgical scholarship, it is eirenic in its approach and successfully transcends the old divisive controversies. In the broad scope of its exposition, it should extend the eucharistic vision of many church members. By the same token it is possible that many will find its general approach too cerebral and too remote from the sacramental experience of the ordinary church member. It includes much that is essentially theological interpretation, not directly based on the evidence of the New Testament. While rightly drawing out the centrality of the eucharist, Lima seems to be in danger of claiming for it much that is to be predicated of the Christian life in general. Once again we would not positively disassociate ourselves from the statements of the text, but we think that in this case there is a degree of over-emphasis that would be alien to the mind of the average congregation.

The chapter begins with a brief survey of the New Testament evidence. One important text that appears to be overlooked (in accordance with the contemporary trend) is 1 Corinthians 11:26—the eucharist as a proclaiming of the Lord's death—which would appear to be central in the prayer book interpretation. Also in line with contemporary exegesis much is made of the link between the eucharist and the other meals of Jesus during his earthly life—a link which seems to us to have minimal significance in our understanding of the sacrament.

Lima attempts to avoid the old controversies that centred around the categories of presence and sacrifice. It does so by concentrating attention on the eucharist as *anamnesis* or memorial. *Anamnesis* is seen as having a dynamic significance. It is not only a calling to mind of what is past. It is the "living and effective sign of his sacrifice, accomplished once and for all on the cross and still operative on behalf of all humankind" (E5). Christ himself is present in this *anamnesis* so that the eucharist is essentially the action of Christ himself. (Similarly the ARCIC report insists on Christ being present *and active* in the eucharistic celebration.) Lima lays stress on the unique and unrepeatable character of Christ's sacrifice (cf. again ARCIC). We cannot think that it has been entirely successful in reinterpreting the Catholic description of the eucharist as "propitiary sacrifice" (see above).

Anamnesis also refers to the content of the preached word. The celebration of the eucharist includes and is reinforced by the proclamation of the word.

An important section of this chapter is devoted to the role of the Holy Spirit. It appeals for restoration in the liturgy of the *epiklesis* or invocation of the Spirit on the community *and* the elements. Some of us hold that this goes beyond our tradition and is unnecessary. The suggestion that the whole action of the eucharist has an "epikletic" character would seem to be more in line with the emphasis in our own formularies on the *spiritual* character of the service as a whole.

We find much to approve in the way that Lima keeps the eucharist firmly anchored in the reality of the church's life in the world. The community reconciled in the eucharist becomes in turn the instrument of reconciliation. The sharing of the eucharist challenges us to fight against injustice and oppression. The love of Christ which we experience sends us out in the service of human need.

The final section on "the celebration of the eucharist" includes a list of the elements that might be expected to be included in a modern liturgy. The Order for the Celebration of the Holy Communion in the Alternative Prayer Book 1984 measures up satisfactorily to the requirements laid down.

It is affirmed that the true president at every eucharist is Christ himself and that "in most churches this presidency is signified by an ordained minister". While we find that there is much to approve in this paragraph (E29), we should require it to be given stronger definition, together with some reference to episcopal ordination.

The commentary on paragraph 28 refers to the use at the eucharist in some churches of local food and drink rather than the bread and wine commanded by Christ. We cannot accept the suggestion that under normal conditions this might be a feature which could be regarded as changeable according to the decision of the church.

Ministry

It is in this area that the descriptive method of Lima becomes most apparent. It has to be content to record the existence of different conceptions of the ministry—episcopal and non-episcopal, those which have preserved apostolic succession and those which lack it, churches which practise the ordination of women and those which do not. Yet against the background of wide diversity of practice, Lima maps out very definite lines of theological convergence. Anglicans will find reassurance as well as hope in the direction suggested for future development.

The first section of this chapter begins by considering the calling of the whole people of God. This provides the broad context in which the role of the ministry must be discussed, as we ask how the life of the church is to be understood and ordered so that the gospel may be spread and the community built up in love.

It is found necessary at the outset to define certain terms. Particularly, the document distinguishes between ministry in the general sense—that is, the service which belongs to the whole people of God, whether as individuals, as a local community, or as the universal church—and the ordained ministry which refers to persons who have received a charism and whom the church appoints for service by ordination through the invocation of the Spirit and the laying on of hands (M7).

We would consider this distinction to reflect clearly the teaching of our own formularies.

The biblical material is again handled very concisely. It demonstrates that from the beginning there were differentiated roles in the Christian community and reaches the conclusion that the ordained ministry is "constitutive for the life and witness of the church" (M8). Ordained ministers are seen as representatives of Christ, leaders and teachers and pastors. Yet they exist only in and for the community, and as such "have no existence apart from the community" (M12). Since the ordained ministry reminds the community of its dependence on Christ, and serves to build it up in him by word and sacrament, its work in the church finds a special focus in its presidency at the eucharist. In this connection Lima defends the use of the word "priest" to designate the ordained minister, although it is not found in the New Testament. The designation points beyond the minister to the priestly ministry of Christ whom he represents and the priestly character of the church of which he is also the representative.

Lima is also helpful in its brief history and analysis of the threefold pattern of ministry, which under the guidance of the Holy Spirit emerged at a very early stage in the church's life, and which was centred on the episcopate. Although other forms of ministry have developed, Lima suggests that

the threefold ministry of bishop, presbyter and deacon may serve today as an expression of the unity we seek and also as a means for achieving it (M22).

Consequently, it insists that churches which do not have the threefold pattern will need

to ask themselves whether the threefold pattern as developed does not have a powerful claim to be accepted by them (M25).

There is much here that is in line with Anglican thought, as there is also in the important section IV on "Succession in the apostolic tradition". Lima shows that apostolicity and succession in the ministry are closely related to life and witness. Apostolic succession in the ministry is

an expression of the permanence and, therefore, of the continuity of Christ's own mission in which the Church participates. Within the Church the ordained ministry has a particular task of preserving and actualizing apostolic faith. The orderly transmission of the ordained ministry is therefore a powerful expression of the continuity of the Church throughout history; it also underlines the calling of the ordained minister as a guardian of the faith (M35).

Lima appeals for recognition of the fact that continuity in apostolic faith, worship and mission has been preserved in churches which have not retained the form of historic episcopate, and also that the reality and the function of the episcopal ministry has been preserved in many of these churches. It suggests that today these churches, without impugning the validity of their own form of ministry, are willing to accept episcopal succession as a sign of the apostolicity of the life of the whole church.

If there is much in all this which Anglicans can accept and approve, Lima also suggests that

the threefold pattern stands evidently in need of reform (M24).

This is, of course, a matter which is exercising the mind of our own church at present in the work of the commission on ministry and elsewhere. Lima pleads for a restoration of the diaconate as an independent order in the hope of regaining its original significance as a link "between the table and the needy" (M21).

The final section deals with the difficult question of the mutual recognition of the ordained ministries. As a first step this must involve all churches in looking more deeply at their own theory and practice. Apostolic succession is probably the most important issue, and some churches need to recover episcopal ordination as its outward sign. The ordination of women also raises a problem for the mutual recognition of ministries, but Lima does not see it as a "substantive hindrance" (M54).

22 January 1985

BAPTIST UNION OF GREAT BRITAIN AND IRELAND

In receiving the WCC Faith and Order Commission report "Baptism, Eucharist and Ministry", the Baptist Union Council welcomes it as a notable milestone in the search for sufficient theological consensus to make possible mutual recognition among separated churches. In general, it would not serve the positive purpose of the report to put the weight of comment on unacceptable words or questionable phrases. To draw attention to major points of difficulty or hesitation may however serve to indicate areas where reservations remain.

Baptism

We welcome the careful attention that has been given to Baptist convictions on this issue and the keen attempt made to do justice to them. We concur with the five strands that are woven together to set forth the essential meaning that baptism enshrines. We thankfully note the significant place accorded to faith within the baptismal reality and the clear recognition of the danger of the indiscriminate baptism of infants. We rejoice in the clear setting of baptism within the lifelong process of preparation, growth, and nurture in Christ. Three specific reservations must however be noted.

1. At the second sentence of B1 language is introduced which continues to mark the subsequent discussion. We are told that baptism *is...gives...initiates...unites...effects....* It has to be asked what is meant by "baptism" where this sort of language is constantly used. Is it the actual performance of the rite? If so, the language seems at best hyperbole and at worst objectionable. It may be strongly affirmed that the efficacious work of the gospel can rightly

---

● 166,688 members, 2,070 congregations, 1,490 pastors.

be spoken of in this way, and that baptism relates scripturally to the heart of that gospel. In this sense, the focal and profound significance of the rite in its relationship to the total work of Christ may and must be maintained. What is not clear is the extent to which the report *identifies* the actual performance of the rite with this vast penumbra of meaning and significance.

2. At B13 it is affirmed that "any practice which might be interpreted as 're-baptism' must be avoided". This statement is wholly unacceptable in its present form since, on some interpretations, nothing could pass through so restrictive a sieve. In cases of infant baptism which are neither accompanied nor followed by any of the significant features of the initiatory process to which the report amply draws attention, and where the individual involved is convinced out of an instructed conscience that Christian obedience requires believer baptism, we cannot agree that an *a priori* universal bar should operate.

3. It has for long been clear that a total process of Christian initiation wherein, at some point, all the necessary elements—including responsible faith-commitment—find a place offers the most promising way forward to mutual recognition on the baptismal issue. This fact underlines the problem of the report's arguable ambiguity in its references to "baptism". Statements that may be defensible where and if "baptism" is a shorthand term for total initiation become suspect when applied *simpliciter* to the baptismal rite as administered to infants.

Eucharist

We welcome the careful way in which the report seeks to define some traditional eucharistic emphases such as sacrifice and real presence in a manner that should assist removal of misunderstandings. We note appreciatively the attempt to encompass the richness of many-sided meaning that belongs to the eucharist. We further welcome the clear statement of the implications of eucharistic worship for the life and mission of the church. Two specific reservations must however be noted.

1. In E1 the eucharist is set against a rich and diverse biblical background within which the Last Supper occupies a crucial but not isolated place. That last meal is described as "a liturgical meal employing symbolic words and actions". Even when maximum realistic weight is given to the term "symbolic", it seems that a large and arbitrary leap has been made to arrive at the formulation of E 13:

> Christ's mode of presence in the eucharist is unique. Jesus said over the bread and wine of the eucharist: "This is my body... this is my blood..."

What Christ declared is true, and this truth is fulfilled every time the eucharist is celebrated.

The use of the word "unique" is question-begging. The affirmation that "what Christ declared is true" seems to assume without argument a quite contestable meaning for his declaration.

2. At E15 it is asserted "that the bread and wine become the sacramental signs of Christ's body and blood. They remain so for the purpose of communion". This manner of formulation leaves the impression that "communion" is some sort of postlude to the real "occurrence". We would wish to affirm that the eating and drinking is a central if not the central point of the eucharist action. While we recognize the concern to focus on debated aspects of eucharistic understanding rather than to offer a coherent and rounded presentation, we still have to observe that the aspect of communion with Christ gets scant attention, since the section on "Communion of the Faithful" moves in other directions.

The overall result in Section II is that a collection of valid emphases does not produce a presentation that throws major weight where we believe it should belong, and a theology of the "elements" seems dominant rather than a theology of "action".

Ministry

We welcome the positive and unqualified grounding of the ordained ministry in the total ministry and mission of the whole people of God, which is itself founded in the total ministry, mission and work of Christ.

We further welcome the explicit recognition of the diversity of patterns of ministry evidenced in the New Testament and the ongoing history of the church. We acknowledge appreciatively the careful attempt to set apostolic "succession" within the wider controlling framework of apostolic tradition and continuity.

Two specific reservations must however be noted, both relating to that major problem for mutual recognition, the desirability (even necessity) of the threefold order of ministry (bishops, presbyters, and deacons).

1. After the concessive opening of M22, which admirably represents Baptist conviction, the report inserts its "nevertheless", and goes on to affirm that the traditional threefold ministry "may serve today as an expression of the unity we seek and also as a means for achieving it". We recognize that the report does not say "*the* expression . . . *the* means . . ." But is this almost an implicit assumption? We recognize a certain flexibility in §§ 28, 37 and 49, but note too the more restrictive tone of § 53, especially (b). We recognize also

that the report does not use the language of a threefold *order* of ministry. It needs however to be clarified how far the notion of a threefold order really underlies the current emphasis upon the adoption of this pattern as a prerequisite for mutual recognition.

2. That the presence of a threefold *order* of ministry is really the divisive question at issue seems reinforced by the shifts of language in the report when diaconal ministry is under discussion. We begin at M20-21 with deacons as *functionaries* assisting the bishop. At M22 we hear of "diaconal aspects and *functions*". On reaching M24 we hear of *deacons* who have lost the *function* of diaconal witness. By the time we reach M31 we are presented with a vision of deacons who on the one hand are diaconal in *function* (servants in the world) but who in the next few sentences become omnibus *functionaries* liturgically, catechetically, *et* innumerably *al*. This confusion suggests a striving to justify a threefold *order*. In this connection, the importance of the distinction between *cheirotonein* and *ordinare* (Commentary 40) indeed bears pondering.

Questions and answers
Four specific questions are put to us for reply.

1. *"The extent to which your church can recognize in this text the faith of the Church through the ages."*

We do not find this form of question particularly meaningful or significant. We can recognize in this text a multitude of emphases in harmony with the witness of the New Testament, and in our response we have thankfully acknowledged key areas where this is judged to be so. But tradition is a dynamic process with inevitable admixture of truth and error; and formulations of faith change through the ages, not least because of changing contexts and situations. What we register is a valuable contemporary movement towards common understanding on divisive issues.

2. *"The consequence your church can draw from this text for its relations and dialogues with other churches, particularly with those churches which also recognize the text as an expression of the apostolic faith."*

It will already be clear that our recognition of the text as an "expression of the apostolic faith" while in many respects real is in important respects qualified. The more significant and related question is the extent to which the text enshrines a basis for mutual recognition. It is just here that fundamental assumptions need exposure and assessment. The preface to the report (p.ix) speaks of "consensus" and "convergence". Consensus is affirmed to involve "that experience of life and articulation of faith necessary to realize and maintain the Church's visible unity". What arguably requires much keener debate is what measure of articulated baptismal agreement, eucharistic agreement, agreement on patterns/orders of ministry, is necessary for "living in communion with one another".

This is but a variation of the question as to what measure of diversity of interpretation and expression is commensurate with unity, and as to the proper limits accorded to contextualization. We do not pretend to offer a clear and coherent answer. We acknowledge that the question presses upon us particularly in relation to the issue of baptism. We believe it presses on others in relation to eucharist and (particularly) ministry. We discern in the report different assumptions surfacing at different points in text and commentary. We are not quite persuaded that this reflects balance of truth rather than incoherence.

3. "The guidance your church can take from this text for its worship, educational, ethical, and spiritual life and witness."

This report was referred to our Baptist communities for study and discussion, and our response takes account of reactions received. It is our hope and intention that this process will continue to inform reflection and practice at all levels of our life. It has however to be recognized that the report—particularly in its treatment of eucharist—uses concepts and language that are still in many respects foreign to Baptists.

4. "The suggestions your church can make for the ongoing work of Faith and Order as it relates the material of this text on Baptism, Eucharist, and Ministry to its long-range research project 'Towards the Common Expression of the Apostolic Faith Today'."

It would seem that any further work on baptism could be usefully done only in the wider context of Christian initiation. The place of diversity in relation to consensus needs sharper enunciation. The fact that varied understandings of the church lurk behind some of the issues discussed in BEM confirms the wisdom of setting subsequent Faith and Order study within the context of the "apostolic faith" project.

A supplement to the Baptist Union Council's response to "Baptism, Eucharist and Ministry" prepared by the Advisory Committee for Church Relations

As a result of discussions on the BEM report prompted by the Baptist Union, comments have been received from 16 Baptist associations, the Superintendents' Board, two Baptist theological colleges, and a number of other groups. Though the Baptist Union's own response has been made the background of constituency comment, it remains necessarily a Union response. Faith and Order discussions at the world level need to hear and take account of reactions from the widest and most localized contexts possible. In what follows the attempt is made to report and interpret such Baptist reaction and to pinpoint some of the basic issues thus uncovered. Such an attempt must be prefaced by recording that many have received the report with deep appreciation and have expressed appreciation both of the riches it contains and the challenges it poses.

Language

There is a widespread feeling that it is largely in terms native to other Christian traditions that issues have been posed and language employed It may be part of the ecumenical task and responsibility to learn a language that is strange. It is certainly true that discussion in so far as it is confined to a Baptist constituency and does not venture into the ecumenical arena at local level restricts such a learning process. Nevertheless, it remains a fact that what is *heard* by one tradition is generally subtly and significantly different from what another tradition *intends*. The problem is compounded by what may well be an inevitable feature of ecumenical statements, namely, an ambiguity of language which allows formal assent in the teeth of suspected unbridged disagreement. The problem is further compounded when doubts arise as to what modes of language are being used, especially if there are signs that some statements are to be taken in fairly literal fashion while others perhaps speak symbolically or have a heavy metaphorical loading.

Baptism

Behind the report's discussion of baptism lurks a basic unanswered question: "What is a Christian?" The simplistic assumption not far from the surface seems to be that, for purposes of the BEM report, the yardstick is baptism. Questions immediately arise on several fronts. Does this mean that the baptized infant is a Christian? If so, in what sense? Since the report seems in general to assume that it is the baptized who share in the eucharist, does this automatically authenticate "infant communion"? Alternatively, are all unbaptized believers not Christian? What of the Society of Friends, or the Salvation Army? If the starting point is a New Testament inseparability of conversion and baptism, certain conclusions may arguably follow. If the starting point is tradition, the implications may be importantly other. It may be objected that such questions are falsely posed because they proceed from a starting point which is not that of the report. It must be retorted that this is in fact the baseline from which many Baptists by conviction move.

Eucharist

The report's discussion of eucharist is felt by many to carry an almost intolerable theological overload. Partly this arises from a descriptive usage, unfamiliar to Baptists, which can sometimes embrace the totality of worship in word and sacrament in the one word "eucharist". Partly it arises from an exploitation of symbolism that is judged to be "catholic" rather than scriptural. Partly it arises from an apparently settled determination to ascribe to the eucharist unique and total significance. It is thus that we are told that "every Christian receives this gift of salvation through communion in the body and blood of Christ" (E2). It is thus that stress—perhaps unnatural stress—is placed on notes such as the celebration of creation, the offering of the world's life, the participation in mission (E. A.-E). It is not that the eucharist is seen by Baptists as wholly unrelated to these emphases. Certainly corporate worship *in its totality* will comprehend them. But those for whom the celebration of the Supper is less than a weekly act will particularly demur at the apparent implication that they are thereby impoverished strangers, removed from such eucharistically-tied imperatives, promptings, and understandings.

Ministry

The report's discussion of ministry is widely felt to reflect an underlying doctrine of the church not easily reconcilable with Baptist convictions as to the centrality of the local congregation of gathered believers and the place of the ordained ministry in relation thereto. It is not found reassuring to be confronted with the affirmation that the ordained ministry "is constitutive for the life and witness of the Church" (M8)—even when the situation is partly retrieved by a later recognition that the ordained ministry "has no existence apart from the community" (M12). Baptist concern in this general area has widely been expressed in relation to the issue of lay presidency at the Lord's Table. It is of course importantly true that the report does not absolutely confine such presidency to the ordained ministry (Commentary 13,14). Yet the directive thrust of M13,14 is heard as an affirmation of a basic distinction between "ordained" and "lay" that raises questioning. It is not that Baptists in general deny the calling and gifting of different people for different functions within the church of Christ. If a lay person presides at the Supper it is by commission of the church, so authorizing him or her for this "ministry". The differentia is that it is the *local* church that so commissions on (so it is believed) the authority of Christ entrusted to it. It should be clear that important questions about both the nature of ordination and the centrality and authority of the local church are here posed.

Consensus

In its preface, the BEM report states: "If the divided churches are to achieve the visible unity they seek, one of the essential prerequisites is that they should be in basic agreement on baptism, eucharist and ministry." Comment from our Baptist constituency makes clear that this apparently self-evident statement conceals as many questions as it answers. What understanding of visible unity is here intended? What measure and kind of basic agreement is here required? Part of the felt difficulty with the total presentation of both baptism and eucharist is a sense that these sacraments are being filled with an exclusive theological weight which is more properly attributed to the deeper realities of which they are the visible signs and to which they bear witness, and that it is upon these deeper and more pervasive realities that unity is properly founded. This in turn reflects a widespread unease that the model of visible unity assumed and the nature of consensus sought make inadequate allowance for a diversity which is arguably compatible with living in communion one with another. In this context, the heavy insistence on the "threefold order" of ministry becomes a centre of deep concern.

METHODIST CHURCH OF NEW ZEALAND

From the letter of the general secretary

The resolution was prepared by the Faith and Order Committee of the Methodist Church of New Zealand, distributed throughout the church, and passed without dissent in a slightly modified form by the Conference.

Our basic response as a member church of the WCC is that we clearly recognize in the text the faith of the church through the ages. To this basic affirmation the church has added some comments, responding to the series of questions outlined in the preface to "Baptism, Eucharist and Ministry". The section numbers in the resolution relate to the four questions asked here.

A few background comments might be helpful. As we seek to discover appropriate responses to the gospel as Maori, and Pakeha (European) in Aotearoa (New Zealand) and as we relate to Polynesian people and are involved with the Asian church, we are led to ask questions about the "Northern" and "Western" nature of the text (1.3). This has to do, in part, with language, but also with imagery and concept. We recognize that a document prepared for worldwide use will inevitably have to be general, and will arise out of a particular tradition and style. But we wish to make the comment from our perspective in our context. We have been grappling with this as part of our expressed intention to move towards becoming a bi-cultural church (3.2). Conference made this commitment two years ago, and the church is seeking ways of expressing that. We do not have final answers, but our consciousness is being raised, and we have the question continually before us.

In general, we are finding "Baptism, Eucharist and Ministry" to be a helpful stimulant in the life of the church. It is a valuable resource as

---

● 19,682 members, 188 parishes, 365 ministers.

we grapple with the questions raised above, and as we seek to serve the ongoing life of the New Zealand Methodist Church and its ecumenical endeavours.

Official response

We, gathered in Annual Conference as the Methodist Church of New Zealand, make the following response to the document "Baptism, Eucharist, and Ministry".

1.1. We recognize the core of the faith of the church through the ages in this text.

1.2. As Methodists, we miss a clear emphasis on God's grace. We recognize this underlies the whole document, but feel the lack of its direct expression. We note that "initiation" is not presented explicitly as an aspect of baptism's meaning and role within the church. We would also tend to see ministry more in terms of functions carried out within the overall ministry of the whole people of God than the text emphasizes, with *episkopé* being exercised as one function within this overall ministry. It is from that viewpoint that we have reinstated a permanent diaconate, along lines similar to those expressed in the statement.

1.3. We note that Northern hemisphere cultural perspectives dominate the text, and we are concerned that other cultural perspectives and heritages may not readily relate to the way Christian faith is expressed in this text. We also consider a rather institutional view of the church permeates the document, and, out of our NZ Methodist history, the definite place given to bishops may be uncomfortable for some people.

2.1. The text continues to challenge us to seek avenues of mutual understanding, further dialogue, and closer cooperation in the search for unity with other churches.

2.2. Specifically, this document is a reminder that baptism is into the whole church and therefore that many barriers are already broken down by baptism, if not recognized in our attitudes and actions. The text also calls us towards mutual recognition of one another's ministries. This seems to us a key step in the move towards unity. We are also encouraged to take further opportunities for eucharistic sharing, especially with those churches whose eucharistic understanding and practice we have considered significantly different from ours.

3.1. The text challenges us at a number of points. It calls us to underline the importance of baptism, and to continue to grapple with the consequences of differing views on baptism within our church. It reminds us of the proper links between worship, and particularly the eucharist, and our life in the world, with a responsibility for issues of social justice. This text also confronts us with the question of the centrality of the eucharist in our worshipping life, especially as this may be expressed by more frequent, perhaps weekly celebration. We are also challenged to look closely at our understanding of ordination and ministry, and of the way episcopal oversight is exercised. We must also be open to the different styles and emphases in ministry, including those contributed by women.

3.2. In all the areas covered by this text, we are called to be open to a diversity of views and practices, each of which may express the faith and witness of the church. Particularly, we are called to enable and affirm expressions of baptism, eucharist and ministry which arise out of various cultures. As Methodists in Aotearoa (New Zealand), that means moving towards bi-cultural and multicultural expressions of our faith and life.

4.1. We would suggest that the Faith and Order Commission of the WCC pick up as part of its ongoing work a clearer expression of a theology of grace. Out of our Methodist heritage we regard the theology of grace as a central part of any theology, and feel it requires greater explicit stress than is present in this text.

4.2. We would suggest also further work on the issues surrounding the unrepeatability of baptism. This touches on an issue of real concern, relevant both for many churches, in their ongoing life and also for the cause of unity. A bald statement of unrepeatability does not meet the need. Related to this is the question of appropriate symbolic and ritual expressions of faith and forms of baptismal reaffirmation.

4.3. The ordination of women obviously still needs addressing. We would not rest until a clear statement can be made that women have a proper and rightful place in ordained ministry, and that to exclude them is a clear injustice. As well, we suggest more work could helpfully be done on the perspective and style women bring to ministry.

4.4. More work is needed to make clear that ministry must not be built on an hierarchical model.

PRESBYTERIAN CHURCH IN CAMEROON

Introduction

We, Christians of the Presbyterian Church in Cameroon, a member of the World Council of Churches since 1961, cannot but praise the efforts of the Faith and Order Commission of the World Council of Churches for this detailed statement on "Baptism, Eucharist and Ministry". In doing so we recognize how far the varying practices of baptism, eucharist and ministry have become rites which have shown the church's disunity rather than its unity as the body of Christ. We regret how far these rites have pushed Christians away from each other, and have even led to failures in union attempts among churches which were close to the goal of church union.

We praise the persistence with which the Faith and Order Commission has carried on its work on this since 1927, coming up with revisions in Accra 1974, and Bangalore 1978, and finally with the Lima text in 1982 to which the member churches of the WCC are now called upon to give their assent. We note with gratitude the ecumenical dimension of the text, involving even Roman Catholic theologians. Their collaboration in drawing up the Lima text is a step in the right direction leading us towards more visible unity, if the text will be accepted by all the churches so that the world may believe.

Our position on baptism, eucharist and ministry

Baptism is the visible sign and means of the forgiveness of sins, of our union with Christ in his death and resurrection and the mark of our entrance into the visible body of the church. It is not the act of baptism in itself which ensures our forgiveness and participation in Christ but it is the Holy Spirit who unites the believer with him.

• 179,352 members, 1,049 congregations, 187 pastors.

Through baptism of infants the church promises to lead its children in faith until they may know their Lord and walk by themselves towards the great destination, the coming kingdom of God.

The Lord's Supper is the visible sign and means of the forgiveness of our sins, of our continuation in the union with Christ in his death and resurrection. It is given to the people of God as the spiritual food on their way to the Last Supper in the coming kingdom of God. By it Christ feeds his people on their pilgrimage and ensures them in their struggle on earth of his final victory. It is not the ceremony of the Lord's Supper in itself which ensures the forgiveness of our sins and our union with Christ, but it is the Holy Spirit who makes the believers partakers of him, through the visible means of bread and wine. Through the word and sacraments (baptism and the Lord's Supper) the church partakes of the one body of Christ and in him shares the fellowship of those who are also members of the same body whatever may be their tribe, race, nation or language.

Ministry: We recognize in the Presbyterian Church in Cameroon the one ordained ministry of the pastor. We understand that the church is composed of ministries. There is the basic ministry of the people of God which is common to all Christians baptized in the name of the Father, Son and Holy Spirit, and a special ministry which is that of the pastor. The setting apart of these servants of the church for a full-time exercise of their ministry is done in the context of a public service (an ordination service). Those to be ordained are presented before the congregation, and the moderator along with all ordained pastors present at the occasion lay their hands on those to be ordained and invoke on them the gift of the Holy Spirit.

Recognition of the faith of the church
We recognize in the text the expression of the belief of the Christian church concerning the central rites of baptism, eucharist and ministry especially as the text anchors the rites in the scriptures which bear witness to the unrepeatable achievement of our Lord Jesus Christ for our salvation.

In baptism believers are incorporated in the death and resurrection of Christ, and henceforth oriented towards a "new ethical orientation under the guidance of the Holy Spirit". The eucharist becomes for God's people not only a memorial of Jesus' suffering, death and resurrection, but also a meal of "anticipation" of the total fulfilment of what Jesus has done for the world in his coming kingdom. The ministry is seen as a common ministry of the people of God within which we find a set-apart ministry for the service of the Christian community and the world. All these aspects of baptism, eucharist and ministry as analysed in the Lima text contain that which the Christian church has confessed through the ages.

We are also glad to note the areas wherein a positive diversity of practice may exist in the celebration of these rites within the Christian church. The Cameroonian church in recent years has encouraged the indigenization of the church's liturgical formulation and practice of worship. Cameroonian musical patterns are used, important cultural observances are integrated, and for us the celebration of the eucharist for instance should be influenced deeply by its cultural given in order to bring its meaning nearer the people. The ministry could also adopt patterns, especially in the attire of the minister and the collegial understanding of service in an African community spirit. There is no doubt that Christianity as it enters into certain cultural modes of existence has to lose its foreignness and adopt new patterns which are essentially at one with the church universal. In Africa where each new status acquired confers on the person a new name, receiving a new name at baptism is no problem but it should be a new name that has meaning for that cultural environment, and that carries with it the significance of the rite that person has undergone. While recognizing the importance of the Lima text on "Baptism, Eucharist and Ministry" for the Christian church throughout the ages, we pray that in its actual living with given cultural set-ups variety and diversity will be tolerated, and this too will become an expression of the richness of the church's way of living out its belief.

Consequences for our church and other churches
There are possible consequences of the Lima text on "Baptism, Eucharist and Ministry" for our church, and for other churches to which we may be related.

The mutual recognition of the Lima text by our church and other churches may become a basis for a new understanding between our churches on the practice of baptism, eucharist and ministry. Each church will be led to reconsider its practice in these areas as suggested by the text and see how those specific features of differing practices could be reshaped, modified and adapted so as to be mutually acceptable. The PCC has gone a long way, even before the publication of the Lima text, in removing hindrances between the sprinkling and immersion methods of baptism as carried out in our church and the Baptist churches in our country. Although the PCC does not practise rebaptism for baptized members of other Christian denominations wishing to join it, it recognizes clearly that both methods of baptism are valid and could be practised in our very church by new members wishing to be baptized. We try to overcome the superiority mentality of those churches which claim to be more at home with immersion as the only form of baptism.

In the practice of ministry, baptism and eucharist, the Lima text will continue to deepen our understandings of these rites, as churches already in communion with the PCC foster "greater growth together". For a church like the PCC which insists on a proper understanding of the eucharist for the one participating in it, we do not foresee a general consensus in our church on children's participation in it, although the participation in it of children of other churches in communion with the PCC will constitute no hindrance of growth together.

The frequency of the eucharist and the form it should take, however, remain for our church open questions which are still under study.

We as a church have no bishops. We have the ordained ministry of the pastor. We have elders who are not ordained but dedicated at a special ceremony before they start serving as elders. For administrative purposes of the church, the moderator and synod clerk (both ordained pastors) are the two highest officers in our church. However, the PCC will live with an episcopal church as long as the latter recognizes our ecclesiastical standing as a church.

Briefly, relations with churches recognizing the Lima text will become healthier, and dialogues on serious questions leading to visible church union may increase. As long as churches can talk on issues dividing them, in an atmosphere of mutual respect, suspicions may be dissipated and greater understanding and growth made possible.

We are convinced that, depending on the measure of understanding gained from the Lima text, many areas of the church's life will be affected. The social implication of "Baptism, Eucharist and Ministry" would have to be applied concretely in given situations. The guidance the PCC will draw from the Lima text cannot now be prejudged and determined precisely. The church has yet to grow in the spirit of the Lima text, especially as most of its practices in these rites are not essentially opposed to the text.

The only suggestion we can make for the ongoing work in the area of the rites is that the theoretical preparations should now lead the churches of the WCC into a practical demonstration of the fact that "Baptism, Eucharist and Ministry" can become uniting rites within the churches. It is more into the "*concrete* expression of the apostolic faith" that churches should be ready to enter at this time.

Conclusion

Having carefully considered the Lima text on "Baptism, Eucharist and Ministry", and making clear our practical areas of differing practice in our church, we members of the Presbyterian Church in Cameroon hereby approve this text as incorporating valuable understandings of our church on baptism, eucharist and ministry.

CHURCH OF SCOTLAND
(REFORMED)

Response of the church: Deliverances of the General Assembly on the Report of the Board of World Mission and Unity (Edinburgh, 27 May 1985)

Baptism, Eucharist and Ministry (IV: 2. App. IX)

24. Recognise in "Baptism, Eucharist and Ministry" an up-to-date statement of "the faith of the Church through the ages" and resolve to discern the consequences such recognition may have for the Church's relations and dialogues with other Churches.

25. Affirm that Baptism constitutes a basic unity among Christians which is fundamental; agree with "Baptism, Eucharist and Ministry" that Infant and Believers' Baptism should be "equivalent alternative" forms of administration in any reunion between paedo-baptist churches and churches which practice only Believers' Baptism; and recognise that the historical reason for the division of the Church at this point would thus be removed.

26. Welcome the basic theological agreement as expressed in "Baptism, Eucharist and Ministry" concerning the real presence of Christ in the Eucharist, and concerning the relation between Christ's sacrifice and the Eucharist, and affirm that while many differences in eucharistic interpretation and practice persist, for the most part they have the capacity neither to cause eucharistic separation nor to justify its perpetuation, and that the basis has been laid for full eucharistic communion.

27. Resolve to examine the Church's structure to see whether the communal, the collegial, and especially the personal dimension of oversight are adequately discharged; affirm the principle of the people's participation in the life and decision-making of the Church

---

• 2,000,000 members, 1,780 parishes, 2,030 pastors.

and commend to episcopal churches the eldership as one historical embodiment of that principle; and undertake to consider whether further development of personal leadership in ministry at area and regional levels would be beneficial for the life of the Church and the prosecution of its mission to the world.

28. Consider that the "ministry of the whole people of God" has implications for patterns of ministry and structures of authority in all Churches.

29. Consider that the Reformation emphasis on (*a*) the centrality of Christ in whom "all parts of our salvation are comprehended" and (*b*) the place of scripture as the word of God are essential to a full understanding of "Baptism, Eucharist and Ministry".

30. Instruct Presbyteries, the Panel on Doctrine and other Assembly Boards and Committees to consider the consequences of the above resolutions and affirmations.

31. Instruct the Board to transmit to the World Council of Churches Faith and Order Commission the reply on "Baptism, Eucharist and Ministry" which it has prepared for the Church, together with the Board's Reports to the 1984 and 1985 General Assemblies and other related documents and studies.

Report of the Board of World Mission and Unity to the General Assembly 1985

Preamble

The Board brings to this Assembly the final Report on Faith and Order Paper No. 111, "Baptism, Eucharist and Ministry", together with the proposed reply to the Faith and Order Commission. The report to the Assembly concentrates on the principal issues which the document presents to the Church of Scotland itself, and which call for the Church's action. The reply to the Commission (Appendix IX), requested by the end of 1985, gathers together the wide range of reactions and comments on the document which have been made by the Church over the last two years. Both these submissions, the report to the Assembly and the reply to the Commission, are the fruit of the discussions in the Church—in Presbyteries, Assembly Committees and special conferences and consultations; these have been summarised and presented by the Board, in accordance with the charge given to it by the Assembly.

Although the first submission is addressed to the Church, it is proposed to send a copy of it also to the Faith and Order Commission, along with the second submission, which is directly addressed to that Commission. The report to last year's Assembly will also be forwarded to the Commission, together with a number of essays and articles written for publication by individual members of the Church.

Report

1. The main overall reaction in the Church, as in other churches, to the Faith and Order document "Baptism, Eucharist and Ministry" has been appreciation, gratitude and an awareness of its great significance for the church throughout the world. The length of preparation for its appearance, no less than fifty-five years, the breadth of participation in its production, which involved all major Christian traditions drawn from many countries and continents, and the disciplined nature of the work that went into it, which combined biblical, systematic theological and liturgical studies—all these factors underline its significance.

2. In its use within the Church so far it has been taken with great seriousness, has been received generally with openness and cordiality, has been more widely and more carefully studied than any other ecumenical document in recent times, has already been in itself both a stimulus to and a medium of inter-church meeting of a specially open kind, has belied its specialist character by its accessibility to general groups of church members, has assisted bilateral church conversations by its multilateral nature, and by its international character has given new and more creative perspectives to controversies previously handled in more narrowly national terms.

3. The handling of it within the Church has been principally through study by Presbyteries and by Assembly Committees. It has also been used both in more formal inter-church studies and conversations, bilateral and multilateral, and in miscellaneous informal and local inter-church discussions. It has been the subject of some consideration in exchange of thinking with partner churches overseas. It has been widely used in theological education.

4. The main comments from Presbyteries were briefly summarised in the report to the 1984 General Assembly, and are further reflected in the appended reply to the Faith and Order Commission. This report confines itself to the principal issues in the document which call for the Church's response.

5. "Response" is only one of the two reactions to the document which the Faith and Order Commission invites from the Churches. The other is "reception". "Response" is asked for now; but "reception" will continue for many years after this initial response this year. As churches discern and work out the practical consequences which their responses entail for their relations with

other churches, they will be swept beyond mere endorsement of a text: they will enter upon a process of receiving other churches as churches—Rom. 15.7: "Receive you one another as Christ also received us". Reception of this kind is what the ecumenical movement exists to promote. Only when we are a little way along this road can we arrive at a really just and of course not uncritical appreciation of what the churches are saying.

6. In this more sustained process of reception in the coming years, three uses of the document may stand out. It is likely to be:

a) a frame of reference for inter-church conversations, aimed at mutual learning, joint working and growing unity; it can serve as such a framework in that on the one hand it shows established agreements and convergences (and thus prevents misunderstandings and unnecessary controversies), and on the other hand it shows areas of difference or obscurity or calling in some way for further exploration; above all it distinguishes clearly between differences that divide and differences that do not or need not divide;

b) an instrument of education and reflection on important aspects of the Christian life, and one which is as useful within as between churches;

c) a warrant for explicit acts of mutual recognition, acceptance and commitment between churches, showing as it does the absence of many previously supposed impediments to unity.

7. But the principal issues in the document which call for the Church's immediate response are three. They are profound and important ones for this Church as for the other 302 churches that constitute the World Council of Churches and others which, though not members of the World Council of Churches, are members of the Faith and Order Commission. In presenting them the Commission is not seeking to impose a particular understanding of them upon the churches, but rather to intimate what may be said to be the "state of play", i.e., what the churches show themselves to be thinking about the issues, and the degree of consensus that has emerged.

8. There is consensus on Baptism—that it constitutes a basic unity among Christians; that essentially the same thing is done in Infant and Believers' Baptism; and that remaining differences of understanding and practice are not of the kind that need cause or perpetuate division.

9. There is consensus on Eucharist—that the presence of Christ in it is real and unique; that in its sacrificial character it neither repeats nor supplements the all-sufficient sacrifice of the cross; and that a basis has been laid for full eucharistic communion.

10. There is consensus on Ministry—that it derives from, and is modelled on, the ministry of Christ; that Ordained Ministry is within the ministry of the whole church; and that it should be exercised, at local and wider levels, in personal, collegial and communal ways.

11. In the light of this consensus the Assembly is invited to make appropriate affirmations and resolutions, as expressed in the sections 20, 21 and 22 of the proposed deliverance on the Board's Report. In making these affirmations and resolutions, the Church will be reasserting the centrality of Jesus Christ, from whom alone baptism, eucharist and ministry derive all their significance; baptismal unity, eucharistic communion and fullness of ministry are all grounded in the unity given in Christ, in whom by grace we are accepted and made one with the Father and with each other.

12. In considering the document, nothing is of greater importance than to realise that "we do not need consensus about everything". In other words, differences differ. Some differences must be resolved if full and unconditional communion is to be reached, while others in matters less central and fundamental can properly be left unresolved as permissible diversities within a united Church. To achieve unity, churches must be agreed on that which is required and on no more than is sufficient. Nice judgement is needed to make the necessary distinction here. It can be achieved only through utterly frank and dispassionate dialogue.

13. "The faith of the Church through the ages" (p. x)* retains an identity through many diverse historical expressions and embodiments. The document tries to express this faith in up-to-date terms and upon the basis of a measure of agreement among the churches unprecedented since the year 787 (Second Council of Nicaea). From what the document says flow consequences for the relations and dialogues of the churches among themselves which they are obliged and resolved to work out and implement.

14. The document makes it abundantly clear however that Christians should not be concerned with the inner life of the Church or its worship, or even with Christian unity, as if they were purely domestic ecclesiastical concerns. The life and worship of the Church are signs of the Kingdom, anticipation of what God has in store for all humankind. Unity in worship, in ministry, in fellowship is the condition for mission: "that they all may be one; ... that the world

---

* This and subsequent references are to the original text of the document: Roman numerals refer to pages of the Introduction; B. E. and M. refer to the sections on Baptism, Eucharist and Ministry respectively; C. refers to the sections headed "Commentary"; numerals refer to paragraphs.

may believe" (John 17.21). The life, worship and service of the Christian community should prefigure the Kingdom and the reality of the reconciliation wrought in Christ. Thus the matters with which the document is concerned are integral to the Gospel itself, and the document itself reminds us repeatedly and rightly that we cannot be concerned with baptism, eucharist and ministry without seeing that this implies and demands a profound commitment to peace and justice and the development of fellowship in the world. (Ephesians 1.9-10.)

15. On Baptism—the document finds that the same thing is done in Infant and Believers' Baptism—the two different forms of administration are "equivalent alternatives" (Bc 12). Churches that practise Infant Baptism as norm, and Believers' Baptism as a frequent necessary and legitimate variant from the norm, cannot do otherwise than endorse this understanding. The question whether Baptism may rightly be deliberately postponed, such churches, as a rule, answer in the negative; but they understand the practice of such deliberate postponement to be a legitimate variant incapable of destroying the fundamental agreement concerning Baptism itself.

16. On Eucharist—the document notes growing consensus among churches on two matters that historically have deeply divided and indeed separated them. There is agreement upon the fact of "the unique presence of Christ in the Eucharist" (E13), and on the fact that the Eucharist is sacrificial in character (EC8, MC17). There remain different understandings concerning the "mode" (E13) of the real presence; and the relation of the Eucharist to the once-for-all and sufficient sacrifice of Christ is differently interpreted. In these areas, diversity is legitimate, provided that, in interpreting the real presence, no injury is done to the integrity of the person of Christ, and, in expounding the sacrificial element in the Eucharist, any repetition of or supplement to the unique sacrifice of Christ is clearly abjured. There are other matters in which different views may be held without disrupting the fundamental eucharistic communion, e.g., frequency of celebration and reservation of elements. Churches holding one view may well learn from churches holding another, without being obliged to assimilate or conform.

17. On Ministry—the document declares that the ministry of Jesus Christ is the model of all ministry. Into this ministry he admits his followers, the whole Church, all members of the People of God, to engage, each in his or her own appropriate way, in service, mission and Gospel witness in the world. The Church's order and structure are to be shaped to and for this end; and similarly its leadership is to be fashioned to promote it.

18. Within the ministry of the whole Church, the Ordained Ministry occupies a special place and discharges special responsibilities. The document declares that the exercise of Ordained Ministry has personal, collegial and communal dimensions (2*b*). For this, New Testament precedent supplies scriptural warrant; Jesus Christ chose persons as individuals, as pairs, as a Twelve, for varying roles within the whole community of the developing Church. Accordingly Ordained Ministry properly discharged contains the following elements: leadership of a personal kind; fellowship of a collegial kind; and solidarity with the whole Christian *koinonia* of a communal kind.

19. There is evidence that the Roman Catholic Church is considering ways of developing the collegial dimension, and that episcopal churches are paying more attention to the communal dimension; it is incumbent on churches of the Reformation to give similar special consideration to the personal dimension.

20. The personal dimension operates at congregational level in all churches: every congregation has at least one person as leader of worship, president at the Eucharist, and pastor of the flock. In some churches the personal dimension operates beyond the congregation on the regional level; and in other churches this is extended to the patriarchal and universal level. Does extension of the personal dimension promote the Church's missionary and pastoral task?

21. Many in the Church of Scotland find that discharge of the personal dimension at congregational level alone is inadequate: the life of the Church is impoverished by the lack of a *pastor pastorum*; the mission of the Church is debilitated by lack of the drive, initiative, and vision that one person in permanent official position can impart. If these are real defects, they are not made good by "Moderators" as presently operating. At Presbytery level, the personal oversight discharged by a Moderator is terminated after (usually) one year; at national level, it lasts for only one week in the year, and for fifty-one weeks personal authority in the Church as a whole is in suspense. This leaves some areas of church life unattended.

22. Two suggested remedies are presently before the churches. The document asks non-episcopal churches to consider whether episcopacy and episcopal succession have not "a powerful claim to be accepted" (M25,53*b*). It is of the utmost importance to note that the episcopacy set forth is deliberately low-key. It does not impose upon anyone recognition of an essential character (though this understanding is not ruled out as illegitimate); and accordingly adoption of it does not for the first time make a church a church. It is commended as a visible sign, though not a guarantee, of unity and especially of the

continuity of the Church, a historical strand in apostolicity, fortifying the invisible doctrinal strand, much as the sacrament fortifies preaching.

23. The other remedy is proposed by the Report of The Multilateral Church Conversation in Scotland (1984). The proposal is that Moderators of Presbytery be set up with long-term continuance of office. Such continuity in office would amplify the personal dimension of ministry and discharge it in areas where purely synodal exercise of oversight is defective or wholly absent.

24. If non-episcopal churches are required to reassess the personal dimension in Ordained Ministry, so episcopal churches are required to reassess the communal dimension. As they engage in the renewal of the diaconate, they will wish to bear in mind the presbyterian eldership (with similar elements in other synodal church polities) as one historical embodiment of the principle of the people's participation in the life and decision-making of the Church at all levels (powerfully commended in M26,27). Thus is established a certain reciprocity, the episcopal and the non-episcopal strands each contributing for the enrichment of the other an element from the heritage with which the Holy Spirit in the course of history endowed it.

Reply proposed by the Board of World Mission and Unity

I. VALUE OF THE DOCUMENT — WHAT IT GIVES US

Baptism

(1) Aid to our own teaching and guide to our own practice, notably in the summary of the main elements of meaning.

(2) Rediscovery of the drama and lively symbolism of baptism.

(3) Rediscovery of the universal or catholic and unified nature of the baptised community, with its implications for relations among Christians (e.g., inter-church marriages) and within the total human community (e.g., apartheid, war).

(4) Basis for constructive conversation with believers' baptists on the complementarity of the grace of Christ and the response of faith, and of personal and communal dimensions of the gospel.

(5) Stimulus to explore possibility of "equivalent alternatives" practice, despite its difficulties.

(6) Stimulus, to us as to believers' baptists, to clarify understanding of the whole process of Christian initiation, and in particular of the relation between baptism, profession of faith and admission to the eucharist.

(7) Stimulus, to us as to all, to improve the Christian nurture of children.

(8) Encouragement to avoid "indiscriminate" infant baptism.
(9) Stimulus to enhance the commitment of adult believers, giving more opportunities to re-affirm their baptism.
(10) Stimulus to act on the mutual recognition of baptism among British churches and their common baptismal certificate.

Eucharist
(1) Aid to our own teaching, notably in the summary of the main elements of meaning.
(2) Classic statement of the rich many-sidedness of the eucharist, converting bones of contention into facets of complementarity.
(3) For us especially, the emphasis on celebration, joy, thanksgiving (the sense of the word "eucharist" if not the word itself).
(4) For us especially, the emphasis on present and future, as well as past, reference.
(5) The emphasis on the central significance of meal and the "convivial" nature of the eucharist (the sense of the word "supper" if not the word itself).
(6) The emphasis on the Spirit.
(7) The emphasis on the action of Christ on the presence of the world in the eucharist, especially in the elements as symbols of the world, with its plenty and its pain.
(8) Strong case for frequent celebration, belonging to a long and broad tradition, including our own, but not part of our recent practice.
(9) Basis for constructive conversation with other churches including notably the Roman Catholic Church on the traditionally difficult issues of memorial, sacrifice and real presence.

Ministry
(1) The clear statement of the grounding of all ministry in the ministry of Christ.
(2) The clear statement on ministry as belonging to the whole church.
(3) The statement of the close relation of the ministry of the whole church to the ministry of the ordained.
(4) The recognition of the complementarity of the personal and communal dimensions of ministry.
(5) Stimulus to us to apply the complementarity of the personal and communal dimensions to ministry at more-than-local levels.
(6) Stimulus to us to acknowledge failures and seek improvements in our pastoral care of ministers and in our co-ordination of mission.
(7) Stimulus to us to greater appreciation of the function of ministry as sign and focus of unity and continuity across time and space.

II. LIMITS OF THE DOCUMENT—WHAT IT DOES NOT GIVE US AND WHAT
WE CAN OFFER

A lack of explicit Christological grounding, exemplified in clauses
in which "baptism" or "the eucharist" is the subject, when the subject
would more properly be "Christ", e.g., "Christ in baptism gives..."

Baptism

(1) Not surprisingly, despite its significant formulation of the
relation between baptism and faith, it leaves untouched some of
the fundamental disagreements between infant baptists and
believers' baptists over timing.

(2) This being so, many in our Church believe that it does less than
justice to the case for infant baptism.

(3) More clarity is needed on the relation between incorporation into
Christ and membership of the church.

Eucharist

(1) While there is agreement on the primary matter of the *fact* of
"real presence", further work is clearly necessary on the secondary matters of modes of interpretation, particularly regarding
    (a) the nature of the uniqueness of the real presence of Christ
    (b) the nature of His relation to the elements as distinct from
    His relation to the action
    (c) the nature of any change in the elements
    (d) the change within ourselves in response to the presence of
    Christ in the celebration.

(2) The same is true of the precise nature of the sacrifice element in
the memorial, and the sense in which Christ's sacrifice is
"represented".

(3) We recognise the danger of thinking everyone except ourselves to
be out of step over the word "eucharist", and acknowledge that, if
one word is to be used, the case for "eucharist", as most widely
distributed and as stressing thanksgiving, is strong, and that
therefore those to whom it is unfamiliar may simply have to get
used to it. Nevertheless we submit that it *is* unfamiliar to a
sizeable minority including our Church, that in English it is an
esoteric and not a common word, that "meal" words like
"supper" have positive merit, that "Lord's Supper" is particularly appropriate, and that several words rather than one may
have merit.

Ministry

(1) The stated complementarity of personal and communal ministries, and of individual and synodal episcope, is not followed
through, and the synodal dimension is seriously undervalued.

(2) The stated importance of the ministry of the whole church (the whole people, all the people, the least people) and of the integration of ordained ministry with the ministry of the *laos* is not followed through to its implications for structured "lay" participation in ministry and government, i.e., in pastoring, liturgy, decision-making and "spiritual" functions generally. This may be because of a lack of emphasis on the royal priesthood of the whole church as a necessary consequence of its union with Christ as Great High Priest, who in himself presents the Father to humankind and in himself offers humankind to the Father.

(3) Consequently, the responses required of episcopal and non-episcopal churches are uneven, with structured change required of non-episcopal churches but not of episcopal churches.

(4) Similarly, there is no treatment of Presbyterian eldership or diaconate—whether within congregations or in full-time church service; of Congregational and United Free Church diaconate; of Methodist Class leadership; etc.

(5) Similarly, the 1927 Lausanne recognition of three main orders, Episcopal, Presbyterian and Congregational, though acknowledged, is not followed through.

(6) While the place of ordered succession in ministry for the sake of apostolic fidelity is rightly emphasised, the place of continuity of doctrine as distinct from that of order is underemphasised.

(7) The significance of the three-fold pattern of ministry both as work of the Spirit and as unitive is overstated and the case for it is not made; ambiguities of terminology and diversities of practice over time and space are elided.

(8) There is no recognition of the theologically more profound two-fold pattern of ministry, of Christ, as both true proclaimer of the grace of God, in word and deed and true responder to it in worship and service.

III. AND WHAT WE CAN OFFER TO OURSELVES

In being stirred by the document to offer our tradition's contributions to the Faith and Order Commission and to other churches, we are led to offer them to ourselves, i.e., to turn our own slogans into reality; in particular

(1) our synodal *episcope*—to make it more effective in its pastoring, of people and of pastors, and in its concerting of the church's mission;

(2) our lay ministry and government—to clarify our understanding of our eldership and to improve its practice, resolving if possible the question whether it is ordained ministry (diaconal) or lay

ministry, diversifying its composition (age, sex, social class), reviewing its lifelong character and mode of appointment, and complementing it with wider congregational meetings;

(3) the participation of the whole membership, with the diversity of their gifts, in the life, ministry and government of the church—to make that real.

IV. More general needs not met by the document

These are expressed for the interest and possible guidance of the Faith and Order Commission, not as a criticism of the document. Though some have been voiced as criticisms, they may not be valid since they may be asking of the document what it could not or did not intend to give. But the needs and worries are real.

Two related concerns on sacraments in general

(1) The centrality of sacraments —many of our members considered that the document makes sacraments too central; some had regard to Christians who have no sacraments, but most were reflecting on their own experience and understanding.

   Does this simply reveal an impoverishment of experience of sacraments in our Church or does it represent a deeper theological disagreement about the relative importance of sacraments within the total Christian life and life of the church?

(2) The nature of a sign, in particular whether its relation to that which it signifies is internal or external. Many of our members have interpreted the documents as implying an "*ex opere operato*" view of baptism, eucharist and ordination. The reasons for this reaction may be diverse—a Calvinist understanding of sign as part of that which it signifies and therefore not to be separated from it and viewed in isolation, or a safeguarding of the once-for-all character of Christ's saving work, or a spiritualism that devalues things physical, or a scientific rationalism that rejects "magic".

If the Faith and Order Commission has clarified for itself the nature of signs and resolved the old controversies concerning them, the church at large would be greatly served by an explicit and extended treatment of them. When the document, for example, makes a statement of the form "baptism is or does..." or "the eucharist is or does..." it is not clear whether this refers to the whole action of God including the rite or the rite "in itself"; the notion of the rite "in itself" may be inadmissible to the writers; but this is not obvious to all readers.

Three related concerns on ministry
(1) The need to give more attention to the actualities of ministry in its great diversity and continuing evolution, and to acknowledge failure in incorporating more recent developments of ministry into ecclesiological self-understanding, one notable example being the inclusion of women in ministry.
(2) The tendency to absolutise past forms and to close a "canon" of sacred tradition at particular historical points.
(3) Lack of attention to the social, cultural, political and economic influences on church order throughout history.

V. Reformed insights missing from the document
In addition to a certain lack of appreciation of the positive value of the Reformation and its particular development both of faith and of order, there is more specifically
(1) an undervaluing of crises in the church's history, with their attendant conflicts and discontinuities, which may be of the Spirit and not merely aberrations and disobediences;
(2) a related undervaluing of the principle of *reformanda*, the need for constant renewal and conversion of the church, as complementary to its continuity;
(3) as already mentioned, the need for a synodal dimension to *episcope*;
(4) as already mentioned, the need for full lay participation.
Some in our Church think that the document is more "catholic" than "reformed"; this may be partly because all traditions are specially aware of the elements in this common document from outside their own tradition, but it may be partly because of its seeming lack of these Reformed insights.

VI. The document and the faith of the church throughout the ages
(1) The document has made plain to us that we inherit two kinds of tradition, a special Reformed one and a general catholic one. To some among us this is a new discovery, either welcome or unwelcome. Some of us recognise only our own Reformed confessional standards, and are either perplexed about or resistant to the notion of catholic standards.
(2) If scripture is regarded as the sole standard, the notion of a body of centuries-long tradition, whether catholic or confessional, serving as an authoritative standard, is either unfamiliar or uncongenial.
(3) If tradition other than and subsequent to scripture is recognised,

there is consciousness of the divergences within the tradition, making it more "traditions" than "tradition"; from this perspective the document has been studied not so much to test it for its conformity or otherwise to that tradition (singular) as to use it as an aid to resolution of the differences between those traditions (plural).

(4) Another reaction has been not to treat the tradition (or traditions) as a given standard against which to measure this or any other such document, but as a dynamic succession of different (whether compatible or incompatible) historic realisations of the common faith within a process which properly continues into the future.

From this perspective it has been said that the document is too little directed to the future of the continuing tradition and too much directed to its past. This criticism of the document is matched by a corresponding enthusiasm for the Faith and Order Commission's continuing project on "Common Expression of Apostolic Faith Today".

VII. DANGERS IN THE DOCUMENT?—OLD DIFFERENCES AND NEW DEMANDS

The aim of the production of the document has been to resolve old differences within the Church in order to let it be and do what its Lord wants now. It seeks to free the body from a certain chronic "neuralgia". This task has its obvious merits. But does it also have its hazards?

(1) Can the resolution of old differences distract from the meeting of new demands? Is the relief of the pain a prerequisite of active exercise or active exercise a prerequisite of the relief of pain? How much needs to be or can be resolved in such conversation, and how much *solvitur ambulando*?

(2) Can one concentrate on neuralgic points without losing a sense of proportion and exaggerating their importance, possibly obscuring more fundamental questions about the nature and calling of the church?

For example, while the primacy of the ministry of Christ is not in dispute among the churches, it may be that the ministry of the church and of ordained ministers cannot be really understood without a great deal of more profound joint study of the content of the ministry of Christ (cf. *God's Reign and Our Unity*: the report of the Anglican-Reformed International Commission, 1984).

Similarly, while the ministry of the whole church is not "neuralgic" the present rediscovery of ministry as belonging to ordinary people, as in base ecclesial communities, may yet challenge the understanding and polities of all the churches—and create new neuralgia!

(3) While the document relates baptism and eucharist and ministry widely to the world and not narrowly to the church, can one really understand them and entirely avoid a limiting ecclesiasticism unless one sets them more clearly and explicitly within the context of the whole human community in its present predicaments and its ultimate destiny? Therefore let not the study of "The Unity of the Church and the Renewal of Human Community" be separated from this study; let them be fully integrated as soon as possible.

UNITED REFORMED CHURCH IN THE UNITED KINGDOM

1. Procedure
The General Assembly of the United Reformed Church meeting at Brighton in 1983 passed the following resolution:

> The Assembly welcomes the publication of "Baptism, Eucharist and Ministry", encourages provinces, districts and local churches to study the text and consider its implications; and requests each synod to set up a panel to monitor discussions and forward a provincial response to the Doctrine and Worship Committee by 30 November 1984; and further requests that wherever possible, debate should take place within an ecumenical context.

The way "Baptism, Eucharist and Ministry" was handled varied from province to province: some approved in general terms a report prepared by their panel; others passed resolutions based on a more general report; some made no provincial response at all. The number of formal responses received both at provincial and national level was disappointingly low. But discussion in the church was wider than this number suggests, and it was frequently pointed out that the timetable laid down by the General Assembly required a response earlier than was compatible with the request for discussion in an ecumenical context wherever possible. This response was prepared by the Doctrine and Worship Committee of the General Assembly on the basis of material submitted to it, and was approved by the General Assembly of 1985.

2. A welcome document
There has been a general welcome of "Baptism, Eucharist and Ministry", many expressions of appreciation for the theological

---

● 190,941 members, 1,898 congregations, 1,080 pastors.

reflection it contains, and support for the continuing work of the Faith and Order Commission which it represents. There have also been some individuals and congregations within the United Reformed Church who have expressed grave reservations about the text. In our response we have tried to indicate the main areas of concern. Many of us feel that the text can contain the differences of emphasis we might wish to make: others doubt whether their disagreement can be so contained. Nevertheless we receive the text as "a significant theological convergence", recognizing that it does not represent full consensus, understood "as that experience of life and articulation of faith necessary to realize and maintain the Church's visible unity" (p.ix). This response has been largely framed in terms of the questions raised in the preface, rather than as a detailed theological critique of the text; but the United Reformed Church's member of the Faith and Order Commission can comment in more detail on behalf of the church as need arises.

3. The experience of the United Reformed Church
Our response draws on our experience as a united church. The three churches which came together to form the United Reformed Church in 1972 and 1981 did so on the basis of what they judged to be sufficient, though not total, theological agreement. No single pattern of church life was taken to be normative and elements of the traditions of all three churches are included in the United Reformed Church, the formation of which involved structural changes for all. On the matters treated in "Baptism, Eucharist and Ministry" the church contains a variety of belief: some, for example, believe that infant baptism is a positive expression of the gospel of grace, whilst others believe that New Testament teaching is most clearly represented by believer's baptism; some believe that holy communion should be celebrated weekly, others monthly and others quarterly; there is a variety of views about the role of the ordained minister of word and sacrament within the congregation and the wider councils of the church. We recognize that the union we have entered is still incomplete and also that it is very recent. But we testify:
—first, that to come together in one church before reaching total theological agreement has provided both a context for, and a sense of commitment towards, continuing theological reflections which are decisively different from those which existed while we were still separate churches;
—and second, that experience so far since union suggests that there will be no rapid move to limit the range of belief and practice which currently exists among us.

4. The nature and extent of the agreement required
We therefore believe that more attention needs to be given to the nature and extent of the agreement required for visible unity. Our discussions of "Baptism, Eucharist and Ministry" show that members of our church find it relatively easy to agree that a certain position may be held within a range of positions; and also that they are more open to the insights of other Christian traditions than in the past. But they are reluctant to ascribe theological priority to one position within the range rather than another, and are particularly hestitant to agree to changes of practice, for example in the exercise of *episkope*,* which seem to involve such an ascription of priority. Some are prepared to justify the existence of denominations as ways of embodying different theological emphases in practice, but even those who believe that the concept of a denomination is incompatible with the New Testament understanding of the church, believe that the church must be comprehensive enough to include a wider variety of belief and practice than is contained in any existing organized church.

It is necessary to consider also how many need to agree as well as how much needs to be agreed. The task of reaching agreement requires theological knowledge and skill which are not possessed by every church member; and those with such knowledge and skill, speaking representatively, can remove distrust and suspicion of heresy: but such a group cannot by itself decide what everyone in the church should believe. How can theologians speak in such a way that ordinary members can receive and accept what they say? The answer to this question involves a discussion of authority as well as comprehensibility.

In making this comment we do not minimize the importance of theological agreement, nor underestimate the value of theological training, which has always been prized in our tradition. On the contrary we affirm the importance in the church of doctrine, which is fashioned as its members join together in prayerful study of "the Tradition of the Gospel testified in Scripture, transmitted in and by the Church through the power of the Holy Spirit" (p.ix), and share their experience of Christian discipleship.

5. Ambiguity in the understanding of the sacraments
One anxiety about the text which frequently emerged was whether the convergence in the understanding of the sacraments depended on

---

* Here, and in paragraphs 7a and 9c, Greek words are used because the various possible English translations have been identified with particular theological interpretations. *Episkope* and *diakonia* are referred to in M14 Commentary and M21 Commentary; *anamnesis* is discussed in E1, 5-13.

ambiguities of language. We accept that no deliberate ambiguity was intended, but we think that at certain points the variety of meaning in the language should be more clearly acknowledged.

For example, the term "rite of commitment" (B1) may mean either a rite in which an individual makes a personal commitment to the Lord or a rite in which an individual is committed by the church to the Lord, or both. The theological implications of the phrase are subtly different according to the meaning understood, and this difference has been historically significant. Both meanings can and should be clearly acknowledged to avoid suspicion that only one is intended.

Or again, the exposition of the real presence of Christ in the eucharist (E13 and E15) posed few difficulties for our members. But in saying "some are content merely to affirm this presence . . ." the use of the word "merely" in the Commentary on E15 seems somewhat dismissive of a refusal to attempt human explanations of divine mysteries; and this reluctance to define the relation between the presence of Christ and the signs of bread and wine is crucial for any decision on whether the convergence set out in E13 is adequate. Attempts to define or explain seem to us likely to limit the variety of ways in which the presence of Christ may be understood.

6. The use of history

There is also some ambiguity in the way history is used in the text. For example, it is not clear what is meant by "the faith of the Church through the ages" referred to in the Preface (p.x). Does it refer to the range of belief seen in history, or to some kind of theological core or norm? Is it a criterion by which those who stand within a particular tradition test that tradition, or is it one which people use to test traditions other than their own?

Or again, it is not clear whether all historical developments are to be regarded as the work of the Holy Spirit, or only some. Whereas in the texts on baptism and eucharist an exposition of the institution of the sacrament is followed by an exposition of its meaning, largely based on biblical material, in the ministry text the historical material in M8-14 is much more closely intertwined with theologically interpretative material. Also paragraphs M19-25, whilst noting the variety of forms of ministry both in New Testament and more recent times, nevertheless interpret the history and theology of ministry in terms of a threefold pattern of ministry which seems to involve more than noting the historical existence of three orders of ministry. Thus it is not clear why the Spirit might not have been as much at work in the breakdown of the threefold pattern in the sixteenth and seventeenth centuries as in the creation of it in the second and third. Is not ministry multifold rather than threefold? The question of the criteria for judging which historical developments are to be regarded as theologically significant requires further attention.

7. Implications of "Baptism, Eucharist and Ministry" for the United Reformed Church

(a) The richness of the meaning of both baptism and eucharist set out in the text has been widely appreciated and needs to become part of our life. It is felt that we often do not adequately appreciate baptism as participation in the life, death and resurrection of Christ, or as a sign of the kingdom (B3,7); nor do we emphasize sufficiently celebration and thanksgiving in the eucharist, or its implications for mission (E3-4,24-26). The exposition of *anamnesis* in E5-13 has been widely welcomed. All this suggests that we should seek to enrich our celebration of holy baptism and holy communion by drawing on these insights. This will involve revision of our orders of service, but since the use of our service book is not binding, the task of renewal is one for every local congregation, and we shall seek to encourage this.

(b) Our experience suggests that different views of baptism can be held together, as suggested in B12 Commentary; but this does require the development of understanding and acceptance of different views, and a willingness to regard neither infant nor believer's baptism as the rule. We accept that baptism is an unrepeatable act (B13), and also that opportunities need to be provided for baptism to be reaffirmed in the context of worship (B14 Commentary (c)). We further believe that care needs to be taken to ensure that parents bringing infants for baptism accept the implications of what they are doing and that those baptized in infancy are nurtured within the church (B16). There is some feeling that the text on baptism does not sufficiently consider the pastoral opportunity (and problem) presented by requests for baptism of infants made by parents with only a slight connection with the church's life. (These points are touched on in the *URC Guidelines on Baptism*, 1983, pp.16–7.)

(c) We believe that further careful consideration needs to be given to the principle of children receiving the bread and wine in communion (B14 Commentary (b), E19 Commentary). Although this is closely tied to the view taken of the relation between baptism, church membership, faith and communion, it cannot be settled by reference to that relation alone. It also raises particular problems in a church such as ours with a dual practice of baptism, where not all children are baptized.

(d) Many of our members found difficulty in separating the question of the eucharist as "the central act of the Church's worship"

(E1) from the frequency of its celebration (E30-31). It was generally agreed both that the question of frequency of celebration needs to be examined afresh by local congregations, and that maintenance of a variety of practice is desirable. The increasing use among us of a completely integrated service of word and sacrament with the elements set out in E27, replacing an earlier practice of adding on communion at the end of a service of the word, has been welcomed. However, the growing practice of having only one service of public worship on a Sunday makes it more difficult to increase frequency and retain opportunities for services of the word alone.

(e) The importance attached to the notion of Christian growth in B8-10 has been welcomed, and it is felt that we need to develop a greater commitment to Christian nurture in relation to both baptism and communion. We also need to enable those who preside at and those who share in the eucharist in the United Reformed Church to participate in the wider experience which comes to us through "Baptism, Eucharist and Ministry" and through increasing familiarity with the liturgical traditions of other churches.

(f) It has been suggested that further consideration should be given to setting the ordination of ministers in the context of eucharist (M41), now that this is usually the context for the ordination of elders.

8. The ecumenical consequences of "Baptism, Eucharist and Ministry"

(a) We believe the statement on baptism does provide a basis for the mutual recognition of baptism, and testify to the value of the Common Baptismal Certificate which has been used increasingly in Great Britain since 1970.

(b) In celebrating the eucharist, churches which stress the sacramental dimension need to learn the richness of the word, and those which stress the word need to learn the richness of the sacramental.

(c) Whilst we welcome the richness of meaning in the sacraments of baptism and the eucharist, we feel some unease about the possibility that non-sacramental Christian bodies such as the Society of Friends or the Salvation Army may be, or feel themselves to be, unchurched by this emphasis. This concern may be linked to the anxiety expressed by some about the link between baptism and church membership, or the centrality of the eucharist. It recurs in the question posed by some as to whether the observance of sacraments effects a change in the participants, or declares a change which God effects by his general dealing with us in grace. More work needs to be done here.

(d) We rejoice in the emphasis on the ministry of the whole people of God (M1-6), and believe this is a growing point for all the churches.

(e) We regret the omission of any reference to the ministry of the ordained elder in the Reformed Churches. Opinion is divided as to whether this may be helpfully or appropriately described as a way in which the Reformed Churches have developed the ministry of deacons (cf. M31 Commentary), partly because this can look like a concern to fit the development of ministry into a threefold pattern. But despite the reference to the gifts exercised by the laity (M5), there is no suggestion there that lay people may be called by a congregation and ordained to exercise a particular ministry, which is a charism in the same sense as that term is used for the ministry of word and sacraments.

(f) Our church provides that in certain circumstances particular lay persons may be authorized to preside at baptismal and communion services. This does not minimize the significance of ordination, but asserts the primacy of meeting the pastoral needs of the people of God. This needs to be noted when the ordained ministry is discussed (e.g. M14), and may assume greater importance if weekly celebration of the eucharist increases, especially in those pastorates where one ordained minister serves several congregations. (This point is made clearly in the Report of the Anglican-Reformed International Commission, *God's Reign and Our Unity*, 1984, pp. 52–53.)

(g) The Commission's treatment of the ordination of women was described by one province as "evasive and unhelpful". These words were blunter than most, but the feeling was widespread. It was felt that the comment about discrimination on grounds of handicap, race or sociological grouping (M50) should be extended to include sex as well. We value the sense of wholeness in ministry experienced as a gift of the Holy Spirit through the ordination of women, which has been practised since 1917 in one of our constituent churches.

9. Suggestions for the future work of Faith and Order

Many of the comments made so far will themselves suggest future work for the Faith and Order Commission. The following topics have also been raised:

(a) Christian initiation. It is felt that more elucidation of the relation between baptism and salvation (B3-4,8), and baptism and church membership (B6,12,14) will expose more sharply the question of the way in which the church is a people called out by God. Also the question of what is completed and what is begun in baptism has much to say about the nature of the Christian life.

(b) The meaning of ordination. If ordination can have a different intention according to the specific task of the office to which it takes place (M39), the sense in which the ordained ministry may be spoken of without distinction of office (M8-18,26-27) needs further definition. Again the adequacy of the concept of a threefold ministry is thrown into question.

(c) Episcopacy and the threefold ministry. We are convinced that the essential elements of *episkope* are exercised in a proper and orderly way among us. We note that "differences in ordering the diaconal ministry should not be regarded as a hindrance for the mutual recognition of the ordained ministries" (M31 Commentary). When therefore we are asked whether "the threefold pattern as developed does not have a powerful claim to be accepted" (M25), this seems in practice to be a question about episcopacy rather than the threefold pattern. Why are differences in ordering the ministry of *episkope* more significant for mutual recognition than differences in ordering the ministry of *diakonia*?

(d) The nature of episcopacy and apostolic succession. We welcome the recognition that churches which have not retained the historic episcopate have preserved continuity in apostolic faith, worship and mission, particularly in ordination (M37). We believe that further work needs to be done on whether or how the sign of episcopal succession can be recovered (M38) in a way which does not in fact throw the existing continuity with apostolic faith, worship and mission into question. We believe that the pattern of ministry today should be determined by the missionary task of the church. The commission of our Lord and the consequent enabling gifts of the Spirit produce a manifold ministry which is apostolic.

(e) Diaconal ministries. We agree that further work needs to be done on the way in which diaconal ministries appropriate to contemporary needs may be developed. We believed that this may be best done if such diaconal ministries do not have to be fitted into a single order within a threefold pattern.

(f) The nature of visible church unity. We live in a constant tension between awareness of a unity which transcends our divisions and awareness of a division which mars our unity. Too great an emphasis on either will suggest either that nothing need be done or that everything must be changed. We believe that further work needs to be done here which will set the experience of churches which have moved into union alongside that of churches which understand unity in terms of unbroken continuity.

(g) The role of agreement on baptism, eucharist and ministry in achieving visible unity. This task, which could well be linked to the project of reaching a common expression of the apostolic faith today, should pick up the kind of points referred to in paragraph 4 above.

We believe it is important that this further work is linked to the two studies on "Towards the Common Expression of the Apostolic Faith Today" and "The Unity of the Church and the Renewal of Human Community". Both are vital to a proper appreciation of "Baptism, Eucharist and Ministry", which inevitably seems to some to place too great an emphasis on the ministry and the sacraments.

10. Conclusion

The publication of "Baptism, Eucharist and Ministry" has provided an opportunity for a large number of our church members to study these matters in a fresh context. The discussions have been stimulating, whether they led to agreement or disagreement with the text. Though many other issues in the world today claim our attention, those raised in "Baptism, Eucharist and Ministry" still concern us because they have divided the church. In our Basis of Union we said:

> The United Reformed Church has been formed in obedience to the call to repent of what has been amiss in the past and to be reconciled. It sees its formation and growth as a part of what God is doing to make his people one, and as a united Church will take, wherever possible and with all speed, further steps towards the unity of all God's people.

We reaffirm that commitment as we submit this response to the Faith and Order Commission, with our prayers and good wishes for its future work.

CHRISTIAN CHURCH
(DISCIPLES OF CHRIST)

In the 180-year history of the Disciples of Christ, one concern that has always been close to our hearts and minds is a deep commitment to and belief in the unity of Christ's church. We have taught and preached that division within the church is sin, and that all Christians have a responsibility and an obligation to work for reconciliation. It is therefore with joy and anticipation that Disciples respond to "Baptism, Eucharist and Ministry" (BEM). But if we are bold in our commitment, we are also painfully aware of the depth of divisions, and the difficulties which lie ahead of the church.

While it is with realistic eyes that we look at BEM, at the same time we see in this document an extraordinary opportunity for the church to move beyond the status quo, to accept the demands of the gospel for unity and the resulting opportunities which should come for the church to witness to the gospel, to preach and teach God's love, mercy, justice, and forgiveness.

Disciples recognize that what BEM offers is not a blueprint, a road map to re-union for Christians. It is, rather, a "convergence", a coming together of theological perspectives, but not yet consensus. But even in convergence there is expressed a sense of unity, a commitment to unity, an awareness of the validity of the diverse expressions of the faith without endorsing the divisive history of some of these expressions.

Because of the unity already represented in BEM, and the ways in which differing theological positions are stated, Disciples join other Christians in appreciation for the significance of this document. Indeed, we see here a witness to the apostolic faith through the ages. If

---

● 1,217,750 members, 4,362 parishes, 6,578 pastors. This text was voted by the general assembly of the Christian Church (Disciples of Christ) in the USA and Canada, Des Moines, Iowa, 2-7 August 1985.

the churches will take this seriously, we may find the Holy Spirit pulling the church together towards new levels of witness, filling the church with a world-transforming power. Disciples note with promise the international character of the document, a factor that by its very nature speaks a word of peace and hope to the world.

Disciples also observe that the vision of the church in BEM is congruent with that expressed in the theological consensus proclaimed by the nine-church Consultation on Church Union and by the international Disciples of Christ-Roman Catholic Commission for Dialogue. Disciples believe that this indicates something of the breadth and depth of the convergence of views in BEM, and it is evidence that the ecumenical movement is proceeding in a common direction.

Further, Disciples see wisdom in addressing the three issues of baptism, eucharist and ministry. For it is in and over these issues that Christians have been most divided throughout Christian history. It is only as these issues are addressed that progress towards visible unity can be achieved. There is a painful irony in the fact that baptism, the act through which we are brought into Christ and the church; the Lord's Supper, through which we share in the one body broken for us; and the ministry, through which the office and function of servanthood is expressed, are the very places where our sins of disunity are most evident.

The consideration and reception of BEM is an opportunity to face directly the founding ideals which called the Disciples into being. If we believe in the unity of the church, we must take this document seriously, engage it with rigour, and speak a word of response to the church universal.

Disciples engaging BEM: a process of consideration

Soon after the publication of "Baptism, Eucharist and Ministry" in 1982, the Council on Christian Unity designed a wide-ranging process for study and consideration of the text across the life of the Christian Church (Disciples of Christ). Three resourcing materials were developed, especially for use in congregations by pastors and lay persons, to help understand the importance of BEM and to enable discussion of the issues at stake in the theological convergence. First, *A Guide for Study* was prepared by Michael Kinnamon and Robert K. Welsh for use in Disciples congregations and ecumenical study groups. The purchase of 5,350 copies of this guide, published by the Christian Board of Publication, reveals the eager response of Disciples to BEM. Second, five video-tape presentations by Paul A. Crow, Jr, were prepared by the Disciples Seminary Foundation of the

Claremont School of Theology to open up the issues and implications of BEM. Copies of these video-tapes have been available to study groups for purchase or rental since September 1984. Third, a special issue of the quarterly publication of the Council on Christian Unity, *Mid-Stream: an Ecumenical Journal* (July 1984), was devoted to exploring the meaning of BEM for North American Christians.

In seeking wide participation in this initial stage of reception of BEM throughout the Disciples of Christ, personal letters inviting individuals and groups to join in study of the text were sent to over 150 congregations, to each Disciples seminary and seminary foundation, to professors of religion in Disciples colleges, to all members of the General Board of the Christian Church (Disciples of Christ), to general unit staff and their boards of directors, and to the network of twenty-three regional commissions on ecumenical concerns. The positive replies received to these letters as well as the large number of response forms returned from groups which had used the *Guide for Study*, indicate that Disciples across the life of the church are, in fact, engaging in discussion and consideration of the text. Often these studies have taken place in the context of ecumenical groupings or programmes designed by local or state-wide councils of churches (e.g. the Washington Association of Churches, the New Mexico Conference of Churches, the Greater Dallas Community of Churches, the Canadian Council of Churches, the Greater Cleveland Interchurch Council, Ecumenical Ministries of Oregon). In many ways the responses received from these ecumenical settings and studies have been the most positive and, at the same time, the most critical. The importance of BEM is thus seen most clearly in its wider ecumenical context of enabling reconciliation among Christians and renewal within the churches.

One of the key learnings reported in many study groups was the importance of linking the study of BEM to occasions of worship, especially to celebrations of the so-called "Lima Liturgy". Special services using this order of worship for the Lord's Supper have been held at the 1983 general assembly, the 1984 meeting of the general board, regional assemblies, and local communities across the United States and Canada. Many Disciples have come to an appreciation of both the potential and the promise of BEM as they have experienced the theological convergence set to the language of worship.

In designing this study process among Disciples, it was clear that consideration of and reaction to the BEM text would be only a first, initial stage in a much longer term process that will require *claiming* the theological convergence in its implication for our church's education, witness, worship, ethical and spiritual life. This report will seek to identify specific areas where such ongoing tasks and opportunities may now be pursued by the Christian Church (Disciples of Christ).

A general assessment of this first stage of study of BEM is that it has generated a new appreciation and much-needed interest in serious theological reflection among Disciples regarding fundamental aspects of our faith in the areas of the church, sacraments, and ministry. And we have seen that the vision of the church articulated through the BEM text is in some sense the same vision which Disciples wish to claim in our ecclesiology and our pursuit of unity.

BEM and the faith of the church through the ages
The basic question posed to all churches in consideration of BEM is to state "the extent to which your church can recognize in this text the faith of the Church through the ages" (preface).

From the responses and reports received across the life of our church—in its congregations, regions, institutions of higher education, and general administrative units—it would appear that the Christian Church (Disciples of Christ) in the United States and Canada is prepared to affirm that "Baptism, Eucharist and Ministry" does reflect the faith of the church through the ages. The extent to which this general recognition is qualified may be discovered in the specific items noted in the material which follows on "Issues on the Way Towards Reception" (e.g. the importance for Disciples to claim the ordination of women in any movement towards the reconciliation of ministries).

In making this affirmation, the Christian Church (Disciples of Christ) wants to underscore and highlight five specific aspects of the BEM text:

1. Disciples affirm the themes of baptism, eucharist, and ministry as central theological issues for ecumenical advance among the churches in overcoming historic divisions among Christians.
2. Disciples find that some of the language and terminology in the convergence text is not familiar to our tradition, and therefore, we are challenged to grow in our understanding of the faith as it has been expressed in different traditions and histories.
3. Disciples applaud BEM's concept of "unity with diversity" as a model for ecumenical growth, i.e. a unity which offers an openness to a variety of interpretations of the faith without diluting the essential understandings of the meanings of baptism, the Lord's Supper, and ministry. Unity is never achieved by conformity in language and practice, but in allowing our diversities and gifts to be shared in communion.

4. Disciples understand that the greatest challenge of BEM is finally not in the approval of a document, but in the spiritual process of moving to live out the implications of the one faith in its call to ecumenical action, new church-to-church relationships, and mutual accountability to our sisters and brothers in other traditions.
5. Disciples claim BEM as a theological convergence while recognizing it is not yet a full statement of theological agreement or consensus. There are several issues on which we would welcome further ecumenical discussion as we move with other churches in pursuing mutual recognition of members, reconciliation of ministries, and sharing at the one Table.

Issues for Disciples on the way towards reception
Part of the Disciples response to BEM has been to point to those levels of agreement as well as disagreement or hesitancy. Many of the problems which Disciples have with BEM are related to questions of language which is simply unfamiliar in our tradition. In some cases Disciples are confronting language which has been self-consciously rejected at various points in our history.

One such usage is the word "sacrament". The early Disciples leaders made a strong case for overcoming division by trying to follow not only New Testament patterns of church life, but also New Testament language. "Bible names for Bible things" was a frequently used motto in the nineteenth century. Thus the word "sacrament" was seen as problematic. Because baptism and the Lord's Supper were clearly understood to be commanded or ordered by Christ, the early Disciples chose to use an alternative word for "sacrament". That word was "ordinance", a word widely used in the Reformed tradition (from which most of the early Disciples came). However, in the past thirty years, more and more Disciples have returned to the language of "sacrament". The Disciples understanding of sacrament/ordinance has always been essentially that of the broader Christian community: visible signs of spiritual graces, avenues of God's grace. Even more important, the Disciples have always seen the church as a community in which these graces of God are mediated, and baptism and the Lord's Supper have been central to the life of the Disciples community.

Baptism
Disciples of Christ find in this section a witness to the essential meaning of the sacrament of baptism. BEM, as well as "The COCU Consensus" (1984), go a long way in bridging the differences which have divided the churches for centuries.

The Disciples teaching on baptism is not an isolated doctrine, but is seen in the context of the church and its unity. Baptism is the sacrament of unity. Through the waters of baptism the Holy Spirit binds all Christians together and impels them to make real and visible their unity in Christ.

We celebrate the theological meaning of baptism articulated in the five aspects developed in BEM in paragraphs 2-7: as liberating participation in Christ's death and resurrection, as conversion of the heart, as a seal of the Holy Spirit, as incorporation into the body of Christ (not a denomination), and as a sign of the kingdom of God and the life to come.

Disciples greet with appreciation the emphasis upon the dynamic relation between faith and baptism (§§8-10,12). The personal profession of faith of the believer is for us essential for responsible membership in the church. At our best we know such faith is neither a momentary act nor totally individualistic, but an expression of the faith lived in a believing community, the church of centuries.

While Disciples affirm believers baptism as the practice of the apostolic church, we look towards a united church in which both believers' baptism and infant baptism/confirmation can be fully practised. Most Disciples believe both witness to the same faith and can be shared in the same fellowship (*koinonia*). Indeed, by official action of our general assembly (San Antonio 1975), our church practises the mutual recognition of the baptism and membership of our partner churches in the Consultation on Church Union.

At the same time Disciples value the deliberate affirmation of immersion as a vivid expression of "the reality that in baptism the Christian participates in the death, burial and resurrection of Christ" (§18). Our witness to immersion is not a sectarian principle by which we seek to exclude other practices or persons. Rather, it is offered as a witness to the full understanding of baptism and the catholicity of the church.

Disciples historically baptize by using the trinitarian formula, "Father, Son, and Holy Spirit", which BEM points out is the common practice and confession in Christian history. Alexander Campbell believed that according to the New Testament witness we are baptized not only "in the name of" (by the authority of), but also "*into* the name of the Father, Son, and Holy Spirit". Such an interpretation emphasizes the profound union with God that comes by virtue of our being baptized "*into* the name".

BEM's clearest challenge to Disciples practice comes in the brief paragraph 13: "Baptism is an unrepeatable act. Any practice which might be interpreted as 'rebaptism' must be avoided." Disciples do not consciously practise "rebaptism". Our spiritual growth since the nineteenth century has led the majority of Disciples congregations to receive into full membership those from other traditions which practise infant baptism and confirmation. A minority of congregations, however, do immerse those adults who were baptized in infancy but whose conscience now leads them to ask for believers baptism. Such a service is performed as an act of pastoral care for those persons and as a witness to the New Testament practice (which BEM acknowledges).

Clearly Disciples must confront the ecumenical implications of this act which others interpret as "rebaptism". Our practice must seek to be inclusive. Educational materials must be developed which teach the common Christian witness of the diverse forms of baptism. Liturgical services can be prepared which both reaffirm a person's earlier baptism and serves his or her pastoral and spiritual needs. Disciples are learning about this duality as they live in united churches in North India, the United Kingdom, and elsewhere. Surely an important part of transcending this difficulty will be a genuine acceptance and practice of both forms of baptism as belonging to the fullness of the church.

Another area of growth for Disciples is related to the act of confirmation. Disciples have not practised confirmation, and thus need to understand the historic roots and theological meaning of the act. Disciples also need to have a clearer understanding of the relationship between our practice of "dedicating children" and the process of providing nurture in the faith. There are strong parallels between the Disciples procedure of dedication of children followed in later years by confession of faith and baptism, on the one hand, and the baptism of infants followed by confirmation, on the other.

Eucharist

Disciples discover in BEM's text on eucharist several perspectives which confirm our historic teaching and practice regarding the centrality of the Lord's Supper to the life of the Christian community.

First, we affirm the Lord's Supper (holy communion, eucharist) as the central event in the church's worship and life (§1). Second, we share an understanding of the Lord's Supper which would include the five aspects set forth in relation to the meaning of the eucharist (§§2-26); Disciples, however, need to be clearer in teaching an understanding of the eucharist as "Invocation of the Spirit" (§§14-18) and as "Meal of the Kingdom" (§§22-26). Third, we strongly endorse the paragraphs which point to the importance of the frequent celebration of the Lord's Supper as a means to deepen Christian faith: "As the eucharist celebrates the resurrection of Christ, it is appropriate that it should take place at least every Sunday" (§§30-31).

The text offers several *areas for theological growth* among Disciples of Christ as we seek to build upon our historic teachings related to the Lord's Supper, and as we seek with other churches to reclaim the eucharist as central to the church's life and witness. One specific area is related to recovering the meaning of the eucharist as an *anamnesis*, or memorial of Christ. In the New Testament *anamnesis* is not an inspirational recollection or remembering a past event, but rather a bringing into the present of a past act in all its significance and reality. Christ is truly present at the Lord's Supper, but Disciples affirm that the text does not require any particular metaphysical interpretation of "real presence". Christ's presence at the Lord's Supper was usually articulated in the understanding of Christ as "the host at the meal". The rediscovery of the biblical meaning of *anamnesis* in the ecumenical discussion offers a way in which "real presence" may be widely embraced.

A second challenge is found in the strong linkage made between the celebration of the eucharist and participation in "restoration of the world's situation and the human condition", that is, between celebration of the Lord's Supper and "participation in God's mission to the world" (§§20-21,24-26). Too often Disciples have seen the Lord's Supper either as only a personal act of worship (between the person and God) or as an internal activity of church life (worship separate from mission). BEM challenges us to an understanding of church which is both sacramental and in mission.

Our responses expressed some difficulty with the list of elements included in a eucharistic liturgy. Are all these elements necessary? Of equal value? Disciples affirm six of the elements as important parts in a celebration of the Lord's Supper: the prayers of the people, the proclamation of the word, the offering of gifts, the unfailing use of the words of institution, prayers for invocation of the Holy Spirit (*epiklesis*) on the community and the elements, and the receiving of the bread and the cup. Further ecumenical discussion and work in the preparation of eucharistic services of worship will be a constructive phase in the years to come.

Ministry

It is not surprising that the section on "ministry" presented the greatest problems and raised the most serious questions for Disciples. The text itself, with a length almost equal to the sections on baptism and eucharist combined, and the frequent paragraphs of commentary which in themselves indicate disputed issues which are still in need of further dialogue and reconciliation, illustrate that this section has not reached the same level of mature convergence as that of baptism or the eucharist. Further, it should be noted that many of the sharpest divisions and most intense controversies among the churches have centred upon the issues, interpretations and practices of the ministry. Nevertheless, Disciples of Christ view as important the significant, though partial degree of convergence which has been achieved in the text. We recognize our responsibility to continued ecumenical discussion and action on the unresolved issues as Christians seek further consensus-building on these critical areas related to the nature and calling of the church.

Disciples celebrate the recognition that the whole people of God is called in baptism to serve Christ and to proclaim and show forth the kingdom of God. It is important to understand that the authority of the church's ministry is founded upon the faithfulness of the whole people—lay and ordained together—and not upon an hierarchical understanding of authority which is given to the ordained alone. An implication from this view of ministry is that the ordained ministry is seen to be inter-related and interdependent with the calling to the whole people of God.

We also affirm the setting forth of the essential character of the ordained ministry as *re-presentative*. They are persons publicly and continually responsible for pointing to the church's fundamental dependence on Jesus Christ. They present again and again the calling of the whole church to service, witness, and proclamation. Ordained ministers are thus more than enablers or reflectors of "public opinion". Their ministries are to be expressions of the ministry of Christ to the whole church and of all the baptized to the whole human community.

Disciples respond favourably to the relation between ordained ministry and authority (§§1c Commentary, and 15–16) which teaches ministerial authority as that of a servant life offered for the upbuilding of the whole body and responsible to the whole church.

Disciples of Christ are coming to see the value of the threefold ministry of bishops, presbyters (pastors) and deacons. We know these three dimensions are already present in our own life, and need to be clearly expressed in persons and offices. We also realize these three offices constitute the possible ministry of a future united church. For us, this growing appreciation of the threefold ministry is conditioned by two insights: (1) in the midst of the diversity of patterns which are often reasons for and expressions of continuing division among churches, we affirm the threefold ministry as an expression of the unity we seek and also as a means of achieving it; and (2) we understand that affirming the threefold pattern is not merely to accept any existing or previous pattern, but is to claim a pattern which both expresses the ministries of all churches and challenges all churches to reform and renewal.

In recent decades in our own reflections about the church and through our participation in the ecumenical movement, Disciples have increasingly come to appreciate the ministry of shared oversight (*episkope*) in the teaching, sacramental, and pastoral care of the church. Our emerging theological understanding of *episkope* sees the role of the "bishop" as not simply identified with administrative oversight or some external exercise of authority beyond the congregation, but as a ministry which is primarily pastoral and sacramental, related to the continuity and unity of the church, and leading in the church's mission. Our contacts with churches in the Consultation on Church Union who have bishops and with the Roman Catholic Church have opened for us some of these wider theological understandings of *episkope* in the practice of oversight, nurture, pastoral care and continuity.

With our particular historical roots in the nineteenth century we were among those churches which reacted against any view which defined apostolic succession through bishops as the only valid expression of guarding the continuity of the faith. Neverthless, Disciples applaud BEM's understanding of apostolic succession which grounds continuity not only in ministry but in the apostolic tradition of the church as a whole (§35) in its faithful teaching, preaching, and witness. We understand that the Christian Church (Disciples of Christ) is a part of this apostolic Tradition. We are coming to accept the importance of ministers of oversight beyond the congregation—regional and general representatives—participating in the laying-on-of-hands in ordination. This sign of the continuity and unity of the church is a critical area for growth as Disciples reflect about the church and its ministry. We welcome the suggestion that all churches explore the possibility of reconciliation of ministries as a witness to seeing our present patterns of ministry as differing forms of continuity. The reconciliation of our ministries would thus involve the uniting of our different expressions of continuity of the apostolic tradition.

Another issue for serious theological reflection among Disciples is the ministry of congregational officers who share in leadership at the Lord's Table, namely, elders. For Disciples, elders are sacramental officers chosen by the congregation because of their spiritual gifts. Our consideration of BEM challenges us to discover the place of elders in the understanding of ministry as set forth in the ecumenical theological convergence.

One of the most critical unresolved issues in BEM is that of the ordination of women. For Disciples it is not simply a matter of practice but of theology. If the churches are to move ahead towards reconciliation of ministries, this issue cannot be left open. While we understand the reasons for caution expressed in the document especially in relation to the Orthodox church, we applaud the call for further ecumenical consideration of this critical issue (§54). We cannot, however, accept any interpretation which could view the ordination of women as a "hindrance". Rather, we see the ministry of women as a gift to the church from the Holy Spirit.

Implications of BEM for the Christian Church (Disciples of Christ)
There are at least four specific areas of work and dialogue which stand as a challenge to the Disciples as immediate implications for our reception of BEM. First of all, BEM as a document and as a fruit of historical process represents what may be the moving of God's Spirit in the church of the twentieth century. By this providential document Disciples may find themselves able to reclaim Christian unity as their "polar star", to quote a much beloved phrase of Barton W. Stone.

Specifically, the unity of the church will be served as BEM is accepted as one of the teaching documents for Disciples. This would suggest that BEM be used in such areas as the development of church school curricula, materials for membership classes and lay study groups, teaching in theological seminaries, providing direction for the work of regional commissions on ministry, and the ongoing work of the Council on Christian Unity.

Secondly, BEM offers help as Disciples enrich their worship through liturgical renewal. BEM will come to life for Disciples by its use in the development of services, celebrations, and orders of worship, and in our teaching the meaning of baptism, eucharist and ministry.

Thirdly, Disciples are called to relate the ecumenical theological convergence represented in BEM to our present efforts in understanding and articulating the nature of the church. This is especially true in such areas as statements on the order of ministry, the meaning of ordination, and the work of the Commission on Theology. Further, other ecumenical relations and activities of the Disciples, e.g. in local, regional, and national councils of churches, will be deepened and enhanced by a careful consideration of BEM.

Finally, BEM calls us to greater faithfulness in pursuing justice in the world and reminds us of the ethical dimensions of the faith, the life of the Christian in society. In its call for acceptance of diversity, the celebration of community, the centrality of the Table, and the fundamental character of Christian ministry as servanthood, BEM calls all Christians to proclaim and live a gospel of love, a message of reconciliation and forgiveness. This gospel of Jesus Christ is preached out of unity; it is grounded in God's justice and mercy. If in baptism we are buried and raised up to be one family, and in the Lord's Supper Christ leads us in sharing the fundamental necessities of life and eternity, and in ministry we enact the gospel, then we will know what it means to be church. BEM gives us an opportunity to move towards being God's church, Christ's body. For this reason, BEM is indeed an extraordinary document in which Disciples discover both their heritage and calling to be God's people.

INTER-ORTHODOX SYMPOSIUM ON BAPTISM, EUCHARIST AND MINISTRY

I. Introduction

1. We give thanks to the Triune God that we, hierarchs and theologians representing the Eastern Orthodox and Oriental Orthodox churches, members of the World Council of Churches, were able to gather together at the Holy Cross Greek Orthodox School of Theology in Brookline, Massachussetts, USA. Our task was to help clarify a number of questions which might arise for the Orthodox churches when they consider their official response to the document on "Baptism, Eucharist and Ministry" (BEM) adopted in Lima, 1982, by the Faith and Order Commission of the World Council of Churches.

2. We would like to express our gratitude to the hosts of the meeting, the Greek Orthodox Archdiocese of North and South America and the Holy Cross Greek Orthodox School of Theology, as well as to the Orthodox Task Force of the World Council of Churches and the Faith and Order Commission which made possible such a widely representative gathering. We are also grateful for the opportunity of meeting with several Orthodox parishes in the Boston region.

His Eminence Archbishop Iakovos, Primate of the Greek Orthodox Archdiocese of North and South America, formally welcomed at the opening session the members of the symposium together with other distinguished guests from the Orthodox and the other churches from the region.

3. The moderator of the symposium was His Eminence Prof. Dr Metropolitan Chrysostomos of Myra (Ecumenical Patriarchate of Constantinople). Papers were presented on the following topics:

● The symposium was held at Holy Cross Greek Orthodox School of Theology, Brookline, Mass., USA, 11–18 June 1985.

"General Introduction on Baptism, Eucharist and Ministry in the Present Ecumenical Situation" (Rev. Dr Günther Gassmann, Rev. Dr Gennadios Limouris); "The Meaning of Reception in Relation to Results of Ecumenical Dialogue on the Basis of BEM" (Prof. Dr Nikos Nissiotis, Response by Bishop Nerses Bozabalian); "The Significance and Status of Baptism, Eucharist and Ministry in the Ecumenical Movement" (Archbishop Kirill of Smolensk); "The BEM Document in Romanian Orthodox Theology—the Present Stage of Discussions" (Metropolitan Dr Anthony of Transylvania); "The Question of the Reception of Baptism, Eucharist and Ministry in the Orthodox Church in the Light of its Ecumenical Commitment" (Rev. Prof. Dr Theodore Stylianopoulos, Response by Rev. Dr K. M. George); "Tasks Facing the Orthodox in the 'Reception Process' of Baptism, Eucharist and Ministry" (Rev. Dr Prof. Thomas Hopko, Response by Metropolitan Prof. Dr Chrysostomos of Myra).

4. On the basis of these papers, plenary discussions on them, and deliberations in four discussion groups, the participants in this symposium respectfully submit the following considerations and recommendations.

II. The significance of BEM and the responsibility of the Orthodox

1. It appears to us that we, as Orthodox, should welcome the Lima document as an experience of a new stage in the history of the ecumenical movement. After centuries of estrangement, hostility and mutual ignorance, divided Christians are seeking to speak together on essential aspects of ecclesial life, namely baptism, eucharist and ministry. This process is unique in terms of the wide attention which the Lima document is receiving in all the churches. We rejoice in the fact that Orthodox theologians have played a significant part in the formulation of this document.

2. In general we see BEM as a remarkable ecumenical document of doctrinal convergence. It is, therefore, to be highly commended for its serious attempt to being to light and express today "the faith of the Church through the ages" (preface, p.x).

3. In many sections, this faith of the church is clearly expressed, on the basis of traditional biblical and patristic theology. There are other sections in which the Orthodox find formulations which they cannot accept and where they would wish that the effort to adhere to the faith of the church be expressed more accurately. As often stated in the document itself, in some areas the process needs to be continued with more thinking, further deepening and clarification.

4. Finally, there are sections in which a terminology is used which is

not that to which the Orthodox are accustomed. However, in some such cases, beneath the unfamiliar terminology, one can discover that the meaning is in fact close to the traditional faith. In other parts of BEM we notice a terminology which is familiar to the Orthodox but which can be understood in a different way.

5. We also think that the Orthodox churches have the duty to answer responsibly the invitation of the Faith and Order Commission mainly for three reasons:

a) because here we are concerned with a matter of faith—and it has been the insistence of the Orthodox churches for some time that the World Council of Churches should focus its attention especially on questions of faith and unity;

b) because the Orthodox have fully participated in the preparation of the text from the beginning and made a substantial contribution to it;

c) because it is important to have the response of all the Orthodox churches, and not just some of them.

III. Response and reception

1. Both at the Sixth Assembly of the World Council of Churches at Vancouver (1983) and at the last meeting of the Central Committee (1984) of the WCC, the Orthodox undertook to respond to BEM as a matter of obligation and commitment with a view to furthering the ecumenical movement.

2. We would like to distinguish between the immediate response of the individual Orthodox member churches of the World Council of Churches to the BEM document and the long-range form of the reception of the text in the Orthodox tradition. We hold that the notion of reception of the BEM document here is different from the classical Orthodox understanding of the reception of the decrees and decisions of the holy councils.

3. Reception of the BEM document means that we recognize in this text some of the common and constitutive elements of our faith in the matter of baptism, eucharist and ministry so that we may stand together as far as possible to bear witness to Jesus Christ in our world and to move towards our common goal of unity. Thus reception at this stage is a step forward in the "process of our growing together in mutual trust..." towards doctrinal convergence and ultimately towards "communion with one another in continuity with the apostles and the teachings of the universal Church" (preface, p.ix).

4. Reception of the BEM document as such does not necessarily imply an ecclesiological or practical recognition of the ministry and

sacraments of non-Orthodox churches. Such a recognition would require a special action of the Orthodox churches.

5. As an initial step towards this kind of reception we would wish to see official action on the part of the Orthodox churches to facilitate the use of the BEM document for study and discussion on different levels of the church's life so that the church evaluates the document with a view to the ultimate unity of all churches.

6. In this process of discernment the Orthodox churches should be sensitive to the similar process of evaluation of the text and of the process of bilateral dialogues in the member churches of the WCC and the Roman Catholic Church. Thus our evaluation will be fully informed of the ecumenical reflections and experiences stimulated by this text.

IV. Some points for further clarification

1. We Orthodox recognize many positive elements in BEM which express significant aspects of the apostolic faith. Having affirmed this initial appreciation of BEM, we offer some examples among the issues which we believe need further clarification and elaboration. There are also issues which are not addressed in the text.

2. In the section on baptism, we note:
a) the relationship between the unity of the church and baptismal unity (§6);
b) the role of the Holy Spirit in baptism and consequently the relationship between baptism and chrismation (confirmation), linking water and the Spirit in incorporating members into the body of Christ (§§5,14);
c) the role of exorcism and renunciation of the Evil One in the baptismal rite (§20);
d) the terms "sign", "sacramental sign", "symbol", "celebrant" (§22), "ethical life" and other terms throughout the text.

3. In the section on eucharist, we note:
a) the relationship of the eucharist to ecclesiology in the light of the eucharistic nature of the church and the understanding of the eucharist as "the mystery of Christ" as well as "the mystery of the Church" (§1);
b) the relationship between participation in the eucharist and unity of faith;
c) the role of the Holy Spirit in the eucharist, with special reference to *anamnesis* in its relation to *epiklesis* (§§10,12);
d) the relationship between the eucharist and repentance, confession, and reconciliation to the eucharistic congregation;

e) the meaning of sacrifice (§8), real presence (§13), ambassador (§29), and the implications of "for the purpose of communion" in regard to the reservation of the eucharistic elements (§15);

f) the participation of baptized children in the eucharist.

4. In the section on ministry, we note:

a) the link between ordained ministry today and the ministry of the apostles and apostolic succession (§§10, 35),

b) the distinction between the priesthood of the entire people of God and the ordained priesthood, especially in light of Pauline teaching on the different functions of the members of the one body of Christ (§17 and commentary);

c) issues related to the ordination of women to the priesthood (§18), including the way in which the problem is formulated in the text of BEM;

d) the relation between bishop, presbyter and deacon;

e) the relation between *episkope*, the bishop, and the eucharist.

V. Tasks facing the Orthodox churches

In view of future work in connection with BEM, we offer the following considerations and recommendations.

1. Steps should be taken to enable translation and distribution of the BEM document in the languages of all Orthodox churches.

2. Orthodox churches should see to it that the BEM document is studied and discussed in clergy and laity groups, theological faculties and seminaries, clergy associations, as well as in interconfessional groups.

3. Orthodox churches should be open to reading BEM and to responding to it in a spirit of critical self-examination, particularly in the area of current practices in churches and parishes. They should also use this process as a stimulus and encouragement for the renewal of their life.

4. In studying and evaluating BEM, the Orthodox should move beyond the theological scholasticism of recent centuries by re-appropriating the creativity and dynamics of biblical and patristic theology. This will enable them to move towards broader perspectives and to think more deeply about certain issues.

5. In their ongoing bilateral conversations, Orthodox churches should take BEM into account.

VI. Perspectives for future Faith and Order work

In view of the future work of the Faith and Order Commission and the WCC as a whole, we recommend the following perspectives for a proper inter-relationship between BEM and the Faith and Order study projects "Towards the Common Expression of the Apostolic Faith Today" and "The Unity of the Church and the Renewal of Human Community".

1. The process of an ecumenical reappropriation of the apostolic faith and tradition as it was begun in the BEM document should be consciously continued in the two other study projects.

2. There should be a clear understanding that baptism, eucharist and ministry are essential elements of the apostolic faith and tradition. At the same time, they are fundamental expressions of the witness and service of the church for today's world and its needs, its concerns, and its renewal. Renewal of both the life of the church and of the world cannot be separated from the liturgical and the sacramental life of the church nor from its pastoral responsibility.

3. These two other projects should also be open to insights and suggestions expressed in the responses of the churches to BEM and profit from them.

4. The Lima document highlights the important relationship between the "rule of faith" and the "rule of prayer", to which the Orthodox are so deeply committed. Therefore we hope that in the two other study projects of Faith and Order this significant insight is seriously taken into account as well.

5. We further recommend that one important point in future work of the Faith and Order Commission in relationship to BEM should be the clarification of theological terminology and of linguistic problems in translations. This seems to be necessary in view of the heading "Ministry" of the third section of BEM and terms such as "sign", reception", and "believer's/adult baptism".

6. Starting from a clarification of the vision of the church which undergirds BEM, the future work of Faith and Order should concentrate on ecclesiology by bringing together the ecclesiological perspectives in BEM, in the responses of the churches to BEM, and in the other study projects of Faith and Order.

*   *   *

We, the participants in the symposium, experienced this meeting as an occasion for exchanging our views and clarifying common perspectives. We saw in it also an important means for furthering contacts and cooperation among the Orthodox churches and thereby promoting our conciliar spirit.

List of participants
Host
Archbishop Iakovos, Primate of the Greek Orthodox Archdiocese of North and South America, Exarch of the Ecumenical Patriarchate

Participants from member churches of WCC
Metropolitan Prof. Dr Chrysostomos of Myra, Ecumenical Patriarchate of Constantinople
Metropolitan Parthenios of Carthage, Greek Orthodox Patriarchate of Alexandria
Rev. Prof. Paul Tarazi, Greek Orthodox Patriarchate of Antioch
Prof. Dr George Galitis, Greek Orthodox Patriarchate of Jerusalem
Archbishop Kirill of Smolensk and Vysma, Russian Orthodox Church
Rev. Prof. Dr Athanassios Yevtič, Serbian Orthodox Church
Metropolitan Dr Anthony of Transylvania, Romanian Orthodox Church
Mgr. Joseph, Bishop of Velyka, Bulgarian Orthodox Church
Dr Benedictos Englezakis, Church of Cyprus
Metropolitan Dr Chrysostomos of Peristerion, Church of Greece
Bishop Jeremias of Wroclaw & Szczecin, Polish Orthodox Autocephalic Church
Rev. Fr Ambrosius, Finnish Orthodox Church
Archpriest Dr Jaroslav Suvarsky, Orthodox Church of Czechoslovakia
Rev. Leonid Kishkovsky, Orthodox Church in America
Bishop Nerses Bozabalian, Armenian Apostolic Church, Etchmiadzin
Bishop Bishoi of Damietta, Coptic Orthodox Church
Archbishop Gregorios of Shoa, Ethiopian Orthodox Church
Archbishop Mesrob Ashjian, Armenian Apostolic Church
Rev. Dr K.M. George, Orthodox Syrian Church of the East

Theological schools
Prof. Dr (Mrs) Nikolitsa Nikolakakou, Department of Pastoral Theology, University of Athens, Greece
Prof. Konstantinos Skouteris, Department of Theology, University of Athens, Greece
Prof. Dr Ioannis Anastassiou, Department of Theology, University of Thessaloniki, Greece
Prof. Dr Nicholas Lossky, St Sergius Theological Institute, Paris, France
Rev. Prof. Dr Alkiviadis Calivas, Holy Cross Greek Orthodox School, Brookline, USA
Rev. Prof. Dr Thomas Hopko, St Vladimir's Seminary, Crestwood, USA

Advisers
Prof. Dr Nikos Nissiotis, Department of Pastoral Theology, University of Athens, Greece
Dr Alexandros Papaderos, Orthodox Academy of Crete, Greece
Prof. (Mrs) Catherina Chiotellis, Center of Translation and Interpretation in Corfu, Athens, Greece

Rev. Dr David Burke, Lutheran World Ministries, New York, USA
Rev. Fr John Long, SJ, National Conference of Catholic Bishops, Bronx, USA

Guest
Metropolitan Emilianos of Sylivria, Ecumenical Patriarchate

Other participants from the United States
Prof. Dr George Bebis, Holy Cross Greek Orthodox School of Theology, Brookline
Bishop Prof. Dr Demetrios of Vresthena, Holy Cross Greek Orthodox School of Theology, Brookline
Rev. Prof. Thomas Fitzgerald, Holy Cross Greek Orthodox School of Theology, Brookline
Rev. Prof. Dr Theodore Stylianopoulos, Holy Cross Greek Orthodox School of Theology, Brookline
Rev. Prof. Dr John Travis, Holy Cross Greek Orthodox School of Theology, Brookline
Prof. Dr Kyriaki A. Fitzgerald, Holy Cross Greek Orthodox School of Theology, Brookline
Ms Elaine Alexis Gounaris, Ecumenical Office of Greek Orthodox Archdiocese, New York
Archpriest Sergiy Suzdalstsev, Dean of the Russian Orthodox Cathedral of St Nicholas, New York
Rev. Fr George Corey, Orthodox Church in America, Boston
Mrs Susan Arida, Orthodox Church in America, Brookline
Ms Constance Tarasar, St Vladimir's Seminary, Crestwood
Rev. Fr Yeprem Kelegian, Armenian Apostolic Church, Etchmiadzin, New York

WCC staff
Rev. Prof. Ion Bria, Moderator of Orthodox Task Force
Rev. Dr Emilio Castro, General Secretary of WCC (12 June only)
Rev. Dr Günther Gassmann, Director, Faith and Order Secretariat
Rev. Dr Gennadios Limouris, Executive Secretary, Faith and Order Secretariat
G. Protopresbyter George Tsetsis, Representative, Ecumenical Patriarchate of Constantinople

Coopted staff
Ms Carol Thysell, National Council of Churches of the USA, Faith and Order Commission (secretarial assistance)
Mr Mstislav Voskressensky, Russian Orthodox Church (interpreter)

Chanukah 2006

10659096

Barry,

I was privileged to be able to provide except for this book. Now I have 2 more angels in my life. You are a primary there!

Kathy

WAR TRAUMA:

Lessons Unlearned,
from Vietnam to Iraq

WAR TRAUMA:

Lessons Unlearned,
from Vietnam to Iraq

Vol. 3
of A Vietnam Trilogy

Raymond Monsour Scurfield

Algora Publishing
New York

© 2006 by Algora Publishing.
All Rights Reserved
www.algora.com

No portion of this book (beyond what is permitted by
Sections 107 or 108 of the United States Copyright Act of 1976)
may be reproduced by any process, stored in a retrieval system,
or transmitted in any form, or by any means, without the
express written permission of the publisher.

ISBN-13: 978-0-87586-485-3 (trade paper)
ISBN-13: 978-0-87586-486-0 (hard cover)
ISBN-13: 978-0-87586-487-7 (ebook)

Library of Congress Cataloging-in-Publication Data —

Scurfield, Raymond M.
War Trauma: lessons unlearned, from Vietnam to Iraq: vol. 3 of a Vietnam
trilogy / Raymond Monsour Scurfield.
     p. cm.
Bibliographic references.
ISBN-13: 978-0-87586-485-3 (trade paper : alk. paper)
ISBN-13: 978-0-87586-486-0 (hard cover: alk. paper)
ISBN-13: 978-0-87586-487-7 (ebook: alk. paper) 1. Post-traumatic stress
disorder—Treatment. 2. Veterans—Mental health. 3. Vietnam War, 1961-1975—
Veterans—Mental health. 4. Iraq War, 2003—Veterans—Mental health. I. Title.

     RC552.P67S3747 2006
     616.85'212—dc22
                              2006025959

Front Cover: Afghan War Veterans Playing Soccer
A soccer player on crutches from the football team "Afgan", and a boy tackle for
the ball during a training match. The team, which includes players disabled from
the Soviet war in Afghanistan (1979-1989), trains three times per week for international competitions between teams of handicapped players.
Image: © Sergei Supinsky/epa/Corbis
Photographer: Sergei Supinsky

Printed in the United States

Some Terms And Definitions

Bazooka: a shoulder-fired weapon used primarily against armored and other vehicles, fortified firing positions, etc.

CO: commanding officer

CONUS: Continental United States

COSC: (Combat Operational Stress Control) Actions by US Military mental health to prevent and manage combat stress reactions among deployed personnel.

CSR: Combat Stress Reaction. US military mental health term to describe temporary negative psychological reactions of military personnel exposed to stressors in a war zone, such as preoccupation with anxiety, fear, unresolved grief, depression.

DOD. Department of Defense

FOBs: Forward Operating Bases

Friendly fire: Bullets, shells, rockets, etc., that have been fired by your own side.

Friendly fire casualties: Personnel injured or killed by friendly fire.

Kuhlmann Group Debriefing Model: A method of psychological debriefing used to counsel military personnel who are secondary and tertiary survivors of a traumatic event, usually those who had a close relationship or acquaintance with the person(s) killed but who were not immediately present at the time of the deaths.

Humvee: The approximately 5,200 pound High-Mobility Multipurpose Wheeled Vehicle (HMMWV). Used as a primary means of personal transport in the military, it has replaced the jeep. The platform of the HMMWV also is the baseline vehicle for 11 other military vehicles.

IEDs: Improvised Explosive Devices (such as home-made remotely-detonated bombs placed in a roadway).

IZ: International Zone, aka The Green Zone. Considered the safest location in Baghdad, heavily secured and protected by US military personnel.

Med-evac: Medical Evacuation.

OEF: Operation Enduring Freedom, the name Washington uses to describe the US military presence and overall mission in Afghanistan.

OI or OIF: Operation Iraqi Freedom, the name Washington uses to describe the US military presence and overall mission in Iraq.

Psychiatric casualty: a person who has a psychiatric or emotional reaction severe enough to miss at least some days of duty to receive mental health treatment.

PTSD: Post Traumatic Stress Disorder

RPG: Rocket-propelled grenade.

SASOs: Stability and Support Operations.

Theater: A war zone or area where military operations are being waged.

VA: US Department of Veterans Affairs.

VBIEDs: Vehicle-borne Improvised Explosive Devices, or vehicles loaded with explosives that are used as weapons. Also known as "vehicle-borne IEDs".

VC: (Viet Cong) The irregular enemy forces indigenous to southern Vietnam who were opposed to the Saigon-based Vietnamese government.

TABLE OF CONTENTS

PREFACE

This book is written to provide vital information to veterans, their families and communities, and the nation about the full human impact of war — both shorter and longer term. It makes no difference if readers are pro-military or pacifists, for or against the Vietnam or Iraq Wars, or simply concerned citizens. If you are interested in knowing the truth about how past and the current wars affect the participants, their families and America, and want to know what to do — read on.

This book completes *A Vietnam Trilogy*. The first two volumes, *Veterans and Post-Traumatic Stress, 1968, 1989 & 2000*, and *Healing Journeys: Study Abroad with Vietnam Veterans*, together describe more than three decades of the continuing journeys of hundreds of Vietnam veterans who have been indelibly marked by the Vietnam War and its aftermath. The current volume applies the lessons that should have been learned in prior wars. If these lessons are not learned by veterans of subsequent US wars, to include the Persian Gulf and Iraq Wars, untold numbers of additional war veterans and their families will experience needlessly prolonged misunderstandings, loss and pain, and may be tortured with the belief that they are doomed to a life of continuing pathos. It does not have to be so.

It is not essential to first read either Volume 1 or 2 of *A Vietnam Trilogy* to appreciate the current work. However, the earlier volumes provide an important background and context to the events and developments that characterized military psychiatry in Vietnam — and that remain similar to military psychiatry today. The first two books also shed light on the universality of the nature of the trauma of the Vietnam War and the strategies used to survive during war, as well as the impact on the in-country and post-war lives of veterans. Finally, they illustrate veterans' return trips to peace-time Vietnam in 1989 and 2000, experiences that were extremely different from each other yet offered lessons about the long-term post-war recovery of war veterans.

1

I served in 1968-69 as an Army social work officer on one of the Army's two psychiatric teams, the 98th Medical Detachment, attached to the 8th Field Hospital in Nha Trang. The medical mission was to assess and treat psychiatric casualties to "conserve the fighting strength." This experience began a 30-plus year mental health career in PTSD treatment, education and research of veterans from the Vietnam War, as well as from World War II, Korea and the Persian Gulf.

From *1979* to *1989*, I was a clinician and program leader involved in the development of several regional and national mental health programs for war veterans. As such, I was both an observer and participant in the midst of powerful national political and social upheaval centering on veterans. An insider's viewpoint is offered of the Department of Veterans Affairs Headquarters in Washington, D.C., to include a counseling and outreach operation during the national dedications of both the National Vietnam Veterans Memorial and statue. Then, I led the implementation of an internationally acclaimed 33-bed PTSD treatment program in the Pacific Northwest. The program's experiences with such highly innovative action-based activities as helicopter-ride therapy, Outward Bound Adventure-Based program and extensive involvement with American Indian veterans and their healers and healing rituals, influenced my fateful decision to undertake a return to Vietnam two decades after the war. These are the main topics of the first volume, *A Vietnam Trilogy. Veterans and Post-Traumatic Stress, 1968, 1989 & 2000.*

1989: The first peace-time return visit by a therapy group of Vietnam veterans with PTSD took place in 1989. The VA and the State Department refused to sanction this controversial trip, but we did succeed in revisiting sites where most of the nine veterans had served during deployment and overall they later judged the experience extremely helpful in furthering their recovery from long-standing war-related problems.

Other issues explored include questions around the stereotype of "troubled veterans" — how troubled are they? Are all war veterans disturbed? And how is it that so many war veterans go on to lead relatively successful post-war lives, and yet are still conflicted regarding their war experiences? In any case, who says it is a sign of psychiatric disorder to be troubled by war-related problems?

HEALING JOURNEYS: STUDY ABROAD WITH VIETNAM VETERANS. VOL. 2 OF A VIETNAM TRILOGY

1990-2000: The Persian Gulf War had an immense impact on all war veterans. There was a resurgence of selective amnesia and denial about the true impact of war. As a national faculty member for joint VA-DOD training programs, I was involved in improving the mental health response readiness for anticipated psychiatric casualties. Also, some remarkably therapeutic people-to-people meetings were arranged between US veterans of the Vietnam War and Soviet "Afghantsi" veterans that belied what the respective governments had been saying about each other for decades. These meetings offered a glimpse of the power of "a healing circle" that occurred between former adversaries and could be replicated with veterans returning to peacetime Vietnam.

Vietnam 2000: My second return to peacetime Vietnam was in May, 2000, as one of three college professors who led a precedent-setting Study Abroad course under the auspices of the University of Southern Mississippi. This unique program for 16 university history students and three Vietnam combat veterans covered an integrated curriculum of military history and the mental health implications of war, and incorporated the personal Vietnam histories of each of the three veterans. The interactions of the veterans and the students and the people they met in Vietnam produced many powerful healing experiences and lessons.

The book includes a comprehensive analysis of the pros and cons of returning to a former war zone.

LESSONS UNLEARNED FROM VIETNAM TO IRAQ: WAR TRAUMA, VETERANS, FAMILIES AND HEALING

September 11, 2001. The terrorist acts of September 11, 2001 had an impact on the psychiatric state of large numbers of civilians, an impact similar to what can happen in a war zone. Panic and other emotions are normal reactions to such a cataclysmic event and must be expected. Also normal, although perhaps not constructive, is the tendency to dehumanize the enemy and to use racism and xenophobia to justify national policies. Emotional and cognitive reactions in the wake of 9/11 both fuel and complicate unresolved issues from prior traumas that have been experienced and drive one's support or opposition to various national and international policies that are associated with, or are cast as responses to, the event.

Iraq and War Zone Mental Health Casualties. Parallels are shown between US military mental health interventions now in Iraq and almost 40 years ago in Vietnam. Given the lack of significant change in understanding and approach, in all likelihood we will see similar high rates of acute and other psychiatric casualties. Indeed, military surveys already have documented disturbing levels of PTSD and other mental health problems in personnel returning from deployment. Some of the changes that are needed are discussed.

War-Related Blame, Guilt and Shame. A step-by-step description of three different cases, a World War II veteran, a Vietnam veteran and a Korean War veteran, illustrate a combination Gestalt Therapy and cognitive reframing strategy, and a special cognitive reframing technique that I have developed over 20 years to bring relief to suffering veterans. Finally, there is a discussion of Traumatic Incident Reduction and alternative interventions that can be considered for use in a war zone with psychiatric casualties.

The Return Home from Deployment: The Ricochet Effect. The impact on the active duty personnel and the family following deployment is described. There is some basic information that active duty personnel and their families need to be told, such as the warning signs of lingering problems in the aftermath of the war, triggers that precipitate symptoms, and the war-time survival strategies that may pop up back home and cause difficulties.

The Expanding Circle of Healing. I provide the elements of one model of recovery that is necessary to promote optimal healing for many veterans, incorporating expanding levels of relationships into veterans' healing journey: non-veterans, veterans' communities, government and society at large, the people of the country where they were deployed, both the negatives and the positives of the trauma experiences and religious/spiritual faith and/or a belief in the interconnectedness of humanity.

In closing, I have lived and worked with hundreds of my fellow and sister war zone veterans from all across the United States, and several from Canada, Australia and the Soviet Union since 1968, in joint journeys of recovery and healing. We all have been a part of the long effort to provide veterans and their families what they have so fully earned. And that is respectful, enlightened and responsive medical, psychiatric and social services, and understanding and acceptance by citizens and communities.

Pax mentis,

Raymond Monsour Scurfield

> *Pax mentis (Latin for "peace of mind") was the unofficial unit motto of the 98th Medical Detachment psychiatric team in Vietnam.*

Chapter 1. Lessons Unlearned And The Context of War: From Vietnam And The Persian Gulf To 9/11, Afghanistan and Iraq

Many lessons should have been learned by now about the psychiatric impact of war on combatants. Those lessons, which for the most part remain unlearned, are at the center of this book and this trilogy. The hundreds of thousands of veterans who returned from Vietnam, and their families, are all case studies of post-war social and psychological readjustment. A number of these have been described in the two previous volumes of *A Vietnam Trilogy*. [1]

The perspective provided is through four primary sources: my four years on active duty during the Vietnam War, including one year as a social work officer on an Army psychiatric team in Vietnam (1968-69); 25 years as a mental health clinician and director of several regional and national post-traumatic stress programs throughout the country with the VA (Department of Veterans Affairs); co-leading two return trips to peace-time Vietnam in 1989 and 2000; and most importantly through the words and hearts of over a thousand combat veterans from several different eras with whom I have worked for more than three decades.

Many of the lessons are briefly identified herein, as well as crucial factors that have characterized the Vietnam War and the veterans and families who are still adjusting after the war. These lessons offer a context and a bridge of understanding concerning about what should and must be applied in the context of

---

1. *A Vietnam Trilogy. Veterans and Post Traumatic Stress, 1968, 1989 & 2000.* (New York: Algora, 2004); and *Healing Journeys: Study Abroad with Vietnam Veterans. Vol. 2 of A Vietnam Trilogy.* (New York: Algora, 2006).

more recent wars, including in Afghanistan and Iraq. In the following chapters, we will explore:

- the social and psychological aftermath of 9/11, and the Iraq and Afghanistan Wars
- what needs to be done today with and for members of the Armed Forces (and their families) both while they are deployed in Iraq and Afghanistan and in the initial weeks and months following their return from deployment. (As of July 2006, more than 300,000 have served one or more deployments, and the number is increasing monthly.)
- what needs to be done differently to help veterans of all wars and their families in their longer-term post-deployment readjustment.

Such discussion is vitally important for those returning from Iraq and Afghanistan, and is still relevant for Vietnam, Persian Gulf and other veterans still suffering from their war experiences, and the families who suffer with them.

Furthermore, past experience holds implications regarding governmental agencies that employ or serve active duty military personnel and their families, particularly the Department of Defense (DOD); and those agencies that serve veterans and their families, particularly the Department of Veterans Affairs (VA). Also, there are crucial implications for the government's domestic and international policies and for society at large. Finally, there are implications for what needs to be done to help war veterans and their families from all eras to have more peaceful and satisfying post-war lives. They deserve no less. These areas are briefly identified here and then are discussed in detail throughout this book as they apply to Iraq and Afghanistan veterans and their families, as well as to veterans from previous wars who may still be suffering from war-related trauma and post-war readjustment challenges.

THE ENDURING IMPACT OF SURVIVING WAR

I had two pivotal experiences with veteran casualties of war before I even got to Vietnam in 1968. As these encounters dramatically altered my world-view and attitudes about war and its impact on combatants, I will recapitulate them here although they are also mentioned in the first volume of *A Vietnam Trilogy*.

Marine Psychiatrically Evacuated from Vietnam

In my second-year internship as I was earning my master's of social work (MSW), I was assigned to a locked psychiatric ward at the Veterans Administration Hospital in Sepulveda, in the San Fernando Valley outside of Los Angeles. I was to be the social worker for a young Marine Vietnam veteran, among others, who was diagnosed with schizophrenia, a profound psychiatric disorder.[2] He had suffered a psychotic breakdown while in combat and had been medically

6

evacuated home. Even with his schizophrenia, he was at times lucid. During one such period, when he was aware of his surroundings and my presence, he looked me in the eyes and revealed a desire that obsessed him, a desire he would never be able to fulfill. His eyes swimming in tears, he pleaded for me to help him return to Vietnam, "so that I can prove that I am a man."

His plea pierced my heart and was seared into my memory. Of course, he was never going to be accepted back onto active duty, let alone be sent back to Vietnam. He could "never make right" what, as I later came to understand, is perceived as perhaps the most unforgivable and egregious shame that can befall any combat soldier — "deserting" or otherwise "letting down" one's buddies in the heat of battle. The image of this tormented soldier stays with me still.[3]

This scene would be repeated in various guises as I worked in Vietnam — and it is being replicated in today's wars as well. As I gained experience with military psychiatry, I came to see that "prematurely" removing a soldier from war condemns him to "never work out" his psychiatric reactions. Just like this tortured young Marine, tens of thousands of psychiatric casualties are haunted for life about having "failed" in combat. And this belief and perception continues to be promulgated today by military psychiatry personnel in Iraq and Afghanistan. However, there was another side to this story that I was not to learn until much later.

On the Plane to the Vietnam War

The second incident occurred while I was onboard a civilian airplane, dressed in my Army uniform. I was leaving my home in Pittsburgh to fly to the West Coast and then onward to duty in Vietnam. A severely disabled Vietnam veteran (double amputee, with forearm crutches and a black patch over his eye) came onboard after we all had been seated and he moved ever so slowly down the aisle to take the only remaining empty seat — right next to me. I found myself feeling awkward and could not think of a thing to say; instead I became preoccupied with my own worst fantasies of injuries that I might incur in Vietnam. He finally initiated a conversation with me — and I still remember two things that he said. He told me about friends back home who had told him that it was a shame that he had "lost his legs and eye for nothing." And he ended our conversation by mentioning that he considered himself to be very lucky — as no one else in the foxhole had survived.

---

2. I completed Army ROTC at Dickinson College, Carlisle, PA, and was commissioned a 2nd Lieutenant in the US Army, Medical Service Corps in June, 1965. I then received a two-year deferment from being activated to complete two years of study for the MSW degree at the University of Southern California in Los Angeles.

3. *A Vietnam Trilogy*, pp. 10-11.

This seminal interchange heightened my awareness about two things. First, when the war is morally controversial and politically divisive, it can make the returning veteran's post-war readjustment extremely problematic. A similar divisiveness is growing in regard to the nation's newest cadre of US veterans of Iraq and Afghanistan.

Secondly, I was struck by what an extraordinarily positive view this severely disabled (but not handicapped!) veteran had fashioned. Somehow, he had been able to look beyond his extensive physical trauma. Rather than dwelling on the morbid aspects of his physical condition, he was able to recognize and appreciate a positive element. This recognition of the positive, embedded in the most horrific of trauma experience, has become a central element in my clinical work with veterans and in the expanded circle of healing described later in this book.

Military Mental Health In Vietnam — And Implications For Iraq

The parallels between what military mental health specialists did during the Vietnam War and what is going on in Iraq today are compelling. Aspects of the military approach to mental health in the war zone that are still being replicated today include the following.

The Military Medical Mission

The overall mission of the military medical establishment is to conserve the fighting strength — whether or not that is in the best interests of the long-term mental health of the individual soldier. They are effective at enabling military personnel with psychiatric difficulties to return to duty in the war zone. However, there has been an unwillingness to recognize and admit that the frequency and duration of exposure to trauma is the single greatest predictor that someone will be at risk to develop post-traumatic stress disorder (PTSD). And in fulfillment of the military medical mission to conserve the fighting strength, the vast majority of psychiatric casualties are sent back to duty — where they almost certainly will face further trauma in the form of witnessing of, participation in and immersion in death, killing and maiming.

Additionally, due to a shortage of volunteers enlisting in the military coupled with increased troop strength required in Iraq and Afghanistan and elsewhere, a large proportion of the Armed Forces find their war tours are extended, or they are being redeployed to face yet more combat trauma. These dynamics dramatically increase the risk that a high number of military personnel today will subsequently develop PTSD. But neither the combatants, their families nor the public are fully and properly informed about this or several other critical factors.

THE PSYCHIATRIC MANTRA

The overriding operational principle in treating psychiatric casualties in the war zone is that it is almost always very bad for the short and longer term mental health of deployed personnel to evacuate them out of the war zone, as "psychiatric symptoms may well become fixated and permanent." Therefore, military mental health personnel are trained to return the psychiatric casualty to duty ASAP and only medevac out of country as an absolute last resort — "as this is in the best interests of the psychiatric casualty."[4]

This mantra, "do not prematurely evacuate," is embedded in the consciousness of military mental health workers. That was practically all the training we had, and on this one point we were trained very thoroughly. Throughout my Vietnam tour, I kept hearing that young Marine's words on the VA psychiatric ward, and I believed, I truly believed. Don't prematurely evacuate out of country, or you will create more chronic psychiatric casualties, hundreds more, like that young Marine.

Of course, the issue is much more complicated. As the reader will discover later in this book, what is happening today in Iraq is a perpetuation of the assumptions and beliefs about psychiatric casualties that were promulgated during and following the Vietnam War — and they can have devastating longer-term impact following return from deployment.

THE PROFOUND PSYCHIATRIC PARADOX

The psychiatric mantra about the dangers of evacuating someone prematurely was juxtaposed with the painful realties of the war and the horrendous impact it was having on deployed military personnel, day after day. The convergence of these two realities — the injunction not to send anyone Stateside to recover, and the ongoing traumas of war — obliged military mental health personnel to make a painfully paradoxical decision:

---

4. R. Scurfield, "Olin E. Teague Award Ceremony Acceptance Talk" (Washington, DC: VA Central Office, December 2, 1988). Unpublished manuscript presented at the award ceremony when I received this national Department of Veterans Affairs Olin E. Teague award for "outstanding achievements and continuing work in the psychological rehabilitation of veterans with combat-related post-traumatic stress disorder."

Is this man too crazy to be sent back to killing, or is he crazy enough to be evacuated out of the war zone?

This oxymoronic situation is founded on the unquestioned overriding military psychiatry mantra: it is much worse to err by prematurely evacuating someone out of country than it is to err by sending him back to war duty. And, yes, I bought it — hook, line and sinker. By all accounts, this continues to be the guiding ethos of military mental health today in Iraq and Afghanistan.

SURVIVING WAR HAS A PRICE

Military personnel typically learn and become conditioned to survive in a war zone in a number of ways (several of which also apply to civilians in a war zone). It is vital that mental health clinicians, veterans and their families understand these dynamics today. Only two of the most salient will be briefly mentioned here. Eleven survival modes are described in detail in Volume 1 of *A Vietnam Trilogy*.

The Survival Mantra in War

For both front-line combatants and support personnel in such roles as medical services, graves registration, truck drivers, in-country prison duty and intelligence, the primary means of surviving the risks, the constant threats and unpredictability of danger, is to learn how to detach oneself from the realities of what is happening. This strategy was boiled down into the blunt saying among combat troops in Vietnam: *F— it, it don't mean nothin.'*

This was the first reaction to anything bad that happened to anyone — Vietnamese or American. This attitude enables a person to protect and take care of himself (or herself), take care of "number one," and resist being overwhelmed.

This survival strategy is important today in the war zone. This is how many vets, and civilians in a war zone, can survive repeated exposure to the traumas of war. One learns to "be removed" or "be somewhere else" while in the middle of unspeakable horror. And what we did not realize in the 1960s is that many vets bring this conditioning home with them after the war, creating a ricochet effect on them and their families. And, it is still happening today with Iraq and Afghanistan veterans and their families.

Dehumanizing the Enemy

To prepare personnel for war, the military reinforces the ability to detach through training and conditioning that dehumanizes the enemy.

You are immediately and incessantly told not to call Vietnamese "Vietnamese". Rather, everyone is called gooks, dinks, slant-eyes and not talked about as people and not to be treated with mercy or apprehension. That's what they engraved into you. That killer instinct. Just go away and do destruction. [5]

Yes: do not consider the enemy as human beings, like you and me. In this way, the killing and death become a more manageable task that one can perform repeatedly and efficiently. In effect, you engage in "cognitive reframing" — to change the definition or perception of reality to make it more tolerable or understandable. You can't think that a dead civilian lying alongside the road is someone's parent or brother or mother or child — or you wouldn't be able to make it through your tour.

In addition, many Vietnam veterans found that the inculcation of dehumanization and its companion, racism against the Vietnamese, became intertwined with racism in Vietnam *between Americans* of different races. And then, this sentiment was brought home. But this is one of the dirty secrets of war that has been kept mostly silent.

Then it happened again in the throes of the Persian Gulf War,[6] and later we will see how it is beginning to happen in the midst of the Iraq and Afghanistan Wars.

The Guerilla Nature of the War

The fighters opposing the American military in Iraq and Afghanistan today use guerilla warfare tactics reminiscent of what we faced in Vietnam. The Viet Cong would operate clandestinely and used terror and deception, murder and public executions to coerce and/or intimidate other villagers. They sometimes used children and women to deliver their attacks or to mask their activities.

In such situations it is difficult or impossible to distinguish enemy from friend. It was natural to become extremely prejudiced against almost anyone who was Vietnamese; and for such combat troops the lives of almost any Vietnamese became unimportant.

Indeed, there were many stories about American troops finding out that Vietnamese whom they had befriended turned out to be VC, like a Vietnamese barber on the base who cut the hair of American military during the day and returned at night to attack, as a Viet Cong. This makes it all the more necessary for combat personnel to dehumanize the enemy and to generalize that dehumanization, whether moderately or strongly, to the local population over all.

And the troops in Iraq and Afghanistan find themselves in the middle of a war against just this sort of non-uniformed forces, forces that use violence and terror tactics not only against the US but also against local citizens who cooperate with the Americans or their allies — or against innocent by-standers. It is

---

5. Haywood T. Kirkland, in W. Terry, *Bloods. An Oral History of the Vietnam War by Black Veterans.* (New York: Ballantine Books, 1984), 90.
6. See Scurfield, *Healing Journeys,* 2006.

an excruciating challenge to be tasked with "trying to win the hearts and minds" of the people while waging war against their neighbors and family members who consider cooperation to be collusion, a betrayal of their nation. The impossibility of knowing who is an "insurgent," "terrorist" or "guerilla" and who is an "innocent civilian" brings with it enormously conflicted and tragic consequences. This brought ongoing suffering to many Vietnam veterans and it is hurting untold numbers of Americans deployed to Iraq and Afghanistan as is described later; and they will bring those conflicts home with them and into their families and communities.

The Collision of Morality with War Zone Reality

War inevitably creates sharp moral conflicts for anyone caught up in it. Most of us were raised with some idea of principles that are promptly broken in a war zone, including these:

- Thou shalt not kill (especially women, children or the elderly).
- Do unto others as you would have them do unto you.

However such moral principles, which may never have to be given much thought at home, are suddenly and violently confronted, if not grossly violated, by the realities of war — and especially guerilla warfare. Indeed, many military personnel consider that military chaplains fill a paradoxical role. They appear to be in the position of "invoking God's blessing for Americans and for our safety" and that we had the moral right to kill — but just how was it so different from murder? [7]

The pretence that "God is on our side and the enemy is God-less" is widespread. Of course, this is what the Muslims in Iraq and Afghanistan say about America today — that they are fighting for Allah and against the infidels. Is it not perhaps the ultimate dehumanization of the enemy to say that we are "God's children" and they are not?

This perception and belief may help combatants to do what they have to do to survive in the war zone, and it is encouraged by the military. However, for many combatants, after the war it became very problematic to realize what horrific acts they had committed "in the name of God." And this conflict, which is being repeated among Iraq and Afghanistan veterans today, has enormous import to the healing strategies that need to be considered and implemented.

7. Haywood T. Kirkland, "Specialist 4 Haywood T., 'The Kid' Kirkland (Ari Sesu Merretazon), Washington, DC", in W. Terry, Bloods. An Oral History of the Vietnam War by Black Veterans (New York: Ballantine Books, 1984), 91. For a description of war and chaplains and God, see Vietnam veteran Bill Mahedy's book, *Out of the Night: The Spiritual Journey of Vietnam Vets* (New York: Ballantine, 1986). Also, there is the excellent book by Walter Capps, a professor who taught at the University of Santa Barbara and who was a pioneer in inviting Vietnam veteran guest speakers: *The Unfinished War: Vietnam and the American Conscience* (Boston: Beacon, 1982).

THE LEGACIES OF WAR FOLLOW THE VETERANS BACK HOME

It was not until around 1974-75, several years after returning from Vietnam, that I found my awareness gradually set in about the continuing and indelible influence of Vietnam on Vietnam veterans — and on myself. And it was not until the National Vietnam Veterans Readjustment Study Findings were reported in 1989 that the country learned for the first time the true and full enduring impact of the Vietnam War. The findings were astounding:

> More than 800,000 Vietnam veterans — almost one in every four — were found to have full or partial PTSD 13 to 20+ years following their deployment in the Vietnam War. [8]

Some readers may be tempted to dismiss the above figures as limited to "that troubled Vietnam vet generation." Wrong. A recent report by the Army Surgeon General indicates a marked — and growing — problem among Iraq and Afghanistan veterans:

> Thirty percent of US troops returning from the Iraq war have developed stress-related mental health problems three to four months after coming home. . . . The 30 percent figure is in contrast to the 3 percent to 5 percent diagnosed with a significant mental health issue immediately after they leave the war theater. . . . A study of troops who were still in the combat zone in 2004 found 13 percent experienced significant mental health problems. [9]

The implications of these recent findings for veterans and their families today are a central focus of later chapters.

ANGRY VETERANS, THE DEPARTMENT OF VETERANS AFFAIRS (VA) AND POLITICS

I was a director of several prominent regional and national programs in the Department of Veterans during the time that the concept of PTSD in war veterans was being developed and started to become understood (1979-1997). I had extensive experiences with more than a thousand veterans of different wars and different generations who were struggling with post-war recovery and with their families. Such experiences are the heart and soul of my perceptions and understanding concerning war, its impact and recovery.

---

8. R.A. Kulka, William E. Schlenger, John A. Fairbank, Richard L. Hough, B. Kathleen Jordan, Charles R. Marmar, And Daniel S. Weis, *Trauma And The Vietnam War Generation: Report Of Findings From The National Vietnam Veterans Readjustment Study* (New York: Brunner/Mazel, 1990).
9. "More troops developing latent mental disorders. Symptoms appear several months after returning from Iraq, military says." MSNBC.com July 28, 2005.

In the late 60s and 70s, many Vietnam Vets were extremely mistrustful of the military and of the government, to include Veterans Administration health care services. Indeed, many veterans considered the VA to be just like the military — except without the uniforms.

However, the sheer number of 3.14 million Vietnam veterans who were continuing to have great difficulty adjusting to civilian life was so immense[10] that inevitably more and more of them started coming to the VA for medical and psychiatric services. Many, especially those who were physically wounded and/or disabled from the war, as well as those with mental problems, were extremely angry and distrustful. There was a deep bitterness burning inside them. Their rage was grounded in the horrors and the recurring memories of war, the sense they had been used up and thrown away by their country and government, being made to feel unwelcome or simply ignored when they returned home.

In spite of the development of specialized knowledge about the impact of combat and operational stress in active duty military programs, and the development of PTSD programs and the innovative "help without hassles" Vet Center program in the VA system, many active duty personnel and veterans and their families today are reporting that their experiences with the DOD and the VA are, indeed, help *with* hassles. This affects the healing strategies of all war veterans today.

---

10. Many different estimates have been published of the number of US personnel who served in Vietnam during the war. The actual number is difficult to pinpoint due to various factors, i.e., (a) a number of persons were on classified operations in Laos and Cambodia, (b) others flew or were inserted into combat missions in Vietnam but their official duty station was elsewhere such as Thailand, and (3) there is disagreement as to who exactly should be counted as Vietnam veterans — what about persons who served prior to 1964, and those who served in ships in the waters contiguous to Vietnam, etc.? I have most confidence in the figure of 3.14 million persons who served in Vietnam and in the contiguous waters and airspace as defined and calculated in the (previously cited) National Vietnam Veterans Readjustment Study (NVVRS)—the largest and most sophisticated national psychiatric epidemiological study ever conducted on the veterans of any era, a study that required an accurate estimate of the numbers who had served. I also have confidence in this source as it is not a government agency that may have an ulterior motive for over- or under-reporting the figures — and I personally know almost all of the central investigators and am extremely impressed with their integrity. See R.A. Kulka, W.E. Schlenger, J.A. Fairbanks, R.L. Hough, B.K. Jordan, C.R. Marmar & D.S. Weiss: (1) *Trauma and the Vietnam War generation: Report of findings from the National Vietnam Veterans Readjustment Study* (New York: Brunner/Mazel, 1990); and (2) *National Vietnam veterans readjustment study (NVVRS): Description, current status and initial PTSD prevalence estimates* (Washington, DC: Veterans Administration, 1989).

As the first National Associate Director for Counseling operations of the Vet Center program (1982-85), which now has over 200 store-front counseling centers, I was there for many challenging and provocative experiences while at VA Central Office in Washington, D.C.[11] Particularly revealing were two discoveries.

PTSD CONSIDERED TO BE ANTI-WAR

In my naiveté, it was startling to discover that many high-ranking VA officials and conservative politicians considered the concept of PTSD to be an anti-war concept. Their concern was that the social and psychological problems that many war veterans developed would be emphasized too much and the Vet Center Program would be seen as indirectly promoting opposition to the war effort. They worried that this "negativity" or unvarnished truth about veterans could make it harder to recruit new troops.

Indeed, in their minds, the establishment of such programs on a large scale would suggest that many of the nation's veterans faced significant long term post-war problems — as if the solution created the problem. This is part of the collusion of sanitization and silence about the true impact of war that has characterized many of the nation's political and military leaders over the decades, described in detail in Volume 2 of *A Vietnam Trilogy*. Such collusion resurfaced during and after the terrorist acts of 9/11 (described in the following chapter) — and are happening now in regard to the Iraq War.

PRO-MILITARY VERSUS PRO-VETERAN

Another discovery that surprised me was that the pro-military, pro-DOD and pro-war forces in Washington, D.C., were not necessarily pro-veteran. In fact, many considered veteran disability benefits and health programs to be in competition for federal funding that they wanted to go to the DOD.

---

11. To include discovering that many of the higher-ranking VA officials, as well as many Chiefs of Psychiatry throughout the VA hospital system, were antagonistic to there even being a Vet Center Program See *A Vietnam Trilogy*, 2004, for a detailed description of the dynamics in the nation's capital regarding Vietnam veterans and the Vet Center Program. For an even more in-depth discussion of the Vietnam veteran's movement in the 1970s and 1980s, see Jerald Nicosia, *Home To The War. A History of the Vietnam Veterans Movement* (New York: Crown Publishers, 2001).

Disturbingly, this same dynamic is in place today; veterans and their families seem to be competing with the DOD and the war effort for funding. Resources and services are required to bring new and innovative healing strategies to many Vietnam veterans today, as well as to veterans of more recent wars and their families.

IN-ACTION THERAPEUTIC EXPERIENCES: FROM "THE WALL" TO RETURN TO PEACETIME VIETNAM IN 1989

From 1982 through 2000, I was a leader and a participant in a number of post-war healing interventions that "went beyond the traditional four walls" of the counseling office. These interventions had a dramatic impact in their own right, and they demonstrated that bold new ideas can make a difference. Mental health clinicians, veterans and their families of today and tomorrow need to be aware that innovative in-action therapeutic experiences can offer a distinctive post-war healing contribution that goes well beyond even the best applied office-based therapies for post-war issues and recovery.[12]

Here, readers will be alerted to such opportunities. These are examples of meaningful complements to complement traditional office-based therapy. The foundation for some of the critically needed post-war healing strategies for today and tomorrow are grounded in the rationale of such in-action therapeutic activities as:

- Visiting the Wall (national Vietnam Veteran Memorial) and other state and community war memorials, and accompanying grief and loss rituals
- Participation in properly-run and sanctioned American Indian warrior rituals
- Outward Bound adventure-based activities
- Helicopter-ride therapy
- Returning to the war zone years later, during peace time

All of these therapeutic activities have helped veterans to confront lingering war-related memories and the associated powerful emotions. For example, returning to peace-time Vietnam gave US veterans and Vietnamese veterans both the opportunity to meet each other in a non-war setting, which resulted (for most of them) in a powerful release of long-held fears, hatred, guilt and mental anguish. And the new and overwhelmingly positive mental pictures of a peace-time Vietnam that were in such contrast with war memories jolted the entrenched images and provided positive new memories and experiences.

---

12. These in-action therapeutic interventions are described in detail in the first two volumes of *A Vietnam Trilogy*.

Iraq and Afghanistan war veterans are also bringing home distinctive war-related sights, sounds, smells and vivid images that will be with them forever. And what is and should be the nature of post-war help available to address such ingrained stimuli?

Perhaps the most critical aspect of this series of positive people-to-people interchanges was that such affirming interactions began to crumble or obliterate a rigidly held set of attitudes and beliefs that had been instilled in combat veterans and then reinforced in the war zone as a way to survive what had to be done in war. And the need to treat "the other side" as less than human, or inhuman, is continuing to fuel chronic or recurring states of pain, guilt, horror, and rage among newly returned veterans. But when Vietnam vets and Vietnamese civilians and former enemies were brought together for the first time after decades, to meet each other as human beings, it led to very strong positive (and in a few cases negative) reactions.

This revelation is crucial information as we seek to invent further innovative healing strategies that so many veterans still need today.

Those who have served in Afghanistan and Iraq may never have the opportunity, or the desire, to return to a peacetime Iraq or Afghanistan some day in the future, as part of their healing process. Even so, there are critical steps they can take but that are almost never included in the prevailing current-day treatment and healing strategies.

THE PERSIAN GULF WAR INTERSECTS WITH VIETNAM VETERANS

The Persian Gulf War in 1991 aggravated many issues for Vietnam veterans. Three salient issues are relevant to Vietnam veterans, Gulf War veterans and their Iraq War and Afghanistan counterparts:

• Medical evacuation from a war zone. Not much has changed to reduce or facilitate awareness of the traumatic experiences that confront wounded personnel from the moment they are wounded until after they are discharged from a stateside hospital.

• The collusion of society and government to hide and deny the full impact of war. Powerful forces in this country contribute to the "politically correct" "media spin" that plays down or even denies the disastrous impact of war on all humans who are touched by it — including military and support personnel and their families, and the people in the country where the US was fighting.

• Racism in war. The Vietnam War brought out serious race-related issues both between American military personnel and the Vietnamese people they supposedly were defending — and the residue of that enflamed racism was brought home. And the Persian Gulf War also provoked disturbing anti-Arab sentiment and behaviors in the US.

Interactions between US and Soviet veterans of the wars in Afghanistan also provided insights that should be used to help today's military personnel. As veterans of countries that supported opposing sides both in Vietnam and the Soviet-supported war in Afghanistan, these meetings kindled Americans' long-held issues about Russian involvement in Vietnam and about how the governments, both US and Soviet, had been less than forthcoming with their nations about the progress and human costs of that war and the Soviet war in Afghanistan. If you didn't know their names, you wouldn't know if you were listening to a Soviet Afghantsi, to a Vietnam veteran — or to a US Iraq or Afghanistan War veteran.

> "You feel you have stepped into a room where the only way out is death, and you don't want that," Kalandarishvili said. "So, somehow you arrive: you fight, you hide, you yourself kill, and you survive. But it changes you, it changes your soul, and afterward you are not the same, never what you were before, never what you might have been, never what people still expect you to be."[13]

RETURNING TO PEACE-TIME VIETNAM IN 2000

My second career began in 1998 as a graduate school faculty member in the school of social work at the University of Southern Mississippi. To my great surprise, I still could not get away from Vietnam. I became involved in a precedent-setting university study-abroad Vietnam history course that combined military history and mental health educational and therapeutic objectives for sixteen history students and three Vietnam veterans.[14]

There were stark differences as well as clear similarities between the 1989 trip and this 2000 trip to Vietnam.[15] One similarity was that returning to former battle sites and meeting the Vietnamese people and former enemy Vietnamese veterans were profound in mitigating decades-old psychological wounds of war. One of the major differences was the inclusion in 2000 of university students along with returning veterans — an inclusion that had a remarkably healing impact. There were also many more substantial people-to-people interchanges in 2000 that brought invaluable cross-cultural sensitivity and learning. The combination of substantial, positive sociological and cultural experiences and poi-

---

13. Michael Parks, "Vietnam vets go 'soul to soul' with Soviets," *St. Petersburg Times*, (Oct. 19, 1988), 1-A, 8-A.
14. The description of the many remarkable experiences on the Vietnam Study Abroad Course in 2000 is a major component of Volume 2 of *A Vietnam Trilogy, Healing Journeys: Study Abroad with Vietnam Veterans*.
15. These similarities and differences, as well as a thorough analysis and critique of the pros and cons of veterans returning to their former war zone, are described in Volume 2 of *A Vietnam Trilogy, Healing Journeys*.

gnant positive interactions between the students and the veterans generated an almost entirely and extremely positive set of experiences among all of the course participants.

Finally, such interchanges further revealed the many ways the legacy of war can continue to persist in hundreds of thousands of combat veterans and impact their families, even three decades after their deployment. And how many more recent veterans will suffer a similar fate? The impact of war is too overwhelming for it not to leave a lasting and troubling imprint — both negative and positive — on a substantial percentage of soldiers from today's wars.

FROM VIETNAM AND THE PERSIAN GULF WARS TO 9/11, AFGHANISTAN AND IRAQ

I was finishing writing about my experiences with well over a thousand active duty military personnel, veterans and their families from 1966 to 2000. And then along came September 11, and then the Afghanistan War; and then the Iraq War. Apparently, there was more work — and writing — to be done. There were too many powerful lessons that should have been learned, but were not, from the Vietnam War and in the post-war problems facing hundreds of thousands Vietnam veterans and their families in the four decades since their deployment.[16] The areas of concern are manifold:

• Strategies that continue to be utilized by military mental health in war zones demand careful examination and a re-think.

• Critical information must be provided to Armed Forces personnel and their families but is not.

• Very specific strategies are needed to deal with returning Iraq and Afghanistan veterans and the impact of their return on the family.

• Better strategies are needed to address the enduring problems of war-related blame, guilt and shame issues.

• The similarities between the Vietnam War and more recent wars in their impact on the psychiatric, psychological and social functioning of veterans and their families must be mined for clues on what we can do to reduce the harm and increase the chances of recovery.

Several areas of enduring war-related and post-war issues that continue to haunt veterans many decades later require a much expanded understanding and broader-based creative approach to post-war healing. This is necessary for veterans of all combat zones, their families and the nation. That is what this book is all about.

---

16. The "combat cocktail" is a metaphor to describe the dialectic relationship between the adrenalin-rush highs and horrific lows of war that insures that so many veterans of all wars will continue to re-experience troubling war-memories for decades. It is discussed in depth in the first book of a *Vietnam Trilogy*, 2004.

The title *A Vietnam Trilogy* was originally intended to refer to my three stays in Vietnam: 1968, 1989 and 2000. As the writing unfolded, that meaning has been transformed to three books in a series about the universality of war and its impact across the decades on veterans and families.

CHAPTER 2. 9/11 AND POST-TRAUMATIC STRESS: INTER-CONNECTIONS TO VIETNAM AND IRAQ

> We were mesmerized at the office, gathered around the television, as we watched the towers burning and clouds of smoke, people jumping from the towers like they were falling from the sky, the panic as people were fleeing, the sights and sounds of the emergency vehicles and rescue teams. Who and when are they going to attack next? [17]

Just a year after the Vietnam history study abroad course a major event occurred — the attacks on September 11, 2000. Like millions of others, I was deeply affected by the idea that terrorists could (and would) attack New York City and Washington, DC and result in additional deaths in Pennsylvania. For me and for millions of other observers (not to mention those more directly affected) the shock of realizing our vulnerability, and the horror of the human carnage, triggered hurts from previous wounds that I still carried from long ago. And, like so many others, my personal reactions fueled my feelings, beliefs and actions concerning the country's national and international policy issues regarding terrorism, defense, and the moral questions around the precedent set by the first pre-emptive military strike in the nation's history in Iraq. And like so many others, my personal reactions have fueled my evolving opinion and issues regarding the Iraq War and US involvement. [18]

Understanding these factors can help one to better comprehend how military personnel survive in a war zone; such survival is not infrequently accompanied months and years later by continuing or resurgent and painful

---

17. R.M. Scurfield, J. Viola, K Platoni and J Colon. "Continuing psychological aftermath of 9/11: A POPPA experience and critical incident stress debriefing revisited," *Traumatology: The International Journal of Innovations. Vol. 9* (1) (2003, March), 4-32.

recollections and reactions. Much of what is described herein is universal to the experience, short and longer-term, of being exposed to and surviving human-induced trauma — be it in the shadows of the jungles of the Mekong Delta, the twin towers in New York City, in the block-to-block search and destroy operations in Fallujah, or in the shadows of your living room as modern technology brings the distant horrors right into the home — day after day.

IMMEDIATE AND LONGER-RANGE REACTIONS TO 9/11

My immediate reactions on September 11 were very similar to my survival reactions during the Vietnam War, my early responses to Operation Desert Storm and the pending invasion of Iraq at the onset of the Persian Gulf War, and my responses to the devastating Hurricane Iniki in Hawaii and several hurricanes on the Mississippi Gulf Coast.

The most common survival reactions during a trauma are denial, tunnel vision and task-focus. Throughout the day of September 11, I chose to remain in my office at the University of Southern Mississippi, door closed, working on a long-overdue project. Simultaneously, I kept one ear partially attuned to conversations in the hallway but my main focus was on completing the task at hand. After all, this is how I had managed to continue to function in Vietnam.

That this was an extraordinary trauma did not begin to fully sink into my consciousness until later that afternoon when I got in my car to drive home and turned on the radio. Then the enormity of what was happening hit. I turned that evening's graduate social work seminar into a session of sharing about how each of us was reacting to the event. Several of the students were partners of active duty military personnel. After class I started writing down what I was experiencing, and wrote and re-wrote my commentary numerous times over the following several months. Yes, this is one way that I deal with trauma: I continue to stay task-focused and at the same time I use writing as a vehicle through which to express and release the many emotions I am experiencing. Similarly, I felt compelled to write a commentary in 1991 as the Persian Gulf War was unfolding.[19]

18. Most of the information in this chapter is adapted from two sources: primarily from R.M. Scurfield, "Commentary about the terrorist acts of September 11, 2001," *Trauma, Violence & Abuse*, Vol. 3 (1) (2002, January), 3-14 and also from Scurfield, Viola, Platoni & Colon, 2003.
19. R.M. Scurfield, "Post-Katrina aftermath and helpful interventions on the Mississippi Gulf Coast," *Traumatology*, Vol. 12 (2), in-press, summer, 2006.

NORMAL AND EXPECTABLE VERSUS PSYCHIATRICALLY DISORDERED REACTIONS TO 9/11

9/11 was an extraordinarily savage and horrific human-induced carnage that claimed some 3,000 lives. And modern technology brought the horror right into our living rooms, whether we were watching in Minot, Togus, Anchorage, Gallup, or Gulfport, Mississippi. Millions of people were witnesses to this tragedy as it was happening and as it was replayed again and again afterward. It was vividly, intimately, and repeatedly viewed and experienced through the graphic visual and auditory media coverage, day after day, for months.

Never before had there been such widespread "distant" witnessing by so many of something so horrific. The massive, repeated national and international exposure to a trauma of this magnitude brought a critical question to the fore: what was a "normal and expectable" range of emotions and reactions to exposure to such a trauma, even for those who were witnessing it from many miles away?

The severity, nature and wide-ranging impact of the tragedy of 9/11 challenged our usual thinking about "normal" responses. This is the very same challenge that is present when we attempt to understand what are normal versus disordered reactions among military personnel in the abnormal milieu of a war zone, be it Korea, Vietnam, the Persian Gulf, Afghanistan or Iraq. (This is discussed in detail in the following chapter).

NORMAL AND EXPECTABLE REACTIONS

The following categories of normal and expectable reactions to 9/11 and its aftermath reflect the reactions of tens of thousands, or even millions of viewers. People need to be able to recognize, understand and address such reactions in order to be able to properly heal. And the same may be said of what happens in a war zone and to veterans then and in the years following their return stateside, and what happens in the aftermath of natural disasters such as Hurricane Katrina.

Being Immersed in the Media Coverage

Many Americans were mesmerized in the initial days and weeks, and even months post-9/11, and immersed themselves in the media coverage. For many people this caused a significant disruption in daily life routines. Was this abnormal? Only if an addiction to such extensive media viewing had existed over a longer period of time and only to the extent that it continued to significantly interfere with one's life long after.

Avoidance, Denial and Detachment

Other survivors and long-distant witnesses did the exact opposite. To help themselves cope with the enormity of the shock and tragedy, they avoided or ignored the media coverage as much as possible, and studiously avoided talking or thinking it:

> Why are people spending so much time just thinking and talking about this and watching the seemingly endless television commentary and pictures about this? After a point, what good does it do? Life has to go on, you know. [20]

Many people seemingly were able to go on with their lives as if nothing had happened. In some cases this might reflect an uncaring attitude that 3,000 people had been murdered within a few hours. More often, being able to avoid, deny or detach from one's emotions was a very effective way to maintain focus and thus keep on functioning. In still others, such avoidance and detachment was a way to prevent the tragedy from triggering a resurgence of pain from previous traumas. And each of these reactions falls within a range of normal reactions to such an extraordinary trauma — or to the trauma of war.

Tunnel vision and task-oriented behaviors are, indeed, quite functional forms of avoidance and denial that provide a dual benefit. The person is able to move ahead, taking care of daily tasks, and the detachment at least to some degree ensures that one is not overwhelmed by tragic memories, mental pictures and emotions.[21] Conversely, if such attitudes and behaviors persist at a substantial level for too long, what was a functional way to cope can turn into an unhealthy denial or avoidance of accepting and dealing with extremely powerful emotions, reactions and real issues raised by the traumatic event.

Triggering of Trauma Wounds from the Past

For 9/11 to trigger painful memories from a previously experienced trauma is normal. This is similar to how many Vietnam veterans experienced a painful resurgence of Vietnam War memories and issues concerning grief and loss while watching the media coverage of the Persian Gulf War in 1991. [22] And families of those killed or maimed in the Oklahoma City bombing or other persons who had suffered personal losses through violence also were quite likely to have such old hurts reopened. It is vital to understand that this was a normal and expectable reaction to the 9/11 trauma, to find oneself either having a minimized or non-reaction to 9/11, alternating between emotional reactions to 9/11 and emotional

---

20. Scurfield, 2002, 4-5.
21. See: K.W. Hammond, R.M. Scurfield & S.C. Risse. "Post-traumatic stress disorder." In D. L. Dunner (Ed.), *Current psychiatric therapy* (288-295) (Philadelphia, PA: W.B. Saunders, 1993); and Scurfield, *A Vietnam Trilogy*, 2004.
22. Scurfield, 1992.

reactions to a previous trauma or having an intermingling or convergence of both reactions to 9/11 and to a previous trauma.

This resurgence of painful wounds can be quite terrifying, with the person wondering whether he or she is going crazy. Not so. It simply means that such persons still have unresolved issues from prior trauma, which they have been able to keep suppressed to some degree. The enormity of 9/11 was sufficient to trigger a resurfacing of such prior trauma.

Similar reactions may well occur in the face of future traumas, such as subsequent terrorist attacks, or having someone near and dear killed or maimed in a war zone, or a natural disaster, or even through media exposure to other cataclysmic events that trigger memories and feelings about one's personal trauma.

Getting Back to Normal Routines

After the tragedy of 9/11, considerable argument ensued over what seemed like trivial matters. Should the upcoming football or baseball games or NASCAR race be cancelled or not? Was our continued merriment demeaning to those who were killed? Some may feel that it was; others claim that such carefree pastimes are part of the "freedom" Americans fight for. Nonetheless, it is essential for trauma survivors to return at some point to the normalcy of daily life as a part of the healing process.

> Hey, you can't dwell on this forever; you've got to move on. There's no harm in getting away from it for awhile; and it might help alleviate some of the pain a little.[23]

A careful balance and timing must be negotiated between reflecting and grieving versus moving on with life. Struggling to find the right timing and balance between these two necessities is part of a normal post-trauma reaction — be it from 9/11, war or other personal trauma.

Strong Reactions that are Somewhat Disruptive

Some of the preoccupations that disturbed people in the aftermath of 9/11 are understandable and expectable:

• Shattering of basic assumptions about what to expect in daily life: "Why would they do this to our innocent people?"[24]

• Preoccupation with environmental dangers, and associated fear, anxiety or isolation: "When are they going to attack again?"[25]

• Loss of a personal (and indeed a national) sense of safety:

---

23. Scurfield, 2002, 7.
24. Scurfield, Viola, Platoni & Colon, 2003, 40
25. Ibid., 36.

I need to rethink traveling by airplanes for awhile, or taking our family on that vacation; it just isn't safe. [26]

Other strong reactions included suddenly breaking down and crying, a pervasive sense of sadness and grief, irritability, mood swings, nausea or body aches. Survivor guilt was a problem for some, mainly those who were present at the 9/11 site or who lost someone they knew:

I should have gone back to help others, but I kept running away from the building instead.[27]

Still others had severe feelings of helplessness or pessimism ("There's no way you can stop such nuts from doing this again") and/or extreme frustration ("I have all these heavy feelings, but nowhere to put them and no one to take them out on.").[28]

Continuing Adverse Reactions

In the aftermath of 9/11, some people continued to have adverse reactions. And this, too, is not an unusual or disordered reaction in the face of human-induced trauma or natural disasters:

Before 9/11, I was a free-spirited, outgoing person. A year later, I experienced an emotional roller-coaster ride that entails bouts of depression and fears of loud noises, airplanes and tall buildings. . . Sure I'm grateful I was spared, but many people don't live with the graphic images I witnessed as I made my way out of the Trade Center. Thoughts of burning flesh haunt me daily. [29]

The *Diagnostic And Statistical Manual* of *Mental Disorders* (DSM-IV-TR) excludes guilt or blame as a core inclusionary criterion for PTSD; nevertheless, very strong feelings of guilt or blame are especially common among survivors of human-induced trauma such as terrorism or war. Survivors oftentimes are tormented by what they did — or did not do — to survive:

I couldn't believe it when I saw the first tower going down . . . we ran like hell to get away from the billows of white clouds rolling down the street. I felt glad that I was safe, but felt so guilty at the same time.

I should have run back into the building to save others. You could see them falling from the sky, and I just ran the other way. [30]

And these very painful issues of guilt and blame are some of the most troublesome for combat veterans, as well.[31]

---

26. Scurfield, 2002, 7.
27. Scurfield, Viola, Platoni & Colon, 1993, 33.
28. Scurfield, 2002, 8
29. Carlisle, D. Letter to the Editor. *USA Today* (2002, September 11). 12A.
30. Scurfield, Viola, Platoni & Colon, 2003, 36.

The Immorality of the Terrorist Acts

Another instance of the range of normal and expectable reactions to 9/11 would be the reaction of abhorrence that such acts were immoral, savage, unthinkable:

> This was an extremely immoral act. How could anyone perpetrate such horror onto other innocent human beings?[32]

While the vast majority of people in the US and abroad agreed with this reaction, there are others who felt that the US was long overdue to "get what was coming to them" because of US policies such as supporting Israel and not the Palestinians, supporting autocratic rulers in various countries, running paramilitary schools to train Latin American forces in torture and terror tactics, and for being the world's largest merchant in weaponry. And, of course, terrorism or guerilla warfare tactics are justified by those who use them as the only tactics available in the face of the overwhelming military superiority of the United States (and Israel). Such tactics are used against the easiest targets to inflict maximum terror with the meager weaponry available, and with the ultimate aim of making the cost of war so steep so that the other side's will and commitment are lost. This means that no targets are off-limit — be they women, children, the elderly or uniformed military.[33]

The irony is that those who are described as "faceless cowards" or "terrorist savages" by one side are esteemed as "heroic resistance fighters" or "martyrs" by the other side.[34] This also applies in Iraq today, with yet a further twist. There is a contingent of Iraqis who contend that "the American occupation of Iraq" makes US-led troops terrorists, rather than a legitimate military force:

> "Don't you consider all the actions conducted against us by the Americans as terrorism? Do you consider killing women and children, making them homeless, legitimate actions for an occupier?" said Talaat al Wazan, a Mosul native who's Secretary General of the Iraqi National Unity party. "All the actions done by Americans are terrorism, so it is the right of anyone treated with this cruelty to use and means to act against the terrorists."[35]

---

31. The therapeutic technique that I have developed over the years to address trauma-related self-blame and guilt with war veterans, "determining the percentage of responsibility technique", is described in detail in a later chapter. This approach also is quite relevant to survivors of other types of trauma.

32. Ibid., p. 8.

33. O. Ayalon, "Posttraumatic stress recovery of terrorist survivors." In J.P. Wilson and B. Raphael (Eds.), *The international handbook of traumatic stress syndromes* (855-866). (New York: Plenum, 1993).

34. Scurfield, 1992.

35. Alam Hannah, "Mess Hall Massacre." Sun Herald. Biloxi, MS (2004, December 22), A4.

Every side in every war comes up with a rationale to support the rightness of its own killing tactics and to denigrate those of the enemy. Then, is it all relative, based on one's subjective perceptions and values? When it comes down to it, what factors truly are meaningful in labeling either who is the "right" side or what are the "right" killing tactics in any or all wars? The reality of wars, especially protracted ones, is that an increased cycle of back-and-forth viciousness inevitably seems to develop. And it appears to be happening in Iraq today.

Feeling Cursed or Blessed

Frequently, exposure to trauma substantially affects the survivor's faith in God or a higher power and/or belief and faith in the basic goodness of humanity. This was no less so in the aftermath of 9/11. The trauma may challenge, test, disrupt, confuse or even shatter one's beliefs.

Why did God let this happen to our innocent people? Where was he?[36]

What is wrong with them? Why do they hate us so?[37]

Conversely, trauma can impel a dramatic reaffirmation or even strengthening of one's beliefs:

God must have been looking out for us that my son got out of the tower before it collapsed.[38]

Such a belief in divine intervention, or in fate, can offer great solace and comfort. On the other hand, others perceive such viewpoints of those "who were blessed" as somehow denigrating to those who were not so fortunate; isn't it tantamount to saying that they were punished by God, or cursed; that God did not look out for one family as he did for another?

No matter what one's particular religious and spiritual beliefs, one of my social work students offered a poignant reflection about 9/11: "God must be weeping at what happened."[39]

INAPPROPRIATE BEHAVIORS AND REACTIONS

Trauma can bring out the best — or the worst — in people. In the aftermath of 9/11, looters were reported beneath the twin towers at the very time that rescue teams were desperately searching for survivors above them. Gas sta-

---

36. Scurfield, Viola, Platoni & Colon, 1993, 34.
37. Ibid., 41.
38. Scurfield, 2002, 10.
39. Ibid., Mary Plaskon, MSW student, University of Southern Mississippi-Gulf Coast. Personal communication (September 13, 2001).

tions were reported raising gas prices as high as $4 per gallon.[40] Others made crude, crass jokes — either a sign of ignorant and demeaning attitudes or an attempt to use humor to deflect the horror. Still others made inappropriate or ill-timed comments that were offensive, perhaps reflecting poor judgment or poor taste, and perhaps seeking unconsciously to be "tough" and shielded from the anguish of the moment. None of these are unusual reactions in the face of protracted or repeated trauma.[41]

The polar extremes of reactions to 9/11 paralleled to some degree what happened during the Vietnam War and is now being replicated in today's wars. Many are consumed with fear, hatred and a desire for revenge.

> One year later, I still look up whenever I hear an airplane, not knowing what to expect. In December, I flew to Brazil to spend New Year's Day on the beach with friends. I felt safer on that flight than I do walking across the center courtyard of the Pentagon. — Survivor of the 9/11 attack on the Pentagon [42]

> Why don't we just go over and blow up Afghanistan?[43]

> I hate what they did, and I would get into a New York cab on purpose, just to aggravate a cab driver that looked Arabic or wore a turban. I wanted him to punch me so that I would really give it to him.[44]

Racist stereotyping and behaviors increase at an individual level and xenophobic reactions at a national level; and anyone who is associated or who somehow reminds us of the alleged perpetrators and their supporters can be a target. As early as September 17, less than one week after 9/11, the FBI had opened 40 cases of hate-crime investigations concerning reported attacks against Arab Americans, to include two killings apparently provoked by anti-Arab sentiments.[45] As I am a third-generation Syrian-American, such attitudes and behaviors struck particularly close to home. Indeed, in the aftermath of 9/11, I had an uncle and aunt who were preoccupied with the safety of their (third-generation US) sons who looked very Arab and had obviously Arabic names.

I was vividly reminded of similar acts and behaviors reported by the media during the Persian Gulf War a decade earlier: racist comments about Arabs, pejorative stereotypical generalizations about the Islamic faith, lack of knowledge or appreciation of various Arabic and other cultures and traditions in the Middle East (no, Iranians are not Arabs), and the controversy over the FBI

40. Tortorana, D. "Moore pounces on reports of gasoline price gouging." *Sun Herald*, Biloxi, MS (2001, September 12), A6.

41. Scurfield, *A Vietnam Trilogy*, 2004.

42. C. Polk, "Strangers became friends." Letter to the Editor. *USA Today* (2002, September 11), 12A.

43. Scurfield, Viola, Platoni & Colon, 2003, 44.

44. Ibid., 46.

45. S. Sobieraj, "Bush visits mosque, pleads for tolerance." *Sun Herald*, Biloxi, MS (2001, September 18), A1, A6.

aggressively interviewing Arab-American leaders here in the US "in the national interest." And my still painful and angry memories resurfaced about how so many of US military personnel in Vietnam had constantly referred to any and all Vietnamese with callous slurs — and so many Vietnam veterans still do.

> And yet, in spite of the racism, the xenophobia, the dehumanizing, the most noble and humanitarian of virtues and behaviors also were a common response in the aftermath of 9/11. These included those who staunchly defended Arab Americans and Muslims from undeserved attacks; there were many acts of strength and sacrifice; large-scale donations of blood, food, money and increased voluntarism; and, yes, heroism. Everyone remains impressed by the fact that firefighters and police were running up the stairs in the World Trade Center while the building's occupants were running down.

Many people reported an enhanced appreciation of the freedoms and rewards of living in America. Others found themselves strongly reaffirming what was really important in their lives — their families, their friends, their community, their faiths. And especially in those days and weeks in the immediate aftermath of 9/11, more appreciation was shown for firefighters, policemen, and emergency medical technicians, and there was an unprecedented outpouring of support, cooperation, and compassion from people in many cities throughout the United States and in many countries abroad.

Some of that outpouring reflected the necessity for survivors of trauma to pull together, to look beyond the pain and grief, and to recognize and appreciate that there always is a "positive" aspect to what is broadly perceived and experienced as negative and tragic. And this is no less true for war veterans in their post-war readjustment.

THE RELATIONSHIP BETWEEN PERSONAL REACTIONS TO 9/11 AND US POLICIES REGARDING TERRORISM AND IRAQ

The horrific events of 9/11 could have been tailor made as a catalyst for influencing voters' convictions on major policy issues at a time when the nation and the international community were building a response to what has been called the threat of global terrorism.

Some people articulated a new mindset suggesting that this happened because "we let the military grow weak." They used the occasion to call for a bigger and stronger military force, no matter the cost, saying we cannot afford to do otherwise; we must curtail many of this country's long-held procedures and freedoms regarding wiretaps, due process, arrest and detention. And we must rescind the policy prohibiting the assassination of enemy leaders and collaborators.

They castigate Americans for criticizing the president's decisions about invading and occupying Iraq, or about how the war is going, or about how much money is being expended in the name of fighting terrorism. They say that criticism is unpatriotic and harmful and demeaning to the military forces and maintain that we have the right to strike "the enemy" and "suspected enemy" and "their collaborators" anywhere, anytime, and to use whatever tactics are required to get the job done.

Others find such viewpoints to be dangerous, disturbing and distinctly un-American. If the Administration and the military are allowed to essentially write a blank check, especially at the expense of many social programs here in the US, if long-cherished freedoms are diluted or tossed out altogether, if any protest or criticism of the government and military policies and actions is branded unpatriotic, immoral and harmful to the nation's vital interests — isn't that the end of the America we cherish and fight to defend; isn't it a start down the slippery slope of becoming more like the regimes we call "the enemy"?

My point is not to convince anyone that one of those perspectives is right and the other wrong. Rather, that it is important to be extremely careful to be aware and understand how *personal* reactions to human-induced trauma, especially if laden with fear and/or hatred, can fuel not only personal attitudes and behaviors but also support for or against various national and international policies and issues. It happened during World War II; fear and hatred fueled support for the internment of loyal US citizens who happened to be of Japanese-American ancestry, and also the less-publicized internment of a number of Italian- and German-American citizens.

It happened for many veterans whose Vietnam War experiences convinced them that the war was moral and just and that the US would have won if not for the anti-war protestors and the politicians' reluctance to "let us do what was necessary to win." It happened for many other veterans whose Vietnam War experiences convinced them that the war was immoral and unjust and that US forces were in a no-win situation. Almost 60,000 US military died, many times that number were severely disabled, and an estimated 2.4 million to 3 million Vietnamese died. From this perspective, the tragic loss was due to US forces being inserted into the middle of a civil war that a foreign military force could not possibly win without literally exterminating the northern half of Vietnam. People with this latter viewpoint are staunch supporters of veteran rights and are much more critical, if not downright disbelieving, of the country's leaders, their professed intentions, and their characterization of the morality of most wars.

And it happened decades later. Unresolved rage and bitterness continues to fuel the hatred of a number of World II veterans toward Germans or Japanese, and for many Vietnam veterans their hatred continues to fuel their negative reactions towards Vietnamese. It happened after 9/11 and today: there were hundreds of reported incidents of harassment of Muslims and even some who were mistaken for Middle Easterners, North Africans and South Asians in the United States in the aftermath of 9/11.

31

Go back to your own countries, you stinking A-rabs and Muslims.[46]

And now there are many innocent and proud American citizens and immigrants and would-be immigrants who are being discriminated against, assaulted, persecuted and even killed — simply because of the color of their skin and other identifiable physical features, their Arabic-sounding names or their religion. This does not represent Martin Luther King's noble dream or the America that many, like me, willingly went into harm's way to defend.

Once pre-emptive killing and reactive killing starts, where and how is the line drawn between acts of murder, acts of terrorism, and the "morally justifiable" versions?

> The Palestinians are partying in the street! [as news was transported world-wide of the 9/11 attacks] I say, "Bomb those idiots! Wipe them off the map. Enough of this!"[47]

Vitriolic feelings of vengeance, hatred, retribution can fuel just about any personal action against anyone — and can be used or manipulated to rationalize just about any national military policy and violent action, to include pre-emptive military strikes, against just about any country. This is what happens when trauma wounds are so deep and painful that they over-ride more thoughtful responses.

> If I let go of my very justified rage, is that not violating the memories and valor of all the innocent people who died?[48]

Many people who lose someone tragically find that years later they continue to hold onto the grief, because a part of them fears that letting go of the grief means letting go of the person and the memories of them.

How can survivors of 9/11 be helped, those who were directly impacted and those who were more indirectly yet still so powerfully impacted from a distance, to explore and understand, to think and vent, to remember and reflect, in ways that do not kept them prisoners to the horrors that will never be forgotten? It is sobering to realize how these challenges are exactly what hundreds of thousands of Vietnam veterans have been struggling with, and what Iraq and Afghanistan War veterans will be facing for decades to come.

> I'm stuck in my 9/11 nightmares. I just can't move on![49]

> Those rag-heads should die![50]

---

46. Ibid. 10-11.
47. D. Cauchon and P. O'Driscoll, "Harsh reality of terrorism hits home." *USA Today* (2001, September 12), 8A-9A.
48. Scurfield, 2002, 12.
49. Scurfield, Viola, Platoni & Colon, 2003, 33.
50. Ibid., 48.

Other fire and rescue workers ran into the WTC as those inside were running out, but not me. I should have been here with my buddies.[51]

Many people will never understand what I deal with inside. Perhaps it's easier to expect me to move on a year after the attacks because my wounds reside mostly inside of me. Even those close to me, though they try, struggle to relate to my experience.[52]

The events of 9/11 were reported to still haunt Pentagon workers and WTC rescuers almost three years later, both among those who were there (22%) and to a lesser extent to those who were not there at the time (6%). [53] For some at the Pentagon, seeking help "may imply weakness — that the terrorists have won." Stigma and concerns about confidentiality also may stop workers from getting help[54]

LET THE HEALING CONTINUE — OR BEGIN

The only emotion I can recall with clarity [from September 11] is being very frightened. But as I come to terms with things, I feel more of a sense of loss . . . this was my first real contact with death.[55]

For many veterans and trauma survivors the path of healing can be tortuous, interminable and seemingly unattainable. But there can be a light at the end of the tunnel.

As time has passed since that horrific day we have all seen the incredible resilience of the American human spirit. . . . Tragedy makes us stronger and pulls us closer. May we all learn from September 11 just how fragile life really is — and how blessed we are to have our families. Let's also keep in mind how lucky we all are to live in a country that provides freedom and opportunity.[56]

I feel more relaxed. It's an appreciation of life. I don't stress about stuff like I used to. I feel more family focus . . . I feel a much greater respect for police and firemen. I look at them differently. Every one of them puts his or her life on the line every day. I'm thankful for being able to choose from an array of food. What a gift it is to be able to have our abundance of choices. I have a new feeling of thankfulness for the country we live in.[57]

---

51. Ibid., 48.

52. Ibid., 48.

53. Marilyn Elias, "Events of Sept 11 still haunt Pentagon workers, WTC rescuers." *USA Today* (2004, May 4), 7D.

54. Ibid.

55. C. Polk, "Strangers became friends," Letter to the Editor. *USA Today* (2002, September 11), 12A.

56. J. Boyle, "Importance of family holds true." Letter to the Editor. *USA Today* (2002, September 11), 12A.

Those eloquent comments were made about a year after 9/11. One wonders whether that new level of consciousness and awareness and appreciation will continue 5, 10 and 20 years later? And now we have increasing numbers of combat and support personnel exposed to new traumas. What will be the legacy, both the good and the bad, on US and Coalition forces, on families, on communities, on the nation — and on the millions of men, women and children of Iraq and Afghanistan?

REACTIONS TO 9/11: A WINDOW INTO THE IMPACT OF WAR

The terrorist acts of 9/11 have been particularly provocative for at least four groups of readers:
- those who are veterans of any war or are close family members of such veterans;
- those who have suffered other personal tragedies prior to 9/11;
- those who suffered personal tragedies in the terrorist acts of 9/11;

and those who were not at the immediate sites on 9/11 yet were deeply impacted — whether one mile or 2,000 miles away watching it unfold on television.

It is the three groups who are not war veterans or family members of war veterans that will be addressed here, as they may not already realize how their reactions to 9/11 can enhance their understanding of the impact of war. The following is in no way meant to minimize the horror of 9/11. However, beyond the scope of the number of deaths and injuries that occurred within a few hours, 9/11 was a microcosm of what happens in war zones, especially in non-conventional wars in which guerilla warfare and terrorism are the battle tactics and civilians are targets. Reactions to 9/11 can be used as a window into the realities of war and its impact.

Time and again during their deployment, day after day, members of the Armed Forces face the very real risk of death and maiming. They are constantly at risk even when they are not near a designated "front line," even in their myriad daily encounters with the local populace of the country where they are deployed. This includes civilians who consider them to be liberators and protectors and defenders of liberty, civilians who have very ambivalent feelings about their presence for varying reasons and are caught between the opposing enemy forces, and civilians who resent or detest their presence and actively support the enemy forces. And, of course, there is exposure to those who are actively trying to kill and maim them — the enemy.

---

57. P. Firmin, "Life takes on new meaning after attacks." *SunHerald.* Biloxi, MS (2002, September 10), A4.

During and after 9/11, were you impacted by raging emotions of terror, horror, hate, grief, sadness, helplessness? Or numbed or stupefied by shock and denial? Or jolted, energized, incredulous at the carnage, at the live bodies tumbling from the upper floors of the WTC. Or mesmerized at the ash-covered and terrified people fleeing ground zero? Or swelled with pride at the remarkable sight of fire, police and emergency rescue personnel running into the burning buildings at the very moment when everyone else was running out? Do you still have vivid memories or feelings about it — or of your own idiosyncratic and powerful reactions? Or are they buried so that you can read about it all in a matter of fact and non-consequential way?

This is what people face day-after-day, in a war zone — and afterwards. Except that *they know* the enemy is waiting, lurking under cover, choosing the exact moment to strike. They are shot at, or a buddy is injured, or another soldier is killed, or nothing happens — today. Then an attack hits their convoy directly, or destroys the vehicle next to them, or kills someone they are sitting alongside. Or a mortar or rocket lands and kills and maims people in the very same location that used to seem relatively safe in the past. Or they witness an attack 200 yards ahead but are unable to do anything about it because the attackers are gone by the time they get there — or the car bomb has already exploded. Or they come across the charred remains of US military vehicles and dead American bodies stripped and mutilated. And perhaps youths are dancing in the streets, celebrating what has befallen yet another American soldier or sailor or marine or downed aircraft crew member — or civilian contractor.

And the all-too-familiar feeling of helplessness come over them. And perhaps their mind goes blank, or the rage swells up inside and threatens to burst out, or the tears are pushed back — maybe until later. Or, perhaps a hardness and numbing and detachment have been steadily building and they find themselves becoming more and more hardened, where perhaps "winning the hearts and minds of the people" is no longer important (if it ever was). For too many, what seeps in and takes hold is a nonchalant attitude about anything except two things: the survival of oneself and his and her comrades. And perhaps retribution and revenge become a preoccupation and obsession.

And always there are the "what-ifs" What if I had not been sick and Jack hadn't had to take my place? What if our convoy had passed by 30 seconds earlier, or later? What if I had *not* hesitated for a split moment before firing, would my buddy still be alive? Or what if I *had* hesitated for a split moment before firing; would those three civilians still be alive? What if I had listened to my gut, and not to my head that told me it was okay to have my squad go into that building? And what if I hadn't got myself here in the war zone in the first place?

It is a sign of the rich variety of human coping mechanisms that some combatants experience feelings of euphoria and adrenalin, feelings of being more "alive" in the midst of death-defying episodes. For them, emotional and physiological highs and "positives" dominate their war experiences — and their post-war memories. For others, their war experiences are a volatile and uneasy mixture of the tragic along with the rush, the thrill. And for still others, it is the terror, the hurt, the senselessness that dominates and haunts.[58]

Combatants are likely to face one or many recurring personal 9/11s while they are deployed. And often there is one singular mother of all personal 9/11s, a moment that has devastating consequences that can never be undone and can never be totally forgotten.

Then one day — hours, days, weeks, months, years, or even decades later — the numbness and denial and detachment and isolation and frenetic urge to keep the memories of one's personal 9/11s at bay don't work so well anymore. And, as the freeze-dried traumatic memories of war thaw, they return, as fresh and real as the day they were originally frozen in time.[59] They become part of the entrenched legacy of war for too many veterans, and for their families as well who live daily with these personal traumas through their intimate contact with their Persian Gulf War, Vietnam, Korean, World War or other veterans.

As of late 2006, more than 300,000 US military personnel have been deployed to Iraq and there is no end in sight. And there are approximately 23 million Iraqi civilians, who all have traumas of their own to carry with them for decades, or forever.

---

58. See the related discussion of the "combat cocktail" in the last chapter of *A Vietnam Trilogy*.

59. Chaim Shatan coined the graphic phrase, "freeze-dried memories," to describe war-trauma memories. C.F. Shatan, "The Grief of soldiers: Vietnam combat veterans' self-help movement." *American Journal of Orthopsychiatry, 43* (4) (1974), 640-653.

Chapter 3. Iraq and War Zone Psychiatric Casualties

The war is still going on in Afghanistan, in fact, it seems to be heating up again. Afghanistan had already turned into the forgotten war of this generation — *even as it was still being waged*. It is seldom covered on TV or the major press, nor is Afghanistan mentioned often by military authorities or by governmental officials. Afghanistan War veterans are not mentioned very much in this book precisely because so little information is available. However, the conditions faced by US and Coalition forces in Afghanistan are formidable:

> They're facing guerillas who were born here, hardened by poverty and backwardness, and steeped in a centuries-old tradition of resisting foreigners . . . The Taliban have killed more than 40 US soldiers and more than 800 Afghan officials, police, troops, aid workers and civilians since March . . . the war has evolved into a bloody game of cat and mouse, a classic guerilla struggle with echoes of the much larger and far bloodier conflicts in Iraq, Chechnya and Vietnam . . . The Taliban operate in small bands, staging hit-and-run attacks, assassinations and ambushes, laying mines and firing missiles and rocket propelled grenades before melting back into local populations. US intelligence reports indicate that Taliban leaders constantly change locations. "One day, they could be firing at you and serving you chai [tea] the next . . ."

> [This is a] country ravaged by decades of civil war and overwhelmed by destitution, corruption, overpopulation, disease and despair. The guerillas stash their arms in the wheat stacks, wells, thick groves and the off-limits women's quarters of adobe compounds. Their hiding places are scattered in the small oases of almond and apple trees in valleys wedged between mountains that seem to roll ever onward like immense, dun-colored tidal waves. Hiding in mountaintop caves and crevices, the Taliban track US troops and aircraft — sometimes for scores of miles — and pass intelligence to each other in coded-language via walkie-talkies that are extremely to get a fix on. "A lot of times it's like chasing ghosts . . ."[60]

Knowing the difficult conditions that face the still sizable US and Coalition military force in Afghanistan, it is safe to assume that whatever problems exist in Iraq apply just as well to Western forces serving in or returning from Afghanistan.

Furthermore, since those who served in Afghanistan have already been ignored or forgotten, there is an additional problem. A warrior being forgotten brings its own legacy of resentment, alienation, despair, rage, misunderstanding — as has been experienced by so many Vietnam and Korean War veterans and their families. And so during the following discussion about what is going on in Iraq and with Iraq veterans, please remember that at least the same degree and depth of issues and difficulties, and perhaps more, most assuredly are applicable to the forces currently in Afghanistan and to Afghanistan veterans and their families.

SOBERING FACTS ABOUT DEPLOYMENT IN IRAQ AND IRAQ VETERANS

Increasingly, it appears that the high numbers of chronic and longer-term psychiatric casualties we saw in the Vietnam War (verified at more than 800,000)[61] may be replicated in the aftermath of the Iraq War. Indeed, this concern goes back to earlier wars and up to Iraq.

> I have visited 18 government hospitals for veterans. In them are a total of about 50,000 destroyed men . . . men who were the pick of the nation 18 years ago. Boys with a normal viewpoint were . . . put into the ranks . . . they were made to "about face" to regard murder as the order of the day.
>
> Then, suddenly, we discharged them and told them to make another "about face." Many, too many, of these young boys are eventually destroyed mentally, because they could not make that final "about face" alone.
>
> — Major General Smedley D. Butler, 1936[62]

By many accounts, difficulty with the "about face" that US troops in Iraq must accomplish, both to function in the war zone and to be able to function again back home, is very sobering. A survey of 2,530 troops prior to and after deployment to Iraq reported in the *New England Journal of Medicine* in July, 2004 that at least one in eight Iraq combat veterans (between 15 and 17%) was reported to suffer from major depression, generalized anxiety or PTSD. Yet, only

---

60. Jonathan S. Landay, "It's not over. Fighting in Afghanistan intensifies as guerillas try to sabotage elections." Knight Ridder Newspapers. www.sunherald.com (2005, August 18), B1-2.
61. Kulka et al, 1990.
62. Stevan Smith, *Two Decades and A Wake-Up*, 1990.

23-40 percent of Iraq combat veterans with such problems sought mental health care.[63]

Another study, the Army's first-ever of mental health conducted in a war zone, showed that about 17% of Army soldiers serving in Iraq in 2003 were assessed to be suffering traumatic stress, depression or anxiety and were deemed to be "functionally impaired."[64] And the actual number may be substantially higher, since soldiers who were injured in combat and did not redeploy with their units were unable to continue in the study.[65] Earlier estimates suggested that about one in six troops deployed in Iraq would suffer war-related psychiatric symptoms and difficulties; however, conditions in Iraq have gotten much worse.

This leads to the very real possibility that the rate of psychiatric casualties among troops deployed in Iraq will be similar to the Vietnam War. Some 30% of Vietnam veterans have suffered full-blown PTSD at sometime since leaving the war zone.[66]

Another military survey of nearly 3,000 Iraq veterans looked at the possible link between PTSD and physical health symptoms.[67] The 17% of soldiers reported to have PTSD symptoms were much more likely to report all kinds of pain — headaches, backaches, gastrointestinal complaints such as nausea and indigestion, and more. PTSD symptoms such as nightmares and flashbacks can interfere with sleep; this further damages one's health. Indeed, about one out of five soldiers without PTSD symptoms said they were in fair to poor physical health; and almost one-half of those with PTSD symptoms said the same. Charles Figley, a PTSD expert who is Director of the Traumatology Institute at the College of Social Work, Florida State University, Tallahassee, stated that these numbers are, "if anything, conservative. . . . When they come in with back pain, doctors are going to have to keep asking what happened to them in the war, not just now but five years from now."

This strong association between PTSD and physical health symptoms should not be surprising, as there is strong evidence in civilian studies that trauma survivors need more health care, at a higher cost.[68]

---

63. C.W. Hoge, C.A. Castro, S. Messer et al. "Combat Duty in Iraq and Afghanistan, Mental Health Problems, and Barriers to Care." *New England Journal of Medicine, Vol. 351* (1) (2004, July 21), 1-10. See also: VA Braces for More Mental Health Cases. United Press International. Retrieved from *Military.com Military Headlines* (2004, October 10).

64. M.L. Lyke, "The unseen cost of war: American minds." *Seattle Post-Intelligencer* (2004, August 27). Retrieved on-line November 18, 2005.

65. Lesley Kipling, "Fighting Combat Stress," *www.Military.com.* (2005, February 7).

66. Ted Koppel. *Coming Home. Invisible Casualties.* ABC Nightline (2004, December 15).

67. Marilyn Elias, "Stress disorder linked to soldiers' ill health." *USA Today* (2006, May 22). Assessed on-line, Health and Behavior, May 24, 2006.

68. Ibid.

The incidence of suicide among Iraq and Afghanistan military personnel also is of serious concern. There have been 53 suicides reported among service members fighting in Iraq and nine among those in Afghanistan.[69] Most suicides occur *after* troops return home. For example, the Associated Press reported that three men who had served with the Army's 10th Special Forces (Iraq) committed suicide shortly after returning home.[70] Other suicides among Iraq veterans have been reported in the media.[71]

The recent study conducted by the DOD (Vedantam, 2006),[72] based on the military's Post-Deployment Health Assessment that is required of all returning soldiers since May, 2003, further suggests the extent of mental health problems among military personnel returning from Iraq (19.8%) and Afghanistan (11.3%).

Some 35% of Iraq veterans sought mental health care, and of those, 12% were diagnosed with PTSD, depression or another serious disorder. Furthermore, this study reaffirms that exposure to combat was the one factor most closely associated with mental problems. As impressive as these statistics are, concern has been raised that they significantly under-report the actual figures.

Psychologist Richard McNally of Harvard University pointed out that almost 90% of those soldiers ultimately diagnosed with PTSD did not meet the criteria for PTSD according to the original questionnaire administered by the DOD; this indicates that the survey has little predictive value (Chong & Maugh, 2006).[73]

Of course, these figures are in regards to active duty Armed Forces personnel who have been willing to admit to the military surveyors that they have emotional problems or PTSD. More typical is the Iraq War soldier who was suffering from combat stress reaction; when he was handed PTSD fliers in the field and asked if the questions applied to him, "I said 'No,' and tossed them."[74]

Another soldier has said that if his returning buddies were asked whether they might be suffering from emotional problems or PTSD,

---

69. Arline Kaplan, "Hidden combat wounds: Extensive, deadly, costly." *Psychiatric Times*, *XXV* (1) (January, 2006).. Accessed on-line 1.25.06.

70. Associated Press, "Special Forces suicides raise questions." (2005, October 19). Available at: www.military.com/NewsContent/0,13319,78508.html. Accessed November 17, 2005.

71. Kaplan, 2006. See also M. Ivins, "Only lunacy can explain this," www.sunherald.com (2006, May 17), p. E4.; G. Zoroya, "Strain and battle fatigue hit home front," *USA Today* (2006 February 21), 13A; and David Mclemore, "For troops, stress a lingering hazard." *Dallas Morning News* (2005, December 8). Accessed on-line 12.9.05.

72. S. Vedantam, "Veterans report mental distress. About a third returning from Iraq seek help." *Washington Post* (2006, March 1). Accessed on-line 3.2.06

73. J-R. Chong and T.H. Maugh, "Study details mental health of war veterans." Los Angeles Times (2006, March 1), A10.

74. M.L. Lyke, "The unseen cost of war. American minds."

"many would answer, 'Not me, sir' — Simply because they wanted to go home. Immediately.

"If you say 'yes' to any question, you will be held back from going home on leave."[75]

In other words, despite the laudable effort by military mental health to survey military personnel while they are in Iraq or upon returning home, it is reasonable to assume that the number of soldiers reporting emotional problems or PTSD, while substantial, significantly under-represents the actual case. There also is a disturbing report that some military commanders have told their troops prior to completing the survey forms that "you get to go home if you do not indicate any problems, but you will have to go to Ft. Lewis and put on Medical Hold if you check any (mental health) problems."[76]

This concern of under-reporting has been further affirmed in a very recent study by the Government Accounting Office (GAO).[77] The GAO uncovered that *only* 23% of the Army and Air Force military personnel who screened positive for possible PTSD (per the four-item PTSD screen used by the military) were actually referred by the military to a mental health professional for further evaluation. The percentages of Navy (18%) and Marine (15%) personnel who screened positive for PTSD and were referred were even less. In the words of US Representative Mike Michaud of Maine:

> When 78% of the service-members who are at risk of developing PTSD do not get a referral for further evaluation, then it's clear the assessment system is not working.[78]

The serious under-reporting is further underscored by another survey that assessed the presence of barriers that stopped military personnel from seeking mental health help. This survey included both Army and Marine Corps soldiers. Such perceived barriers included: "I would be seen as 'weak'" (48%), "My unit leadership might treat me differently" (45%), "members of my unit might have less confidence in me" (45%) and "It would harm my career" (37%).[79]

Indeed, "just to seek [mental health] treatment in the military is an act of courage" due to the fear of stigma from peers and the fact that soldiers are dis-

---

75. Ibid.
76. Dana Hull, reporter, San Jose Mercury. Personal communication, August 3, 2006. Dana told me, that she had heard this from returning Iraq soldiers whom she had interviewed. There is no reason to doubt the veracity of these comments, but there also is no way to know how widespread such prejudicial comments has been from commanders prior to completing the forms. Nonetheless, this is very disturbing information that further casts doubt whether the findings reported by the military reflect the true psychiatric impact of the war.
77. G. Zoroya, "Many war vets' stress disorders go untreated," *USA Today* (2006, May 11), 3A.
78. Ibid.
79. Hoge et al, 2004.

couraged from sharing emotions.[80] This reluctance is exacerbated by the still prevailing "suck-it-up, soldier on, deal with it" culture.

> There's a strange pressure on these soldiers not to have any problems with what they are doing. It's the old idea that a real man and a true warrior will stay strong.[81]

Besides the "macho warrior" mentality, the very real fear that to seek mental health treatment will harm one's military career is at least partly related to concerns reported about the confidentiality protections of military medical records. While confidentiality protections have improved, unlike the vast majority of civilian employers military commanders have the right to invoke a need to know prerogative to access a soldier's medical history and counseling records. Thus, mental health problems have the potential to block security clearances, promotions and even retention on active duty.[82] Military personnel are quite aware of this.

These barriers to seeking mental health services undermine the chances that military personnel will actually go to see a military mental health professional in the first place. A recent survey conducted by the Army in Iraq reported that about three-quarters of the soldiers suffering from traumatic stress, depression or anxiety and those who are functionally impaired had received no help at any time while in Iraq from a mental health professional, a doctor or a chaplain, and overall, only one-third of soldiers who wanted help actually got it.[83]

Further, up to 40% of the American fighting force deployed in Iraq are from the National Guard presents adds another critical problem, given the delayed onset of many war-related psychiatric symptoms. National Guard members are only entitled to receive free mental health services from the Department of Veterans Affairs for two years following their discharge from active duty.[84]

What should make the above figures even more troubling is a little publicized fact: the acute or short-term psychiatric casualty rate in a war zone appears to be substantially less than the longer-term rate. This is what happened in Vietnam. There were widely announced and optimistic pronouncements by military officials about how low the overall acute psychiatric casualty rate was and that this rate was about half that during the Korean War, which in turn was about half that in World War II. Such pronouncements led to the early bold statement that "military psychiatry had worked" in Vietnam.[85]

---

80. Ibid.
81. Ibid.
82. Sara Corbett, "The Permanent Scars of Iraq." *New York Times Magazine* (2004, February 15), 34-35, 38-41, 56, 60, 66.
83. R. Burns. "Report acknowledges shortfalls in addressing troop morale, stress." *Army Times*. Associate Press, 2003. Retrieved on-line 3.29.04
84. Peg Tyre. "Battling the Effects of War." *Newsweek* (2004, December 6).

However, what was not reported to the public was that by only giving the overall acute psychiatry rate over the entire Vietnam War masked the very disconcerting fact that the acute psychiatry rate during the last few years of the war had skyrocketed. This was at a time during which it was becoming clear that there was no end in sight to the fighting and a quick victory as predicted by a number of the nation's leaders was not going to happen.

These facts, along with increasingly vocal and strident anti-war protests back home, hit the morale of the troops. All of these developments were correlated with the explosion in the acute psychiatric casualty rates during these latter years of the war. And then, two decades later, it was documented that over 800,000 Vietnam theater veterans had brought their war-related PTSD home with them.[86]

And so, if the violence in Iraq remains anywhere near its current levels and US armed forces remain in Iraq for several more years, we face the specter of rates of psychiatric casualties similar to those that occurred among Vietnam veterans. Indeed, the Chairman of the US House Veterans Affairs Committee stated that (as of March 2005), "as many as 100,000 Iraq and Afghanistan veterans could have PTSD."[87] These sobering predictions have been reinforced by the recent report of the Army Surgeon General that fully 30% of US troops returning from the Iraq War have developed stress-related mental health problems by three to four months after their deployment.[88]

These numbers are likely to increase as the numbers of dead and wounded and disabled inevitably rise, as protests increase against continuing military involvement in Iraq, and if and as society becomes more divided in its view of the war. As an indicator of the growing anti-Iraq War movement, about 800 anti-war marches were reported in all 50 states on March 19, 2005, the two-year anniversary of the day the Iraq War began.[89]

---

85. See *A Vietnam Trilogy*, 2004.

86. Kulka et al, 1990. Also, see much more in-depth discussion in A Vietnam Trilogy, 2004.

87. Tom Philpott, "VA Chairman: In wartime, all vets aren't equal." *SunHerald*, Biloxi, MS. (2005, March 13), A11.

88. The Associated Press, "More troops developing latent mental disorders. Symptoms appear several months after returning from Iraq, military says." Accessed on MSNBC.com, 7.28.2005.

89. As reported by the group United for Peace and Justice which helps coordinate antiwar activities. Jonathan Finer, The Washington Post, as reported in the SunHerald, Biloxi, MS (2005, March 19), C-2.

There also may be an increase in questioning about US military involvement in Iraq among active duty military personnel.[90] Some cases already have been reported.

> When they [Iraq veterans] grew cynical about the Iraq War, the Vietnam veterans in their family immediately recognized what was happening — that another generation of soldiers was grappling with the realization that they were being sent to carry out a policy determined by people who cared little for the grunts on the ground.... Now you realize that the people to blame for this aren't the ones you are fighting.

> It's the people who put you in this situation in the first place. You realize you wouldn't be in this situation if you hadn't been lied to. Soldiers are slowly coming to that conclusion. Once that becomes widespread, the resentment of the war is going to grow even more.[91]

To the extent that public opinion shifts away from support for the US involvement in Iraq, this problem is already affecting today's military personnel.

MILITARY MENTAL HEALTH RESPONSES IN IRAQ AND IN OTHER WARS

The Good

The military has adopted the term "combat stress" or "combat stress reaction" (CSR) rather than using the psychiatric diagnoses of Acute Stress Disorder (ASD) or Post-Traumatic Stress Disorder (PTSD) to describe most acute reactions to combat stressors while in the war zone. Combat stress reactions or battle stress is not considered to be an abnormal response to exposure to combat stressors in a war zone. The nature of such exposure is graphically described by a military psychologist in Iraq:

> The greatest difficulties experienced by our troops surround the extremely dangerous and unpredictable conditions faced continuously by an unseen enemy. The dangers inherent in the global war on terrorism surround living in and living through a relentless series of traumatic and horrific events. There is no way to stop driving through this. It is the nature of the war, which is far from over in this theater . . .

> When leaving "the wire" or the somewhat protected environment of the FOBS (Forward Operating Bases), soldiers are exposed to the relentless possibilities of attacks from those indistinguishable from civilians and normal objects of everyday living turned into instruments of injury and death: soda cans, dead animals, abandoned vehicles, all of which can be easily converted into deadly IEDs (Improvised Explo-

---

90. Opposition to US military involvement in Iraq is also growing among other groups, such as some of the families of Iraq veterans. For example, see Military Families Speak Out at *www.mfso.org*

91. David Goodman, "America's Soldiers Speak Out Against the Iraq War." *Mother Jones* (2004, November-December), 55.

sive Devices) or VBIEDs (vehicle-borne IEDs). They maim, torture, and kill their victims with grisly burn and blast injuries. There is no end and no escape from the danger they pose. We even hold our breath every time we leave the safety of our compound in the IZ (International Zone, aka Green Zone).

No one could possibly be completely immune to peril here. It erodes one's ability to carry on over time, renders one less able to deal with and push through those endless hours in which your life dwindles down to the prospect that this day might be your last. We are all susceptible . . .

The level of danger seems to be an ever-increasing problem, as insurgents become more clever and perfected in their game. This is why we wear over 35 pounds of body armor, Kevlar helmets, weapons and ammunition whenever leaving our facility. The level of security and numbers of checkpoints increases with the tempo. The illusion of safety rapidly disappeared during the recent elections and forced us to maintain more intensive force protection measures like sandbagging, roving guards in a tower on our roof comprised of our own soldiers, both male and female, in full defensive posture . . . .

In addition, stability and support operations (SASOs) can be as overwhelmingly stressful as major combat operations, as the level of danger and risks do not diminish in the face of "unfriendly" civilians whose major job it is to kill American soldiers, more restrictive Rules of Engagement and the changing Laws of War, and missions that are ambiguous in nature. It is very difficult to gauge the effectiveness and visible progress of our military operations as a result. [92]

Combat stress reaction describes a not uncommon response among military personnel; and it is a reaction rather than a psychiatric disorder. Indeed, military psychiatry has broadened the definition of combat to include operational stress.[93] This is a term that includes more than just fearful reactions to battle experiences *per se*, but to the broader range of stressor that deployed persons face, i.e., deprived working and living conditions, the threat of disease, and stress simply from being in a war zone and far from home.

Again, in the words of LTC Platoni:

In addition to issues surrounding combat, the most frequent psychological issues faced by our soldiers are those stemming from problems on the home-front, poor or inexperienced leadership, uncertainties about extended tours in theater or a back-to-back deployments, physical and psychological exhaustion, complicated grief and self-blame over the loss of fellow soldiers and surviving when buddies didn't, tremendous hatred for an often unrecognizable enemy, and the loss of the will to keep on living in the face of precarious battles that seemingly have no end . . . Add to the mix the lack of privacy, often extreme boredom waiting for something, anything to happen upon which to act, restricted movements within "the wire", and the long-

---

92. LTC Kathy Platoni, Combat Stress Control unit, Iraq. Personal communication (2005, March 18). Dr. Platoni can be contacted at: 50 South Main Street, Centerville, OH 45458-2362; 937.321.4020.
93. Patrick Peterson, "Combat stress centers opened." *SunHerald,* Biloxi, MS (2004, April 22), A-1, A-4.

term separations from home, family and all that is familiar. Undeniably the level of stress and distress remains high in OIF (Operation Iraq Freedom).[94]

CSR is understandable in the context of the extraordinary stressors of war; its acute manifestations are temporary and short-term precisely because they are reactions and not a psychiatric disorder. CSR symptoms among US troops in Iraq have been described as including "feelings of anxiety, upset stomachs, somatic complaints — anxieties that are converted to body illness — twitching, as well as emotional and maybe even spiritual problems."[95] LTC Platoni further describes the classic or typical signs and symptoms of combat stress or battle fatigue that the Combat Stress Control Units are seeing in Iraq:

> tremendous anxiety, hyper-vigilance, jitteriness and shaking; sleeplessness, haunting nightmares; irritability, anger, rage, outbursts of unresolved grief, self-doubt, excessive self-blame and guilt; inattentiveness, loss of confidence, carelessness and recklessness; loss of hope and faith, impaired ability to perform duties; depression that does not lift; freezing and immobility; erratic behaviors and actions, terror and panic, running away; loss of skills speech and memory; impaired sensation, hearing and vision; exhaustion, apathy and indifference to life itself; extreme fatigue, weakness and paralysis; delusions, hallucinations; vivid re-experiencing or re-living of images that cannot be forgotten; confusion about the taking of other lives and the fear of the loss of one's humanity in the face of doing so.[96]

The use of CSR terminology is an excellent practice as the difference between CSR on the one hand, and PTSD and ASD on the other, is immense. After all, ASD and PTSD are official psychiatric diagnostic labels for people who suffer a *disordered* response to trauma.[97] CSR terminology prevents the application of a "disorder label" being applied to large numbers of military personnel who are, in fact, reacting normally in the middle of a war zone. It is a fundamental fact that what is "normal" in the far-from-normal environment of war is far different from the behaviors that are "normal" in typical civilian life.

In fact many of the symptoms of post-traumatic stress (PTSD) and acute stress (ASD) that the APA describes as psychiatrically disordered in the civilian

---

94. Ibid.

95. B. Weinraub, "Therapy on the Fly for Soldiers Who Face Anxiety in the Battlefield." *New York Times* (2003, April 6), B-4.

96. K. Platoni, 2005.

97. The core symptoms of PTSD: (1) psychological re-experiencing symptoms that include reliving the event through very intense memories, mental pictures, thoughts or dreams; (2) persistent avoidance of stimuli associated with the trauma and numbing of general responsiveness symptoms to include denying or minimizing the reality of what happened, and detaching from one's emotions; and (3) persistent symptoms of increased physical arousal, to include sleep difficulties, difficulty concentrating, hyper-vigilance, and exaggerated startle response. American Psychiatric Association. *The Diagnostic and Statistical Manual of Mental Disorders, IVth Edition, Text Revision.* (Washington, DC: American Psychiatric Association, 2000), 463-472.

world are not only commonplace in a war zone, but indeed they are functional to survival in a war zone. These include:

- detaching from or numbing one's emotions.
- denying or minimizing the horror of what one is seeing and experiencing.
- hyper-vigilance.
- exaggerated startle response.
- experiencing the environment as unreal. [98]

In a war zone (or very soon after returning from deployment) it would be foolish and unproductive to consider such behaviors to be symptoms of a psychiatric disorder. Yet hundreds of thousands of veterans from the Vietnam War, for example, after returning from deployment or following their discharge from active duty, were later given the psychiatric disorder label of PTSD. And this is a "disordered" label that they keep forever. The decision of the military mental health establishment to make a distinction between CSR and ASD and PTSD appears to be quite appropriate.

On the other hand, the military denies that it is reluctant to diagnose PTSD. They say officially that they are not. However, in a public statement to the GAO (Government Accounting Office) Dr. William Winkenwerder, Assistant Secretary of Defense for Health Affairs, explains why clinicians ought not necessarily diagnose PTSD when patients present with symptoms, but to "watch and wait." This is a term that comes from cancer research and for which there does not appear to be any support in the mental health literature:

> Watchful waiting. The concept of watchful waiting is common in medical practice. Symptoms may present for any number of reasons that do not reach clinical significance or cannot be readily diagnosed. Frequently, individuals are provided the advice that they should pay attention to the symptoms and return if they do not dissipate or if they get worse. Watchful waiting is a clinical relevant position to take in the case of PTSD-related symptoms at the point in time at which the Post Deployment Health Assessment (DD Form 2796) is conducted [the military's screen for PTSD that is administered after deployment and six months after coming home]. [99]

This is an interesting, and controversial, stance. When someone meets full diagnostic inclusionary criteria for a psychiatric disorder per the *DSM-IV-TR*, diagnostic convention is that the diagnosis is given — although a "provisional" diagnosis is considered appropriate when there is doubt about the diagnosis but the working assumption is that the diagnosis applies. The concern here is if the

---

98. For an enlightening description of how the DSM has pathologized what would otherwise be considered "normal" reactions in the abnormal reality of war, see the chapter, "Bringing the War Back to DSM" (pp. 100-125) in H. Kutchins and S. Kirk. *Making us Crazy. DSM: The Psychiatric Bible and the Creation of Mental Disorders* (New York: The Free Press, 1997).

99. Mark Boal, "Fight for Mind of the Veteran" (working title), Playboy Magazine, in press, October, 2006.

military is overtly and/or covertly coercing or influencing diagnostic practices to purposely discourage military mental health clinicians from applying the PTSD diagnosis in spite of their clinical judgment to the contrary?

More Good — Up To A Point

Viewed in the above context, there are logical military mental health responses to combat stress reactions in a war zone, responses that have been provided in various forms since as far back as World War I.[100] Indeed, in congruence with ethical principles of treating post-trauma reactions, the argument can be made that the time and logistical constraints and realities in a war zone dictate severe limits on what can realistically be done therapeutically with psychiatric casualties other than the classic military psychiatry interventions that are based on long-standing principles known as PIES: Proximity, Immediacy, Expectancy and Simplicity. Along with PIES, there is the military mental health principle of Centrality. [101]

In Iraq the multi-faceted mission of the Combat Operational Stress Control (COSC) units is described as operating within the basic principles of PIES but with an unprecedented insertion of COSC personnel with combat units:[102]

> To treat from the front lines (as there is no longer a rear echelon), to improve access to our services, and to liaison with all "boots on the ground" in theater to meet all the needs and demands of every unit, commander, and soldier. Our Prevention Team missions involve treatment of battle fatigue by providing comprehensive support for stress casualties as immediately as time and location allow, always with the expectation that soldiers can recover and will return to duty.

> If primary preventive measures are insufficient, soldiers are referred to one of our two Restoration Teams for rest, physical replenishment, three hots and a cot, neuropsychiatric triage and evaluation, stabilization, brief supportive counseling, mission stress education that promotes coping with any number of combat stressors, work hardening to allow them to better perform their missions (occupational ther-

---

100. For a detailed description, and critique, see Scurfield, *A Vietnam Trilogy*, 2004.

101. For a more thorough description of military mental health in the war zone, see *A Vietnam Trilogy*, 2004.

102. The following description of military mental health today is based on three primary sources, my first-hand knowledge from my experiences in Vietnam and through my clinical work with veterans over the decades; media accounts over the past year that include statements by active duty military mental health personnel, DOD officials and Iraq soldiers and their families; and comments from mental health professionals in the Department of Veterans Affairs who are working with OEF and OIF veterans and their families. One military mental health expert in particular is Harry Holloway, Uniformed Services University of the Health Services, who gave a presentation on "Military Psychiatry, Then and Now" at the International Society for Traumatic Stress Studies, Annual Meeting, New Orleans, LA (2004, November 16).

apy), and disposition, including med evacuation to a higher echelon of care in Land-shtull (Germany) [103]

The five principles of PIES plus centrality can be considered as falling into two categories: functional and clinically specific.

The functional principles include Proximity, Immediacy and Centrality and have to do with the way how mental health services are structured or organized. The objectives are to have mental health professionals strategically located to be able to provide mental health services in accordance with the military mental health principles.

Proximity: they are easily accessible to provide mental health services to front-line and indeed all military personnel, and as close as possible to their duty stations.

Immediacy: they can very quickly provide needed assessment and consultation and direct counseling services, and

Centrality: the authority to medically evacuate anyone out of the war zone is limited to specific medical officers in order to insure that a centralized quality control is uniformly applied throughout the war zone. This arrangement prevents decisions about medical evacuations from occurring through the individual medical judgment of numerous medical officers scattered throughout the war zone and is said to ensure more uniform assessment and disposition decisions.

Critics contend that centralization is actually a strategy to suppress the number of psychiatric of casualties being evacuated out of country. In other words, experience has shown that if individual medical physicians were left to their own judgment, they would be more likely to consider the health of the injured individual when making decisions about an appropriate medical disposition. Far more medical evacuations would thus be authorized. Under military mental health practices both in Vietnam and in Iraq today, restricting medical evacuation authority in-country to medical officers who primarily factor in the medical mission of conserving the fighting strength results in more military psychiatric casualties being sent back to duty rather than being medically evacuated.

The remaining two principles of military mental health are the clinically-specific principles and provide the framework, ethos and methods for the provision of clinically specific interventions.

Simplicity: interventions are to be simple and uncomplicated and easy and quick to administer. As such, they do not give the message to the military personnel that they are "sick" or "disabled."

Expectancy: the providers are instructed to be very clear and repetitive with the message that the patient is suffering a temporary and understandable

---

103. LTC Kathy Platoni. (2005, March 18).

reaction to a powerful situation or incident, will recover within a very quick period of time, and will soon be returning to duty.

> These latter two principles prescribe the limits of the range and depth of interventions that will be provided to psychiatric casualties. [104]

> "Three hots and a cot" in a safe environment to rest and be given a brief respite from dangerous duty.

> Education about combat stress reactions and recovery from them, i.e., it is normal for soldiers facing combat to also face fear and stress. [105]

> Crisis intervention related to traumatic combat experiences, to include losses during combat and accompanying guilt and grief, sadness and anger reactions.[106]

Within this context of very time-limited and directive counseling, patients are provided an opportunity to talk briefly, vent any pent-up feelings and issues, and reexamine what is troubling them and what they need to do to get themselves back together again and return to their duty station.

COSC personnel in Iraq have benefited from adopting mental health interventions developed since the Vietnam War — especially Critic Incident Stress Debriefings or Critical Event Debriefings, to include the Kuhlmann Group Debriefing Model that originated in the 785th Medical Company, Combat Stress Control, during the late 1990s. (For a detailed description of the Kuhlmann model, please see Appendix II.)[107]

Besides using crisis intervention and debriefing strategies that include simply allowing the emotionally troubled combatant to talk and vent, relaxation and cognitive-behavioral techniques are provided. The combatant may be taught simple breathing and other relaxation techniques to help allay anxiety, and cognitive reframing to help combatants look at what they are experiencing as a normal or "natural" reaction.[108]

When necessary, and depending on the prescribing proclivities of military physicians, some amount of psychotropic medications, typically anti-depres-

---

104. Much of the following information is from four sources: B. Weinraub. "Therapy on the fly for soldiers who face anxiety in the battlefield." *New York Times*, B-4.; Stoesen, L. (2004, July). "Social worker helps soldiers cope. US Army major deployed in Iraq offers support to the troops." *NASW News* (2004, July), 9; M. Friedman & H. Hollaway, "Military Psychiatry, Then and Now," presented at the International Society of Traumatic Stress Studies, New Orleans (2004, November 18); and my personal familiarity with the functioning of psychiatric teams in the war-zone (see *A Vietnam Trilogy*, 2004).

105. Weinraub, 2003, p. B4.

106. Stoesen, "Social worker helps soldiers cope," 2004.

107. D. Patterson, T. Austin and D.D. Rabb, "Introducing the Kuhlmann Group Debriefing Model in Operation Iraqi Freedom 2," power point presentation. Rabb, M. Stalka, C. Kampa & G. Grammer, "55th MED CO (CSC) power point presentation.

108. Weinraub, 2003, April 6, B4.

sants and anti-anxiety medications, are provided to mitigate particularly severe anxiety, depressive, sleep deprivation/exhaustion (or, in very rare cases, psychotic) symptoms in the immediate.[109]

CSR mental health units in Iraq have gone beyond what was offered in Vietnam in terms of having a substantially more extensive role of being a force multiplier:

> This means going out to the Forward Operating Bases to provide one on one or group support, command consultation to assist commands in confronting widespread problems, providing on-the-spot training and briefings, from combat operational stress management, conflict resolution, anger management, coping with grief and loss, to dealing with human remains. We provide critical incident stress management defusings and debriefings after significant events, particularly when there have been casualties and fatalities.[110]

Combatants who are seen at CSR units often are sleep deprived and exhausted, combined with the cumulative and unrelenting stress of repeated exposure to death, dying and the constant threat of unpredictable surprise attacks. Army mental health in Iraq claims that about 80% of soldiers treated by the combat stress unit are able to return to their operational units after several days. It is reported that soldiers who do not respond so positively and quickly can be placed in a headquarters relatively near to their units for 7 to 10 days, assigned low-stress jobs like kitchen duty, and given further rest.[111]

However, an Army survey of mental health services in Iraq reported that more than half of the mental health providers surveyed whose mission was combat stress control reported that they had inadequate supplies of antidepressant and sleeping drugs. Half also said they did not receive enough pre-war training in combat stress and more than half said they either did not know the Army's combat stress control doctrine or "did not support it."[112] These findings strongly suggest that the actual practice of mental health in the Iraq war zone may not be entirely consistent with official military mental health principles and doctrine.

Without question the official military mental health doctrine is intended to give a consistent message that such soldiers are not having abnormal reactions

---

109. I am not privy to, and there may not be accurate information available, as to what the exact medication dispensing practices are by the various physicians throughout the Iraq war-zone. Certainly the official doctrine is to use as little psychotropic medication as possible. And this policy is affirmed in a report that states that anti-depressants and anti-anxiety medications are not prescribed for soldiers, at least not in the early stages of treatment. Weinraub, "Therapy on the fly for soldiers who face anxiety in the battlefield", 2003.

110. LTC Platoni, 2005, March 18.

111. Weinraub, 2003, 4.

112. R. Burns, "Report acknowledges shortfalls in addressing troop morale, stress." *Army Times* (2004, March 26).

and hence are not "patients." Rather, reactions such as fear and anxiety are normal; it is the environment that is abnormal, and the soldier will very soon be able to return to duty. This is military mental health in a war zone; it sounds exactly like what was provided in Vietnam in 1968-69.[113]

And it works — up to a point. It enables the maximum numbers of combat-stressed soldiers to return quickly to their units and minimizes the number of acute psychiatric casualties who would be medically evacuated out of the war zone. In other words, these military mental health principles have an excellent track record in reducing the acute psychiatric rate in the war zone and the number of military personnel who are medically evacuated out of country. After all, the goal of the Combat Stress Control teams in Iraq is to: "provide high quality combat/operational stress control service and to manage fear, fatigue, and traumatic experiences of soldiers, thereby preserving unit cohesion and fighting strength of combat units."[114]

The Not-So-Good

The military has extolled the advances in psychiatry strategies and service-delivery improvements, to include having dispatched combat stress teams to Iraq early on, having mental health personnel embedded with combat units, and their forward thinking in terms of the quick interventions provided. Such advances are laudable in that they have helped to alleviate acute combat stress reactions. However, they belie a sobering reality.

Military mental health differs distinctively from civilian practices in that it is not the personal problems of the soldiers, or their mental health *per se*, that are the primary focus of clinical attention. Rather, the military medical mission is to conserve the fighting strength of the unit, and thus to return the combat stress reactive soldier back to his or her unit in the field ASAP.

From a strictly military perspective, this makes total sense. But while military mental health practices in a war zone almost assuredly help keep down the numbers of acute psychiatric casualties in the war zone, I am aware of only one study that affirms that this approach is conducive to the longer-term mental health of that soldier. That singular investigation was a 20-year longitudinal study of psychiatric casualties in the Israel Defense Forces. Preliminary findings indicate there was a significantly lower PTSD rate 20 years later among psychiatric casualties who were treated at the front lines versus those medically evacuated to rear-echelon areas (31% vs. 41%).[115] However the study was conducted in Israel, where circumstances are different; it is risky to assume that any

---

113. Readers are encouraged to read *A Vietnam Trilogy*, in which such psychological operations are described in detail, as well as the range of psychiatric reactions of psych casualties, and other military mental health strategies.
114. Rabb, Stalka, Kampa & Grammer, power point presentation.

findings on Israeli forces would be identical in the US. To my knowledge no such study has ever been done on any era of US military psychiatric casualties.[116]

Furthermore, while a reduction of ten percent is to be welcomed, the fact that 31% of psychiatric casualties continue to have PTSD twenty years later is still appalling. The Israeli study findings argue for the US to conduct its own such studies. Until such longitudinal studies are completed in the US, there is no empirical evidence to support the military's assertions that American military mental health practices in war zones is conducive to either the shorter- or longer-term mental health of US combatants. One can only wonder why it is that the military still has refused to mandate such a study of US military mental health practices.

The scientific literature overwhelmingly confirms that increasing one's exposure to repeated high magnitude stressors or trauma is the single greatest risk factor to developing PTSD.[117] Indeed, a broad survey of the diverse literature concerning the psychological consequences of combat exposure strongly reiterated the linear relationship between combat exposure and negative psychological outcome:

> Combat exposure studies of all wars identify higher level of exposure as a significant contributor to PTSD development. Certain malignant types of combat exposure also appear to place service members at particular risk [veterans who handled human remains, and injured soldiers] . . . In conclusion, despite certain limitations, multiple studies regarding psychological sequelae of war show a clear association between combat exposure and PTSD, with greater levels of exposure leading to greater prevalence.[118]

The irony is this is exactly what military mental health practice in the war zone is geared to do. The focus on returning psychiatric casualties to duty ensures that traumatized personnel will return to combat — where they will face yet additional and recurring traumas.

Reports from the first study ever conducted by the military on the mental health of troops who fought in Iraq or Afghanistan confirmed the salient role of exposure to direct combat stressors with developing PTSD. Soldiers surveyed in Iraq showed a higher rate of PTSD (12%) than Afghanistan (6%). However, the

---

115. Z. Solomon and associates, "Front Line Treatment of Combat Stress Reaction — A 20-Year Longitudinal Evaluation Study." This study was of Israeli Defense Force psychiatric casualties of the 1982 Lebanon War. In this study, it is reported that there was a significant positive impact on reduce rates of PTSD in 2002 of Israeli psychiatric casualties treated near to the front lines (31%) versus those who were evacuated away from the war-zone and then treated back in Israel (41%). Findings reported at the "Military Psychiatry, Then & Now" Workshop at the International Society for Traumatic Stress Studies. New Orleans, LA (2004, November 18).

116. For example, there is a universal draft and it is almost universally supported by Israelis; the perceived threat from all the surrounding Arab countries is omnipresent and is reinforced daily.

troops in Iraq saw more combat, including firefights and attacks. The higher PTSD rate among those soldiers surveyed in Iraq confirmed the very strong relationship between exposure to direct combat stressors and PTSD.

This linear relationship between increased exposure to combat stressors and psychiatric problems among combatants is not a new finding. It reported in the National Vietnam Veterans Readjustment Study some 15 years and two wars ago,[119] and it was reported 60 years ago in a study of World War II veterans. Sustained exposure to direct combat over about 30 days had almost a 100% association with becoming a psychiatric casualty.[120] This is just one more critical lesson that apparently needs to be learned and relearned.

It may, indeed, be true that "if combat is bad, evacuation is hell." [121] The negative emotional impact of the medical evacuation process is without a doubt extremely stressful, if not traumatic.[122] Yet returning psychiatric casualties back to duty clearly puts them at increased risk in terms of their longer-term mental health.

> It appears to truly be a mental health Catch-22 of war: conserve the fighting strength while dramatically increasing the risk of PTSD by returning psychiatric casualties back to duty, or medically evacuate out of country and avoid further exposure to combat trauma yet expose evacuees to the emotional trauma of the evacuation process and "deserting" their comrades. Pick your poison.

117. Ibid. See also: R.A. Kulka, W.E. Schlenger, J.A. Fairbank, R.L. Hough, B. Kathleen Jordan, C.R. Marmar & D. Weiss, *Trauma and the Vietnam War Generation. Report of Findings From the National Vietnam Veterans Readjustment Study.* (New York: Brunner/Mazel, 1990); J.P. Wilson & G.E. Grauss, "Predicting post-traumatic stress disorders among Vietnam veterans." In W. Kelly (Ed.), *Posttraumatic Stress Disorder and the War Veteran Patient* (102-148). (New York: Brunner/Mazel, 1985); D. Kaysen, P.A. Resick & D. Wise, "Living in danger: the impact of chronic traumatization and the traumatic context of posttraumatic stress disorder." *Trauma, Violence & Abuse: A Review Journal, 4* (3) (2004), 247-264; N. Breslau, G. Davis, P. Andreski & E. Peterson, "Traumatic events and posttraumatic stress disorder in an urban population of young adults." *Archives of General Psychiatry, 48,* 216-222. Further evidence of the salient role of exposure to traumatic stressors as predictive of PTSD is the psychometric development work that has been accomplished on trauma exposure scales such as the PTSD Checklist, e.g., E.B. Blanchard, J. Jones-Alexander, T.C. Buckley & C.A. Forneris, "Psychometric properties of the PTSD Checklist," *Behavior Research Therapy, Vol. 34* (8) (1996), 669-673; and D. Forbes, M. Creamer & D. Biddle. "The validity of the PTSD checklist as a measure of symptomatic change in combat-related PTSD." *Behaviour Research and Therapy, 39* (2001), 977-986.

118. Cozza, S.J., "Combat exposure and PTSD." *PTSD Research Quarterly, 16* (1) (2005, Winter), 1-7.

119. Kulka et al, 1990.

120. Grinker, T. & J. Spiegel, *Men Under Stress* (Philadelphia: Blakiston, 1945).

121. H. Holloway, "Military psychiatry then and now." International Society of Traumatic Stress annual meeting. New Orleans, LA (2004, November 18).

This is a complex issue that, other than the Israeli study, is devoid of any empirical evidence to support either position. Is it really in the long-term mental health of those who are suffering combat stress reactions to be stabilized, re-invigorated and returned to duty versus being medically evacuated out of country? It should be of great concern to all of us that in spite of the dearth of empirical data, this premise is completely accepted and promulgated by military mental health officials.

The acceptance and promotion of this unsubstantiated and certainly debatable premise is further buttressed by the fact that once a person is in a war zone, the pressures are enormous to reinforce returning psychiatric casualties to duty. First and foremost, in a war zone one gets caught up in the fervor of war, and the pride and esprit de corps. When you encounter people acutely suffering from exposure to horrific events and consequences, your heart goes out to do all that you can do to help.

> The satisfaction we derive from being called to duty in support of Operation Iraqi Freedom is pretty overwhelming. It just takes talking to one soldier to know what we do as a CSC team really matters. When we conducted debriefings for the US Embassy staff in the aftermath of the rocket attack few Saturdays ago and allowed them to process their incredible grief and sense of both loss and horror (many of them witnessed the gruesome deaths of 2 colleagues and injury of 5 more) and their completely selfless acts in tending to the wounded with little regard for their own lives (many of them are civilian personnel), our reason for being here truly took shape. It is a gift to be called to serve one's country for the cause of freedom. As I always say, there are few more noble deeds.[123]

I can identify with this powerful drive to help people and the sense of gratification and pride at doing the best you can. Besides the inevitably intoxicating combination of wanting to help and the adrenalin stimuli rampant in a war zone, there are other powerful factors that influence the decision to return psychiatric casualties to duty rather than medically evacuate them. If they are evacuated, who is going to take their places? Will they be (even more vulnerable) "newbies"? (Anyone who has been in war knows that a newbie is the most dangerous person to have in combat situations, until he can learn the ropes.) Or will it mean that others will be forced to have their tours extended to make up for the personnel loss, or that others will be redeployed from the US back to Iraq to fill the absences? None of these alternatives is appealing.

And there is one additional and extremely powerful dynamic that further "loads the dice" towards a disposition of return to duty rather than medical evacuation out of country. During the Vietnam War, the primary performance factor in the annual evaluation by the commander of the psychiatric team was "reduced medical evacuation rate out of country," used as the benchmark to ensure that

---

122. See Scurfield & Tice, "Medical Evacuations from War-Zone to Stateside: A Trail of Tribulation." In Volume 2 of *A Vietnam Trilogy, Healing Journeys*, 2006.
123. LTC Kathy Platoni, 2005.

the psychiatric team was successfully carrying out the mission. And in Iraq today performance evaluations of Combat Stress Control units are also based primarily on returning psychiatric casualties to duty versus med-evac to Landshtul, as well as the length of stay at the Restoration Program for those who need to temporarily be in a 24-hour mental health environment.[124]

Such performance benchmarks dramatically load the pressures on military mental health personnel, obliging them to have tunnel vision on conserving the fighting strength rather than to weigh equally the value of preserving and enhancing the longer-term mental health of the individual psychiatric casualty. And all the while the unsupported notion is reinforced that "premature" or "unnecessary" evacuation out of country will be more injurious to the casualty's longer-term mental health than remaining in a war zone and being re-exposed to additional traumatic stressors.

The results are that more psychiatric casualties will be exposed to further trauma by being returned to duty; and second, this exposure to further trauma is the single greatest predictor of being at risk to eventually develop PTSD. Indeed, even the previously referenced Israeli study that showed a 25% lower rate of PTSD 20 years later among psychiatric casualties treated at the front lines versus those medically evacuated and treated still reported a very high PTSD prevalence rate of 31% among the psychiatric casualties treated at the front and returned to duty. To put this PTSD rate in perspective, it is double the rate of PTSD found among Vietnam theater veterans as a whole (15.2%) some 15 to 20 years after the Vietnam War.

Also, it is critical to remember the evidence reported earlier that only a fraction of personnel in a war zone suffering from the effects of emotional stress will ever actually see a military mental health professional in the war zone. And so, no matter how dedicated, skilled and courageous military mental health personnel are in the war zone, it is inevitable that there will be a number of deployed service members who will return home with unresolved post traumatic stress. It cannot possibly be any other way, because exposure to the repeated traumatic stressors is indisputably injurious long-term to the mental health of a substantial portion of those who serve. There is no way around it, other than to stay out of the war to begin with.

Therefore, given the US involvement in at least two ongoing wars, there is an ethical question if not a dilemma. Is it really possible for the military mental health establishment to consider the longer-term mental health ramifications of any interventions in a war zone on an equal basis with the narrow view to accomplish the medical mission of conserving the fighting strength? This would require the military to be willing to develop a balanced medical mission that would officially and equally consider what is good for the individual and what is good for the Armed Forces. The likelihood of this happening is virtually nil —

124. Ibid.

especially when military forces are stretched to the point of requiring multiple repeat deployments back to the war zone, such as in Iraq today.

Hence it would appear to be an ethical imperative that the military mental health establishment be willing to change two things. First, performance evaluations of Combat Stress Control units must not be based on the med-evac rate. Rather, psychiatric evaluations must be based on the accuracy or efficacy of the psychiatric dispositions that are made. In other words, if someone is med-evaced to Germany, does subsequent assessment at Landshtul confirm that the decision to medically evacuate was the right decision? And, out of the psychiatric casualties who are returned to duty, what percentage are able to successfully carry out their duties? Such performance markers get away from the bias to return to duty and to valid mental health performance factors.

Of course, in Vietnam the psychiatric team almost never knew what happened to any of the psychiatric casualties after we treated them, whether they were medically evacuated out of country or returned to duty — unless they happened to end up back at the psychiatric team one day. There was no tracking or feedback system, which meant that all of the psychiatric team's actions were being conducted in a total information vacuum. As far as I can ascertain, the Combat Operational Stress Control units in Iraq today still do not have a tracking system in place,[125] so there can be no meaningful system of tracking.

If there was a desire to close this gap, two wars later a system would be in place. The lack of data prevents health personnel from determining, for example, if psychiatric casualties being returned to duty have a different mortality rate than their counterparts. Or a different rate of failure to perform their duties satisfactorily, or a different PTSD prevalence rate than those evacuated out of country. Or whether being returned to duty may be associated with a higher rate of increased ability to perform and an increased positive mental health longer-term.

The second concern is about the information that is typically provided to veterans and their families. It is critically important that certain information be shared by the military and most mental health providers, and by the government to US military forces and to veterans, to their families and to the country, as to the risks and likely consequences of serving in a war zone.

WHAT TO SAY AND DO DIFFERENTLY: IT'S TIME TO TELL THE WHOLE TRUTH

All of us, including deployed members of the Armed Forces, their families and the country, are entitled to have the truth, the whole truth and nothing but the truth concerning combat stress reactions and post-traumatic stress, and the

---

125. Ibid.

full range of possible short- and longer-term impact of war-trauma. It is supposed to be a hallmark of a democracy to have a fully informed citizenry and not let others decide what is best for us to know.

To my knowledge, important facts are not shared by the military with Armed Forces personnel and their families, nor does the government share this with the electorate. Is there not an ethical responsibility to insure that all military personnel serving in any war zone, their families, and veterans and their communities have access to this information?[126] Following is what I consider to be absolutely vital information that must be provided directly to the active duty member or veteran; some of this is currently provided by some military mental health providers yet other essential aspects of this information are not communicated.

MYTHS AND REALITIES ABOUT COMBAT STRESS REACTIONS, TRAUMA AND PTSD[127]

There are several important myths about the impact of trauma and war.[128]

• Myth: Heroes and "normal" healthy persons don't have (psychological or social) problems after being exposed to war trauma. If they do have such problems, then that means that they already had problems, or were predisposed to having such problems anyhow; "the trauma was merely a trigger."

• Reality: War and other trauma are so catastrophic that they will evoke symptoms in almost everyone regardless of one's background or pre-morbid factors. It is abnormal *not* to have strong reactions to a trauma. As Viktor Frankl, concentration camp survivor and founder of logo-therapy stated: An abnormal reaction to an abnormal situation is normal behavior.[129] Indeed, trauma always has a significant impact, although not everyone necessarily develops PTSD.

————

• Myth: Time heals all wounds.

• Reality: Not necessarily. Long-term follow-up studies of WW II, Korean and Vietnam war-veterans indicate that psychiatric symptoms not only do not necessarily disappear over time, but in a significant sub-group

---

126. Some of the following is discussed in more detail in *A Vietnam Trilogy*, 2004.

127. See also G. Schiraldi, *The PTSD SourceBook*, 2000.

128. These myths and realities also apply to survivors of other human-induced trauma (such as sexual assault, homicide or disappearance of a loved one, child abuse) and most also apply to those who have been traumatized by exposure to a natural disaster.

129. Frankl, V. *Man's Search For Meaning*. (Boston: Beacon, 1959).

the symptoms have become worse, probably exacerbated by the aging process. They may be triggered by a greater likelihood of exposure to deaths of significant others as one grows older, age-related losses of job, career, health. [130]

• Myth: My war trauma was not as bad as what others suffered, so I should not be feeling as badly as I do. Or, I should feel guilty because I was spared what others suffered. [131]

• Reality: Comparing your war trauma with those of others is a no-win proposition. What is essential is to fully admit to yourself that your trauma is your trauma, and what is its impact on you? If you continue to deny or minimize the very real impact of your war trauma experiences on you, you are lying to yourself. You must be willing to face the truth about how the war has impacted you — or it will always have a hold on you. And valid guilt does not come from feeling guilty over that which you had no responsibility for or control over — someone else's trauma. You can have empathy for others without having to put yourself down by denying the impact of your war trauma.

• Myth: I must be crazy or weak to still keep remembering and still be bothered by the war after all this time.

• Reality: Trauma is unforgettable (unless one has psychic amnesia). It is absolutely normal to *not* be able to totally eradicate the memories of war trauma, and to be bothered to at least some degree by the trauma — for months, years or decades afterwards. Therefore, a war survivor will not be able to totally forget salient memories of the war unless they resort to artificial means such as substance abuse, psychotropic medications, constant exposure to current danger, etc.

• Myth: I must have been bad or somehow deserved what happened to me during the war or afterwards.

• Reality: Bad things can happen to good people and through no fault of their own.

However, many survivors tend to blame someone for their trauma: themselves, others, institutions — or God.

-----

130. H.C. Archibald and R.D. Tuddenham, "Persistent stress reaction after combat: A 20-year follow-up." *Archives of General Psychiatry*, 12 (1965), 475-481. For a comprehensive review of studies on older veterans, see P.P. Schnur, "PTSD and combat-related psychiatric symptoms in older veterans. *PTSD Research Quarterly*, 2 (1) (1991 Winter). Accessed on-line 6.17.06.

131. Scurfield, R.M. "Post-Katrina aftermath and helpful interventions on the Mississippi Gulf Coast.," *Traumatology*, 12 (2) (2006, Summer, in press).

• Myth: If I can just forget about the [traumatic] memories of the war, I will be able to move ahead with my life.

• Reality: If you are a survivor of war trauma that happened awhile ago, you are an expert at detachment, denial, minimization, avoidance — because is what you have been doing in an attempt to forget about the unforgettable traumatic experience. If that detachment and denial had worked satisfactorily for you, or continued to work satisfactorily for you, you wouldn't be here at this time for treatment. But the detachment/denial isn't working so well anymore, or you have become so extreme with your detachment/denial that it is causing other problems in your life — in addition to the painful memories and other PTSD symptoms.

––––––

• Myth: I can never trust myself or anyone else again. My judgment during the war was bad, and the environment is not to be trusted. So I need to isolate and be constantly wary and careful of my surroundings.

• Reality: Trust in self or others is not an all-or-nothing proposition. Developing appropriate degrees of trust does involve risks, yet is essential for a fulfilling life. And if isolation and constant wariness are successful strategies, you wouldn't be here in treatment, would you?

––––––

• Myth: My war trauma is the cause of all of my problems that I am having. Or: I'm behaving or feeling this way just because of the war.

• Reality: No one was a "blank tablet" before entering the military and war. We all were persons with strengths and weaknesses, positives and negatives. You may be having problems now that existed before the war, or that are worse in the aftermath of the war. If this is so, you must be truthful with yourself as to the cause(s) of your current problems or you will continue to put blame and responsibility where they do not belong and you will not address what truly needs addressed.

––––––

• I did okay during the war and for awhile afterwards, so I shouldn't be having all of these negative feelings and reactions now.

• Reality: People seldom break down psychologically or have emotions that overwhelm and incapacitate them while in the midst of the emergency or the war or in its immediate aftermath. Rather, most survivors suppress or "bury" painful feelings and thoughts and learn how to detach yourself from your own emotions in order to survive and not be overwhelmed. Typically there is a delay in the onset of problematic emotions and thoughts until sometime after the danger has passed—hours, days or weeks later; in a number of cases, months, years or decades later. Just because you are feeling okay and in control of yourself at this time (or even in the first several weeks or months or even years following deployment) does not necessarily mean that this will be the case later. [132]

———

• Myth: Most war survivors are highly motivated to eliminate or reduce PTSD-related symptoms like isolation, numbing, and physical arousal/hyper-alertness to the environment.

• Reality: A number of PTSD symptoms also are survival modes that were learned during or following the war; and many war survivors are very reluctant, ambivalent or not interested in giving them up. [133] They may: (1) feel that it is quite justified to stay removed and apart from others, because they are different than others and do not feel comfortable in many social situations; (2) believe that to let themselves feel emotions once again will only result in painful reliving of traumatic memories, and (3) believe it is wise not to trust and be wary of the environment, and so hyper-arousal is a necessary protection against a hostile world.

OTHER REALITIES ABOUT WAR AND ITS IMPACT

All military personnel and their families need to be expressly informed that:

• Combat or war always has a significant impact on all who experience it, both shorter-term and longer-term. As one Iraq war veteran stated, "My body's here, but my mind is there [in Iraq]."[134]

• You may have either significant "positive" and/or "negative" outcomes or impact from your war experiences, both while deployed and following your return. This impact may be evident immediately, later or after a very long period of time has elapsed. However, having even many positive war experiences will not necessarily resolve or ameliorate the grief, hurt, fear or loss of war trauma.

• Most vets feel that, overall, their military experiences were more positive than negative. For example, a study of Vietnam vets showed that 56% felt that their Vietnam War and military experiences were an entirely or mostly positive effect on their lives. However 33% felt that Vietnam and the military had an equally positive and negative impact; and 11% felt that the impact of their Vietnam and military experiences were entirely or mostly negative.[135] Major negatives from the Vietnam experience included: loss of

---

132. Scurfield, *Traumatology*, 2006.

133. See R.T. Murphy, R.P. Cameron, L., Sharp, G., Ramirez, C., Rosen, K., Dreschler & D.F. Gusman,, "Readiness to Change PTSD Symptoms and Related Behaviors Among Veterans Participating in a Motivation Enhancement Group." *The Behavior Therapist*, 27 (4) (2004), 33-36.

134. This quote is from an Iraq veteran who stated that he could not get past the memories of Iraq, and that his experience there felt unresolved. Corbett, 2004, 34.

civic pride, of faith in America; cynicism; inability to make friends; and experiences of grief at death and suffering. Such negatives may well be an outcome of the war experience.

• To attempt to suppress or bury painful memories, and to learn how to detach yourself from your emotions while in the war zone is almost certainly helpful to be able to continue to function in the war zone; these strategies also will help you to be able to make it through your deployment. On the other hand, there is absolutely no evidence that doing this will have any impact on whether you will or will not subsequently develop longer term war-related mental health problems.[136]

• People rarely break down psychologically while in the midst of an emergency or trauma, even in a war zone. Rather, typically there is a delay until later — after getting back to a more secure area, or hours or days or weeks later, or in a number of cases months, years or decades after leaving the war zone. And so, just because you are feeling okay and in control of yourself at this time (or even in the first several weeks or months following deployment), does not necessarily mean that this will be the case months or years from now.

• There is compelling evidence that the more anyone is exposed to stressors of war, the greater the likelihood that he or she will eventually develop post-traumatic stress or post-traumatic stress disorder. And so, the longer you are deployed and the more you are repeatedly redeployed back to the war zone, the risk will be increasingly higher that you will ultimately develop PTSD. This is the risk of being willing to repeatedly put yourself into harm's way.

Acute psychiatric casualties in the war zone who are being treated and sent back to their duty stations deserve to be warned about the mental health risks they face, in terms along these lines:

• I want to be very frank with you about what will happen by going back to duty. You may well suffer additional psychological or emotional difficulties if you are exposed to yet more combat stressors and trauma.

• This is understandable, and you should recognize if this is happening and not think that you are going crazy or are a "weak" person. However, you must pay close attention: do what you have to do to protect yourself and survive during the remainder of your tour.

• Be aware that you may have suppressed or delayed emotional problems and issues related to exposure to combat that can surface months or years

---

135. Card, J. *Lives After Vietnam. The Personal Impact of Military Service.* (Washington, DC: Lexington Books, 1983).

136. For example, the research data on the outcome of very brief interventions in the aftermath of disasters is very mixed, with considerable evidence that it may not be at all beneficial in reducing the risk of subsequently developing PTSD.

after leaving the war zone. But as a veteran you can get knowledgeable help through the Department of Veterans Affairs and Vet Centers.

A NEW MESSAGE FOR PSYCHIATRIC EVACUEES

A new message must go out to psychiatric casualties — once the decision has been reached that their medical condition is such that they are going to be evacuated out of the war zone:

> We are planning to evacuate you out of the war zone. As a result, you may feel even more guilt or shame that you "deserted" your buddies or "failed" as a soldier. I want you to remember me telling you this now. This is a natural reaction, and these are issues that you may well have to deal with sometime after you return from deployment. Even so, we believe that it is in your best mental health interests to be evacuated at this time.

How does this differ from what military mental health professionals do now? It is impossible to know how many military mental health professionals give this information, explicitly or less explicitly, to psychiatric casualties. The timing of this message and how it is used are critical. This message has been used as a fundamental rationale to justify keeping psychiatric casualties in the war zone and returning them to duty.

Instead, this message should only, and always, be given after a decision is made to medically evacuate someone out of the war zone. Then it is merely an important piece of information to advise the evacuee about — not an unquestioned and unfounded attempt to persuade psychiatrically troubled personnel to return to duty.

SHOULD MILITARY PERSONNEL AND THEIR FAMILIES BE TOLD THE WHOLE TRUTH?

At a state-wide Florida social work conference in Ft. Lauderdale, I was asked if it is really wise to tell active duty personnel and their families the whole truth about war and its impact — especially before or while they are deployed? There was a fear if military personnel knew the full risks of being in combat, it would have a negative impact on them and they might be more likely to have adverse psychological reactions while in the war zone and afterwards.

US military personnel and their families are not, nor have they ever been given such complete information before, during and/or following deployment; hence there is no empirical information to support or counter this concern. However, by long-standing legal precedent in US society participants in research studies are entitled to be fully informed of the potential and actual risks of their participation in a given project; similarly, the nation has long held that consumers are entitled to be fully informed of potential and actual risks in consuming various products such as tobacco and medications.[137] Finally, a patient deserves to be told all of the facts, probabilities and possibilities about his medical condition and prognosis.

Does not this same principle apply to what mental health professionals do and do not convey to military personnel and their families — before, during and after deployment to a war zone? It is of course necessary to provide such information in a way that is not biased— but that is straightforward and complete (and to be available to discuss the meaning and implications of such information).

A more full and complete set of such information is described in this chapter.

OTHER TRAUMA-FOCUS INTERVENTIONS IN THE WAR ZONE

No data has ever been published to show whether common US military psychiatry interventions utilized in a war zone have had any appreciable benefit on the longer-term mental health of military personnel. And yet, as shown in various studies in this chapter, there is considerable evidence that a significant sub-group of war veterans continue to have war-related problems years and decades later. On the other hand, there is data to indicate that there is a benefit to reducing or ameliorating acute or short-term dysfunction while in the war zone. Therefore, it would seem to make sense to consider whether there are trauma-focus intervention protocols available that might be able to have both more immediate and more longer-lasting effects, and to test such protocols in empirically-sound outcome studies.

Trauma-focus protocols that would be realistic to consider providing in a war zone would have as many of the following characteristics as possible:

• Skills to implement the intervention protocol could be learned relatively quickly by a variety of military mental health personnel.

• The intervention protocols or techniques utilized are simple and straightforward.

Such pragmatic trauma-focus protocols could be administered quickly, in one or several sessions.

• Quick positive results would be expected.

---

137. Ironically, the precedent does not seem to be as well established that employers must fully inform potential or actual employees of any risks inherent in their jobs — such as personnel who were working with nuclear testing or who work at chemical plants.

• Empirical outcome data (or, in its absence, substantial positive clinical usage and results) should be gathered to measure the efficacy of the protocol — at least in application to traumas involving civilians.

Trauma-focus protocols that, at first blush, appear to meet many if not all of the above criteria, include: Eye Movement Desensitization and Reprocessing (EMDR); cognitive re-framing; and Traumatic Incident Reduction (TIR). Specific creative applications of cognitive reframing strategies that I have developed with war veterans, although quite relevant and appropriate to apply in a war zone, will be discussed in a later chapter as they also have perhaps even greater applicability to veterans in their post-war recovery. Here, for illustrative purposes, there is a brief description of TIR, and the rationale to encourage consideration of a pilot application of TIR or EMDR in the war zone.

TRAUMATIC INCIDENT REDUCTION (TIR)

TIR is a brief, individually-administered, simple and highly structured method to address painful negative effects of trauma experiences.[138] The core strategy involves having the trauma survivor verbally describe the traumatic incident thoroughly from beginning to end. This process is immediately repeated, time and again, in the same session. Typically, the viewer over a few repeat viewings will become increasingly emotional and will go into more detail about the event, and reach an emotional peak within several repeats (it may take as many as 15 to 20 times). The negative cognitive and emotional reactions will gradually diminish, and then cease. At this "end point," the survivor is able to verbally describe the incident without having any negative emotion about it; instead, he or she is able to come up with new insights about the incident, about him/herself, or about life, and to display some positive emotion or calm in the face of the trauma memory.[139]

---

138. Three articles about TIR: C.R. Figley, J.L. Carbonnel, J.A. Boscarino and J. Chang, "A clinical demonstration model for assessing the effectiveness of therapeutic interventions: an expanded clinical trials methodology." International *Journal of Emergency Mental Health 1* (3) (1999, Summer), 155-164; Valentine, P. and Smith, T.E., "Evaluating Traumatic Incident Reduction Therapy with female inmates: a randomized controlled clinical trial." *Research on Social Work Practice, V 11* (1) (2001, January), 40-52; Valentine, P., "Traumatic Incident Reduction (TIR): a brief trauma treatment." *Crisis Intervention and Time-Limited Treatment, Vol. 4* (1) (1998), 1-12.

139. www.tir.org. Web page of the Traumatic Incident Reduction Association. FAQ for Practitioners Interested in Using TIR & Related Techniques. Accessed on 3.9.04. The originator of TIR is Frank A. Gerbode. See also: G.R. Schiraldi, *The Post-Traumatic Stress Disorder Sourcebook.* (Los Angeles: Lowell House, 2000).

Particularly distinctive in this trauma-focus protocol is the constrained role of the therapist. The client does all of the work. The therapist role essentially is limited to giving appropriate instructions to enable the survivor to view and review the traumatic incident completely and thoroughly from beginning to end and to determine when a successful "end point" has been reached. The therapist is instructed only to ask the survivor to relate the event, then "rewind" the tape and replay it, again and again.

The therapist offers no reactions to what has been verbalized, no interpretations, no suggestions as to what to focus on or emphasize, no advice, and no evaluations as to what has been expressed.

The appropriateness of applying TIR or any other "uncovering" trauma-focus intervention in a war zone is arguable. The TIR Association itself has articulated possible contra-indications that suggest it might not be appropriate to use with armed force members in a war zone. TIR should not be utilized when clients:

- Are psychotic or nearly so.
- Are currently abusing drugs or alcohol.
- Are not making a self-determined choice to do TIR.
- Are in life situations that are too painful or threatening to permit them to concentrate on anything else, such as a TIR session.

TIR further adds that: "If the client is afraid of being murdered, or is preoccupied about the possibility of having cancer, or engaged in constant fighting with the spouse, such issues/situations would have to be addressed first, by in-vivo behavioral interventions or other means, before the client will be ready to do TIR."[140] In other words, some clinical attention would have to be addressed to assess and facilitate whether and how to help the troubled military person to be sufficiently able to concentrate on "viewing" the identified trauma.

CRITICAL INCIDENT DEBRIEFINGS AND THE KUHLMANN GROUP DEBRIEFING MODEL IN THE WAR ZONE

Some military mental health Combat Stress Control personnel in the Iraq war zone are providing debriefing interventions. Critical event or incident debriefings appear to be a primary intervention strategy to defuse acute reactions. Unfortunately, there is almost no empirical data to support the idea that such debriefings, especially one-shot interventions, have any appreciable impact on outcome when compared with a natural process of recovery from such events. Indeed, I am aware of only one controlled study of group debriefing. This was conducted on platoons that had been deployed on peace-keeping missions who

---

140. Ibid.

were randomly assigned to either a CISD debriefing or an information session where stress information was provided, or to a third group that was administered a survey. On the seven outcome measures, those who received the debriefing did not show any difference from the others.

On the other hand, they reported a very high satisfaction level. They liked participating in the CISD.[141] This agrees with my extensive experience as a debriefing facilitator. And the high satisfaction among those who participate in debriefings, such as after 9/11,[142] is mirrored by most of those who provide such debriefings. Debriefers feel that they are very helpful, and intuitively it seems they are. How it could not be better to give people who have been significantly impacted by a critical event a chance to get together, process the events that happened and check the accuracy of their own recollections, share their emotions and bond in the shared grief and acknowledgement process that occurs?

It may be that such debriefings provide benefits that are not measured in the studies. Having significant positive subjective feelings about engaging in debriefings must be an important outcome in it own right.

Of course, there is another possibility: CISD or CED interventions applied in the war zone may be more efficacious than those applied elsewhere. This is my intuitive sense as a Vietnam veteran who also has facilitated numerous CISD interventions over the years. Debriefings in a war zone, such as in the aftermath of the deaths of members of a unit, may play a very special role. Because of the intensity and intimacy of peer relationships in small operational military units, debriefings may promote several critical outcomes: acute grief resolution, acknowledgement and tribute to fallen comrades, enhancement of the peer and peer-command relationships in the small operational unit being debriefed, re-energizing and re-focusing on the mission and promoting increased resolve to persevere in one's duties in spite of the ongoing casualties, and/or increasing the likelihood that participation in a successful debriefing may facilitate some participants to be willing to subsequently seek further counseling. I would argue that critics of debriefings have not attempted to measure almost any of these outcome indicators — or the following.

Perhaps the most crucial outcome is enhanced morale and satisfaction that the military has provided a meaningful opportunity to honor fallen comrades and allow their peers the chance to vent their feelings. High morale is crucial to mil-

141. B.T. Litz, A.B. Adler, C.A. Castro, K. Wright, J. Thomas & M.K. Suvak,. "A controlled trial of group debriefing." In M. Friedman (Chair), *Military psychiatry, then and now.* Plenary session presented at the 20th annual meeting of the International Association of Traumatic Stress Studies annual meeting. New Orleans, LA (2004, November 18).

142. See R.M. Scurfield, J. Viola, K. Platoni and J. Colon, "Continuing psychological aftermath of 9/11: a POPPA experience and critical incident stress debriefing revisited." [POPPA = Police Organization Providing Peer Assistance]. *Traumatology*, 9 (1) (2000, March), 4-30.

itary personnel. Army mental health officers utilizing the Kuhlmann Group Debriefing Model verbally report such positive outcomes.

Kuhlman Group Debriefing Model (KGDM)

The KGDM was developed by LTC David Kuhlman, a career Army social worker, and colleagues. Among other Army mental health personnel, LTC David Rabb MA, LICSW, ACSW, Commander of the 785th Medical Company, Combat Stress Control, Fort Snelling, Minnesota, United State Army Reserves, was active in using and refining this model since 1994 (LTC Rabb provides much of the following information). The model is a didactic sequential group debriefing intervention that assists secondary and tertiary survivors of a traumatic event in coping with the loss of a person(s) due to a sudden death. Secondary and tertiary survivors are primarily those persons who had a close relationship or acquaintance with the person(s) killed but were not immediately present at the time of the death(s) as a result of urban guerilla fighting (ambushes, sniper fire, mortar attacks, suicide boomers, and improvised explosive devices).

The goal of the KGDM is to stabilize group participants by addressing conflict in their cognitive, emotional, physical, and spiritual reactions to a sudden loss, thereby assisting participants to begin to work through the sequelae of the traumatic event. The model recognizes the traditional grieving process model (Elizabeth Kubler-Ross), but draws from a public health approach in addressing the death(s), substituting other ways of coping to get through temporary disequilibrium, and taking action to remember and pay tribute to the person(s) that died.

The KGDM draws on the debriefing phases that are part of the Critical Incident Stress Debriefing (CISD) model designed by Jeffry Mitchell & George Everly, but branches out to engage group participants in paying tribute, honor and respect to the person (s) who have died. It also includes a teaching phase at the beginning of the process that instructs and examines the subjects of grief, loss and bereavement. This teaching phase, and the discussion that ensues, primes participants for subsequent phases and group activities (brainstorming ways to remember the person(s) that died through small storytelling/collective shared memory). The model has been used with groups as small as three participants and as large as 100 participants.

Critical Incident Stress Debriefing	Kuhlmann Group Debriefing Model
Introduction	Introduction
Fact	Teaching
Thought	Purpose
Reaction	Fact

Symptom	Thought
Teaching	Reaction
Reentry	Symptom
Follow-up	Tribute
	Storytelling
	Reentry
	Follow-up

LTC Kathy Platoni describes the usage of the KGDM in OIF and OEF: [143]

It was not an infrequent occurrence for one of our Prevention Teams to be requested and 'dispatched' outside the wire. Never less than an honor to be called to provide for the psychological welfare of combat arms units, we rarely stopped to consider the risk that we assumed in leaving the unsafe havens of our Forward Operating Bases, often under fire and escaping harrowing death by IEDs.

What was always foremost in the minds of those of us assigned to the Al Anbar Province was to assure that our Soldiers did not shoulder alone the burdens of the horrific deaths of their comrades inflicted by an un-uniformed enemy. Rather, our mission was to facilitate through a peer group debriefing the opportunity to help them find solace in one another and to seek closure in the face of tremendous anguish and grief, regardless of numbers of attendees or recommended time constraints. Without such an intervention as the Kuhlmann Debriefing Model, the loss of mission focus remained a serious consideration for all levels of leadership educated to the critical importance of the debriefing process.

Though not in accordance with recommended guidelines, the seat of the insurgency leaves few choices other than to provide whatever CSC services time and level of danger permit. In some cases, a combination of both the traditional and Kuhlmann Debriefing Models were utilized concurrently in order to provide for the "de-escalation" of two groups of soldiers: 1.) those who were at the actual scene at the time of the catastrophic event and thus directly witnessed, observed and/or were engaged in various actions at the scene; and 2.) those who, while not present at the scene, had been seriously impacted by the loss — such as other unit members who had established relationships with those killed in action. [144]

As an example of using the KGDM, under indirect fire and among piles of rubble as the only seating arrangements, in unforgiving heat and for 3 consecutive hours, more than 35 members of an infantry unit involved themselves in a debriefing process. The purpose was to facilitate their de-escalating from the traumatic experience of witnessing first-hand the deaths by incineration of several of their fellow soldiers. Because of the escalating tide of insurgent attacks and rapidly increasing numbers of WIAs (Wounded in Action) and KIAs (Killed in Action) and ongoing military mission demands, it was necessary to combine the two group (those

---

143. Personal communication, May, 2006.
144. Note: some information is omitted in order to protect the confidentiality of the deceased soldiers, their unit and their mission.

directly at the scene and those who were not present) into one combined debriefing.

The debriefing began with (1) introduction: the CSC debriefers introducing themselves, and insuring that all persons present were known to each other; (2) teaching (the Kubler-Ross Model of grief processing and discussing the various ways in which people deal with grief and loss); and (3) purpose: providing a brief description of common reactions and impact of being exposed to deaths of comrades in the war, the purpose of why this debriefing was being conducted and the steps of the debriefing process. Then, (4) facts: those present were given the opportunity to talk about the facts of what happened so that everyone present would be knowledgeable of the information that each member had about the incident and its aftermath, and (5) reflections: for each person present to share whatever they were willing to share with each other about what had happened to them emotionally in terms of the impact of the deaths of these two unit members at the time and/or immediately afterwards, and to express their thoughts and feelings about their experiences of witnessing such trauma and the loss of two peers.

By facilitating graphic descriptions of the manner in which two of their beloved Soldiers lost their lives, as well as the expression of universal tears and expressions of grief for those who were killed, members of this unit were allowed the opportunity to decompress emotionally from this horrific event. Then, (6) symptoms: they were informed of the range of normal emotional and behavioral reactions that they were and might well experience from witnessing such a traumatic event (i.e., strong feelings of grief and/or rage and/or the opposite reaction — maintaining a numbness from feeling their emotions).

The next step was to (7) pay tribute to and acknowledgement of the two comrades-in-arms who had died. Tribute was closely related to the next step (8) storytelling: giving participants the opportunity to each "tell a story" about their experiences of these two soldiers during the time that they had known them. Stories of antics and mischievous behaviors that memorialized the deceased were not only encouraged, but served to celebrate and immortalize the lives that were lost. These two steps facilitated moving beyond expression of pain and loss, to provide more positive acknowledgement and recollection of the qualities and essence of just who these two persons were and how they should be remembered.

There are enormous and longstanding implications for self-care and for facilitating unit members to be able to better take care of themselves through this debriefing process that typically allowed these Soldiers, many of them justifiably consumed with grief, to continue to perform their dangerous missions. This process also facilitated longstanding bonds between infantry Soldiers and debriefers. These bonds would have enormous follow-up and "continuity of care" implications both during the remainder of their deployment, and long past redeployment to CONUS and through the reintegration process. Soldiers who had been involved in the debriefings who were in need of additional mental health attention would be most likely to avail themselves of such counseling with the CSC debriefers that they had bonded with in the war zone. And for others who had not had personal, direct contact with the debriefers, word-of-mouth from their peers got around that these CSC personnel knew what they were doing and were to be trusted.

From February of 2004 until January of 2005, the Kuhlmann Group Debriefing Model was used in Iraq over 30 times to debrief units and workgroups that experienced single or multiple deaths. In addition the model was used with government (Coalition Provisional Authority) and government contract workers who also experienced the hostilities and casualties of war that were inherent on an asymmetrical battlefield where there were no front lines or safe havens.

LTC David Rabb, SFC Timothy Austin and SFC David Patterson of the 785th Medical Company formally presented the KGDM at the 2nd Medical Brigade Professional Development Seminar in April of 2004, Baghdad, Iraq (International Zone). Prior to completing its tour in Iraq, the 785th Medical Company provided the 55th Medical Company with Combat Stress Control instruction and training on the KGDM. The model continued to be used throughout Operation Iraq Freedom.

The Kuhlman Group Debriefing Model has been described as a tool that when used correctly can greatly enhance the support of secondary and tertiary survivors of a traumatic event. It allows

> participants to fully engage the reality of a significant loss and begin the journey of recovering from it. LTC Rabb emphasized that the purpose of this debriefing model with the military is to "try to get people back on the horse, not cure them — it is not a long-term solution."[145]

There are no empirical studies to document the subjective positive impressions of the impact of the Kuhlman Group Debriefing Model. (Nor are there outcome studies of any other therapeutic interventions conducted in any war zone that the US has fought in.) Any or all such outcomes would be of utmost importance to optimal functioning in the war zone to the extent that the critical event debriefing contributes to reducing the possibility of acute pre-occupation with not only the loss and grief of fallen comrades but also with increased anxiety over one's own vulnerability. And the longer-term consequences of such outcomes are speculative in the absence of meaningful longitudinal outcome research. Intuitively, it does not appear that there would be any significant negative longer-term outcomes for promoting such positive short-term outcomes. However, this cannot be assumed without necessary outcome evaluation studies that verify the overall positive subjective impressions among care providers and participants. These are studies that are extremely overdue.

New Treatment Protocols in the War Zone

What further trauma-focus interventions might be useful in a war zone? Are any of the other trauma-focus technologies more or less applicable, such as

---

145. My gratitude to David D. Rabb, commander of the 785th Medical Company, Combat Stress Control, Fort Snelling, MN, US Army Reserves. Col. Rabb gave permission to use this description of the Kuhlmann Group Debriefing Model that he provided to me in July, 2005.

Eye Movement Desensitization and Reprocessing (EMDR)? EMDR also is a cognitive-oriented trauma-focus intervention in which empirical research studies have reported that up to 90% of trauma survivors with single-incident traumatic events show significant relief in as little as three sessions.

EMDR also can quicken the treatment of multiple incidents of trauma, although this oftentimes will take considerably longer.[146] And EMDR would be subject to essentially the same contraindications and limitations that apply to TIR (i.e., not for use with persons who are psychotic or actively using substances). And, quite frankly, it does not appear that any such techniques have been systematically utilized in a war zone.

But what is known about US military mental health as practiced in war-zones in the 20th and 21st centuries is startling:

> US military psychiatry as it has been practiced in war zones offers no scientific evidence that the interventions that it has been using have a positive effect on longer-term (versus acute) mental health of combatants.[147]

Despite the single Israeli study mentioned above that shows a positive differential outcome for Israeli combatants treated close to the front lines in contrast to those medically evacuated and then treated, even this study still reported a very high PTSD rate 20 years later: over 31% among those treated close to the front lines.[148]

Along with outcome studies, it also would seem long overdue to apply creative and trail-blazing treatment protocols to assess whether emerging evidence-based trauma-treatment technologies used with civilian populations may be viable alternative or complementary interventions in a war zone. The risks inherent in instituting treatment technologies that do not have an empirical track record as applied in a war zone are worth taking.

As a conservative alternative, the same treatment protocols could be designed to be provided to psychiatric casualties evacuated out of the war zone, and to military personnel returned from deployment who report continuing or newly arisen serious symptoms and issues related to their deployment. Such interventions could be compared with other mental health interventions provided by military mental health personnel — and with personnel who received no such interventions but had a "natural" course of recovery.

Many skeptics said early on that combining veterans of WW II, Vietnam and the Persian Gulf War together in the same therapy group was ill-advised and would not work because of the generational gaps. Experience has proven

---

146. See, for example: Schiraldi, 2000; F. Shapiro & M.S. Forrest, *EMDR: The Breakthrough Therapy for Overcoming Anxiety, Stress and Trauma.* (New York: Basic Books 1997); M.L. Van Etten & S. Taylor, "Comparative efficacy of treatments for posttraumatic stress disorder: A Meta-Analysis," *Clinical Psychology and Psychotherapy,* 5 (1998), 126-144.
147. David D. Rabb, commander of the 785th Medical Company.
148. Z. Solomon, 2004.

otherwise.[149] Many skeptics contended that helicopter-ride therapy was too dangerous and would not work. Experience has proven otherwise.[150] Many skeptics worried that taking severely physically disabled veterans with PTSD on adventure-based Outward Bound activities was inappropriate and ill-advised. Experience has proven otherwise.[151] Both the VA and the State Department argued that taking veterans with PTSD back to Vietnam was too dangerous. Experience has proven otherwise.[152] What is dangerous and ill-advised is for the government and the nation not to demand that military mental health and the Department of Veterans Affairs implement and evaluate both short and longer-term outcome of new trauma-focus technologies and critical event debriefings both in the war zone and afterwards.

THE DILEMMA, CHALLENGES AND MANDATE

Why not implement and evaluate alternative, additional trauma-focus protocols that could be integrated along with the classic military mental health interventions in a war zone? Can the best impact of the classic military mental health strategies (proximity, immediacy, expectancy and quick return to duty status) be complemented by protocols that offer both more immediate and longer-term resolution of trauma-associated problems? Or, is it better to continue to primarily offer the opportunity for brief venting or expression, or suppressing, avoiding or burying them until sometime after Armed Forces personnel have left the war zone, and to continue to have them simmer or fester for months or years, remain dormant and then possibly erupt years later?

Let us have the two institutions whose missions include protecting and sustaining US Armed Forces and veterans, respectively — the Department of Defense and the Department of Veterans Affairs — become yet more proactive and pro-creative.[153] There is no scientific evidence that US military mental

---

149. A 66-page companion monograph and three-set video were developed at the National Center for PTSD division in Honolulu, HI (1997) documenting the 20-session trauma-focus therapy group with veterans of WWII, Vietnam and the Persian Gulf War. Copies of this video and monograph are available free of charge as long as copies last from the National Center for PTSD, Pacific Islands Division, Honolulu, HI. Contact Allan Perkal: perkman@hawaii.rr.com or 808.383.7877.

150. See Scurfield, R.M., L.E. Wong and E.B. Zeerocah, "Helicopter Ride Therapy For Inpatient Vietnam Veterans With PTSD." *Military Medicine*, 157 (1992), 67-73.

151. See Hyer, L., R.M. Scurfield, S. Boyd, D. Smith & J. Burke, "Effects of Outward Bound Experience As An Adjunct to In-Patient PTSD Treatment of War Veterans," *The Journal of Clinical Psychology*, 52 (3) (1996), 263-278.

152. See *A Vietnam Trilogy*, 2004. Also, see: Stevan Smith, *Two Decades and a Wake-Up*. PBS Documentary (1989).

health as it has been and is being practiced in a war zone works to promote longer-term mental health of combatants. There is scientifically impeccable evidence that too many veterans continue to suffer from exposure to war-related stressors and trauma for decades if not their entire lifetimes. Of course, there is a disturbing possibility: This just may be an inevitable consequence of being in war, regardless of how effective military mental health interventions may be.

In the meantime, military personnel continue to be exposed, and many through repeated deployments, to war-trauma in Iraq and in Afghanistan and elsewhere. Indeed, nearly 400,000 active-duty, National Guard and reserve military personnel have served more than one tour in Iraq or Afghanistan.[154] And this places them at high risk for PTSD or other longer-term mental health consequences — as well as physical health problems.[155] (And how many of these 400,000 or their families been told by the military that they are at increased risk to develop PTSD!)

Finally, for reasons mentioned above, most military personnel in a war zone never actually see a mental health professional for their problems. This is so even when they report the presence of serious problems of traumatic stress, depression or anxiety.[156] Therefore, even if state-of-the-art mental health services are made available in a war zone, they will almost certainly never be actually provided to the vast majority of military personnel who may need such services. This leads to an inescapable conclusion:

Clearly, an appreciable number of post-war psychiatric casualties are an inevitable outcome of participating in a war.

Even so, for those who are actually seen and treated in a war zone, the implementation of a trauma-focus treatment protocol research project that includes tracking of both short-term and longer-term mental health outcome is many wars overdue.

Until some such level and scope of endeavor is conducted, the military forces, veterans, their families and communities, and the mental health professions, will continue to be in the dark as to the actual impact of military psy-

---

153. The VA National Center for PTSD has developed an *Iraq War Clinician Guide* (2003) that is available on CD and on the Center's website [*www.ncptsd.org/war/guide/index.html*]. The *Guide* contains a wide range of information, including assessment guidelines, treatment of the returning Iraq War veteran, treatment of medical casualty evacuees, military sexual trauma, traumatic grief, and educational materials for veterans and their families. The *Guide* is intended to help VA providers understand the unique circumstances of the war and to prepare them to handle casualties that entered the VA system.

154. L. Chedekel and M. Kauffman, "Emotional wounds don't end their war. Troubled troops are back in battle." *www.sunherald.com* (2006, May 18), B4.

155. M. Elias, "Stress disorder linked to soldier's ill health." USA Today (2006, May 22). Accessed on-line May 24, 2006.

156. See, for example: Burns, 2004; and Hoge et al, 2004.

chiatry interventions on the mental health of Armed Forces personnel. Unanswered questions that beg to be answered through scientific study include:

• What specific treatment protocols offer short-term relief in a war zone?

• What specific treatment protocols provided in a war zone offer longer-term relief or indeed preventive effects?

• What is the true and full human cost of war?

• What funding and programs are required to meet society's obligations to the millions of servicemen and women that this country continues to put in harm's way?

A rationale and recommendations for a research project to test new trauma treatment protocols for long-term impact on veterans' psychological and social health is outlined in Appendix II. The nation must make it a priority to address this tragedy. There is still no valid data to indicate the true long-term impact of mental health strategies and efforts made *during* war on armed forces personnel *following* the war.

And yet major research findings indicate that:

> Exposure to war continues to be injurious to the mental health of at least about one in every six members (and perhaps up to one-third) of the armed forces in a war zone, and such negatively impacted mental health and accompanying physical health continues over years or decades.[157]

In summary, many veterans are not getting the help that they need. No matter how meaningful military mental health treatments might be in a war zone, many members of the armed forces will not go to see them, and large numbers of armed forces personnel will suffer serious mental health problems for decades. War is injurious to not only the physical but also the mental health of many of those who participate in it.

All of the preceding discussion relates to helping military personnel with the wide range of deployment-related stressors and adjustments necessary while they are still deployed overseas. Still, afterward there is an enduring legacy for a high proportion of war veterans — war-related issues of blame, guilt and shame. These enduring issues are addressed in a following chapter. This is one of the most prevalent and troubling war-related issue that continues to plague military personnel.

---

157. See Cozza, 2005; Kulka at al, 1990; and Solomon and associates, 2004.

Chapter 4. The Return Home and the Ricochet Effect on the Family [158]

What should we say and do when the deployment ends and the combat veteran returns home? Returning home, and the first several weeks and months back in particular, is a critical juncture in the lives of returning military personnel and their families. The challenges in readjustment from a war zone to the family and civilian world, and the typical delay in the emergence of war-related and readjustment psychiatric symptoms, led one Iraq veteran to say:

> Like a live grenade. They throw you out in civilian life and say you're now a civilian and thanks for the service.[159]

Sean Huze, Marine corporal awaiting discharge at Camp Lejuene, N.C., says that everyone who saw combat suffers from at least combat stress due to the unrelenting insurgent threat that requires constant vigilance and a numbing of the senses and emotions:

> I saw a dead child, probably 3 or 4 years old. Lying on the road in Nasiriyah. It moved me less than if I saw a dead dog at the time. I didn't care. Then you come back home, if you are fortunate enough, and hold your own child, and you think of the dead child you didn't care about . . .
>
> You think about how little you cared at the time, and it hurts. [160]

---

158. The inspiration for the chapter title, "the ricochet effect," comes from an article by Elliot Blair Smith, "Deaths in combat ricochet here at home." Cover Story, *USA Today* (2004, December 1), 1A, 6A-7A.
159. P. Zahn, "Paula Zahn Now. Family of Soldiers." (2004, June 30). Accessed on-line 3.2.06: CNN International.Com.Transcripts
160. William Welch, "Trauma of Iraq war haunting thousands returning home." *USA Today* (2005, February 28), 6A.

The return from deployment never is simply a "welcome home, we missed you, and now we can pick up right where our lives were before you went to the war." War has far too great an effect and the gap left in the family during deployment is much too deep.

> It may be impossible . . . to fully counteract the shock of going from a 24-hour state of generalized fear-apprehension-paranoia, sustained for a year through wartime, to evenings at home on the La-Z-Boy, [and being] asked to fulfill the requirements of love and tenderness to sustain a family.[161]

A dramatic instance of a problematic readjustment occurred in the summer of 2002. Five soldiers at Fort Bragg murdered their spouses following their return from Afghanistan, and two of those soldiers subsequently committed suicide.

Following an investigation, the Army concluded that the murders could not be totally (nor perhaps even primarily) attributed to problems that these soldiers brought back with them as a result of their very recent deployment to a war zone. Nevertheless after the Fort Bragg murders the Army revamped its entire program of pre-deployment screenings and educational classes and its post-deployment "decompression training" program. This was a very welcome step. The changes included much more thorough medical and mental health screenings prior to deployment, classes on suicide prevention and dealing with depression, tips on adjusting to family life before re-deployment and then following the return from deployment. Some soldiers feel the classes are repetitive and have nicknamed them the "don't beat your wife class," but others find it useful. [162]

A perhaps insurmountable difficulty is that many soldiers don't see the relevance of information being presented because they are too focused on getting home as quickly as they can. Another problem is that most National Guard and Reserve soldiers return home and have relatively little interaction with other soldiers and may be even more likely to isolate and feel as if they are the only ones having readjustment difficulties.[163]

The back into civilian life is colored by the accumulated stress and anger that is infused in many war veterans. One Iraq veteran revealed how impacting various war zone stressors can be.

> We never really know what was going on. We were told, "We're here to do good, to help Iraqis; they want us here!" And we know that's just pep talk from politicians — a bunch of professional liars . . . Everything in Iraq pissed me off. That included extended deployment, the smell of raw sewage dumped outside doors, friends' endless "Dear John" letters, unpalatable rations . . . body armor that weighed 70 pounds in 130 degree heat, orders to knock in doors of Iraqi families

---

161. Corbett, 2004, 56.
162. L. Kipling, February 7, 2005.
163. Ibid.

based on suspect "intelligence." You never knew if the guy was innocent or not, and half the time he was.[164]

Indeed, mental health experts at the Department of Veterans Affairs and the Army have stated that there is reason to believe that the Iraq War's ultimate psychological impact will be much more than was shown in early projections. This lack of optimism is based on the results of a survey conducted within a few days of return from deployment; but it differs markedly from the results of a second survey conducted 3-4 months later. In the earlier survey, only 3% of returned soldiers indicated that they had a mental health problem or concern. However, by the time of the later survey only a few months later, the number had jumped to 13-17 percent.[165] And the most recent survey of Iraq and Afghanistan veterans seen at VA hospitals reported that as many as one in four treated in the past 16 months were diagnosed with mental disorders — a number that has been steadily rising.[166] These survey results confirm that the acute psychiatric casualty rates that are measured in the Iraq war zone, like during the Vietnam War, are substantially lower than the post-war psychiatric casualty rates. There is a delay in the onset of the symptoms or in the veteran's ability or willingness to admit that such exist and seek help — if ever.

And what about those who are wounded? Due to newly developed medical techniques on the battlefield and after,[167] an unprecedented number of wounded, some 90%, are now surviving their injuries.[168] That is the good news. The bad news is that many such surviving veterans have sustained injuries and disabilities that will have long-lasting negative impact on such factors as the "veterans' quality of life, marital adjustment, vocational opportunities, self-image, outlook with regard to the future, and mental health."[169] Furthermore, veterans with war-incurred injuries are among the highest risk group for developing PTSD.[170]

---

164. M.L. Lytle, "The unseen cost of war. American Minds. Soldiers can sustain psychological wounds for a lifetime." Seattle Post-Intelligencer Reporter (2004, August 28). Retrieved from the web, 3.9.05.

165. Esther Schrader, "Iraq War vets to get follow-up mental evaluations." *Los Angeles Times* (2005, January 28). Accessed from the web. 1.28.05

166. Marilyn Elias, "Mental disorders are on the rise among Afghanistan, Iraq veterans." *USA Today* (2005, March 31), A1. Figures are quoted from: Han K. Kang and Kenneth C Hyams, "Mental health care needs among recent war veterans." *New England Journal of Medicine*, Vol. 352: 1289, No. 13 (2005, March 31).

167. G. Zoroya, "Lifesaving knowledge, innovation emerge from war's deadly violence." *USA Today* (2006, March 27), 1A, 4-5A.

168. A. Gawande, "Casualties of war—military care for the wounded from Iraq and Afghanistan." *New England Journal of Medicine*, 351 (2004), 2471-5,

169. M.J. Friedman, "Veterans' mental health in the wake of war." *New England Journal of Medicine*, 235 (13) (2005), 1287, 11288, 1290.

Finally, while there is little data yet to substantiate the concern expressed by many experts that National Guard and Reserve personnel are at a higher risk to develop post-war problems than their regular military counterparts, there is such data from the Persian Gulf War. Factors considered include: 1.) They are not as thoroughly inculcated with and integrated into the military culture and military base community; 2.) They did not volunteer for and perhaps were not nearly as ready to engage in full-time service much less active duty 3.) Consequently, there is a much more severe disruption of family life and civilian careers.[171]

And the vast majority of Americans deployed to the Persian Gulf faced less exposure to combat stressors, and much shorter deployment rotations than many Guard and Reserve personnel have been to Iraq and Afghanistan. And almost none were re-deployed back into combat conditions.

All of these factors are extremely sobering and strongly indicate that this country should be very concerned that the psychological and social impact of the war on Iraq and Afghanistan veterans and perhaps particularly so among those in the National Guard and Reserves.

TRUTHS THAT NEED TO BE TOLD

US armed forces personnel and their families and communities need to understand what happens to people who survive war — both the immediate and the longer-term impact, both the good and the bad. The government, military and mental health professionals are reluctant to alert the public to the negative ramifications of common war-zone survival modes that can hamper the re-adjustment to civilian life, and for good reason. This means getting closer to acknowledging the whole truth about the full and continuing human cost of war.

All who serve in war, whether or not they are or were psychiatric casualties, and their families and communities, need to be told this, verbally and in writing, at least several times and not just once, and in a way that promotes discussion and understanding:

> After the war you may continue to use or be invested, to a little or to a great degree, in the survival skills, attitudes, behaviors, that worked to help you survive during

170. Schlenger, WE, Kulka, RA, Fairbank, JA et al, "The prevalence of post-traumatic stress disorder in the Vietnam generation: a multimethod, multisource assessment of psychiatric disorder." *Journal of Traumatic Stress*, 5 (1992), 333-363.

171. M.J. Friedman, 2005, 1290; and Kang, HK, Natelsosn, BH, Mahan, CM, Lee, KY, Murphy, FM, "Post-traumatic stress disorder and chronic fatigue syndrome-like illness among Gulf War veterans: a population-based survey of 30,000 veterans." *American Journal of Epidemiology*, 157 (2003), 141-148.

deployment; however, many of these are probably not appropriate to your post-war life. For example, while denial, detachment and numbing work very well in a war zone, it can be very difficult to turn the detachment off after leaving the war zone — partly as a way to continue to anesthetize yourself from the painful and recurring horrific memories about death and injury during the war that stay with you.

After returning from the war, for several good reasons you may find yourself not wanting to let go of the "survival mode" that you developed during the war. Firstly, it is familiar, like an old companion that you're comfortable having around or are pretty good at doing. Also, it continues to get you some of the things that you may want: some power, some aliveness, the adrenaline rush, feelings of security or safety.

It is difficult to let go of things that you are familiar with, and that you have been doing for a long time. What would you put in its place? If you have been "running on empty", or have been keeping yourself so busy to avoid painful submerged memories and you let go of the survival mode, that emptiness or those painful memories will rise to the surface, something that perhaps you have kept submerged or have avoided admitting to yourself all these months or years.

You have to recognize if and when you find yourself not being able to "let go" of your war zone survival mode. If you do recognize this in yourself, or you are being told this by loved ones or close friends, and you find yourself unable to do something about it on your own, you need to talk to someone about it. If you are still on active duty, this could be for example with a military mental health professional if you are comfortable doing that, or with a counselor at a military family service agency or with a military chaplain. If you have been discharged from active duty to veteran status, you can go to a VA Vet Center or a specialized VA PTSD program such as a PTSD Clinical Team, or to the OEF/OIF Coordinator at the local VA Hospital or to a Veterans Service Organization officer who may be able to point you in the right direction. But staying isolated and non-communicative will do nothing positive about the problem.

WARNING SIGNS

There are a number of the signs that strongly suggest that the imprint of the war and the transition back home is continuing to plague the returned soldier (assuming, of course, that none of the following were present *prior* to deployment; otherwise, it cannot be presumed that it was the deployment experience that is the "cause," although it may have aggravated or exacerbated pre-existing conditions):

• During waking hours having vivid, repeated painful and unwanted memories about the war.

• Continuing sleep disturbance if not insomnia, and typically disturbing or painful nightmares.

• Being or staying isolated.

• Considerable difficulty concentrating, not remembering things, being unorganized, seemingly not being able to "get it together."

- Being or staying detached and aloof or "distant" emotionally, even if you are around others.
- Unable to feel or express appropriate emotions like others can do, such as not being able to cry at something really sad; conversely, overreacting emotionally and having mood-swings.
- Staying constantly "on alert"; being hyper-vigilant about scanning the environment.
- Having continued marked startle responses to being approached or touched suddenly.
- Guilt at not having suffered like others or at decisions or actions made while in the war zone that may have had catastrophic consequences
- Being profoundly bored with normal living, continually looking for that adrenaline rush and/or possibly exposing yourself and/or your family to unnecessary risks.
- Feeling that life is aimless or has little or no worthwhile meaning and perhaps yearning to be back in the war.

As one Iraq vet said:

> I miss it. At least there was a purpose. I wish I was in Iraq because my buddies are there. [172]

- Becoming or continuing to be very preoccupied with bitter feelings and thoughts towards the government or towards society about broken promises, how they have mistreated or ignored veterans or concerned that they might do the same to you.[173]

This can become a "me-against-the-world mistrust of what's to come, an indistinct but entirely accurate perception that this country has failed veterans of past wars. The war will stay with them, but after a point the Army won't."[174]

- Being confused, pessimistic, angry about your lot in life and seeing only dim prospects of any positive changes in the future.

---

172. Corbett, 2004, 38.

173. For example, many veterans are very aware that while the government boasts it has boosted for the Department of Veterans Affairs in 2004 by $1.9 billion, the government neglects to inform the citizenry that due to an increasingly older veteran population with increased health care needs, and more and more veterans being killed (thus increasing survivor benefit payments to widows/widowers and their children) and wounded in Iraq and even still in Afghanistan, that the VA budget falls considerably short of the $3.1 billion increase the House Veterans Affairs Committee said in February, 2004, was needed just to maintain the current level of services and benefits! It is this kind of double-speak that generates more distrust and rage. Editorial, *Sun Herald*, Biloxi, MS (2004, December 6), B2.

174. Corbett, 2004, 38.

TRIGGERS

There are a number of common triggers that provoke trauma survivors and war-veterans to have surges of unwanted, vivid and troubling memories. Some service personnel will find themselves reacting with marked detachment and isolation. Others will find themselves reacting very strongly to any of the following:

• Sights, sounds, smells, physical circumstances similar/reminiscent of those experienced in the war zone, such as being in an environment similar to war zone destruction — like the aftermath of Hurricane Katrina.[175]

• Strong emotional states similar to those experienced during deployment, e.g., rage, grief, fear, adrenalin rush.

• Subsequent repeated or new exposure to any trauma by you or your significant others, to include being victims of racism, sexism, sudden poverty....[176]

• Anniversary dates or other significant time anchors such as holidays, birthdays, times of the year that are associated with particular events in the war zone.

• Season of the year, weather, climate, terrain reminiscent of duty or catastrophic events in the war zone

• Media coverage of the war, terrorist acts, or other major traumatic incidents (that may or may not resemble in some way the original trauma during the war)

• Theater and television movies that have scenes or themes reminiscent of events that happened in the war zone.

• Music — lyrics and/or melodies that are particularly evocative of or somehow related to the time of the trauma or its aftermath. [177]

• Experiences of loss — divorce, separation, death of significant others, loss of job, sudden geographic relocation, loss of body parts or bodily functions, impending death.

• Contacts or conflicts with authorities: medical, clinical, governmental, religious, job supervisors (which may bring back memories of conflicts or issues with military commanders or other military authorities).

---

175. Discussed in the Afterword of this book. See also R.M . Scurfield, "Post-Katrina aftermath and helpful interventions on the Mississippi Gulf Coast," Traumatology, Vol. 12 (2), in-press, Summer, 2006.

176. For example, VFW officials in 1994 reported a significant increase in disability claims from World War II veterans, whose nightmares were dramatically revived by all of the media coverage surrounding the 50th Anniversary of D-Day. Corbett, p. 40.

177. Thanks to my good friend Angelo Romeo for reminding me of the power of certain songs. For Angelo it is the Beatle's "Hey Jude"—a song that I also found particularly evocative of melancholy states I found myself in while stationed in Vietnam.

WAR SURVIVAL STRATEGIES THAT MAY BE BROUGHT HOME

> I had the misfortune to have a mental breakdown three years ago and as part of that healing process, discovered that my service and my cousin's services to this country were full of soul-rendering terror. I now remember sitting on the back steps at our house in Texas and listening to my cousin, "Dub," wake up the neighborhood with his screaming. I could not imagine what was causing his blood-curdling screams. Somehow along the way, Dub and I both managed to put up a wall around this issue.
>
> There is nothing honorable in killing. Nothing is as horrible as the inner soul-rendering scream that comes with the first time. Then the numbness comes to silence it. Numbness is a narcotic to the soul. Numbness takes over your life and has a death grip on you until (if) you finally reach a point of total security with being home among family and friends. There is nothing to glorify what we do in war. [178]

To assist the returning and returned war-veterans, their families, friends and community to better understand why so many returned veterans may be acting and thinking the way they are, the following additional information about survival modes in a war zone can be very helpful. Just when such information might best be provided is open to consideration. Since these points have been described in detail in vol. 1 of *A Vietnam Trilogy*, they will only be briefly identified here, with the addition of a description of the potential negative ramifications of each survival strategy on Iraq and Afghanistan veterans who return from deployment.

Fight or Flight

You meet and engage the enemy, destroying or repelling them. Alternatively, in the face of overwhelming odds, you choose to strategically retreat to fight another day. These are the two classic and instinctual survival strategies that human beings have used over the millennia.

There is a potential downside. Some vets, after they have left the war zone or even while still there, have found themselves plagued with feelings of guilt, shame, grief or unremitting rage over what they had to do to survive. And so this may be bothering you now, and/or it may come back to haunt you months or years from now.

Detachment, Numbing and Denial

You learn how to protect yourself against the horrors of what you are witnessing and you do so by convincing yourself that "it doesn't matter," no matter

---

178. J.P. McDonald, Letter to the Editor, *The SunHerald*, Biloxi, MS (2004, November 12), D-2.

what happens. You learn to anesthetize yourself to not feel what otherwise would be overwhelming — anxiety, fear, shock, horror, depression, loss, grief.

On the downside, you may get so good at detachment, denial and emotional numbing that you take this with you back to the civilian world. For example, some family members have described their veteran family member as not able to show or perhaps even feel normal emotions like everyone else and have complained that their veteran family member is emotionally inaccessible.

Tunnel Vision

You learn how to maintain an intense, focused, full attention to complete a particular task and become oblivious to whatever else is going on. You learn to focus all of your energies and attention on completing the immediate task or objective — to the exclusion of every thing else.

This can be a good skill and attitude to take home with you. You may find that tunnel vision helps you to get through tough times in civilian life. Conversely, you may find that tunnel vision has become second nature and you have great difficulty or find it impossible to ever turn it off. And this can be devastating to relationships and the ability to enjoy life fully.

External Discharging of Emotions

Finding an outlet for the inevitable cumulative build-up of stress, frustration, grief, fear and rage that are inevitable in a war zone is crucial to surviving. The pent-up emotions demand an outlet. Typically, this is actualized through rage towards the enemy, which can be very functional, but it can also fuel an internal anger and resolve to persevere.

Even during the war, there may be few opportunities to discharge such pent-up emotions — especially in a war against a non-uniformed enemy. Then your rage can erupt unexpectedly, possibly towards innocent or apparently innocent civilians, and even towards other Americans. These emotions have to go somewhere. If they not expressed outwardly, you may well redirect such feelings inwardly. And you can carry this home with you, and find it very difficult to share what is going on with you with your family members. It might continue to build up and then you explode in anger, frustration or grief. Or, you may isolate in an attempt to avoid having your deep emotions and memories triggered or to prevent venting your emotions against others.

Comparing Traumas

It can be functional short-term to compare what you are going or went through with others and realize that your experiences are not so terrible; this can be an excellent temporary strategy to help you get through what you need to get through and not dwell on it.

Conversely, if this becomes a chronic and exaggerated post-trauma response, you can become (1) bitter, dismayed or depressed that you suffered much more than many others did, or (2) decide that your trauma experiences are not as terrible as others'. In this latter scenario, you may:

- Deny that you are entitled to the negative or troubling reactions that you are having and you become very self-critical at your own "weakness," or
- Not allow yourself the right to feel how you are feeling about what you went through, or
- Feel guilty that you are having such negative feelings because "your trauma was nothing compared to so many others."

All of these are no-win propositions. Each person's traumatic experience was his or her traumatic experience, period. It was and is meaningful to that person and to compare different people's traumas is not fair to anyone.

Belief in Fate/Randomness/Higher Power

Many military personnel rely on their long-standing faith in a higher power or Supreme Being to sustain them through the horrors of war. Others find their faith and beliefs severely challenged or decimated when they come face-to-face with the horrors and inhumanity and Catch-22 conundrum: having to kill in order to save the lives of self and others.

The first question that some soldiers ask after something bad has happened is, "Why me, God?" Or, "Why did this have to happen to ___, God?" And other soldiers will ask: "Why me, God", and "There is a God and I need to reconnect."

Also, there is the issue of morality in a war zone. While chaplains are a source of great comfort and counsel to many active duty personnel, their primary mission essentially is the same as that of the mental health staff — to preserve the fighting strength. Many vets perceive a conflict in the chaplains' blessing US troops to kill and emphasizing that "God is on our side," when obviously the enemy is saying and believing the same thing.[179] And some may ask, how could there be a God or higher power who would allow people, and you, to do what they and you do to each other during war? And you may carry such issues back home.

---

179. Frank and realistic dialogue is absolutely necessary to address such real, not just imagined, conflicts in a war-zone — and such dialogue may well have to go beyond private 1-1 conversations and occur in the very circle that is the sustaining life-blood of military combatants — in the small unit peer group. For a more detailed discussion of the conflicts between faith and behavior in a war-zone, see in *A Vietnam Trilogy*, 2004.

PROBLEMATIC WAR SURVIVAL STRATEGIES THAT MAY BE BROUGHT HOME

There are additional survival modes that can be very or at least somewhat helpful in getting through the immediacy of the dangers and stressors of war. However, they almost always have a big down side when it comes to post-war behaviors, mental health, happiness or positive readjustment. Each will be briefly mentioned here.[180]

Rage

If any feelings are allowed to emerge, they are likely to be the one emotion conducive to survival in the war zone — rage; and it is best directed at the enemy. Unfortunately, this is extremely difficult to do for personnel whose role does not entail firing on the enemy, or in a guerilla war or a war fought by terrorists or insurgents, who do not present an easy target and who often cannot be distinguished from civilians. And thus one can become increasingly agitated and frustrated, if not undependable and unstable, or prone to taking inappropriate action against others when there is no appropriate target to attack. And this can result in a generalized anger if not rage against the civilian population (as described next). And military personnel can take these unsatisfied, pent-up rages, impulsive and other inappropriate behaviors home with them.

Dehumanizing the Enemy

Training for war inculcates the new recruit in the classic detachment strategy — dehumanize the enemy. "They are not human beings like we are; they are horrible, evil, heartless, immoral." And racism and ethnocentrism are key dehumanizing strategies.

One Iraq veteran described how what happened to Vietnam veterans parallels what is now happening in Iraq, beginning with the realization that the original mission or justification given for the war proved to be false.

> There was a progression of thought that happened among soldiers in Vietnam. It started with a mission [in Vietnam]: contain Communism. That mission fell apart, just like it fell apart now — there are no weapons of mass destruction. Then you are left with just a survival instinct. That, unfortunately, turned to racism. That's happening now, too. Guys are writing me saying, "I don't know why I'm here, but I hate the Iraqis."[181]

It is much easier to seek out and kill an enemy who seems "less human" rather than an enemy who is regarded as a good person, an honorable adversary fighting for a just cause. You can become cut-throat, cold, uncaring and may gen-

---

180. Discussed in depth in *A Vietnam Trilogy*, 2004.
181. Goan, 2004, 58.

eralize this towards the civilian population as well. And you can carry this denigrating attitude with you for a very long time. I have met a number of World War II veterans who still have a vitriolic hatred towards the Japanese or the Germans — any Japanese or Germans. And I continue to meet too many Vietnam veterans who hate the Vietnamese, any Vietnamese. And this hatred inevitably seeps into and contaminates their attitudes about others, and about life.

Isolating

Isolating oneself from others, not letting anyone get close emotionally, is another common way to promote detachment. The remarkable bonding that occurs among brother and sister soldiers in a war zone is a two-edged sword. It helps you to survive the otherwise un-survivable. On the other hand, when you lose or have a close comrade maimed, it can be devastating. Thus, many soldiers decide not to let anyone get too close. When they carry this attitude home, some vets only want to be around other vets because they find that they cannot feel comfortable with anyone else. Still other vets find themselves avoiding any meaningful discussions or interactions with other veterans, because it brings back too many disturbing memories and too much pain.

Drinkin' and Druggin'

Substance use and abuse are two of the most common tactics for fighting men and women to achieve detachment and relief — and the military historically has made cheap or even free alcohol readily available. To compound this problem, there is an unmatched ingenuity and enterprise in the military for armed forces personnel to procure or manufacture intoxicating substances — even in the middle of nowhere. Many vets who entered the war zone with substance use problems leave with a bigger problem, and many who did not have a substance-abuse problem before the war develop a problem during deployment. And even if they "kick" the habit back home, they may revert to it, especially when things get rough.

Risk-Taking/Thrill/Sex Addiction

It is not uncommon for military personnel in a war zone to become "addicted" physiologically, psychologically and behaviorally to the thrill, the risk, the danger, the adrenaline rush. And sex is always available in a war zone. Sex with local civilians can be bought; or the intensity and loneliness of life in the war zone will spark sexual encounters that are mutually sought — or forced. Some become action junkies, as intense activity can be a powerful elixir; it can also lead to increasingly dangerous attitudes and behaviors. And the craving for this rush becomes extremely difficult to turn off when returning to civilian life.

However, some manage to constructively sublimate the adrenalin habit through successful post-war employment in high-risk, high-thrill occupations and jobs such as emergency medical services, fire and rescue, law enforcement, off-shore and oil pipeline work, and contract positions in support of military operations. Conversely, others satisfy the risk/thrill/sex addiction craving by constantly looking for unsafe high-risk behaviors and/or stay immersed in memories and feelings about war and danger.

As an example of dangerous risk-taking, an alarming number of returned Iraq Army and Marine veterans have been killed in single-occupant vehicle accidents.

> We absolutely have a problem . . . The kids come back and they want to live life to its fullest, to its wildest. They get a little bit of time to let their hair down, and they let their hair all the way down and do everything to excess. They drink to excess. They eat to excess. They party to excess. And then, some drive . . . They want something that goes fast and keeps that high up they had during the war . . . speed fills some indescribable urge for excitement that they've felt since returning from war . . . Going fast is like a drug — the newest crack out there.[182]

Bizarre or Gallows Humor

In the midst of horror and chaos, resorting to what otherwise would be seen as gross or inappropriate humor can be at least a partial antidote to the relentless horrors of war.

> Hey, John: We have an extra leg here. Let's throw it in and give this here guy a third leg — that'll give the body handlers stateside a little surprise when they open up the body bag.

> [This type of joke] helps to stop you from crying, or becoming overwhelmed by what you're facing day after day after day. Instead, you can get a deep belly laugh, a moment of absurdly hilarious respite, a closeness of comradeship with the only people who could possibly get it or tolerate such humor — your war buddies.

Of course, this provides only a very temporary respite; it doesn't erase the horror from your mind or from your heart. And, you can carry that bizarre humor back home with you in either a positive or negative way. Positively, you may be able to have an irreverent attitude, an enjoyable or refreshingly unexpected or amusingly sarcastic or humorous attitude that at least some others may find to be a welcome respite, especially during tough times. Or, you can develop a

---

182. From October 2003 to September 2004, when troops first returned in large numbers from Iraq, 132 soldiers died in vehicle accidents, a 28% jump from the previous 12 months. Two-thirds of them were veterans of Iraq or Afghanistan. And there was a 23% increase in deaths from vehicle accidents in the past seven months. Gregg Zoroya, "Survivors of war take fatal risks on roads." *USA Today* (2005, May 2). Accessed on-line 5.2.2005.

harshly pejorative, insulting, callous attitude, and you can behave inappropriately towards others.

The Returned War Veteran Who Detaches From or Rejects the Family

One of the common dynamics between combat veterans and their family is that that a number of veterans seemingly rejects distance or detach themselves from their families. It happened with Vietnam veterans, and it is happening with Iraq veterans. And I had numerous people approach me after I have given a presentation and tell me that their World War II or Korean War veteran was very distant emotionally after the war.

This first illustration is an excerpt from a clinical session with Mario, a Vietnam veteran. (Irene Powch, clinical psychologist, was a co-therapist in the session.) [183]

Mario: Every time I get flashes [of war] or nightmares, the [Vietnamese] people. I think of my family [who are Filipino-American]. We look like Vietnamese, you know. I can look at my mom and my dad, I can see Vietnamese people that I killed, or I roughed up plenty. I see all that, I don't know what's going on.

Ray: Does it surprise you, you're seeing all this now?

Mario: I . . . think that these things wouldn't come up, I never thought it would . . . I thought I had everything in control . . . but I don't have nothing in control. You can only control so much. You cannot control what's in your head. I tried so hard to control what's in my head. Maybe I tried too hard . . . it just goes, it just comes out . . .

Later in the session

Mario: It's like being back in Vietnam. You're one less person to help another guy. I look at other people [today] as being back in Vietnam . . . I don't want to jeopardize anybody.

Irene:[184] Who are you worried about jeopardizing now, not in Vietnam?

Mario: I don't know. I just don't want to jeopardize anyone.

---

183. Bill Kilauano, peer counselor, was the third co-facilitator in this group. This clinical vignette is from a trauma-focus therapy group session with six combat veterans of World War II, Vietnam and the Persian Gulf War. See *A Healing Journey* video (1997). Honolulu: Department of Veterans Affairs, Pacific Islands Division, National Center for PTSD. This video is available free of charge to helping persons who work with veterans while supplies last; contact Allan Perkal at perkman@hawaii.rr.com or 808.383-7877..

184. Irene Powch, clinical psychologist, now at the Portland VA, was a co-facilitator for the group sessions.

Ray: Are you worried about jeopardizing your family?

Mario: NO! [very angry]. NO. I DON'T GIVE A SH-- FOR THEM! I DON'T GIVE A SH-- FOR MY FAMILY. Why does everybody talk about the family! After Vietnam, I did not give --- about my family. They call me up, ask me how I'm doing? I tell them ... why, I don't want to talk to you guys.

Ray: What's the anger about your family?

Mario: I don't want nobody being close to me. I kept that all the way through [in Vietnam]. I didn't want to be close to nobody. I don't want nobody crying over me. Believe me, I don't want that.

Ray: So, that's the issue — you don't want anyone *close* to you? And your family would be the ones who could [become close] . . .

Mario: No [agreeing with me], I don't want nobody close to me. They tried their best. If you could see what they try to do for me.

Ray: Why wouldn't they?

Mario: I know they care. Inside. I know they care, but I don't want it.

Irene: What feels bad about it?

Mario: What?

Irene: What feels bad about it?

Mario: I don't know. Feels like begging. I don't want people thinking I'm begging for their help. It's like being in Vietnam. You don't beg ... I never beg.

Expressing and receiving emotional closeness with others was not what most soldiers did to get through the war. And many vets continue to feel very uncomfortable or strange with expressing or receiving emotional closeness after they're back home.

Another major problem for veterans who have returned from deployment is that their minds often are back in the war zone. The following vignette describes a returned Iraq veteran and his wife.

> At night, in the quiet of their rented farmhouse, Robert Shrode lets Debra pick the shrapnel out of his body. Over the last six months, she's tugged out 15 pieces as they have worked their way to the surface of his skin. She has picked them from his legs, his face. Sometimes he will study them, these twisted aluminum chunks that have managed to escape while so many more will forever live inside him.

> Barely out of her teenage years, Debra Shrode never pictured her life this way. Never imagined the Army would be calling her up and asking her to hand out advice as some kind of expert wife. Yet someone from the Army's Family Readiness Group wanted her to call another wife whose husband had come home injured. She sighs and dials the number. "I don't know what I can say to make you feel better," she says into the phone. "If he doesn't want to talk, don't take it to heart."

She adds each new piece of shrapnel to the collection they keep stored in a Tupperware container. For awhile, the container sat on their coffee table, but recently Robert moved it into a spare bedroom drawer.

If it seems as if he might be moving on, Debra has only to ask, "What're you thinking about?" "Iraq," he'll say. And then the silence falls again.[185]

"As if by ricochet," each American serviceman and woman killed, wounded or disabled in combat leaves behind a trail of secondary casualties: spouses, children, parents and grandparents, siblings, and friends. As of November 20, 2004, 45% of the 1,374 US service personnel killed in Iraq and Afghanistan since September 2001, were married.[186] Over 18,000 US military personnel have been wounded or disabled as of July, 2006.[187] The toll of casualties continues to rise daily.

And this does not include the readjustment problems for the family members of personnel who were killed or maimed or psychiatrically impaired. Spouses have described how the war tore apart their families.[188] Comments like "he wasn't [still] in Iraq, but in his mind he was there day in and day out," and "he'd never discuss the details of his experiences in Iraq, but they changed him forever," have been heard time and time again.

---

185. Corbett, 2004, p. 66.
186. Elliot Blair Smith, "Deaths in combat ricochet here at home." Cover Story, *USA Today* (2004, December 1), 1A, 6A-7A. See also Dave Moniz, "Monthly death toll reaches record set in April." *USA Today* (2004, December 1), 15A.
187. United States Casualties, Iraq and Afghanistan. Accessed on-line: Iraq Coalition Casualty Count. August 4, 2006
188. Kimberly Hefling, "Army seeks to save marriages torn apart by war." *SunHerald*, Biloxi, MS (2004, December 3), B1.

UNSPOKEN ISSUES THAT THE FAMILIES MAY HAVE

So far, we have focused mainly on the returned veteran. How about the family dynamics[189] while the active duty member is deployed? Often there is a sense of:

• Anger, resentment or fear that the family is "being kept in the dark" or that there is simply a lack of information about where the active duty member is going and what he/she is doing and facing.

• Preoccupation with the continuing media coverage of the war zone and accompanying severe reactions such as anxiety, depression or somatic [physical] symptoms such as back or stomach pains, headaches.

• Preoccupation with worry that the deployed family member will be killed or be physically disabled; conversely, staying extremely busy and denying that anything "bad" will happen.

• Fear that the deployed service member will return and "have problems like Vietnam vets had."

• Confusion and/or anger over the deployed member's priorities — is he/she more committed to the military than to me and our family? One wife cried out to her husband who was back from Iraq:

> You didn't care when you went off to the war and I was worried that you would die. I have absolutely no control over my life![190]

• Possible underlying anger or resentment — and perhaps some guilt about even having such feelings — that it is the deployed member who receives or will receive all the attention [welcome home, etc.] and the family may be ignored or left alone. "What about us and all that we have been through?" A lack of recognition for carrying the load alone at home and "living the war" at home.

• Concern, anger or confusion over the deployed member's symptoms of isolation, moodiness, preoccupation, detachment, sleep disturbance, anger outbursts. One active duty member, following deployment in Iraq said:

---

189. For writings that focus on the family of veterans, see Patience Mason, *Recovering from the War. A Woman's Guide to Helping Your Vietnam Vet, Your Family and Yourself.* (New York: Viking Penguin, 1990); Matsakis, A. *Vietnam Wives. Women and Children Facing the Challenge of Living With Veterans with Post-Traumatic Stress Disorder. 2nd Edition* (The Sidran Foundation. Lutherville, MD, 1996); and Matsakis, A., *Trust After Trauma. A Guide To Relationships for Trauma Survivors and Those Who Love Them* (Oakland, CA: New Harbinger Publications, 1998). There are also web sites that offer guidance. i.e., J.C. Stoppler, "Wartime Stress and Military Families," accessed on the web 3.26.05. See also "Resources for Parents, Teachers, and Family Support Professionals in Times of War. Summary of Conference Call on April 17, 2003. Accessed on-line at http://www.cyfernet.org/hottopic/warres.html.

190. Corbett, 2004, 60.

My family tells me that I am much more moody, more quiet, preoccupied, that I seem to not understand or perhaps don't even care about them as much any more.[191]

In addition to the family's dynamics described above, there also are the following to consider.

- Possible guilt or anger that the family does have important issues and needs that have been put aside and need to be addressed, but feeling very ambivalent about when or even if to insist that the active duty member respond and deal with these issues since he/she may have serious war-related, personal and readjustment-back-to-civilian life issues to deal with.

- Worry about going to any military resource to talk about any problems that the active duty member is having, or that the family is having, out of fear of the negative impact this will have on his or her military career.

- If the active duty member is wounded, disabled or psychiatrically impaired, just not knowing much about, or worried, upset or angry about the possible impact of the deployed member's medical or psychological condition on his/her military career, type of discharge, and what benefits the family is entitled to.

There are excellent resources available through the various branches of the military to help families while the spouse is on deployment, such as the Wives Clubs, the ombudsmen/family readiness volunteer systems and the Family Support/Service Centers that have excellent educational materials and often-times have counseling staff familiar with the stresses faced by military families.[192] Some bases also may have special programs to prepare families before and during deployment, such as at Ft. Carson with their Family Intervention Team of multi-agency representatives that uses a single phone number to direct families to needed resources, to include a special play activity/educational program for the children of such families.[193] Another special program for hospitalized veterans and their families is a unique private public partnership, Fisher House Program. This program provides the families with "comfort homes" at a low cost that have been built on the grounds of major VA medical centers and

---

191. Ibid.
192. The various branches of the military have different configurations of services and names for their programs. However, two basic types of programs have a roughly equivalent element in each branch. For example, family support centers include: Navy Fleet & Family Support Centers; Marine & Family Services; Air Force Family Support Service Centers; and Army Community Service. Volunteer programs that support military families before, during and following deployment include, but are not limited to: Navy Family Ombudsman/Deployment Support Programs; Marine Corps Key Volunteer Networks; Air Force and Army Family Readiness Programs. All these programs have web sites.
193. Jim Sheeler, "Dealing with deployment. Fort Carson develops new ways to take care of families left behind." *Rocky Mountain News* (2005, February 5). Retrieved from the web on 2.9.05.

military facilities.[194] Also, there is a new online Mental Health Self-Assessment screening test that can be that taken anonymously. It is offered through the Department of Defense, Office of Health Affairs and can help both veterans and their family members to identify symptoms.[195]

WHAT TO SAY AND DO AFTER THE VET RETURNS FROM DEPLOYMENT

There is no adequate cookbook recipe of do's and don'ts that all families of all veterans returned from deployment should do and not do.[196] This is for a very simple reason: no one "can package in a bottle" the "appropriate response" to suffering.[197] And words intended for everyone will provealmost worthless.

> For one individual person, if you go to the sufferers themselves and ask for helpful words, you may find discord. Some recall a friend who cheerily helped distract them from the illness, while others think such an approach insulting. Some want honest, straightforward confrontation; others find such discussion unbearably depressing.[198]

Recognizing that there is no magical set of responses for the family to carry out, the following are offered as a general set of principles or precepts and are written specifically to the partner and other family members/significant others of a war zone veteran.

You must consider how each of the following may fit, and whether it is or is not relevant for you and your family and for the veteran. Use your judgment and consider the strengths and shortcomings of all of your personalities, the quality of your past relationship, and any unresolved personal and relationship

---

194. Fisher House, 1401 Rockville Pike, Suite 600, Rockville, MD 20852. See also J. Brothers, "When our troops come home. One-fifth of the soldiers returning from Iraq suffer from major depression, anxiety or trauma. And others need help, too." *Parade* (2006, April 16), 4-5.

195. This program is available 24 x 7 at: www.militarymentalhealth.org. This site also provides information about mental health and substance-use services that are covered by the DOD.

196. For an interesting discussion of implications regarding the families of war veterans ("When a soldier goes to war—the family goes to war" and "turning hearts toward home—preparing to reunite with the loved ones and resolving conflicts"), see Cantrell, B.C. & Dean, C. *Down Range to Iraq and Back. (Seattle: WordSmth Publishing, 2005).*

197. I am indebted to the writing of Philip Yancey for the important general principles that I emphasize before getting into the specifics of relating to veterans who have returned from war-zone deployment. See: *Where is God When It Hurts? A comforting healing guide for coping with hard times* (Grand raids, MI: Zondevan, 1990).

198. Ibid., 168.

issues stemming from before and/or during deployment with your veteran partner.

It has been asserted that what people in pain (physical and/or psychological) most need is love, "for love instinctively detects what is needed."[199] In this regard, Jean Vavnier, founder of the l'Arche movement, said:

> Wounded people who have been broken by suffering and sickness ask for only one thing: a heart that loves and commits to them, a heart full of hope for them.[200]

Never underestimate the power, even if it is not immediately noticeable, of simply communicating through words and actions that you are available, you are here for your veteran partner.

> It is our mere presence [affirming that] . . . The world will go on. I am with you in this scary time . . . We will not leave you alone. We will bear this pain with you.[201]

This is a most powerful gift to offer to your veteran spouse, in that:

> People who are suffering often times feel an oppressive sense of aloneness. They feel abandoned, by God and also by others, because they must bear that pain alone and no one else quite understands. Loneliness increases the fear, which in turn increases the pain, and downward the spiral goes . . . . [202]

These words perfectly describe the *angst* that many veterans evidence, sooner or later, after returning from deployment. Most veterans will not show the depth of their anguish, and family members may not notice such, during the glow of the "honeymoon" period immediately following return from deployment. However, inevitably the glow fades, and then if there are serious underlying issues from the war, they will start to reveal themselves.

Finally, the development of stresses and strains following the veteran's return from deployment, even the most severe problems that are war-related, will not necessarily result in disaster or a splintering apart of the relationship and the family. Nor will it necessarily result in the family pulling together and becoming closer and stronger. This is illustrated by the following conversation with a couple whose relationship was sorely challenged when the wife found herself battling Hodgkin's disease.

> I asked Claudia and her husband why that crisis seemed actually to pull them together, whereas more frequently a life-threatening crisis creates tension and pushes a couple apart. Claudia responded: "In the movies, couples who have fought for years suddenly in the face of danger forget their differences and come together. But it doesn't work that way in real life. When a couple presents a crisis, it magni-

---

199. Ibid., 168.
200. I am indebted to Philip Yancey for quoting Jean Vanier as referenced from: "Hearts awakened by the poor," *Sojourners* (1982, January), 17.
201. Yancey, *Where is God When It Hurts*, 177-178.
202. Ibid. 173.

fies what's already present in their relationship . . . the crisis of the illness merely brought to the surface and intensified feelings already present."[203]

In my clinical work over the past three decades, typically many vets strongly asserted that the source of any post-war problems was the war and the transition back home. "I'm this way because of the war." Many veterans fail to also consider the important role that their life *before* the war may have played. And it is essential to note the word "also", along with what happened during the war. The "blank tablet metaphor" has been very effective in conveying this critically important point when talking with vets (or with their families):

> Let's be very clear. No one went to war as a "blank tablet." We all went as someone, as somebody. We all had personalities, strengths and shortcomings, values, beliefs, prejudices, relationships, successes, problems, issues and dreams. And you, this some-body, entered the military and went to war. And you brought inside of you to the war all of those personality characteristics, strengths and shortcomings, values, beliefs, prejudices, relationships, successes, problems, issues and dreams with you — we all did. And what we brought with us to the war somehow interacted with what each of us experienced during the war, resulting in unique combinations arising out of who were before the war and during war. And so, there is no way to begin to understand the possible impact of war unless you have a clear sense of your personality before, during and following exposure to war trauma — both those aspects that changed and just as importantly, those aspects that remained the same or seemed to go underground during the war but reappeared later. [204]

Long-standing characteristics, personal strengths and issues, and positive and problematic relationship patterns that existed before deployment within the veteran and in the veteran's relationship with partner, children, extended family members, all will come back with the veteran. However, these pre-deployment factors are now mixed inextricably together with the remarkable highs and depths of the experiences of war. And all that, together, comes home with the veteran and into the family. It is inevitable that the mixture of pre-war and deployment factors will be exacerbated by the veteran's post-deployment readjustment. Such long-standing issues and problems will require their own attention and must not be ignored or subsumed by focusing entirely onto the veteran's war-related problems as "the" problem.

The partner back home, the children, significant extended family members all also have their unique combinations of pre-war characteristics, strengths and problems. These inevitably become intermingled with their life experiences

---

203. Ibid. 164.
204. See R.M. Scurfield, "Treatment of Posttraumatic Stress Disorder Among Vietnam Veterans," in J.P. Wilson & B. Raphael (Eds.), *International Handbook of Traumatic Stress Syndromes* (879-888) (New York: Plenum Press, 1993); and R.M. Scurfield, "War-related trauma: An integrative experiential, cognitive and spiritual approach," in M.B. Williams & J.F. Sommer (Eds.), *Handbook of Post-Traumatic Therapy* (179-204) (Westport, CN: Greenwood Press, 1994).

while the veteran has been deployed. And, similar to the veteran, their combination of pre-deployment and life experiences and characteristics and patterns during the partner's absence while on deployment now come face-to-face with the returned veteran who has been extraordinarily impacted by war.

What is the family to say and do in regard to a veteran who has recently returned from deployment and who appears to be quite different or appears to have been significantly affected by the war? Should the partner and family remain silent and avoid talking with the returned active duty about these noticeable changes (that are negative) in the hope that he/she eventually will revert back to how he/she was before being deployed? And, of course, there also could be positive changes.

The family has needs and wants right now. And the family has just as much right and need as the returning veteran to be reached out to, listened to and understood, and to have their issues and feelings respected and addressed. Therefore, it is essential to focus on the big picture, to be very aware and sensitive to the mental and emotional state, and the wants and needs of the veteran, and of the partner, any children and any extended family members important in your lives.

To be of optimal help to the veteran partner, one first must understand the family's primary needs and wants *right now*, as you and the family are readjusting to the veteran being back and adjusting to someone who has been deeply touched by war.

• Are you resentful, relieved, entrenched in daily habits developed while your veteran partner was deployed, resistant or very ambivalent that your veteran partner has disturbed whatever routines and homeostasis you had achieved in his/her absence?

• Do you want to just drop all the responsibilities onto your veteran partner, because you are exhausted if not angry and needy and want your own space that was impossible to have while your partner was deployed?

• Or, are you so happy to have him/her back that you choose to bury or deflect all or most of your or the family's pent-up feelings and issues and defer to your veteran partner's needs and wants?

Of course, you also must pay close attention to what is going on with your veteran partner.

The majority of veterans who are recently returned from war appear to be all right, and do not want to dwell on what has happened to them while they were in the war. Rather, they want to put it aside, deflect it or bury it and get their lives back. This is normal and expectable.

There is a substantial sub-group of returned veterans who remain totally or partially preoccupied with the war and what happened, are obviously impacted about what they have experienced, and are either sorely troubled and/or become quite isolated. Ironically, most of this group of returned veterans, similar to the first group, also do not want to dwell on it, do not want to talk about it, think about it, or feel about it. They too want to put it aside, deflect it or bury it and get their lives back to normal.

A third, small group of veterans reveled in the war, miss it, yearn for it, talk about it, immerse themselves in the memories and happenings about war. This group is of critical immediate concern; they probably are extremely resistant to changing anything about themselves, don't really like much about normal civilian life, and make it almost impossible to connect with them in a meaningful way. Help is required in dealing with such veterans, and they need help (if they have any interest in being back in the normal world) but in all likelihood will not avail themselves of it.

The most fundamental "do" for partners is: take care of yourself. Get help for yourself, learn how to take care of yourself with a veteran partner who wants or seems compelled to relive and stay in the war even though he or she is now stateside. Quite frankly, for some the only "cure" may be for the veteran partner to head off on another deployment. Some relationships stay intact precisely because the veteran partner does go on relative frequent deployments and both partners prefer it this way.

When you put all of the above together, it is clear that this is a most challenging set of tasks. The service member returned from deployment has the personal responsibility to let the family know when he/she is ready or available to connect or not. However, the family also may find it necessary to become adept at the rhythm of contact and withdrawal. "I'm here, my ears and heart are available when you want to talk." Then, you pull back some and give space, repeating this dynamic countless times over weeks, months and perhaps years. You stay around and make it clear that you will be available when your veteran partner is more ready to connect with you and the family.

Furthermore, readjustment requires a balancing act by both the returned service member and the family. The veteran is responsible to be aware of when he or she is struggling with deployment-related issues and problems, and for doing something about it. However, the service member may be in denial about this. And so, the family may have to decide if it is necessary to confront the service member about his/her denial and/or do a balancing or juggling act to some degree between and amongst the array of competing needs and wants of the veteran, partner, any children and any involved extended family members. Thus, the partner may find himself of herself in the position of having to decide if and when to become more assertive in voicing concerns. Don't just allow a bad situation that is not showing much sign of improving to stagnate or become entrenched and chronic.

The vast majority of vets who are trying to deflect, deny, minimize or bury what has happened in the war and what may be going on inside themselves about the war, may need a wake-up call about their denial and avoidance. This might be from a close friend, religious confidant, and/or perhaps from the partner and/or adult children. The family may have to decide if it is willing to engage in strategies of interacting and balancing competing needs and priorities, and perfecting the art of contact with and withdrawal from the partner and/or insisting that the service member become more responsible. Either or both actions may be pivotal to the mental health and happiness of the individual and the family. And the service member, of course, has personal responsibility to do what he or she has to do to deal with possible deployment-related problems and issues. Getting assistance and support may be very advisable.

The Do Not's

Do not say, "I understand," or "I know you feel." No one who was not in the war could possibly understand. And no one knows what another person is feeling.[205] However, you may well understand from your own life experience how it feels to not want to talk to anyone, or how it is to feel that no one will be able to understand about something you have experienced, or how you may have hoped you could just ignore something festering inside you and that it would eventually go away.

Do not push or insist that your veteran talk about the war if he/she does not want to. It is too personal a subject to attempt to pry the details out of someone — you are trampling on hallowed ground.

Do not say, "Did you kill anybody?" Or, "How did it feel to kill someone?" If the vet wants to share this, the vet will share it. Otherwise, this is received as an invasive and unwanted demand for the most extremely intimate of information. One returned Iraq vet is described as he was being interviewed by a reporter at a small coffee shop.

> His voice rose as he talked. It was loud, too loud, his sentences laced with expletives. People moved away as he talked about "stupid" people at home asking him if he'd killed anyone in Iraq. "I just told them to shut up or I'd kill them!"[206]

Don't take it personally when your veteran does not want to talk about it. The fact that you are not a combat veteran is important; your veteran partner will probably be, by far, most comfortable talking about the war experiences in any detail with another combat veteran. The reluctance and difficulty in your veteran partner relating intimate details about the war has much less to do with you and much more to do with the veteran feeling that no one but other combat veterans could possibly understand.

Also, the veteran typically is concerned about "taking the lid off" of all the severe pent-up feelings and memories that have been buried. There is a fear that,

---

205. The exception being those care providers and others who have spent a substantial amount of time talking with and relating to various war veterans and who have been allowed into the veteran's hallowed inner circle.
206. M.L. Lyke (2004, August 28), "The unseen cost of war. American minds."

"If I open the lid [of the memories, emotions, trauma] I may not be able to put it back on again."[207] As one such Vietnam veteran told me:

> When I got back from Nam, the *only* people I could relate to were other Vietnam vets — and they were the *last* ones I wanted to be around.

Don't make ultimatums or threats that have severe consequences and deadlines attached to them unless you are absolutely at the end of your willingness to wait, like, "you need to get it together now, you've been withdrawn, moping around for X weeks. If you don't go see a counselor this week, I'm going to leave you." Big mistake; most combat vets do not respond very positively to threats. This isn't a poker game where bluffing and deception go hand-in-hand with winning.

Don't try to lay a guilt trip on your vet about how it's time to stop being so self centered, or ask if it is a test of your relationship. "If you really loved me, you would share more with me." The veteran partner already has more than enough guilt about what he/she did in the war or about the hardships you and the family have gone through while he/she was deployed. Piling on yet more guilt will only exacerbate the issues and intermingle those with your relationship dynamics.[208]

Does this mean that there is not anything that you *can or should* do? On the contrary:

Do not ignore warning or trouble signs in your vet that there is stuff going on inside or behaviors that indicate potentially serious problems — such as excessive drinking, isolating, mood swings, anxiety and sleep disturbance. Point such things out, but do not dwell on them, at least for awhile, depending on how severe such problems are.

Do not ignore your own needs and wants. You as a person have the right to have at least some of your needs and wants met, no matter how troubled your veteran partner is. And so do your children and perhaps important extended family members such as parents or siblings or grandparents.

Do not ever allow your veteran partner to treat you unkindly, or disrespectfully, or in a threatening way. And absolutely do not ever tolerate your veteran partner

---

207. This preoccupation entails a fear that if you allows yourself to fully feel the underlying emotions and memories about the (war) trauma, you will become so angry that you will hurt someone, or so sad that you will not be able to stop crying, or so full of the memories and thoughts that you will go crazy. This is an extremely important legacy of trauma that the *DSM-IV-TR* does not recognize as a PTSD symptom as described in *A Vietnam Trilogy*. Also, see R.M. Scurfield, "Treatment of Posttraumatic Stress Disorder Among Vietnam Veterans," in J.P. Wilson & B. Raphael (Eds.), *International Handbook of Traumatic Stress Syndromes* (879-888) (New York: Plenum Press, 1993); and R.M. Scurfield, "War-related trauma: An integrative experiential, cognitive and spiritual approach," in M.B. Williams & J.F. Sommer, *Handbook of Post-Traumatic Therapy* (179-204). (Westport, CN: Greenwood Press, 1994).
208. Understanding and treating guilt and shame issues are the main topics of the following chapter.

hurting you or your family. Violence in war is one thing. But to bring it back into the home is quite another matter; it is never excusable. If you can't protect yourself or your family, then immediately go talk to someone who can help you.

The Do's

Do remember to reach down deep within and stay in touch with the love that you have for your veteran — even if it is love more for how he or she was before deployment than how he or she is behaving right now.

Do remember that it is your relationship that should be at least as important as the individual needs and wants of each of you; what is best for your relationship right now, not what is best for you or what is best for your veteran partner. [209]

Do remember that no matter how you might wish otherwise, things are different now.[210] You both have gone through a lot since you were last together and readjustments will absolutely be required by both of you — as well as by other family members.

Do be willing to give the veteran some space.[211] Yes, there can be a fine line between giving the veteran enough space, on the one hand, and fulfilling the family's expectations and needs for closeness and intimacy.

Do understand that many vets need and want to spend time with war buddies or other veterans. Your vet's connection with other vets may be a lifeline that can help mitigate against severe isolation and withdrawal.[212]

Do hold hands and look each other in the eyes. I don't remember much of anything specific that I was taught in almost 10 years of undergraduate and graduate study. But there is one thing I remember very clearly from a favorite social work professor, John Milner.[213] He said, if you and your partner are having a serious argument or harsh words or tempers are rising, both of you stop. Be silent for a moment, compose yourselves, stand in front of each other, hold hands, look each other in the eyes, and now start talking to each other while continuing to hold hands and looking in each other's eyes. You almost surely will calm down and start relating to each other rather than talking hurtfully *at* each other.

Do be out front by saying: Do you want to talk a little with me about the war? Are you willing to share with me some of the good times, some of the bad times? If not now, possibly later? And I need to be able to ask you these same questions again at another time, because otherwise you may never come to me first and start talking about it. Tell me the best way to approach you.

---

209. See W. Glasser, *Choice Theory* (New York: HarperCollins Publishers, 1998).
210. Brothers 2006.
211. Ibid.
212. Ibid.
213. John Milner, Professor, School of Social Work, University of Southern California, Los Angeles, CA. Class lecture, 1966-67.

Do remind your veteran partner about the literature you have in the house that describes the warning signs and triggers about post traumatic stress and lingering combat stress reactions and that are reminding you of him or her. And if you don't have any such literature, get some ASAP from a military family support agency or ombudsman/family support volunteer, a partner support group, a VA Vet Center or a Veteran's Service Organization — or from this book — and become familiar with the contents.[214]

Do recognize that your veteran partner will probably be very resistant to going to talk to anyone, including you, about what is going on. The veteran may not respond positively to your suggestions today or tomorrow or next week, and so you have to be both persistent and diplomatic/gentle in continuing to bring up your concerns.

Do say: I know I can't fully or perhaps at all understand what is going on with you, because I wasn't there in the war.

Do say (if you genuinely mean it): I really do want to better understand, and request that you help me better understand. If you don't tell me anything, then you are shutting me out and it will be impossible for me to ever really understand. Please, don't shut me out completely.

Do say: I don't need or want to hear all the gory details. I just want you to please share at least some of what is going on inside of you, some of what you are feeling angry about, or sad about, or anxious about, or any other important feelings. Are you willing to share at least a little of that with me today? And gently yet persistently make this request at other times.

Do ask your vet: Are there any books, articles or other readings about war and what happens in war, or any movies, or any songs/music that are personally meaningful that you could recommend to me that could give me at least a little better understanding of what it was all about, about what was so meaningful for you? And then I would like to talk with you a little about it. (Many vets will be much more comfortable with you learning in this manner, rather than you expecting your veteran partner to talk in great detail and express heavy pent-up emotions.)

Do say: Please let me know if I am saying something offensive, or that hurts you, or when it feels like I'm trying to pry you open and you feel that I am trying to invade into your most deep and personal feelings and issues. And I really want you to tell me that gently, in a respectful way. Telling me in an angry way doesn't help anything — and I don't deserve or need your anger being directed at me.

And that goes both ways. I am going to let you the veteran know when you may say something offensive to me, or that hurts me, or when it feels like you're trying to invade my deepest and most personal feelings and issues. And I want to

---

214. For other resources, see the VA National Center *Iraq War Clinician Guide; the National Gulf War Resource Center; Iraq and Afghanistan Veterans of America; and the National Veterans' Foundation.*

tell you that gently, in a respectful way. Telling you in an angry way doesn't help anything and you don't deserve or need my anger being directed at you.

Do say: I'm here for you. And I want you to be here for me, even if you can't be here for me as much right now as I want you to. Because I am in this for the long haul. (However, if you are having serious doubts that you still committed to this relationship, then that is another matter entirely that requires your immediate attention.)

And do put on your oxygen mask first. [215] This is the bottom line do or don't—to first take care of yourself. As we all know, the proper procedure on an airplane when the oxygen masks drop down is to put your oxygen mask on first; otherwise you will be in no position to help anyone else. The same principle applies to you at home. Seek help if you are hurting, whether or not your veteran partner does and whether or not your veteran partner wants you to. This is your right. And one of the most powerful sources of support and understanding will be with and from partners of other veterans who have returned from deployment.

These are only some guidelines to consider. Your veteran partner's situation, yours, your family's, may not be similar to what has been described above and you have your own distinctive issues and challenges to deal with. Two most important truths to remember are that:

• war always has a long-standing impact on all combatants and others who serve in a war zone

• this impact on them is brought home and absolutely will have a significant impact on the veteran, you (the veteran's partner), children and significant extended family members and close friends.

Readers are encouraged to look at some the excellent writings that focus on the dynamics of families of veterans mentioned earlier,[216] visit some of the Web sites established regarding children of veterans,[217] wives, or families of veterans[218] and those that offer various forms of assistance to deployed military personnel and their families.[219] There is no need to be a "Lone Ranger." Family of a veteran still on active duty can contact a military family support center or community service center, military base ombudsman or family readiness group, wives support group or military chaplain. Family of veterans no longer on active duty can contact the local VA Vet Center, VA social work department, VA spe-

---

215. This is an expression applied by Charles Figley, School of Social Work, Florida State University, to self-care for clinicians who work with trauma survivors. It also is very appropriate for family members of veterans.

216. Mason, 1990; Matsakis, 1996, 1998.

217. See, for example, the web sites "Children of Vietnam Veterans," "Children of Veterans With PTSD," "Sons and Daughters in Touch" (of a parent who was killed). A Google search on February 12, 2005, under "Veteran's Children" produced 320,000 hits; and a search of "Veterans Children" (no apostrophe in "Veterans") produced 550,000 hits. A Google search for "Veterans Children's Groups" produced 1,550,000 hits.

cialized PTSD program, OIF or IEF case manager, county or state veteran's service officer or veteran's service organization representative for family assistance.

POSSIBLE POSITIVE IMPACT OF WAR AND DEPLOYMENT

The preceding discussion has emphasized the potential and actual negative impact, both short and longer-term, of being in war — because this amount of information typically is never given routinely or comprehensively. There is a whole other side — the remarkable positives, the extraordinary valor, strengths, comradeship, heroism, and humanity that can characterize what goes on in wars, and can be brought home and remain a powerful positive within many veterans.

Families may be blessed with the development of resilience, strength, and a very positive identity as a military family or as the family of a veteran, proud of the service their spouse or parent or sibling has given to this country, and the sacrifices made both by the active duty military person or the veteran and by the family. And there can be a profound appreciation of what the price of freedom is, and it is not free.

Such was revealed in the stories of the brave and proud veterans as described in the first two books of the *Vietnam Trilogy*. In the words of a Vietnam veteran 20 years after the war:

---

218. See, for example, the web sites "Motherspeak," "Occupation Watch," "Veterans & Families," "Vet Wives," "Army Wives," "Navy Wives," "Proud Air Force Wives," "Support4Military Wives," "Soldier's Moms," "Marine Moms," "Home Front Support Web," "Veterans for Peace" and "Raging Grannies." A Google search on 12 February under "Veteran's Wives" produced 16,400 hits that included vet wives e-mail lists, organizations, veteran wives hotlines, handbooks, veteran's wives groups, state organizations, etc.

219. For example: *soldiersangels.org* (Soldiers' Angels — takes donations for Kevlar blankets and "cool scarves" for deployed personnel); *operationuplink.org* (Operation Uplink — Veterans of Foreign Wars program to provide service members with prepaid phone cards to call home); *freedomcalls.org* (Freedom Calls Foundation — provides free videoconferences between soldiers and their families); *opgratitude.com* (Operation Gratitude — care package deliveries to service members); and Any Soldier — has 3,000 contacts in the military who post messages on the website about what their buddies need, with goods distributed to 92,000 troops in 11 countries and at sea). See related article: Oren Dorell, "Websites connecting Americans' generosity, service-members' needs. *USA Today*, June 28, 2006, 7A. See also *www.AmericaSupportsYou.mil* website that includes an informative newsletter. Other resources include USA Cares, Give 2 the Troops, Little Patriots embraced, Operation Shoebox and the Wounded Warriors Project.

Maturity, self-esteem, teamwork, accomplishment, pride, excitement, and adventure are certainly as much a part of the war zone experience as anything else. For these, I am extremely gratified.

In the words of a serviceman in Iraq:

These two deployments have taught me a degree of patience and tolerance that I never thought possible. I have been forced to live in terribly deprived conditions and with ungodly levels of frustration and uncertainty, far more than in any arena of my life as I knew it before OEF and OIF. I have learned to live without the most basic comforts of life for months on end, without privacy and with restrictions I have never known before. To this end, I have learned to appreciate why freedom has a tremendously high cost. I am grateful to be among the finest in this struggle to bring democracy to the people of Iraq so that someday they can live as we do in America. [220]

---

220. Platoni, 2005.

Chapter 5. The Relationship between Active Duty Military, Veterans, Their Families and the DOD and VA

Many readers may think that a discussion of the relationship of active duty personnel and veterans and their families with the Department of Defense (DOD) and the Department of Veterans Affairs (VA) is not of particular relevance or interest to post-war healing. To the contrary; this chapter covers an absolutely critical aspect of post-war readjustment that is virtually absent *from almost all* counseling and treatment strategies offered to active duty personnel, veterans and their families. Let's take a look at this because it is c crucial to optimal post-deployment readjustment, treatment and healing strategies.

To the extent that many veterans and retired military personnel feel that they have been lied to, betrayed, and been left with broken promises by the nation, the issues discussed here are an essential element of the expanded circle of healing that is described in the final chapter. The resulting hurt is too deep to be avoided if post-war readjustment and treatment are to be meaningful.

The Relationship Between The DOD And The VA

Historically, there has been a clear separation between the DOD and the VA. People on active duty, or retired from a full career with the military, were served by the DOD. Those who had been discharged from active duty were now veterans and received care from the VA. Thankfully, there has been an unprecedented level of cooperation between DOD and the VA in response to the Iraq War.

First, there has been an increase in joint trainings of some VA and DOD providers. Several VA medical clinics now offer special deployment-related health services, like the Deployment Health Clinic at the VA Puget Sound Health Care System in the state of Washington. This deployment health clinic provides mental and physical post-combat evaluation and treatment, and some counseling on family issues.[221] A number of VA Medical Centers are providing limited inpatient psychiatric services for active duty members and there now are OEF/OIF case managers, although many are part-time. And the VA Vet Center Program has hired some 50 outreach specialists to focus on Iraq and Afghanistan veterans and their families.

Finally, there is a very welcome and long overdue VA initiative in response to the serious challenges that historically have faced active duty personnel and their families when they move from active duty to veteran status. Such a move requires that any medical services related to military condition must be transferred from the DOD Military Treatment Facilities to VHA Veterans Health Administration facilities. There are a handful of VHA social workers now assigned as VHA/DOD liaisons at seven of the country's major military hospitals. Secondly, many VA medical centers across the country have assigned both social workers and nurses to serve as contact points and case managers for active duty military personnel whose medical services are being transferred from active duty to VA medical facilities.[222]

All of the above are very welcome, and hopefully are just the initial stages of the major collaboration that is required to adequately serve the needs of active duty personnel who will need to continue their health care at a VA facility. Unfortunately, this service is limited at this point and there still is a huge gap in the collaboration and cooperation required to provide anything approaching a seamless transition from active-duty to veteran status. Furthermore, too many active duty military personnel have major problems in obtaining services from the Department of Defense while they are still on active duty and the same for too many veterans regarding the Department of Veterans Affairs.

TRYING TO OBTAIN NEEDED BENEFITS AND SERVICES FROM THE DOD AND VA

Many active duty military personnel, veterans and their families receive state-of the-art and caring services from many outstanding health care, social work, spiritual and benefits providers in both the DOD and the VA. They find very sympathetic and helpful assistance about important information and how to apply for and receive in a timely manner all benefits to which they are entitled.

221. M.L. Lyke, "The unseen cost of war. American minds," August 28, 2004.
222. "Social workers leading VA Transition Project. The Program helps patients and families with the transition to VA care." *NASW News*, (2005, March), 9.

Conversely, there are several factors that contribute to an oftentimes frustrating, challenging and at times dismaying experience for many others. These problems are becoming more frequent in seeking needed medical services due to lack of resources and increasing waiting times.

Don't Do It Alone. Because the DOD and the VA are vast and complex institutions, seemingly saturated with paper work requirements, regulations, procedures and red tape, they are at times very impersonal. There is a fundamental strategy to use in approaching them:

> When having to interact with the DOD or the VA to obtain needed benefits or services, have a trusted and knowledgeable advocate available to help you navigate through the oftentimes murky waters of the system. This expert assistance may be essential to increase the likelihood that you will be able to obtain what you need and want and are entitled to, and in a timelier manner.

You may not need such assistance. However, if you do encounter any significant resistance or difficulties in interacting with the DOD or the VA, do not wage the battle alone. Some of the best advocates are your peers, others who have already been through numerous encounters with large federal institutions and know from experience the do's and don'ts. Some peers participate in self-help organizations, such as the various service wives' clubs and family support systems. Some advocates are present in numerous organizations. DOD civilian social workers and counselors, Family Support Centers, VA OEF/OIF case managers, PTSD Clinical Teams or other specialized PTSD programs, VA social workers and Vet Centers can be very helpful. Veterans Service Organizations, State and County Veteran's Officers, and veteran's assistance officers at some US Congressmen's offices can be invaluable in providing assistance and leverage for filing, tracking and appealing applications for benefits. The bottom line: don't do it alone.

Difficulties in obtaining needed benefits and services may be due in part to the overwhelming demand caused by the ongoing requirements to mobilize, train, support and deploy hundreds of thousands of members of the Armed Forces back and forth to Iraq and Afghanistan. Also, there are severe logistical challenges in mobilizing large numbers of Reserve and National Guard units. Besides logistical complexities, Reserve and National Guard members called to active duty have been described as particularly vulnerable to combat stress reactions and PTSD. Reserve and National Guard members are more isolated and lack the support systems at and surrounding military bases.

> War is not the full-time job of the estimated 160,000 "weekend warriors" now in Iraq — civilian soldiers who have been called up in the largest numbers since World War II. They have off-duty lives, careers and demands back home that increase stress.[223]

---

223. M.L. Lyke, "The unseen cost of war. American minds," August 28, 2005.

In addition, the Government Accounting Office (GAO) reported that a major limitation on VA services is that, in spite of the VA being considered a world leader in PTSD treatment, the VA "does not have sufficient capacity to meet the needs of new combat veterans while still providing for veterans of past wars." The GAO said that the VA had not been able to meet its own goals for PTSD clinical care and education, even as it "anticipates greater numbers of veterans with PTSD seeking VA services."[224]

PTSD DIAGNOSIS VERSUS LEGITIMATE COMPENSATION FOR VETERANS HARMED BY WAR

In an earlier chapter, there was a discussion of the new DOD policy of "watchful waiting" in regards to giving active duty personnel who served in a war zone a PTSD diagnosis. I am not adverse *per se* to the concept of "watchful waiting" regarding giving someone a PTSD diagnosis — especially during or soon after returning from deployment to a war zone.

This is partly because I have great issue with the PTSD diagnosis as it is defined in the *DSM-IV-TR*. It is my experience that the PTSD diagnosis as currently defined largely fails to differentiate between a "normal and expectable" reaction to trauma and a psychiatrically disordered one. Consequently, many trauma survivors are being wrongly labeled as having a psychiatric disorder when in fact they do not — but they *are* legitimately suffering from trauma exposure.

Unfortunately, there is no provision in mental health practice today — nor in the policies that govern "service connected conditions" — that recognizes the significant suffering and dysfunction that are normal outcomes of trauma exposure, such as in a war zone — unless the condition fully meets PTSD diagnostic criteria. This is a catch-22 that unfairly penalizes those who are already injured.

Should a vet be given a psychiatric disorder label of PTSD in order to be able to receive his/her rightful compensation for serving his/her country and having been harmed? Or should we avoid giving the psychiatric label, since he/she is not psychiatrically disordered but instead is suffering immensely, as one might expect, from war trauma exposure)? The latter option will certainly result in depriving the vet of the compensation earned by having served the country. This is, indeed, the choice faced by many veterans and clinicians.

---

224. W. Welch (2005, February 28), "Trauma of Iraq War haunting thousands returning home," (2005, February 28), 6A.

Furthermore, if the vet shows improvement and/or if the clinician documents such in the medical record, then the vet is at risk to have any PTSD (or other mental disorder) compensation reduced or eliminated. And so, in effect, the vet is "paid" to "remain sick" and is "financially penalized" if he/she improves!

This is a terrible conundrum — and would require a major overhaul of the entire compensation system to rectify. This would include authorizing those veterans to receive just compensation for having served in harm's way and who themselves have been indeed harmed — but not necessarily getting a psychiatric disorder label of PTSD. And this revision will almost certainly never happen, if for no other reason than the enormous financial implications that would come with truly recognizing the full impact of war, both short- and long-term.

There is an additional complexity. Part of the problem is that many vets feel (and rightly so) that our country has not lived up to its promise of providing just services and compensation for their war-related hurts. And so, to get a PTSD diagnosis and PTSD service-connection is seen *as their only avenue* to be able to get something back for what they believe they deserve for their sacrifices for our country.

Again, this is a terribly convoluted and long-standing system and arrangement that leads to many of the problems identified above. Veterans (and their clinicians) must essentially falsify or claim a prolonging of symptoms in order to continue to receive "just" compensation; conversely, those who don't want or don't get the PTSD label but are suffering from the war — end up with nothing in the way of compensation.

And I must say that many veteran advocates minimize some of the above issues and focus on others to try to prove their point (that veterans deserve compensation for having been harmed in war). In turn, many in the military, at higher levels in the VA and many conservative politicians focus on other issues to prove their point (that cost containment is of utmost importance, the PTSD diagnosis is problematic, and if someone does not have the PTSD diagnosis, then they will not get compensated). This line of thinking makes it convenient to discourage the giving of PTSD diagnoses, to call into question or discredit the diagnosis of PTSD itself and to downplay recognition of the full human cost of being in wars. [225]

---

225. Readers are encouraged to read critical analyses of the VA's motivations and stealthy actions concerning trying to discredit the diagnosis of PTSD and to reduce PTSD compensation awards. See, for example, Larry Scott, "VA launches PTSD review," November 29, 2005. Accessed on line 8.5.06 at vawatchdog.org; Steve Robinson, "VA's PTSD review continues at the Institute of Medicine." July 3, 2006. Accessed online 8.3.06 at www.veteransforamerica.org; and Mark Boal, who interviewed me for his forthcoming article, "Fight for the Mind of the Veteran" (working title), Playboy Magazine, in-press, October, 2006.

And of course, veterans and their families are caught in the middle — again. Frankly, to me, as a clinician it matters little if an active duty member or a veteran is suffering from full-blown war-related PTSD or from "partial" PTSD or from combat stress. In all cases, it is the *suffering from war-related trauma and stressors* that is what is important to recognize and address.

THE DOD, VA AND FAMILIES OF COMBATANTS

Concern about the DOD and the VA in terms of services available for the families of active duty personnel and for veterans is not meant in any way to be a criticism of many of the staff of the health and mental health services of these two vast institutions. Such staff, by and large, is extremely dedicated, well-intentioned, hard working and deeply caring about the welfare of the family members. And they do the best they can within the constrictions of funding, priority and policy realities that are centrally-directed from the headquarters of both the DOD and the VA. Yet, somehow, the institutions and bureaucracies of both the DOD and the VA almost seem to have lives of their own.

There are true leaders in both institutions at the highest levels and down to the base, unit and program levels who are compassionate, sensitive and creative and who realize that ultimately the strongest organization possible and the provision of the best services possible will be accomplished through maximizing the talents, initiative and motivation of subordinates and front-line personnel. However, they are relatively few in number.

Other factors can make interactions with the DOD and/or the VA very problematic. Far too often, both institutions (as well as other governmental agencies) appear to be much more concerned about minimizing or mitigating financial costs than they are about being responsive to the needs of their clients.

Such a bias is reflected in moves such as reducing eligibility criteria and increasing restrictions on services; reviewing compensation awards under the guise of quality control when it is cost control that is of paramount concern; an unwillingness to over-turn politically-motivated denials of higher-level administrators who are quick to deny that there are short-falls in funding and who adamantly maintain that resources are adequate — in spite of obvious overloads to the system.

Veterans are not stupid; they easily see such pronouncements for what they are, and this is a recurring source of anger and resentment. There is a substantial group of federal employees, including but not limited to a number that have risen to management and command positions, who are mostly concerned with power and control and protecting and increasing their own area or "turf." Such people tend to be very rigid, use punishment and intimidation tactics, and operate from a position of "let's not make a mistake," "just follow my orders", and "don't question or challenge anything I say or do."

Among this group, the provision of quality service to support the active duty population or veterans and their families is not a priority. Also, there seems to be little motivation to promote autonomy, initiative and creativity in their subordinates, to encourage critical thinking or to truly put "customer service" first.

The front-line health care and benefits services providers also are varied in terms of attitudes and commitment. Many such providers are remarkably and consistently dedicated to serving military and veterans. Such providers are concerned to provide expert services that are informed with knowledge and infused with caring about military and veteran dynamics and issues. They truly go above and beyond and are a blessing to active duty personnel, veterans and their families.

Still, too many employees seem to care little that they are serving active duty military or veterans. They are just punching a time clock.

Let us look, respectively, at what some of the dynamics and underlying issues are among those staff and providers in each of these two institutions that affect their relationship with their constituents.

ACTIVE DUTY MILITARY BACK FROM DEPLOYMENT, THEIR FAMILIES, AND THE DOD

Many active duty personnel who were wounded or injured while deployed have reported serious problems in obtaining needed ongoing medical services. For example, Reserve and National Guard soldiers are described in a Government Accountability Office report to have lost or risked losing both medical care services and thousands of dollars of pay for months.[226] The stories are heartbreaking.

Sgt. 1st Class John Allen, a weapons sergeant on a Special Forces A team, suffered brain trauma, leg, torso and vision injuries from a helicopter accident and grenade blast near Kandahar, Afghanistan, in the summer of 2002. But when he applied for an extension of his active-duty status (to be able to continue to receive needed medical services), he was forcibly dropped from the active duty rolls. "I had no pay, no access to base, no medical coverage for my family," and his medical appointments with military physicians were repeatedly canceled. "The broken, dysfunctional system," Allen said, "placed my family under intense and indescribable stress. In short, this by far caused the most burden on my family, my financial situation and my life in general."[227]

---

226. Ann Scott Tyson, "Guard and Reserve soldiers face the equivalent of financial and medical 'friendly fire.'" *The Washington Post* (2005, February 22). Cited in the *SunHerald*, Biloxi, MS, B2.
227. Ibid.

Another testimony at the Congressional hearings on this matter was by Sgt. Joseph Perez, a military policeman with the Nevada National Guard. He was wounded in the knee during a riot in a Baghdad prison compound, witnessed comrades killed in mortar attacks and suffered flashbacks and nightmares. "Flown back to Fort Lewis for care, he said he spent months 'languishing' in a WW II barracks with insufficient heat and moldy walls. 'You feel they don't give a damn whether you get well or not.' Subsequently, his unit was removed from active-duty status, and he and his family were deprived of medical care or access to the local base. 'All this made me feel worthless.'"[228]

US Representative Tom Davis, Republican, Virginia, chairman of the House Government Reform Committee that held hearings regarding such problems, called the impact of the flawed system on troops "the equivalent of financial and medical 'friendly fire.'"[229]

For families where an active duty military person has been killed, "the death of a loved one is only the first in a series of blunt arrangements for the surviving spouse. Civilian wives and children methodically are separated from the tightly structured military hierarchy. Base housing, neighbors, nearby schools and the fabled band of brothers all disappear."[230] In the words of Bonnie Carroll, founder of the Tragedy Assistance Program for Survivors (TAPS) and herself a war widow:

> The Defense Department's mission is war fighting. Once the paperwork is done and the late family is out-processed, they no longer are part of the war machine.[231]

Similar dynamics have been reported by active duty military who suffered severe enough injuries or disabilities to be medically discharged from active duty. There is the perception that the country has failed veterans of past wars and will fail the current generation as well.

> The war will stay with them, they realize, but after a point the Army won't.[232]

The experience of loss, aloneness and being cast aside and forgotten can be a most bitter pill to swallow. This is aggravated by the challenges that may be faced in dealing with DOD (or VA) medical facilities or benefits processing regarding military-related physical and mental conditions that may last a lifetime.

The issue of the responsiveness of the DOD (and the VA) to family members is particularly critical in that there has been a dramatic shift in the demographics of combatants in the Iraq War in contrast to the Vietnam War.

---

228. Ibid.
229. Ibid.
230. Elliot Blair Smith, "Deaths in combat ricochet here at home," 6A.
231. Ibid.
232. Corbett, "The permanent scars of Iraq," 38.

The US now has an all-volunteer military, and about two-thirds of the military personnel are married.[233]

If one understands the implications of deployment to a war zone on the functioning and health of combatants and on the families back home, then it is easy to understand why the military has placed increased emphasis on retention of current active duty personnel as a critical strategy to help maintain adequate levels of military personnel. One also has to be very concerned about how the families of deployed personnel are impacted, and what services are needed beyond those provided directly to the active duty member.

The destructive impact of deployment and war zone duty on families has been well-known among Vietnam veterans for decades, and the military has finally recognized that providing services for families is a critical element in keeping Armed Forces personnel on active duty. The Army is now spending $2 million on a variety of marriage programs. These include marriage enhancement seminars with Fort Campbell-based 101st Airborne Division personnel, vouchers for romantic get-aways, and a 40-hour course with lessons on forgiveness, communication skills, the damage of alcohol and tobacco use, and how to recognize post-traumatic stress symptoms.[234]

However, most such efforts are "pilot" or demonstration programs supported by special funding initiatives. Hence, they have not been part of the recurring DOD budget nor are they routinely available throughout the branches of the military nor are the families of National Guardsmen and Reserve units necessarily served by such programs.

Largely in recognition that many Reserve and National Guard personnel live too far from military bases to take advantage of the Family Support Centers, the DOD has contracted with Military OneSource to provide telephone information, referral and brief counseling assistance.[235] Also, up to six free counseling sessions can be arranged with a social worker in their community through One-Source.[236]

However, there is a concern that the DOD is using a cost-reduction rationale to move towards replacing in-person counseling with such telephone assistance.

This is very troubling for two reasons. First, telephone assistance centers and contract staff cannot duplicate the many advantages inherent in having counseling staff embedded at military bases and co-located with the military community. Second, few mental health professionals (other than those who might benefit from being awarded such a federal contract) would agree that a

---

233. Holloway, 2004.
234. Hefling, 2004, B1.
235. L. Kipling, February 7, 2005
236. The Military OneSource toll-free number is 1-800-342-9647 (US) and 1-800-3429-6477 (international).

telephone counseling system should ever be more than a complement to in-person assistance available at the local community level.

The DOD talks about the need to retain fighting personnel and thus they talk about caring for the family of active duty members. And the DOD is more sensitive to the needs of the families of active duty personnel than almost any other employer, large or small, in the US. Still, the DOD has been quietly implementing an approximately 30% reduction-in-force throughout the military in the staffs of their family support centers.

To reduce on-site resources in the DOD sectors responsible for providing services to families, just when the percentage of deployed service members who are married has increased dramatically, would seem to be irrational. Spokesmen obfuscate with pronouncements like, "We're consolidating services at several sites so that we can be more efficient." Or, "we're not reducing staff, we're shifting resources." This is tragic. Don't be fooled by such bureaucratic double-speak.

There are Family Support Groups affiliated at various unit levels that are active and viable resources for family members. Also, a number of military bases and units maintain a very useful ombudsman system. Spouses and advocates are dedicated, organized, enthusiastic and available 24-7, especially for families of currently deployed Armed Forces personnel who are in need. The viability of such arrangements depends on the attitudes and leadership of the local command and their spouses, and having sufficient numbers of dedicated and competent volunteers available.

And, of course, the supportive military community will not be readily available — if at all available — to those surviving family members who relocate back to their hometowns or elsewhere distant from their spouse's home duty station. This geographical isolation from the support of military base resources and the surrounding military community is particularly likely to be a problem for family members whose spouses have been activated from Reserve or Guard units and may be mobilized some distance away from the families.

VETERANS, THEIR FAMILIES AND THE DEPARTMENT OF VETERANS AFFAIRS (VA)

Many veterans and their family members perceive the institution that the federal government has established for serving veterans, the US Department of Veterans Affairs, as an entity that they have to do battle with just to get the services they are entitled to. One veteran described to me how he had come to understand his long-running battle with the local VA Regional Office to get benefits for a service-related condition. After years of struggle, he realized that he needed to adjust his attitude so he could better marshal his energies and not become so enraged and disillusioned:

I was really not doing well [emotionally] fighting the VA — until I came to the realization that the VA was running a marathon, but that I was running a 100 yard dash.

The bureaucratic complexities within the Department of Veterans Affairs and between the government and many veterans are deeply entrenched. The major Veterans Service Organizations have had to play a yeoman's role in representing veterans and family members in battles over compensation and eligibility issues. No wonder so many veterans and their families feel that they have been betrayed by the government.

It is disconcerting how many veterans report their relationship with the benefits component of the VA to be an adversarial one. Indeed, in the words of a World War II veteran advocate:

It's hard to go against the VA on your own—it's like going to court without a lawyer.[237]

The VA often is perceived as trying to give the veteran the minimum benefit possible. The veteran and family become engaged in what is usually a lengthy and acrimonious struggle just to get the benefits they understand they are legally eligible to receive.

An entire book has been written to help guide veterans: *The Viet Vet Survival Guide. How to Cut Through The Bureaucracy and Get What You Need — And Are Entitled To*.[238] Although I was then relatively new as a national VA official and had to be circumspect in what I wrote, I did contribute to the chapter on Psychological Readjustment (pp. 101-111), along with veteran advocate and psychologist Jack Smith (Cleveland).

There are individual VA medical centers that provide some important services to family members of veterans. However, the vast majority of VA medical and mental health services, by long-standing centrally-directed VA policies, are almost totally oriented to veterans (the VA Vet Center program is an exception). Family members are not seen except for problems directly related to the veteran's service-related condition. For example, if couples' counseling is considered important to the veteran's resolving of PTSD, then the spouse can be seen in conjunction with the veteran for the purpose of helping the veteran with his or her condition.

This is how it has always been. But a change in policy seems to be overdue, given the steep in crease in the number of active duty members with families. Studies document the devastating impact of war zone deployment on those mil-

237. Alison Young , "60 years later, help. Frostbite injury dated to 1944." *SunHerald*, Biloxi, MS (2005, March 8), A1. See also Alison Young, "Veterans struggle lasts for decades." *SunHerald*, Biloxi, MS (2005, March 7), A1.

238. C. Kubey, D.F. Addlestone, R.E. O'Dell, K.D. Snyder, B.F. Stichman and Vietnam Veterans of America, *The Viet Vet Survival Guide. How to Cut Through the Bureaucracy and Get What You Need — And Are Entitled To* (New York: Ballantine Books, 1985).

itary families. The typical rationale given for this very restrictive policy is that broadening it would cost too much money, and limited resources would be denied to the active duty member and to veterans. That is obviously false, since "new" funds are found every year for "new" needs. How can it not be a priority to fund family services for active duty members and for veterans when funding is found, for example, for re-enlistment bonuses or new weapons systems?

The words of Abraham Lincoln that grace the front of VA Central Office in Washington, D.C., come to mind: "To care for he who has borne the battle, and for his widow and orphan."

Survivors benefits are paid to the widows and orphans of deceased veterans. However, family members of deceased veterans are not entitled to any health or mental health services from the VA. This is particularly tragic for widows and orphans and Gold Star mothers and fathers — many of whom could derive enormous benefit, solace and understanding from being able to talk with a knowledgeable VA counselor.

And for the families of living veterans, other than disability payments to veterans with VA-adjudicated service-connected disabilities, there are mighty few noteworthy services.

The problem is compounded by the fact that there is almost no systematic information or significantly-funded research study about the acute and longer-term impact on the families of active duty personnel and veterans.[239] And the two elements of the government that should have considerable expertise to offer in terms of understanding what war and its impact on the family is all about — the DOD and the VA even more so — have yet to give that a priority.

THE PROMISE OUR COUNTRY MAKES TO ARMED FORCES PERSONNEL, VETERANS AND THEIR FAMILIES

The noble commitment by the federal government to help the families of active duty personnel too often remains empty words, another broken promise. This is especially so when the active duty personnel, for medical reasons, are in a "medical hold" status or are being processed off of active duty. Indeed, for many veterans the post active-duty relationship with the government and with the VA is that of a neglected stepchild, and requires a constant battle to retain or obtain promised rights and benefits.[240] This was illustrated in a cartoon on Veterans

---

239. One exception is an $8 million federally funded study by Purdue's Military Family Research Institute of soldiers and their families focusing on retention on active duty, as well as how military life affects children. See: Military Family Research Institute: *http://www.mfri.purdue.edu/*

240. See Kubey et al, 1985. D2.

Day, 2004. A decorated military veteran at a Veterans' Day Recognition ceremony is talking with two school-age children and pointing to the ribbons on
his chest:

> I received this one for combat in Afghanistan, this one for fighting in Iraq, and this
> one for the ongoing struggle to save our VA Health Benefits after I got home. [241]

This struggle to obtain justifiable benefits was highlighted in a three-part
series that chronicled cases where vets did not get benefits they were entitled to
for as long as 60 years.[242]

And just what was the understanding, what were the promises given to
military recruits and to veterans? What are the essential factors that underlie
this relationship based on trust? The factors include that the US government,
leaders and society:

• Are truthful when they say that the country needs to go to war; that it is
in the nation's vital interest to do so; in other words, that this (and any) war
is vitally necessary to the nation's survival.

• Will not unduly risk the lives of any members of the Armed Forces for
any longer than is absolutely required to get the job done.

• Will continue to sanction and provide whatever is needed to enable the
military forces to carry out their mission so that they are optimally trained,
prepared and equipped to win the war in the quickest period of time and
with the fewest casualties. For example, will insure adequate numbers of
trained personnel, equipped with the most advanced weaponry and
protections that money can buy (to include adequate body armor and
properly armored vehicles in a war zone).

• Will honor their commitment to insure that adequate moral, social,
health and economic support is provided to the troops who are in harm's way
and to their families back home — before, during and following deployment.

• Will provide the necessary resources to help active duty armed forces
succeed in making the adjustment when they return to their family and
community life.

• Will continue to provide sufficient resources when the armed forces
have left active duty and become veterans so that they can move on with
their post-war and post-military lives, and will justly compensate them for
their sacrifices, their physical and emotional injuries and scars, and the
indelible imprint of horrific memories that will be carried forever. This
includes appropriate compensation for the families when the serviceperson
has been killed, physically or mentally disabled, and/or dies prematurely due
to service-related medical conditions.

---

241. Jeff Barker, reprinted from the *Florida Today*, in: *SunHerald*, Biloxi, MS, D-2.
242. Alison Young (2005, March 7 and March 8), *SunHerald*, Biloxi, MS (2005, March 7 and
     March 8).

• That when a new war comes along, veterans and military retirees of previous wears are not forgotten or pushed aside and promises that had been made to them curtailed under the guise of there being too limited resources. In other words, that the priority now being given to current active duty military personnel is not ever at the expense of veterans, that the government will be at least as vigilant and forceful to insure that the needs and issues of veterans related to their having gone into harm's way to serve the country are prioritized and fully addressed. And that this commitment will be no less so than the vigilance and commitments being made to recruit, pay, train and equip the next generation of active duty personnel who are being asked to go into harm's way to once again to do that "about face" necessary to protect our nation's vital interests.

If and when any of the above commitments from the government, America's leaders, and society is violated or perceived to be violated, the impact on military retirees and other veterans and their families can be devastating — even beyond the loss or absence of the needed benefits or services that were not received.

> The transcendent trust relationship between our government and society with our active duty military and veterans and their families is vital to help provide a valid rationale, a sanction, a reason for the individual armed forces personnel to be able to justify to themselves why they had been willing to do something that civilians are not asked to do: engage in war and to kill and maim and willingly suffer injury, loss or death of self and one's comrades for the benefit of our country.
>
> However, this willingness and decision can become extremely conflicted and troubled when our government and our society are perceived to have diluted, disrupted or fractured concomitant promises made to our active duty members and veterans. And such diluted, broken or fractured rationale and promises can and do result, for many veterans, in a strained if not broken connection with our government and our society. [243]

And any such betrayal has enormous implications for post-war healing, as is described in the last chapter.

DON'T CHEAT VETERANS TO COVER THE COST OF A CURRENT WAR

A political tactic that has been used much too often is to pit the budgetary priorities of the DOD and the VA against each other, as if funding could not be found to cover both. No less a figure than the Undersecretary of Defense for Per-

---

243. See two classic writings by Robert J. Lifton, "Advocacy and corruption in the healing profession." In C.R. Figley (Ed.), *Stress Disorders Among Vietnam Veterans: Theory, Research and Treatment* (209-230) (New York: Brunner/Mazel, 1978); and R.J. Lifton, *The Broken Connection. On Death and The Continuity of Life* (New York: Simon & Schuster, 1979).

sonnel and Readiness, David Chu, stated that the money being spent on retirees and veterans "is hurtful, and takes away from the nation's ability to defend itself." [244]

When men and women sign on for military duty, they accept a bargain in good faith, and for their part they honor their commitment and put their very lives on the line. When they find themselves fighting peace-time battles to obtain benefits and services that they have earned, their trust is seriously weakened if not destroyed and they can only wonder what kind of nation they were serving. In that context, is it any wonder so many have difficulty with their post-war readjustment? This is seldom incorporated in any meaningful way into the counseling and healing efforts that are provided.

The return trips to Vietnam in 1989 and 2000 revealed that the violation of this trust even impeded what otherwise was an extremely positive healing process for the veterans.

> The return to Vietnam [in 1989] was a healing experience, but I still have a problem with America and mostly with the government for how they treated us on our return from the war. America still needs to recognize the Vietnam vets for what we went through in the name of Freedom! I think we need a trip to the White House and Congress so they can apologize and thank us for what we endured and not fight us every step of the way — especially the VA.
>
> — Dave Roberts

During a time when it seems like the President is willing to ask for (and Congress is willing to sign) blank checks for limitless amounts of money in support of the US military presence in Iraq and Afghanistan, the VA budget is hardly keeping pace with the cost of living. Indeed, large funding cuts in VA psychiatric programs over the past several years are very worrisome in regards to both psychiatric casualties and those seeking medical services. "The soldiers [with post-traumatic stress disorder] didn't come right away after Vietnam, either. If they come in the numbers predicted, the numbers the VA's own studies predict, we could be overwhelmed," stated one VA psychiatrist.[245]

This serious concern is echoed by an analysis of VA funding by Paralyzed Veterans of America. Regarding the president's proposed budget for the VA for FY06, it says,

> of the proposed increase of $111 million in the VA Health Care budget, annual cost increases will consume all but one-fourth of one percent. This paltry increase wouldn't fund existing patients, let alone the new veterans coming into the system. Currently, thousands of veterans wait six months or longer just to see a specialist for the first time because of delays in funding.[246]

---

244. Ray Funderburk, "Don't cheat veterans to cover the cost of war." Letter to the Editor, *SunHerald*, Biloxi, MS (2005, January 30), B-2.
245. Marilyn Elias, "Mental disorders are on the rise among Afghanistan, Iraq veterans." *USA Today* (2005, March 31), A1.

No wonder so many veterans question America's commitment to veterans and their families.

Indeed, early estimates of the "final" price tag for the war in Iraq were between one and two trillion dollars; and as of mid-2006 there is talk of increasing rather than decreasing troop numbers as expected.

Putting those figures into perspective, the highest grossing movie of all time ("Titanic") earned $1.8 billion worldwide. This is about one-half the cost that the US incurs in Iraq every week.[247] But the place to cut costs is surely not at the expense of those who put their lives on the line.

As a result of the promises this country has broken or diluted, many military retirees and other veterans experience despair, rage, pessimism, disillusionment, suspicion and deep distrust, self-reliance or even severe isolation, passivity, disinterest or apathy, and separateness or severe alienation. For many it seems easiest to just give up, and remain embittered.

When any of these negative outcomes occur, a successful post-war recovery is seriously jeopardized. A negative post-war experience with the DOD or the VA requires specific attention. The last chapter of this book discusses what to do about this.

AN ANALOGY: PROFESSIONAL SPORTS AND THE DEPARTMENT OF DEFENSE

An analogy could be drawn between professional sports teams and active duty military personnel and how they are treated, on the one hand, and on the other hand, the treatment of ex-players and ex-military.

Professional sports players and active duty military personnel who perform well are rewarded, while in uniform.

The US military is like a Department of Sports (DOS) with teams that have potential opponents worldwide. (It happens that opponents who can realistically compete in this league are few in number, and most are too poor, too small, and not willing to be scheduled to play against the DOS.)

The owners and coaches have one mission: defeat their opponents. They talk about being a family, they say that to win we must stick together and work towards a common purpose, putting the team head of personal goals. And, they say, we're behind you, we care about you, you're not just an interchangeable part. When you wear this uniform, you are family.

---

246. Roger D. Clark, "VA budget won't meet needs of returning troops." *www.SunHerald*, Biloxi, MS (2005, April 1).

247. Linda Bilmes and Joseph Stiglitz, "War's stunning price tag." *Los Angeles Times* (2006, January 18). Accessed on-line 1.19.2006.

It is understood that the professional sports player will play until he (or she) can no longer contribute to winning. Some will play to the point where their bodies are worn out or broken. But the risks are considered well worth it.

Of course, it is a two-way street. The players love playing: the teamwork, the adrenaline rush, the personal challenge as warriors — and the winning; that's the bottom line. When you are the champion, there is no feeling that can match that. It's also a job, and it pays the bills so you can support your family.

Some of the players who are worn out, or broken, or never did well enough to be in the first-rank of players, or have just gotten too old, will be released. Some won't even make it out of training camp. Others may be put on a reserve squad to call up in case a replacement is needed to keep our active roster full. Many of you will not have very good contracts if you are not in our elite league; too bad you left school early to join. And while some of you will go on to do quite well in your post-sports lives, others will not fare nearly as well.

Because one day the members of the sports teams and the members of the military will retire and become ex-players, or veterans.

And where do you turn after your active days are over, if your physical or mental health has been damaged?

If the analogy could be stretched, there would be an organization just for ex-players who may be in need — the Department of Ex-Players (DExP). Only not every ex-player is eligible to receive the services of the DExP. You now must prove that you need the services or benefits that you seek, even though (and this is where there is a slight deviation from current sports reality) you were told when you signed your contract that you would be taken care of when your playing days were over. Actually, you may not be eligible for various benefits and services, and you may or may not be given any, some or most of the services you want or need. In fact, you should consider getting a lawyer.

Of course, that requires money. Yes, it's always money. Money to fund the DExP is really tight. The owners of the Department of Sports are funded from the same pot of money that the DExP is funded from. Do you think we can keep on winning if we reduce training, salaries, and signing bonuses, or settle for second-rate equipment?

It may seem surprising that the Director of the DExP (equivalent to the Secretary of Veterans Affairs) serves the very same boss (equivalent to the President) as the Director of the DOS (equivalent to the Secretary of the Department of Defense). And the Director of the DExP knows when he is selected what the rules of the funding game are.

- He is to never complain publicly when the lion's share of the annual funding is apportioned to the DOS.
- Nor will he complain publicly that the DExP is not being adequately funded, if he wants to keep his job.
- Indeed, he may well have marching orders that his number one priority is to constrain the costs of the DExP — regardless of the needs of ex-players.

• Let's be frank. How could anyone possibly consider denying funding to retain that sharp competitive edge to not only defeat but annihilate our opponents — just to meet the needs of an ever-growing pool of grumpy and growing older ex-players?

THE IRAQ WAR HITS CLOSE TO HOME

It is one thing to read the latest casualty reports in the local newspaper, lists of names that are not familiar to the reader, and perhaps to pause for a moment to reflect on yet another death or injury. It is quite another thing to see a name you do recognize. Around Christmastime 2004, the husband and father of a mother and young girl I know was just such a casualty, killed in action in Iraq. This tragedy illustrated the horrific human cost of war, as well as the wonderful support provided through the military's casualty assistance program and both the military and civilian communities in honoring a fallen hero and assisting the surviving family members. And the memorial service was remarkably emotional.

I found myself worrying about how both mother and daughter would handle this tragedy, both short and longer term. In particular, I thought about the daughter and how the Christmas season would always be bittersweet — infused with the memories of the traumatic death of her father; and, hopefully, over time, also with treasured memories of him.

And I wondered, if I were the one who had to talk to a child whose parent had just been killed, what would I say? And, while words are never adequate at such a time, the lyrics from a song kept singing in my head. I thought, I might say: "This is what your daddy would have wanted to tell you, if he could, and I am sure that he is thinking it right now, up in heaven."

> I'm already there.
> Take a look around.
> I'm the sunshine in your hair.
> I'm the shadow on the ground.
> I'm the whisper in the wind.
> I'm your imaginary friend.
> And I know I'm in your prayers.
> I'm already there . . .
> I'm the beat in your heart.
> I'm the moonlight shining down.
> I'm the whisper in the wind.
> And I'll be there to the end.
> Can you feel the love that we share?
> I'm already there.
> I'm already there.[248]

And I was reminded of two poignant letters that were left at the site of the Vietnam Veterans Memorial in Washington, D.C. One letter was from a now 23-year-old daughter whose father died in Vietnam, and the second letter was from a son of who was three years old at the time of his father's death.

> Well, here you are, making another lasting impression on me and everyone else who sees you! I love you so much. I have dreamed of the day you'll come home and finally be my dad. You would have been the best daddy in the whole world. You were for the short period of time in my life. I can never forget you. I'm 23 now! I sure look a lot different from six-years old. You'd be very proud of me. They say I'm a lot like you. I can see it too. I have never forgotten you. I knew you were Santa Claus, but I didn't want to spoil it for you.
>
> Your daughter, Sheri [249]
>
> Even though I never really knew you, you still meant the world to me. Thank you, Daddy, for giving me three years of your life. Remembering you through photos, I can only say I love you, Daddy. Happy Father's Day. Part of me died with you.
>
> Love, Your son, Joe [250]

For the current generation, the reverberations of today's wars continue to cut an ever-widening swath through the hearts of families throughout America — and Iraq and Afghanistan and elsewhere. And I hope and pray that the ever-accumulating sacrifices, injuries, psychiatric casualties and deaths, and the escalating number of family members deeply wounded by ricochet, are truly necessary and for the right reasons.

Convince me that they are — please.

---

248. "I'm Already There," by Lonestar, 2005.
249. L. Palmer, *Shrapnel in the Heart. Letters and Remembrances From the Vietnam Veterans Memorial* (New York: Vintage Books, 1987), 42.
250. Ibid., 42.

CHAPTER 6. WAR TRAUMA-RELATED BLAME, GUILT AND SHAME. RELIEF IS POSSIBLE

Shortly after Staff Sergeant Jimmy Mussey arrived in Iraq, his unit manned roadblocks. To signal cars to stop, they raised their hands as vehicles would approach.

> [If the driver kept going] we would just light 'em up. I didn't find until after, after talking to an Iraqi, that when you put your hand up in the air, it means "Hello."

Mussey estimates that his unit killed 30 civilians in one 48-hour period. He can't forget one incident in particular:

> . . . there was this red Kia Spectra. We told it to stop and it didn't. There were four occupants. We fatally wounded three of them. We started pulling out the bodies, but they were dying pretty fast. The guy that was driving was just frickin' bawling, sitting on the highway. He looked at me and asked, "Why did you kill my brother? He wasn't a terrorist. He didn't do anything to you."

And then Mussey searched the car:

> It was completely clean. Nothing there. Meanwhile the driver just ran around saying, "Why? Why?" That's when I started to question.[251]

Many survivors of trauma have a particular problem with guilt and blame issues. War-related guilt involves feeling responsible in some way for a negative result during the war. Unresolved guilt keeps the trauma memories very emotionally charged and part of active memory.[252] Veterans' attempts to forget or resolve long-standing guilt and blame issues from their war experience often

---

251. Goodman, 2004, 52.
252. Schiraldi, *PTSD SourceBook*, 2000.

times are unsuccessful. For them, there is preoccupation with guilt and painful, incessant ruminations of anguish about feeling guilty.

Such veterans carry an exaggerated and distorted sense of guilt, shame, self-blame, self-denigration and/or self-contempt over "being at fault" or "responsible" for some combination of:

- Having been in a trauma.
- Not having prevented the trauma from happening.
- Not stopping the trauma once it began.
- Experiencing problematic behaviors and emotions during the trauma.
- And then at their continuing to be troubled and haunted by painful memories of the trauma.

An Iraq veteran who has become an activist against the Iraq War said:

> A lot of what I'm doing is basically survivor's guilt. It's hard. I'm home. I'm fine. I came back in one piece. But there are a lot of people who haven't . . . I came home and read that six children were killed in an artillery strike near where I was. I don't really know if that was my unit or a British unit. But I feel responsible for everything that happened when I was there.[253]

Finally, shame also can accompany issues of guilt. Shame goes one step further than guilt: "Not only did I do something bad, but I am bad to the core."[254] And while shame can be a very painful and severe outcome of engaging in certain behaviors to survive war, clinical experience with hundreds of veterans is that guilt and blame are much more predominant problems for most veterans. And shame may be very problematic for some veterans.

There is a powerful, confusing and conflicting aspect of the experience of war. And that is being an active participant in, or witness to, acts that are a combination of the seemingly irreconcilable. On the one hand, there is horror and carnage. On the other hand there is the culturally forbidden arousal, the thrill, danger and the intoxication that can come with wielding the ultimate power over other human beings — the power to take another person's life.

The Thrill of the Kill. The inextricable linkage of such polarities is not a problem to some combatants. The "dirty little secret of war" that most civilians do not understand is that, for more combatants than the US would like to admit, there is an adrenalin rush, and for some a joy, at the thrill of hunting down the enemy.[255] This fact was aired in public by Marine Lt. Gen James Mattis, an infantry officer who commanded troops in both Afghanistan and Iraq, and at the time he made this statement was the commanding general of the Marine Corps Combat Development Command in Quantico, VA. He said:

---

253. Goodman, 2004, 50.
254. Schiraldi, *PTSD SourceBook*, 2000.
255. See my discussion of "the combat cocktail" in *A Vietnam Trilogy*, 2004. See also D. Grosssman. *On Killing. The Psychological Cost of Learning to Kill in War and Society* (New York: Little Brown 1995).

Actually, it's a lot of fun to fight. You know, it's a hell of a hoot. It's fun to shoot some people. I'll be right upfront with you, I like brawling . . . You go into Afghanistan, you got guys who slap women around for five years because they didn't wear a veil . . . You know, guys like that ain't got no manhood left anyway. So it's a hell of a lot of fun to shoot them.[256]

Perhaps even more troubling than the general's expression was the official response of the commandant of the Marine Corps, General Mike Hagee. General Hagee issued a statement saying,

Lt. Gen Mattis often speaks with a great deal of candor. I have counseled him concerning his remarks and he agrees that he should have chosen his words more carefully. . . .While I understand that some people may take issue with the comments made by him, I also know he intended to reflect the unfortunate and harsh realities of war.[257]

In other words, Lt. Gen Mattis was rebuked for speaking too candidly about having fun shooting the enemy. But he was not rebuked for the fact that he enjoyed killing other human beings. That combatants may get a kick out of killing is the nasty secret of war — and for some, it is an intoxicating emotional rush. Of course, this is almost always minimized if not denied in public. And some such combatants may feel no guilt or shame or remorse or sadness at all. My former auto mechanic for my 1967 Austin Mini in Woodland Hills, California was a combat vet. Once he told me in the late 1970s:

I will never forget my first combat assault into a hot LZ [landing in a helicopter in an area that was under enemy fire]. As the chopper was approaching the LZ, we were yelling and screaming, rocking up and down, pumping ourselves up. It was such an intense high, I have never felt so alive in my life. And that's why there will always be war — because war is the ultimate thrill.

They have their counterparts in civilian life, who "get their kicks" wielding the power of violence or threat of violence against others. This dynamic was graphically described by some of the prison guards at the Abu Ghraib prison, where US guards were photographed grinning and giving the thumbs up over the bruised and bloated corpse of a prisoner whose death eventually was ruled a homicide.[258]

256. John L. Lumpkin, "Marine leaders says, 'It's fun to shoot some people,'" *SunHerald*, Biloxi, MS (2005, February 4), D-1. And for those who might be concerned that the general was misquoted, his words are reported to have been obtained from an audio recording of the forum he was speaking at in San Diego about strategies for the war on terror.
257. Ibid.
258. "Iraqi died in Palestinian hanging, CIA records reveal," *SunHerald*, Biloxi, MS (2005, February 18), D5.

Engaging in such violence is not bothersome to some; they enjoy doing in war what would be judged psychopathic or criminal in the civilian world. For such people there is no internal conflict.

Others may use the threat of violence for personal gain. For example, dozens of incidents involving Army soldiers involved in mistreatment of Iraqi citizens were in Army files that were only made public under a Freedom of Information Act request by the American Civil Liberties Union. Nine soldiers from Fort Carson's 3rd Armored Cavalry Regiment went unpunished after being accused by other soldiers of stealing over six months from Iraqi citizens or accepting "hush" money from those who did.[259]

The vast majority of veterans are upset by the inevitable immersion in the horror and excitement/arousal that characterize life in a war zone. However, they can tolerate the internal conflict as long as they remain firmly convinced that the violence was inescapable and justifiable either because it was necessary for the survival of oneself or to protect one's blood brothers and sisters in arms, and/or because it was what had to be done to protect and defend the nation's vital interests and security. And the solace derived from such rationale appears to be dissipating dramatically as the massive US military presence in Iraq and Afghanistan seems unable to quell the vicious cycles of killing and retribution.

The final group of veterans, to varying degrees, was and has remained deeply conflicted if not tormented by the awareness of a most startling discovery — that the horror of what one had to do by being both the hunter and the hunted during wartime was accompanied by an intoxicating high. The complex sensation results in terribly ambivalent and conflicted internal forces seething within, or emerging over time as a disturbing, unacknowledged and toxic presence laced with shame. If it is not fully acknowledged and accepted as part of what one was and what one did (admission and acceptance that there is a part of oneself that could have been so turned on by such horrific experiences as a perpetrator or even as a witness) will result in remaining a prisoner to the resulting toxicity within.

THE THRILL OF THE KILL AND THE ANGUISH

This anguish, inexorably fermenting and breeding within as the months and years go by, is illustrated again by Mario, a Vietnam veteran. Mario was a helicopter door gunner, and he also was involved in ground operations. The following clinical vignette is from one therapy session in a treatment group with

---

259. Dick Foste, "Troops accused of theft in Iraq. Some Fort Carson soldiers took money, goods from citizens." Rocky Mountain News (2005, January 27).

five peers — two Vietnam veterans, two from World War II and one from the Persian Gulf War.[260]

Mario: My CO [Commanding Officer] said, "You hurt a lot of people in the village." I said, "the hell with them — you worry about the people in the village, what about all the [US] guys over here . . . It's so stupid . . . The platoon leader asked if I wanted to join them. I said, "no, I'd rather [go into the village and] see the people looking at me where I can do something. Not staying up there [with the platoon on the outskirts of the village and shooting into the village from a distance] just shooting the person. I wanted to see the people [that I was shooting at]

Ray: Why?

Mario: [smiling] I like to watch the guys drop . . . I like to watch their eyes. I wish I could see, watching somebody drop and doing their last shakes [as they are dying].

Ray: And what was driving you? What was pushing you to do all this stuff? What was going on with you?

Mario: Oh, I just wanted to kill as much as I could kill. I wanted to be on the edge all the way, all the time.

Ray: If you could be the part of you that killed, give a voice to that part and be that part. Tell us. Talk to us as that part of Mario.

Mario: [you mean] How I feel about that? [starts smiling again, and laughs] I smile, and I laugh. It's a high. I like . . . hch . . . I like to see . . . heh . . . I like to take body parts a lot of times. I like to . . . heh . . . [continues smiling and laughing, and then becomes silent].

Ray: Go ahead . . .

Mario: It was just fun . . . I don't know about you guys [here in the group], but it was fun and joking for me. I . . . a lot of the guys I knew they were scared . . . but I made a joke out of everything — even though I felt sour inside [gestures with hand to his throat] at what I was doing. But my outer part, it always was a joke, you know. Uh, it was, it was like funny [laughs again]. You make a joke. Hey, we really have to throw some guys [enemy prisoners] out of the helicopter [laughs]. I say, shoot, give me the guys [laughs]. Ah, shoot, heh. I . . . crazy . . . [smiling].

Ray: What's crazy?

Mario: The way I think.

Ray: So, is this the "crazy" part of Mario talking?

---

260. Scurfield & Powch, *Journey of Healing* (1997).

Mario: I don't know . . . I . . . don't know, hmmm, what part . . . I used to go to orphanages on my own to help the kids.

Ray: Then, this isn't the part of Mario that enjoys killing talking now, is it?

Mario: No. I used to go [to the orphanages] just to feel a little better about what I had done to some of the people.

Later in the session, Ed, one of the other group Vietnam veterans, gives Mario some feedback (and demonstrates the empathic abilities of peer veterans to be able to tune in to what is really going on with another vet):

Ed: I tried to listen to the person underneath the saying of the words and, what I see, is, when you're laughing, you're not laughing, you're not happy . . . You're crying underneath.

Mario: Yeah, that's it; crying out.

Ed: I don't know if this is true for you or not, but it seems to me like, you don't really enjoy killing. But you had to survive and you had to tell yourself something, you had to convince yourself that you liked it. That's why you had to make the jokes, and it's like you're acting, like you're pretending like you liked it, and you did it so much that you believed it, too. But I don't think you liked killing.

And Mario sits in his chair, very somber, no longer laughing.

OTHER REACTIONS TO KILLING

Some veterans accept little or no responsibility for their part in having been in a trauma or for their behaviors and they blame others to an exaggerated and distorted degree. They, too, find themselves stuck and preoccupied; they project blame onto others and are unable to honestly look at their own actions and reactions.

To survive trauma, people typically ascribe meaning to the events that occur and may reframe the trauma experience. This reframing may or may not be reality-based. This is partly due to the tunnel vision survival mode, where the veteran is so narrowly focused on surviving that it is impossible to see the whole picture. A common result is that the veteran will assume a much exaggerated sense of responsibility while denying or avoiding recognition of mitigating circumstances. Hence, a war veteran might conclude that he or she should have died "because people I was responsible for died." Veterans also may judge themselves to be immoral or unworthy of success because of their survival behaviors or mistakes, and they severely downplay the role of environmental circumstances.[261]

And when a special comrade is maimed or killed, the guilt is particularly deep. It is as if there can be no excuse for not having saved one's comrade or having somehow prevented what happened — even when there is absolutely no rational basis for such self-blame.[262]

TRAUMA TREATMENT MYTHS AND REALITIES

It is typical for war veterans (and survivors of other types of trauma) to believe in several myths related to the treatment of trauma-related symptoms and issues.

The veteran's beliefs regarding the following should be assessed and discussed prior to attempting to move ahead with more specific treatment interventions.

Myth: These treatment sessions are to help me forget about the war trauma.

Reality: It is unrealistic for a trauma survivor or a clinician to believe that. Trauma-related memories cannot be entirely eliminated. A more realistic goal is to reduce the toxic reactions to such memories and to learn to more peacefully coexist with such unforgettable memories.

> *Analogy:* With successful treatment, it is as if your trauma memories are being telecast through a small black and white television off in the corner of the room, at a very low volume, and you control the off/on button — versus being subjected to a huge-screen, Cinerama, 3-D color movie with loud surround-sound that continually replays the most horrific trauma scenes, over and over again. And you have no access to the volume and on/off controls.

Myth: If I fully remember and re-experience aspects of my original war trauma (through talking about it, thinking about it, focusing on it), I will lose control and either be sucked back into the vortex of that memory and never able to come back out again or I will go crazy, or start crying and not be able to stop, or become so enraged that I will hurt someone or myself.

Reality: Trauma survivors don't go crazy from remembering and talking about their trauma but they may "go crazy" trying so desperately to deny the undeniable that the trauma happened, that it hurt then and it hurts now, that it hasn't gone away and that it needs to be dealt with.

Myth: My trauma-focus treatment was a failure — because I started having increased nightmares about the original trauma, couldn't stop the new flood of intrusive trauma-related thoughts, my sleep disturbance got worse, and I was crying or really angry a lot.

---

261. Schiraldi, 2000, 185.
262. J. Shay, *Achilles in Vietnam* (New York: Atheneum, 1994).

Reality: That is not necessarily a sign that the treatment was not working. Once you engage in trauma-focus treatment or engage at a deeper level, your traumatic stress symptoms will temporarily get worse before they get better. And that is only natural, because you are being asked to put attention on the very experience(s) that you have been trying so desperately to deny, numb, minimize or avoid all these years/months.[263]

COGNITIVE REFRAMING INTERVENTIONS

To understand the reality of the trauma experience, it may be necessary to look at it in a "fresh" or new way. This may allow the veteran survivor to more fully understand and acknowledge a range of factors that have not been fully or at all recognized or considered. And, this might then allow appropriate reframing to occur that allows the veteran to have a much more balanced perspective on what happened and on the issues of blame and guilt (and, where it fits — shame). Otherwise, such distorted or erroneous memories and viewpoints may never be effectively challenged as one tries to just forget the past and move on.[264]

There is one psychological intervention that has a very long track-record in addressing psychological symptoms and various behavioral problems for mental health populations. And this intervention also has been commonly used by military mental health providers. This is the cognitive-behavioral technique known as cognitive reframing.

A psychiatrist on active duty with the 883rd Combat Stress Control Detachment described a version of this approach with a soldier near the Kuwait border.

> He was frightened of going to Iraq and afraid of chemical attacks, couldn't get it out of his mind . . . It seemed like a pretty normal amount of fear. [I] tried to "reframe" the fears of the soldier in order to calm him . . . that it was perfectly natural to be scared, and that, even though a chemical attack would be dreadful, it would probably not prove fatal to many soldiers due to their training and the masks and outfits they were to protect against such assault. We talked about ways to relax . . . He seemed much more reassured when he left.[265]

Cognitive reframing also is essential for many survivors who continually replay the events and then — months and years later — come to the conclusion that somehow it was their fault what happened. This is like "Monday morning

---

263. See also: J.L. Herman, *Trauma & Recovery* (New York: Basic Books, 1992/1997); and G.R. Schiraldi, *The Posttraumatic Stress Disorder Sourcebook. A Guide to Healing, Recovery, and Growth* (Los Angeles: Lowell House, 2000).
264. Schiraldi, 2000, 185.
265. Weinraub, 2003, B4.

quarterbacking" after the weekend game was played. Outside of the immediacy and emergency of the moments during which the trauma has occurred, the survivor is cursed with the ability to go over and analyze what happened time and again. Inevitably, such self-analyses often times bring the survivor to the conclusion that he/she always could have done something differently, or quicker, or better. And the self-blame and guilt set in, and is aggravated every time he/she thinks about what happened.

Therefore, one therapeutic strategy is to move the survivor from sitting here today and looking back as a critical observer who is cursed with hindsight about what had happened years ago. Instead, the survivor must be able to reemerge him/herself back into the memory of what happened — as if it were happening again right now. Gestalt and Existential therapies have very effective therapy techniques to accomplish this, for instance by having the person speak in the first person, present tense when describing what happened.[266] This helps the survivor to therapeutically re-experience the event as if it were happening now and to discover that his/her Monday morning quarterbacking was not realistic.

Second, a "determining the percentages of responsibility technique" that I developed over decades of clinical work with combat veterans offers a strategy to directly address that which Harold Kushner describes as a universal sense that "it's my fault."

> There seem to be two elements involved in our readiness to feel guilt. The first is our strenuous need to believe that the world makes sense, that there is a cause for every effect and a reason for everything that happens. The second element is the notion that we are the cause of what happens, especially the bad things that happen.[267]

SURVIVAL GUILT: CLINICAL VIGNETTE

An application of Gestalt Therapy intervention strategies to a cognitive reframing intervention is illustrated by excerpts from the following therapy session with Chuck, a World War II veteran. This clinical vignette also illustrates how, through several repetitions of telling the trauma story in a here-and-now Gestalt approach, memory is enhanced and a more realistic perspective of what happened is realized.

---

266. For a description of how I have adapted Gestalt Therapy techniques to trauma-focus therapy, see the companion monograph for the video, *Journey of Healing*, by R.M. Scurfield and I. Powch. (Honolulu, HI: Department of Veterans Affairs. National Center for PTSD, 1997).
267. Harold S. Kushner, *When Bad Things Happen To Good People* (New York: Schocken Books, 1981), 92.

Chuck, at the age of 69, has continued to feel anguish and guilt for over 50 years for the death of one of his best friends that occurred on the last day of battle in World War II.[268]

Chuck: We were pinned down by a German machine gun in a pillbox [concrete bunker]. All we had were M-1s [rifles] and a BAR [Browning Automatic Rifle], nothing heavier than that. I told the guys to hold their position and wait until I could [go back to the rear and] bring back a bazooka... And when I came back one of my best friends, Gilfelden, he was dead. He had been shot in the back. But there was no way the Germans could have killed him because he was down, concealed by the building between him and the Germans. The only thing I could figure out was that the GIs on our left [they were behind us], in moving up to be on the same position that we were, had mistaken him for a German or something and had shot him. And that was really . . . I cried . . . And I, God, it was horrible.

Irene: I was touched by the closeness of you with your buddy who was shot in the back, and just the senselessness of losing him in that way.

Chuck: And the worst part that I didn't even say is that . . . that was actually the last day of combat that we ever had. There wasn't any firefighting from then on. Now that made it even more traumatic, although I didn't know that at the time.

Ray: Chuck, and if that buddy were here today and could hear you, what would you say to him?

Chuck: I think I would say, "Gilfelden old buddy, I'm sorry I left you. Maybe if I had stayed behind, uh, we could have protected the rear better and you would never have been killed as you were." I know for a long time after that I felt that I had not really protected the flanks and the rear . . . I figured our real enemy was out in front, and I hadn't realized that the sides and flanks and the rear also had to be protected. We had the whole squad there; we could have built up a circle until I got back with the bazooka.

Ray: That's easy to say in retrospect.

Chuck: Yeah. Right. Right. Nobody blamed me at the time or later.

Ray: Chuck, *based on what you knew at the time*, tell your buddy what you're thinking about what you did. Based on what you knew at the time, what would you now say to your buddy?

---

268. Scurfield and Powch, *Journey of Healing* video, 1997.

Chuck: Well, from what I knew at the time, it was urgent that we get a bazooka and knock out that machine gun because we were pinned down, at least we couldn't move forward, and the orders were to advance. And so, I did. . . the only thing I thought would have broken the impasse was to go for the bazooka.

Ray: And if you had decided to try to take out the nest without the bazooka, do you think you (your unit) would have had any casualties?

Chuck: Oh, yes, an MG-42 fires a thousand rounds a minute. As soon as we went over that wall they would have gotten us. There was no way we would have . . . they were in a [concrete bunker] gun port . . . even with rifle grenades, you couldn't get up to fire a rifle. How were you going to get a clean shot on the machine gun? The only thing I felt was to get the whole squad up, ready to fire, and then bring the bazooka up, let everyone open up on the machine gun and try to pin him down long enough for the bazooka to get a shot at him.

Ray: And, in retrospect, does that seem like the tactical thing to do?

Chuck: I thought so, yeah.

Ray: And today, do you think so?

Chuck: Well, yes. But of course [it turned out that] I couldn't even get a bazooka when I went back.

Ray: Well, but you couldn't have known that [at the time].

Chuck: Yeah, that's right.

Ray: Considering all of this, and if your buddy could hear all this, what would you say to him right now?

Chuck: Well, I think it was just fate that, uh, that we lost you, Gilfelden old buddy. God must have willed it. We wanted you to be with us here today, but it just wasn't in the cards.

How Chuck's words to his dead buddy have changed! After some 50 years of self-recrimination and retrospective thinking, now he could speak based on what he knew at the time of the incident some 50 years ago.

Technique To Determine The Percentages Of Responsibility

Over the past 20 years I have developed and refined a specific cognitive reframing therapeutic intervention with war veterans. Active duty military mental health professionals, as well as those working with veterans, also could use this systematic approach to complement what they already do. It is a quick and powerful intervention.[269]

This technique aids the trauma survivor in arriving at a more balanced perspective and acceptance of personal responsibility versus responsibility that should rightfully be shared with or that belongs to others. This is especially germane to war veterans, in that war trauma always occurs in the context of the small operational military unit and always is interpersonal.

This technique is not an attempt to totally absolve trauma survivor guilt or to minimize legitimate personal accountability for behaviors and non-behaviors. Rather, it is utilized to facilitate a more reasonable and reality-based perspective and to ease the psychological pain associated with an exaggerated sense of guilt or blame. One objective is to clarify feelings of guilt that may be appropriate and necessary; after all, sometimes there is a degree of personal responsibility that has caused or contributed to trauma or suffering, and that responsibility ought to be accepted.[270] On the other hand, there can be an excessive sense of guilt, a tendency to blame oneself more than is actually deserved.[271] Hence, it is necessary to differentiate between what, if any, is appropriate versus excessive or inappropriate guilt.

The therapeutic steps in applying the Percentages of Responsibility Technique to the survivor of any type of trauma are described in detail in Appendix I. Here are two actual case vignettes that involve very different traumatic war incidents. Each had a quite different negative outcome on the veterans, at the time and for decades afterwards. One is a Vietnam War veteran and one is a Korean War veteran. Each case also illustrates a different approach in utilizing this treatment technique.

ACCEPTING TOO MUCH RESPONSIBILITY

This case involved application of all eight steps of the technique in sequence during an actual group therapy session.

---

269. I first wrote about an application of this technique to war veterans in: Scurfield, R.M., "War-related trauma: An integrative experiential, cognitive and spiritual approach." In M.B. Williams & J.F. Sommer (Eds.), *Handbook of Post-Traumatic Therapy.* (180-204) (Westport, CN: Greenwood Press, 1994). The case illustration described herein is taken and expanded from this writing. A version of this case was also described in Schiraldi, 2000. Please note that my development of the steps of this technique owes much to various peer counselors at the American Lake VA PTST Program (1985-91). The details of the technique evolved through many trauma-focus groups that I co-facilitated with various peer counselor Vietnam veterans, such as Steve Tice, Nelson Korbs, Art Owens, Jim Cariaso, Rico Swain and Bob Swanson.
270. Harold S. Kushner, *When Bad Things Happen To Good People* (New York: Schocken Books, 1981).
271. Ibid.

Step #1: Get a clear description of the event and the veteran's perception and rationale for the degree of self-responsibility assumed.

Ray: Please describe the event as best you remember it.

Vet: I had just finished unloading a truck full of supplies to this unit; I was really tired and was just sitting in the cab, resting . . . I happened to glance over and saw a guy in the distance by a tree. I assumed he was on perimeter [guard] duty. I also saw a second guy who was a little ways apart from the first guy and was moving in his direction. I assumed they were both Americans. All of a sudden, I heard this loud sound, a rifle shot. One of those two guys looked like he was lying down next to a tree; the other guy was running away. I found out that the second guy must have been a VC [Viet Cong] and he had killed the American . . . and, I just sat there in my truck and assumed he was an American!

My God, I could have checked closer, or I could have yelled out, or done something!

Ray: Let me clarify something right away; are you feeling totally responsible for this?

Vet: Yes . . . well, almost totally.

Ray: Let's give a percentage to it. If we can assume that there is a total of 100% responsibility for this American's death, what percentage have you blamed yourself for? You don't have to be exact, just give an approximation — about what percentage do you feel responsible?

Vet: About 95 percent.

Ray: Are you sure that your responsibility is about 95 percent? Is it maybe more than that, or less than that?

This therapeutic interaction is to stimulate new thinking by the veteran. The veteran is then challenged to convince the clinician and the rest of the group[272] how it was that he deserves to be 95% responsible.

The clinician must direct the group *not* to rescue at this point in the process in order to force the veteran to fully acknowledge "publicly" (to the clinician and to the peer group) that which he has already decided and been persecuting himself about all these years. It is critical for the veteran to let them know how and what he has been remembering and saying to himself to remain convinced of his (exaggerated) sense of responsibility.

---

272. This session was in a peer treatment group with several other war veterans, which is my therapeutic modality of choice for working with veterans on war-related issues. However, this technique could be applied in individual sessions as well.

Step #2: Challenge the veteran's exclusion or minimization of the role of others who were at the immediate scene of the trauma.

Vet: I would give the other 5% of the responsibility for the death to the vet himself. I guess if he had been a little more careful maybe the VC wouldn't have gotten that close to him.

Ray: Wait a minute. Let's look closer at this guy's responsibility. Were you responsible for sentry duty that night?

Vet: No, actually I think the guy killed was one of the guys pulling sentry duty that night.

Ray: And so, he's only 5% responsible for allowing that VC to get that close to him that night, and he was on sentry duty, and somehow you are 95% responsible for his death? Does that make sense to you?

Vet: Well, now that you put it that way, maybe he was 15% or 20% responsible.

Ray: Really? Are you sure that's a fair percentage to assign to him? Should he get more or less than 15-20 percent?

Once the veteran arrives at what appears to be a more realistic percentage of responsibility that he might assign to the most obvious other person who bears some responsibility, the veteran is further challenged to consider to what extent he is responsible for that other person even being there that night.

Ray: By the way, did you have any responsibility for that guy being in Vietnam? [and being in that unit, being there that night, being on guard duty, obeying the order to stand guard, being in-country or for being in the Army in the first place...]

If the veteran claims that indeed he did have some influence or responsibility over the other person's being in the actual situation that occurred, he then is challenged to convince the group and the clinician that the other person himself had absolutely no responsibility for being there, and how the veteran could have 100% responsibility for forcing or causing that person to be there.

The above strategy is also systematically applied to all other persons who were present at the scene of the traumatic incident:
   • The other veterans who were on guard duty that night.
   • Whoever assigned sentry duty.
   • Whoever was responsible for the selection of the site where the unit was located (would this event have occurred if the unit had been elsewhere?)
   • Any other Americans who were in the area — do any of them have any responsibility for what happened that night?
   • And, last but not least, the Viet Cong fighter who actually shot the American.

Ray: Let's talk for a moment about the enemy. Were the VC any good at what they did? You tell us how good, or incompetent, the VC were at infiltrating behind perimeter lines.

Vet: Well, of course, they were good, they were damned good.

Ray: And if the men in that unit were all doing their jobs to the best of their abilities that night, does that mean that the VC would never have been able to kill anyone? Let's get real: No matter how good a job all the Americans there that night had been doing, does not that VC deserve some of the "credit" and responsibility for the death of that American?

Vet: Well, yes, thinking about it like that, yes, he does.

Ray.   And now that *you* are thinking about it like that, what is your judgment as to how much responsibility he deserves?

Vet: Maybe about 30% or 40%.

Ray: Wait a minute. Isn't 30 or 40% too much to give to someone whom you hadn't given *any* responsibility to all these years? Make sure that you are now giving what you consider to be a fair and realistic percentage to the enemy — no more and no less.

Vet: No, as I think about it now, the VC really does deserve to have about 40% of the responsibility for what happened.

Thus, the veteran comes to his own conclusion that, indeed, his perception and remembrance of the event and delegation of blame have been extremely constricted. It may now be timely to bring to the veteran's attention that the percentages of responsibility that the veteran has now assigned to various people, including his own — now total well *over* 100 percent.

Ray: By the way, you have now allotted well over 100% responsibility for the death of the American who was killed. Do you think that you can recalculate some or all of the percentages that you have assigned? Is yours still 95%, which means that all of these other people split up the remaining 5 percent?

The veteran is not specifically directed to precisely recalculate the percentages at this time. It is best to have a volunteer from the group who will agree to write down what percentages have been assigned to whom and to give this written list to the veteran at the end of the group session. In this way, the veteran does not have to be distracted by keeping track of percentages during the exercise.

Step #3: Challenge the veteran's exclusion or minimization of the indirect responsibility of others who were not at the immediate scene of the trauma.

To not expand the circle of responsibility beyond individuals immediately and actually at the scene promotes a continuation of an exaggerated burden of responsibility for individual acts or non-acts that occur in the war zone. This is "society victim-bashing" of war veterans; that is, blaming veterans for society licensing them to be agents of death and maiming. They carry their own and everybody else's share of responsibility for the consequences of the nation's war policies.

What about more senior military officials in the war zone? Do they deserve any share of the responsibility for the various traumas that occur? In other words, did the military strategies facilitate the most likely positive (military) outcome, was the minimization of loss of US casualties a primary concern, and did their strategies and policies contribute to "unnecessary" loss of life and destruction among the veteran and/or civilian population in the war zone?

Next, the veteran is asked a series of probes to consider and respond to about persons not actually at the immediate scene of the incident.

Ray: Ultimately, doesn't the military command structure at its highest levels in the theater of operations deserve to receive a piece of the responsibility for what happens in the many individual incidents?

Vet: Well, yes, I would give them about 10% of the responsibility.

Ray: Would any of you even have been in-country that night if the US were not fighting in Vietnam?

Vet: Of course not . . . hmm, I can see where I didn't have 100% of the responsibility for being in Nam that night, or even being in Vietnam at all . . .

Ray: And so, what percentage of responsibility for you even being in the Vietnam War at all should be assigned to our political leaders who got us into this war?

Vet: Well . . . I would think that they ought to have at least 20% of the responsibility.

Ray: And, what about all of the civilians who sat around and watched the latest Vietnam casualty reports on television and then proceeded with their lives, irrespective of what was happening in Vietnam? Do they deserve any of the responsibility for you being in Vietnam at all, continuing to be in Vietnam, and being in Vietnam that night?

Vet: Absolutely. But I don't know right now what percentage of responsibility I would give to them.

Ray: That's okay. Just think more about it later and see if you can come up with a fair assignment of percentage of responsibility, if any, for the US civilians during the war.

I must admit that I do have a very strong conviction about civilians during a war being fought by our country. I contend that when a nation goes to war, every adult in that nation bears a piece of the responsibility for each and every single traumatic incident or result that occurs.[273]

Step #4: Re-challenge the veteran's sense of his/her own percentage of responsibility for behaviors and consequences

Ray: Now, let us return to you and what you did and did not do, and how much responsibility you had for being in the military in the first place, for being in the war zone, for being there that night, and for what you did and did not do that night. Because, you were that night, you did sit in that truck, you *did not* say or do anything when you saw the second person [the VC], and an American was blown away.

We are not here to try and help you to explain away any of whatever percentage of the responsibility that you truly believe and feel that you deserve for what happened that night — once you have fully considered all the others who legitimately deserve to be held accountable for some of the responsibility, too.

And so, considering all the other factors and persons, what piece of the responsibility for that American's death do you now believe is truly yours?

Vet: Well, considering all of those people, I would say that I deserve to have about 25% of the blame.

Once the veteran has focused or re-centered on this issue, the clinician moves on to the next step.

Step #5: Challenge the veteran to consider if he/she has been "punished" enough for his/her personal share of the (recalculated) responsibility for what happened

Ray: Now, tell us how much you have suffered and punished yourself all of these years over the 95% or so of the responsibility that you have been blaming yourself for about this American's death. In other words, take into account all the times you have suffered pain from remembering and agonizing over what happened, criticizing yourself, feeling guilty, etc. How much?

Vet: A lot . . . I mean, a whole lot. Not a week has gone by these last 17 years that I haven't relived that event, over and over again and thought about what I did not do.

The group then discusses the degree of responsibility that the veteran has now assigned to him/herself, and how this percentage compares with the self-punishment suffered — which has been based on a much higher assumption of responsibility. The veteran must make a clear statement to all the group members, and decides if he or she has engaged in self-punishment and being

---

273. Scurfield, in Wilson & Raphael, 1993.

punished "enough," "not enough," or "more than enough" — in consideration of his/her *newly assigned* percentage of responsibility.

It is often helpful for the veteran to repeat this statement to several individual veterans in the group, to see if this revised perception of responsibility he/she has assigned feels right to him/her at this moment.

Vet: Yeah, well I now really feel that my percentage of the responsibility is about 25% for that American's death, that 25% is a fair percentage to lay on me.

Ray: That's not too high? Too low? Repeat what you said to each of several different vets here in the room and see if perhaps you want to change your percentages higher or lower.

Vet: Jim, I feel that 25% responsible for my part in that American's death that night seems like a fair percentage. Billy, I now feel about 25% responsible for not having reacted more quickly that night and that American on sentry duty dying. Ron, I am 25% responsible for what happened that night, not 100%, but definitely 25%. I own that, that feels right.

Ray: And now that you have said that to three different vets here today, does this feel like a fair percentage of responsibility for you to have, to accept for yourself right now, not too high or not too low?

Vet: Yes, that feels right. 25%. [And this time it is said with conviction and acceptance. If it is not so stated, the veteran is further challenged to consider what percentage he truly feels he is responsible for.]

Step #6: Explicate a non-self-destructive plan to provide additional "payback" (if any more payback feels warranted) for the veteran's share of the (recalculated) responsibility

Ray: And so, have you suffered enough, have you been punished enough, for your 25% of the responsibility for that American's death?

Vet: Well, you know, now that I am sitting here and realizing, really realizing how much more of the responsibility for his death than I really am responsible for that I have been feeling all these years, I feel like a really big weight has been lifted off my chest.

Ray: That's great. But that doesn't totally answer the question. Have you suffered enough? *Have you been punished enough* for your 25% of the responsibility?

Vet: I don't think I'm quite ready to say that, that I have been punished totally enough. Maybe I deserve just a little more punishment to finish off this feeling of guilt.

Ray: Okay, there's no hurry. You've been carrying this around a very long time. This isn't something that you have to totally and finally make a decision about today. See how this week goes as you review what happened here today, and your discoveries about the other people who legitimately have deserved to share in the responsibility for that American's death, and your revised thinking about your fair share of the responsibility.

Step #7:   Conceptualize and commit to a homework assignment.

Ray: And so, you have a lot to think about this week, and to reflect upon. I want you to consider the following homework assignment.

• Take a little time each day to really reflect back on what you discussed today, and if you feel like it, further adjust the percentages of responsibility that you have assigned for the total to equal 100.

• Also, pay attention to that heavy weight that has been lifted from your chest. And see if you still feel some weight there, some pain, whether there still is some payment that you still feel that you need to make to more fully balance the scales and "pay" yet some more for your share of the responsibility.

If you decide that you still "owe" something more, think about a payback plan that is *not* something to continue to further punish yourself with and to feel bad about, and to continue to mess up your life with. Instead, think of a more "positive," life-sustaining action that would both do honor to that dead American and better satisfy your continuing commitment to pay back. And, if you cannot come up with something that is appropriate and positive and not self-destructive, talk with one or two of the group members to see about ideas that you might consider.

Is this something that makes sense to you, something that you can take a crack at?

Vet: Yes.

Ray: Okay. I want to do one more thing. I would like to ask if there any group members here who would be available for you to contact them if you need to talk with someone about a continuing pay-back plan? (Five different group members volunteer.)

Step #8:   End the session in a way that recognizes and confirms the "work" that the veteran has accomplished today.

Ray: Wow, I really feel like you did some really, really important work here today. I am amazed how much weight you have been carrying around all these years and how much you have been punishing yourself. And, in spite of that, you were willing to re-look at this whole incident and honestly address all the challenges we threw at you today. You must be very strong, that you have been able to survive all these years, even with this terribly heavy weight pressing down on you. I thank you for trusting us enough to go through this with us here today. I am proud to have been a witness today to your work. [And other group members are encouraged to share their reactions to the work this vet did, and how observing his work may have impacted on any guilt or responsibility issues that they might have.]

Vet: Thank you. Yeah, this was a really important session for me today. I'm looking very differently at this heavy guilt issue I have been carrying around all these years. I need to go home and reflect more on this. Thank you all for your patience in bearing with me as I went through this today. I needed your support. Thank you all.

NOT ACCEPTING RESPONSIBILITY: CLINICAL VIGNETTE

The intervention to determine the percentages of responsibility technique is equally effective in dealing with the opposite issue, when someone denies or dramatically minimizes his or her own responsibility and is blaming and putting the responsibility almost entirely onto others.

This is a very critical issue to confront. Sometimes one has caused or allowed something bad to happen and one ought to take appropriate responsibility; an appropriate sense of guilt makes people try to do better.[274] Furthermore, inappropriately blaming others and not accepting our share of responsibility is a way to continue to deny the reality of what happened and to justify "holding on" to damaging feelings and beliefs. It is a way to maintain a "woe is me" attitude, fixate on blaming others and to continue to live in the past.

This clinical vignette demonstrates the systematic challenging of a Korean Vet's 37-year long holding onto rage, projecting 100% of the blame towards his unit, his lieutenant (LT) and the Army for an incident. He was seriously wounded by a land mine and was severely disfigured (face and body) and suffered other physical disabilities. He has continued to not accept any personal responsibility whatsoever for what happened.

This vignette illustrates that all eight steps do not necessarily have to be addressed, nor are the steps necessarily addressed in a strict sequential manner. However, the basic strategy is carried out, challenging the veteran each step along the way about the degree of responsibility that (1) he had originally assigned to himself and to others, and (2) the revised percentages he is now assigning.

---

274. Kushner, 1981.

Step #1: Get a clear description of the event and the veteran's perception and rationale for the degree of blaming others and not accepting self-blame.

Vet: First of all, I was supposed to be in the rear echelon in Korea, but the Army didn't keep their promise and sent me to the front. In Korea, mines were a really serious problem. On this day; our unit [six soldiers who set up battlefield lights to illuminate the surrounding area in case some of the enemy might infiltrate or attack] was supposed to set up a good location for the lights. The LT told us that there was this area that had been checked by the engineers and seemed safe. The Chinese had abandoned some bunkers here, and so the LT thought it was a good idea to use one of the bunkers, rather than build our own bunker. And, we had not yet realized how smart the Chinese were — they would have thought that we would have thought like we were — about taking over an abandoned bunker rather than building one ourselves.

So, I went up over to the area, and then a mine blew up. The next thing I know I'm woozy and am down on my knees, blood pouring out, my guts hanging out, and I'm yelling to the unit — who were over behind the truck — to help me. But they didn't come right away. I could have died! Finally I passed out. Luckily, I was rescued and I remember being in a medical ambulance and being evacuated to a field hospital. I then was taken to Japan, where...

Ray: Hold it. What's the issue for you?

Vet: I'm really angry at being disfigured and at the army and at my unit and at my LT.

Ray: Okay, so if there is 100% responsibility to be distributed around for blame of your having been severely wounded in this incident, how much of the responsibility have you been laying on the unit, your LT and the Army?

Vet: They *obviously* were 100% to blame for what happened.

Step #2: Challenge the veteran's exclusion or minimization (or inflation) of the role of others who were at the immediate scene of the trauma.

Ray: Okay. Let's go over this again: How difficult was it to detect the mines?

Vet: It was pretty difficult, with the terrain how it was and the Chinese were really good at hiding their mines.

Ray: Oh, the Chinese were good at what they did?

Vet: Very good.

Ray: Well, I noticed that you didn't assign any percentage of the responsibility to the Chinese forces who laid the mine in the first place. Don't they deserve to have a share of the responsibility?

Vet: Well, yes, if they hadn't hidden the mine so good, I would have been able to detect it.

Ray: So, what percentage of the responsibility do you want to assign to the enemy who laid the mine that blew you up?

Vet: Well, maybe 50 percent.

Ray: Okay. Now what was the SOP [standard operating procedure] when setting up a light site?

Vet: Well, we would recon [do a "sweep" or reconnaissance] of the area ourselves to make sure there were no mines, or sometimes we would rely on the word of others that the area had already been swept.

Ray: Bullshit — you knew to never trust what some one else did. Didn't you?

Vet: Well, yes.

Ray: And so, per SOP, one person was selected [in this case, you] to go over to the bunker area where the unit had decided to set up the lights, right?

Vet: Yes.

Ray: Did you then assess the area yourself?

Vet: Well, I grabbed a light and kind of walked nonchalantly over there.

Ray: Was that SOP to recon in the way that you did?

Vet: Well, I did look and the area seemed okay at first glance.

Ray: I repeat, was that SOP, to do a quick visual scan like that?

Vet: Well, no.

Ray: Then, how often did you only do such a quick visual scan?

Vet: About 30% of the time.

Step #3: [Step #3 is skipped at this point: indirect responsibility of others not at the immediate scene]

Step #4: Re-challenge the veteran's sense of his own percentage of responsibility

Ray: So, you actually gambled 30% of the time and got away with it — until this incident? Right?

Vet: Right. But the LT said [I interrupt him again]

Ray: Forget what the LT said for now. Did you not assess the area like you should have? Did you goof up your part. Didn't you gamble — and you lost?

Vet: Well, yes, but . . .

Ray: No "buts." Can you accept *your* part of the responsibility? Did you mess up your part, did you gamble, and you lost?

Vet: Well, yes.

Ray: Okay, then what percentage of the responsibility would you assign to yourself right now, for not having followed SOP and only doing a cursory visual scan of the area.

Vet: Uh, maybe 30 percent.

Ray: Okay. Now, how many hills had your unit set lights up on?

Vet: Many. I was really exhausted. We had been setting up and taking down the lights on many different hills over the past several weeks.

Step #3: Challenge the veteran's exclusion or minimization of the indirect responsibility of others who were not at the immediate scene of the trauma

Ray: So, who's to blame for you and your unit being so exhausted by the time you got to this area?

Vet: Well, no one in particular. It was just the way it was. Korea was a harsh country to fight in, there were lots of troop movement going on, the enemy were very dangerous, there were only so many of us to do this important job.

Ray: And who is to blame for there not being more of you on light details?

Vet: Well, we just weren't getting enough troops to take care of it.

Ray: And who is to blame for that? The LT?

Vet: No, not really. He tried to get more men assigned.

Ray: His CO? The head of the Army operations in Korea? How about the Secretary of the Army and the DOD?

Vet: Well, yes, I think all of them had some blame for us not having adequate numbers of men to both scan for mines and set up the lights as much as we had to.

Ray: So, what percentage of the responsibility would you assign to them, as a group?

Vet: Uh, perhaps 30%. Wait, I think the percentages now add up to more than 100%.

Ray: That's okay for now. Let's keep going on like we have been. You are doing great. We'll deal with the total of the various percentages assigned near the end of our session today.

Vet: Okay.

Step #4: Re-challenging the veteran's assignment of personal responsibility:

Ray: And you got tired of being real careful all the time, right?

Vet: Yes. I was only a dumb 18-year-old, and no one's perfect.

Ray: Did you hear what you said, "no one's perfect"?

Vet: Yes, no one's perfect.

Ray: And that includes you?

Vet: Absolutely.

Ray: So, you were guilty of not being perfect, weren't you?

Vet: Well, if you put it that way, yes, I guess so.

Ray: Don't just accept it because I said it. Does it make sense to you?

Vet: Well, yes it does.

Ray: Okay, then what percentage of the responsibility do you deserve because you were a dumb 18-year-old who was exhausted, there weren't enough troops to do the job, you were way overextended, the Chinese were a very formidable enemy, and you found yourself gambling 30% of the time on quick visual scans because of all of this?

Vet: Well, thinking about all of those things, I think I would give myself maybe 20% of the responsibility. Wait, didn't I give myself 30% earlier?

Ray: Yes, you did. But that was before taking all of these things into consideration. So, do you want to change to 20% or go back to your first percentage of 30%. Which feels more accurate?

Vet: I think I would go with the 20%, considering all those things.

Ray: Now, what about when you were hit? Your complaint is that you were yelling, and that your unit wouldn't immediately come to you, and they took so long. In your condition, you *may not have been able to yell!*

Vet: Well, I didn't hear too good, either, because of the concussion from the explosion.

Ray: And, in an emergency, what seems like hours might have been only minutes, right?

Vet: Yes.

Ray: And, what's the SOP when someone gets caught in a minefield?

Vet: You don't immediately send others in. You check it out very carefully first, and then send in one or two . . .

Ray: And, considering the severity of your wounds, it must not have taken them *too* long if you survived, did it?

Vet: Well, I guess they had to call for a medic over the phone — that would have taken some minutes, anyway . . . I guess I don't really blame them.

Ray: You "guess" you don't, or you don't?

Vet: You're right, it's not a guess; I don't blame them now.

Step #3: Re-challenging the veteran's assignment of responsibility to others at the immediate scene:

Ray: Well, considering all of the above factors, what percentage of the blame would you give to your unit members who were hiding behind the truck?

Vet: Well, I guess they did the best they could. They did follow procedure. And they did get medical help for me. So, maybe 10% of the blame.

Ray: Are you sure? Is 10% too little or too much?

Vet: No, that sounds about right.

Getting the veteran to now look at the impact on himself — this is a variant of Step #5: challenging the veteran to consider if he/she has been "punished" enough for his/her personal share of the [recalculated] responsibility for what happened.

Ray: Okay. Now, Rick I want you stop and look at all the feelings you have inside about what was happening to you in Korea, what was going on with you over there. How did being in the war impact on your feelings?

Vet: [Rick thinks, owning the feelings underneath.] Well, I'm a caring person . . . and it hurt — all that death. So, I became angry — the caring person just disappeared.

Ray: And what are you in touch with right now, as you have said all that you said today?

Vet: Well, you know, you've now 'removed an old buddy' I've been carrying around for 37 years [the anger and hostility towards his unit, the LT and the Army]. I now realize that they weren't 100% responsible for what happened. No, not anywhere near that percentage. I've been holding onto this anger and blame towards them for 37 years. This really is feeling different right now. In fact, I'm feeling relieved. Why?

Ray: Well, perhaps because you are now admitting to yourself the realities you and your unit and your LT and the Army had been facing there in Korea, that you had been distorting those realities somehow in reaction to being so severely wounded and disabled. Perhaps you needed to put the blame somewhere, on someone — and you picked those closest to you. Does that sound at all like what was going on?

Vet: Yes, *exactly* like what was going on.

Ray: And so, if you truly deserve 20% of the blame for what happened, can you live with that? Does that make sense?

Vet: Yes, I can and yes, it does. After all, shit happens being in war, and it sure happened to me. It's so unfair.

Ray: Yes, it is unfair. I am truly sad that it was so unfair to you, and what you have been going through.

Vet: Thank you. . . . But I do feel much better right now about this.

Step #7: Conceptualize and commit to a homework assignment:

Ray: Okay. Let's see how the coming week goes, as you reflect back on our discussion today. Spend a little time reflecting back and play with the percentages for all who deserve some share of the responsibility for what happened to you that night. And if you would let us know next week what you have decided about the percentages at that time, okay?

Vet: Yes, actually, I am really looking forward to doing that.

After the session was over, I felt such ambivalent emotions. On the one hand, this Korean War veteran had accomplished some really important clinical work that now made it possible for him to be able to move beyond the rage that he inappropriately had been projecting onto others for three decades. Now, he could begin to truly look at and deal with the real issues — his grief over what had happened to him, and the lost years spent mired in his anguish. On the other hand, I was saddened. How tragic it was that this veteran had suffered so much more than he had needed to *for over three decades* and had not been able to move on with his life. Better now than never. And I pray that not many Iraq veterans also have to wait several decades to obtain relief from war-related issues.

What more can be done to help ease this inevitable negative legacy of war?

From my three decades of working with hundreds of war veterans, and from being in Vietnam three different times over three decades, I have come to an additional series of strategies, the concept of an expanding circle of healing.

Before presenting the components of an expanding circle of healing, I want to briefly identify the impressive number of factors that describe the parallels between Vietnam and Iraq in terms of the psychological and social impact on combatants and civilians. These parallels underscore the lessons unlearned from Vietnam that continue today regarding the Iraq War in terms of the impact of war.

CHAPTER 7. BACK TO THE FUTURE: FROM VIETNAM TO IRAQ

Just what does the Iraq War, not to mention Afghanistan and other wars that may yet occur in the Middle and Far East, have to do with *A Vietnam Trilogy*? Everything.

The Iraq War is not an exact replication of the Vietnam War. There are significant cultural, political, historical, religious and military differences. And all wars that are fought have their differences — even the wars currently and concomitantly being waged in the predominantly Moslem countries of Iraq and Afghanistan. On the other hand, there is a universality of the social and psychological impact of war that transcends any differences between Vietnam and Iraq or Afghanistan.

There are too many "once agains" about the Iraq War that are strikingly parallel to the Vietnam War. These include:

• US military men and women are put in harm's way in a far-off land, fighting, killing and dying "in the vital interests of our national security."

• There has been a massive investment in and deployment of state of the-art military technology in support of American military forces that are, arguably, the best equipped, and best trained and most lethal and effective fighting force in the world. Early on, there were very optimistic predictions of a quick victory. Yet what was described as a *quagmire* some three decades ago has become a *slog* today.[275]

• US military might and state-of-the-art weaponry and technology have been accused of buttressing or arranging the "election" of a "native government" that has been labeled by some of the local people as lackeys of the US, a puppet government that does not represent the majority of the people but serves someone else's interests.

153

• US military men and women are being hailed by different factions of the populace as liberators, or as invaders and occupiers, and others in between. And perhaps most painfully Iraqis, even children, have been captured in media photos openly rejoicing over the charred wreckage of choppers and Humvees where Americans have died. And the initial "hero's welcome" accorded many of our entering military forces are a distant memory.

• US military men and women are fighting in a war zone where it is close to impossible to discern friend from foe. Once again we are immersed in nasty guerilla (now called terrorist or insurgent) warfare, in which notions of formal warfare between uniformed enemies, the so-called "accepted rules of engagement" and "moral" behaviors in a war zone, have been discarded. Strategies of subterfuge, intimidation and terror are waged by an enemy who was largely disarmed before the war by international inspectors who located or even destroyed the weapons systems; locals seemingly will do anything now, will maim or kill anyone, to include non-combatant children, women and the elderly, to expel the Americans and the US-controlled government — or to kill other Iraqi's who they hate.

• In an effort to defeat guerilla/terrorist/insurgent warfare, US military men and women have been instructed to "win the hearts and minds" of the populace while simultaneously carrying weapons, invading communities and homes to do block-by-block and house-by-search searches, destroying schools, power grids and sewage plants, maiming, killing or taking away family members and friends who are suspect, inadvertently maiming and killing innocents who happen to be in the wrong place at the wrong time or who become frightened or confused and don't understand or don't obey the rules about curfews and check-points — all of which sows further seeds of hate and retaliation.

• For every enemy you kill in a guerilla war, you create two new ones.[276]

• US military men and women are put in an excruciating position. On the one hand, they must maintain essential vigilance, suspicion and proactive self-preserving instinctual and lethal, split-second responses if they are to survive physically. On the other hand, they are trying desperately to remain

---

275. My gratitude to Secretary of Defense Donald Rumsfeld for adding the word "slog" to my vocabulary when he angrily declared that Iraq was not a "quagmire" (like the Vietnam War) but a "slog." Slog: — v. 1. to walk or progress with a slow, heavy pace; plod: slog across the swamp. 2. To work diligently for long hours: slogged away at. Latin. — tr: 1. To make (one's way) with a slow heavy pace against resistance. 2. To strike with heavy blows. — n: 1. Along exhausting progress, march or hike. 2. Long hard work. *The American Heritage College Dictionary, Third Edition.* Boston: Houghton Mifflin Company, 1997, 1282.

276. Joseph Galloway's rule of thumb about guerilla warfare. J. Galloway, "War in Iraq: It's got to be about more than numbers." www.*SunHerald*, Biloxi. MS (2004, September 18), C2.

caring and moral human beings and not let the rage and revenge and self-preservation become so overwhelming that nothing else really matters — and which are often easier to justify *during* the war than it is *after* returning home.

• US military men and women are flooded with the ultimate adrenaline pump. They feel incredibly alive and experience what seem to be the very ultimate of highs and successes, forged in the crucible of life-and-death moments.

• At the same time, they are experiencing the ultimate of tragic depths as they are placed repeatedly in positions where they have to make instantaneous decisions that inevitably will involve mistakes or errors in judgment. These are split-second decisions with life-changing impact that pierce, if not shatter one's psyche, one's heart, one's humanity, one's soul.

• Military medical authorities describe a healthcare system that is state-of-the-art and will save untold numbers of lives that otherwise would have been lost. Yet again they fail to mention that there will be vast numbers of severely disabled veterans who will require substantial resources to cope with not only the life-long physical wounds but the accompanying emotional and spiritual wounds as well — as will an exponentially larger number of their family members.

• Government and military authorities issued highly optimistic predictions that the acute psychiatric casualty rates would be very low, based on expected limited tours of duty, adequate rest and relaxation respites for war zone soldiers, and the placement of trained mental health teams in the war zone. However, the public was not told that a reduction in the acute psychiatric rate tells us absolutely nothing about how many longer-term or chronic war-related psychiatric casualties will be created.

• US military men and women are being emotionally and psychiatrically damaged, maimed and/or killed, and are returning home in body bags, as medical evacuees, or as part of routine rotations back to Stateside. At first, all casualties were individually recognized in the front pages of newspapers, with photographs and stories. Inevitably, as has already happened in Afghanistan, such personal acknowledgments move to back pages, then disappear. While the very few high-profiled "heroes" are adulated, medical and psychiatric casualties and other returnees become mere numbers in the continuing onslaught. They will remain nameless and faceless — except of course to their loved ones — although they are still recognizable by their uniforms.

• The initial attention from the military and the media passes, as does the initial euphoria and attention and understanding from loved ones and community, and the initial phases of elation and thankfulness of having survived begin to dissipate. And then returnees mostly become anonymous out-of-uniform veterans who meld back with little or no fanfare into communities across the land. Many of the recruits attracted by military public relations campaigns such as the Army of One become proud veterans; they are rightfully proud of their service to their country — before they will move on to become very proud and/or perhaps very invisible, lonely and isolated Veterans of One.

• For many, it starts to sink in — or it bursts into the consciousness — that the war isn't over for them. "How do I get on with my life — now that I have a gaping hole in my job resume, and in my relationships, missing limbs, missing body functions, missing comrades, missing youth and innocence, missing tranquility free from unexpected, excruciating and vivid combat images and missing nights of restful sleep?"

• Many veterans discover they do not miss — and yet they crave — those days when life was spiked with emotional highs and lows more intense than civilian life can provide.[277] War can bring out the best — remarkable valor, sacrifice and accomplishments. And war can bring out the worst — depravity, cruelty and failures. "War is the catalyst that brings out the best and the beast in man" (and, presumably, woman) — from My Lai to Abu Ghraib.[278]

• Many veterans discover that their lives have been immeasurably enhanced by their military experiences, to include a sense of being able to transcend anything that life might bring along. Conversely, other veterans are punctured with self-torture, guilt or shame, rage, and/or a spiritual void.

The readjustment is colored by the increasingly fractious public dialogue as voters get over the initial patriotic rush to support whatever their nation's leaders tell them is needed. The disparity begins to sink in between the words, values and priorities of elected leaders and "pro-war" contingents of both major political parties, versus what is shown by daily media coverage about the realities of the war and what many troops on the ground in Iraq are saying.[279] It was proven that even Colin Powell was misled about the official excuse for waging war in Iraq (weapons of mass destruction, which it turns out some in Washington knew were long since gone). No wonder a substantial number of responsible US citizens question the validity or perhaps the truthfulness of government pronouncements about:

1. why this war (Vietnam, Persian Gulf or Iraq or Afghanistan) really was necessary in the first place
2. how the war is really progressing, and

---

277. See the discussion of "the combat cocktail" in *A Vietnam Trilogy*, 267-211.
278. Eugene G. Verret, "Kerry respects those who fight for their country." *SunHerald*. Biloxi, MS, B2.
279. Tom Lasseter, "On Baghdad streets, soldiers see an Iraq that's unraveling." McClatchy Newspapers, *www.sunherald.com*, August 5, 2006, C-1, C-6.

3. why it continues to be necessary to put our uniformed men and women in harm's way.[280]

• American protestors are placed in a double bind. They are accused by pro-military forces of "not supporting the troops," when in fact bringing the troops home might be the most supportive thing we could do; of "hurting troop morale" by asking the government to justify its policy regarding the war, when that is in fact the sort of freedom Americans supposedly fight for. The schisms grow more acrimonious as increasing numbers of soldiers and their families more openly ask, "for what?" while others say we've invested too much to turn back now, and remain firmly convinced we should "stay the course," right or wrong.

• And, once again, the numbers of civilian casualties are mind-boggling yet dramatically downplayed — from perhaps some three million Vietnamese killed during the Vietnam War to untold tens of thousands of Iraqi civilians killed to date in the Iraq War. And all citizens of all political persuasion hope that the enormity of such losses is necessary and for a just cause.

THE EXISTENTIAL SLOG

Pictures of Iraq wind and rewind in his mind: the starving children crawling out from beneath homes of old rubble and debris as US troops roll in; the cheers for Americans with water systems and food supplies, come to make everything OK; the warnings from commanding officers that any villager could be armed with explosives.

"These people are happy to see you, they're cheering, and you're wondering if the same guy cheering for you might blow you up. . . . I just don't want all of it to be for nothing . . . This took a big chunk of my life away — and I want it to count for something."

His head falls into his hands. When he looks up, there are tears welling in his eyes. "Sorry," he says softly. "I'm sorry." No one understands. And he can't translate.[281]

---

280. The political statements about an exit strategy from Iraq have been critically described by a number of observers as very similar to what was stated during the Vietnam War. "Yet again, an American exit strategy depends on building up indigenous security forces virtually from scratch, before US public support for the war disappears." "To some Americans, the US exit strategy is a haunting echo of 'Vietnamization', the American plan a generation ago to train and equip South Vietnamese troops to fend for themselves against Vietcong and North Vietnamese communists, so that US forces could return home. They did, but South Vietnam quickly collapsed in the face of attack." Bob Deans, "Exit Strategy an echo of Vietnam War." *SunHerald*, Biloxi, MS (2005, February 1), A-4.

281. M.L. Lyke, "The unseen cost of war. *American* minds." (2005, August 28).

And so, once again, returning war veterans are grappling with issues that are not clean, abstract philosophical questions that one writes about in a school term paper. Because they may be immersed in a difficult post-war existential slog out of which there appears to be no easy path of recovery:

Who am I . . . this person who did and experienced things in the war zone that no one should ever have to face, but did — and survived, while others did not?

Why am I here . . . and repeatedly subjected to vivid memories and pain of what I did and did not do, and witnessed, during the war?

Where am I going . . . what now? Is this what I have to look forward to for the rest of my life, being so very alone with my own personal demons from the war, and never again really feeling like I am truly understood and a part of my community or my country?

A *New York Times* reporter interviewed a soldier who was paralyzed in Iraq.

> But when I asked this soldier, Eugene Simpson, Jr., a 27-year-old staff sergeant from Dale City, VA, whom he had been fighting in Iraq — who, exactly, the enemy was — he looked up from his wheelchair and stared at me for a long moment. Then, in a voice much softer than he had been using for most of the interview, and with what seemed like a mixture of sorrow, regret and frustration, he said: "I don't know. That would be my answer. I don't know."[282]

The unanswered questions, the confusion that can never be cleared, are haunting.

Too Many "Continues To Be"

The pain of the expanding ranks of damaged veterans and families cannot be assuaged until America deals with a series of issues that continue to be in place, decades after we learned about the problem. These include:

- The military medical mission to conserve the fighting strength, rather than to conserve the physical and mental health of the individual uniformed man or woman. Throughout history, front-line ground combat troops *always* have been the cannon fodder.
- A prevailing stigma, both among one's military peers and infused in the chain of command and especially in combat units, that those men and women who manifest psychiatric problems are "less than" real men and women.
- The knowledge among uniformed men and women that seeking mental health services can be disastrous to their military careers. And military

---

282. Bob Herbert, "Letting Down the Troops," *New York Times* (2004, October 29).

medical records do not have nearly the same measure of confidentiality protections that civilian medical records have.

• A lack of full DOD/VA collaboration in the transition from active duty to veteran status. The long-standing military attitude is "to discharge the unwanted and the unfit and let the VA take care of them."[283]

• A lack of VA programs, other than Vet Centers and some exemplary hospital-based exceptions, that provide state-of-the-art trauma-focus treatment services for veterans with war-related Post-traumatic Stress Disorder. Many PTSD Clinical Teams and specialized PTSD Programs are providing less and less, or minimal, trauma-focused treatment in which the troubling experiences during the war are directly addressed in a meaningful way. There is an increasing emphasis either on removing psychiatric symptoms or avoiding underlying traumatic issues, and little emphasis on helping the veteran to transcend negative symptoms and to enhance positives, hope, and spiritual wellness.

• An almost total absence of meaningful VA health or mental health services for the partners or children of veterans — loved ones, the veterans' primary support group, who are themselves entrenched in, confused about and dramatically impacted by living with the veteran and his or her post-war angst. Most families are left on their own to sort it all out.

• A focus in mental health treatment programs for veteran-only treatment, singly or only with other veterans. There is still extremely minimal direct intervention to enhance veterans' ability to integrate back into their families, into their communities, and into larger society.

• Thinking that the VA can handle it all, many communities continue to take little or no initiative and no sustained effort to understand and to welcome home, and to accept veterans back — and to actively help them over the years, if not decades, to integrate satisfactorily back into their families, communities and country. Once-a-year Veteran's Day acknowledgments don't do it.

• A US foreign policy to send large numbers of men and women to engage in military and peace-keeping actions, especially sustained ones, throughout the globe and where there often is not overwhelming support from the populace. This repeatedly exposes uniformed men and women to the no-win situation of being in the midst of harm's way ostensibly to protect the welfare of people who do not want them there and see them as foreign occupiers. How else would they be viewed? Occupying troops are at best briefly heralded as saviors. But then, the longer they remain, the more

---

283. There are encouraging signs of collaboration as was described in an earlier chapter. An additional example is the development of a VA/DOD Clinical Practice Guideline for the Management of Post-Traumatic Stress. See: http://www.oqp.med.va.gov/cpg/cpg.htm.

resented if not loathed they become. In the history of the human race, has a prolonged foreign military presence ever been considered otherwise?

• There continue to be considerable grounds to argue for and against what seems to be a mislabeling of the "Department of Defense." The decision to initiate a pre-emptive invasion of Iraq is consistent with the influence of war-hawks in the Administration and in Congress and the DOD over the years to operate more as a "Department of Offense." There has been a redefining and justifying of pre-emptive military interventions anywhere, anytime, rationalized by the threat of global terrorism and the possibility of weapons of mass destruction being or becoming available to nations we don't control. Regardless of one's political persuasion, the results are stark. This precedent-setting policy puts hundreds of thousands of Americans in harm's way. The Armed Forces are dispersed so widely that many individuals continue to be redeployed, time and again, very much to their personal detriment and beyond the agreement they thought they'd signed up for, and increasing significantly the risk they will be killed, crippled or mentally hurt.

• Finally, the public is increasingly polarized about national and international policies regarding the use of military force as an instrument of peace and a promoter of the grand aspiration of democratic nation-building. This polarization ensures that combat veterans will return to a nation deeply divided about whether their military service and sacrifices were the most noble and worthwhile of endeavors — or tragic and misguided.

BACK TO THE FUTURE — IS IT INEVITABLE?

Depending on how many of the aforementioned factors "continue to be," substantial numbers of future war veterans will suffer acute and decades-long psychiatric, moral, social and spiritual sequelae. These are inevitable legacies of war. Indeed, only the complete cessation of US military involvement in all wars and military occupations would stop this suffering among yet more generations.

It is extremely unlikely that wars will end, or even that the US would undergo such a regime-change that it would dramatically change its international policies and reduce its proactive and sustained military activities worldwide.

However, that does not mean that strategies of helping people to recover from war cannot be improved, based at least in part on the vital and courageous lessons learned by a number of veterans. These strategies must be considered for combatants both while they are on active duty and beyond. And that must start with two vital understandings:

1. a full acknowledgement and recognition of the universality of the experience of war and the shorter- and longer-term social and psychological impact of war, and...
2. what is needed and what is yet to be done to help our active duty military, our veterans, all their families, and our country, to heal from war.

This means that veterans of every war and more limited combat deployments, and their families, need to consider going beyond an emphasis on how unique and special each war and era of service has been. Can there not be recognition of both the unique contributions and experiences of each era of veteran and each war, as well as recognition that there are universalities that cut across wars, generations and continents in terms of what is experienced in war and what the range of social and psychological impact for decades is?

Indeed, the more one knows about veterans' experiences, the more clearly the similarities, not the differences, stand out. And it is the impact of war itself, of all wars, where the healing is needed.

Is Nonviolence No Longer A Viable Alternative?

In many ways the profession of arms [military service] appealed to Tolstoy. The quality it most demanded, courage, was one by which he himself set great store, and the alterations of danger and austerity with wild living suited his temperament . . . and even after he had become an out-and-out pacifist, he would confide to his diary how ashamed he was of the excitement and partisanship still stirred up in him when Russia was at war . . . Yes, eventually this huntsman and soldier who gloried in shedding blood became passionately convinced that killing, either of men or of animals, could never be justified.[284]

Everything has gone so far — the hatred, the killings, the counterattacks, the continuing threats, the retribution, the seemingly never-ending and ever-escalating cycle of violence — and the vow that America "will stay the course." The nonviolence espoused by luminaries in world history — such as Buddha and Jesus Christ, Mahatma Gandhi, Martin Luther King, Jr., and Mother Theresa — remains almost unthinkable, almost impossible to believe in and use as a guiding principle for how nations treat each other.

And yet, some people do see it. A letter to the editor in a local newspaper provides a breath of clarity and wisdom that actually speaks to some of the root causes of terrorism. Talk about winning the hearts and minds...

Why more violence?

---

284. Malcolm Muggeridge, *A Third Testament* (Farmington, PA: The Plough Publishing House of the Bruderhof Foundation, 2002), 127.

> Why must everything someone does to us be answered with more violence? I, for one, am proud to be called a dove. There is nothing to fear from me. If retaliation is on the people's minds, hit them where it really hurts. Destroy them with worldly goods. Randomly drop everything we can all over their countries. Target the women and children with the necessities and joys of life. A new set of pots and pans will go a long way in our quest for peace. Yes, I served in the armed forces and I'm 61 years old. [285]

No, I am not a pacifist. However, I do believe that war is, at best, a horrific alternative to be used only when there is no other way to secure a country's very survival. (I do recognize that good, honest and virtuous women and men may differ markedly in their convictions as to when this is actually the situation.) And yes, of course the above veteran's statement is somewhat whimsical — but it is no less in touch with reality than the belief that a war can be won against an indigenous guerilla or terrorist opponent strictly (or even primarily) through military means.

> When you fight in urban terrain, in the streets and alleyways of cities teeming with people, the killing you do today breeds new enemies tomorrow. [The] rule of thumb is that for every enemy you kill in a guerilla war, you create two new ones . . .

> Worse, machine guns and tank guns and Bradley chain guns and Air Force and Marine bombs inevitably kill the innocent as well as the guilty. The ordnance destroys homes and automobiles, and the pitiful possessions of the dispossessed, and it creates even more recruits to the war against the Americans. You blow up my house and kill my mother, and I will soon be waiting on a rooftop with an AK-47 and an RPG launcher and hatred in my heart for all Americans.

> That is why the main emphasis in counter-insurgency warfare is, or should be, on the political side of political-military operations. This is why there can be no purely military solution in Iraq. This is why, until and unless some political solution is found, Americans and their allies will continue to be maimed and killed in Iraq on a daily basis. [286]

A new public report by the National Intelligence Council (an advisory board of top intelligence analysts that is independent of the CIA) concluded that "instead of diminishing terrorism, US-occupied Iraq has replaced pre-war Afghanistan as a breeding and training ground for terrorists who may disperse to conduct attacks elsewhere." The report goes on to say, "The Al-Qaeda membership that was distinguished by having trained in Afghanistan will gradually dissipate, to be replaced in part by the dispersion of the experienced survivors of the conflict in Iraq. Iraq and other possible conflicts in the future could provide recruitment, training grounds, technical skills and language proficiency for a new class of terrorists who are 'professionalized' and for whom political violence becomes an end in itself." [287]

---

285. Why more violence? [anonymously written e-mail sent to Soundoff@sunherald.com, Biloxi, MS (2001, September 16), A 2].
286. J.L. Galloway (2004, September 18), C2.

The voter turnout of about 58% of the Iraqis for the elections on January 30, 2005, was a very hopeful step. Indeed, the United States, "a country where voting can be discouraged by the threat of rain has to marvel at the people who voted Sunday in Iraq under threat of death."[288] There is the contrary viewpoint that the heavy turnout for the Iraqi elections "was due in part to a declaration of martial law by the interim Iraqi government, the deployment of thousands of police and military, and a daylong ban on driving, depriving terrorists of both a favorite weapon and a means of escape."[289] A critical Arab viewpoint stated that the election installed "a democracy under occupation, on the corpses of 100,000 Iraqis, and ignited racial and ethnic divisions."[290] Also, the protracted failure of the elected Iraqi officials to form a government acceptable to the various factions in Iraq was a long and frustrating process that illuminates the deep fractures within the Iraqi peoples. Whether it was a remarkable success or a sham vote tainted by a foreign military occupation, the high voter turnout (other than in dominantly Sunni areas) was impressive.

On the other hand, another viewpoint would argue that the brutal regime of Saddam Hussein had kept a lid on internal Iraqi divisions and dissension, and that the violence there today was inevitable once dictatorial repression was eliminated — and will be inevitable whenever the American forces leave—and, indeed, maybe even if we stay. Recent reports reflect how top US generals who are still on active duty have stated that "the growing sectarian violence between Shiite and Sunni Muslims threatens to plunge Iraq into civil war." The United Nations has reported that 14,000 Iraqis are thought to have been killed by each other this year, and 3,000 in the month of June alone.[291] And reports from many of our ground troops in Iraq state that the possibility of civil war has already begun: "villages have been abandoned by Sunni and Shiite Muslims; Sunni insurgents have killed thousands of Shiites in car bombings and assassinations; Shiite militia death squads have tortured and killed hundreds, if not thousands, of Sunnis; and when night falls, neighborhoods become open battlegrounds."[292]

All agree that under the most optimistic scenario there is a long and very challenging road still ahead, and that the outcome of an ultimately peaceful and

---

287. Warren P. Strobel, Jonathan S. Landay & John Walcott, "Outlook bleaker, latest intelligence reports full of dire scenarios." *SunHerald*, Biloxi, MS (2005, January 18), B1-B2.

288. Editorial "Surprising turnout bodes well for challenges ahead." Detroit Free Press, Detroit, MI. As cited in the *SunHerald*, Biloxi, MS (2005, February 2), B-2.

289. Ibid.

290. Abdel Bari Atwan , editor, pan-Arab newspaper Al-Quda al-Arabi. "Arab governments get the jitters," *Dallas Morning News*, as reported in the *SunHerald*, Biloxi, MS (2005, February 2), B-2.

291. Drew Brown, "Top generals see Iraq slipping away." McLatchy Newspapers. SunHerald.com, Biloxi, MS, August 4, 2006, D-1, D-5.

292. Tom Lasseter, "On Baghdad streets, soldiers see and Iraq that's unraveling." McLatchy Newspapers, SunHerald.com, Boloxi, MS. August 5, 2006, C-1, C-6.

stable Iraqi government and country is far from a given—and may well be spi-raling out-of-control in the vicious, wide-spread and sustained cycle of violence and retribution.

And if the US does not win the battle for the hearts and minds of the Iraqi people (whom we said we are fighting to protect), there will be no chance of winning the war on the military front either. That was the stone-cold reality in Vietnam. It is the stone-cold reality in Iraq and in Afghanistan — and in any other country where the US might choose to send troops.

CHAPTER 8. THE EXPANDING CIRCLE OF HEALING

The full impact of war — physically, socially, culturally and spiritually — runs deep and cuts across us all. It is true whether one is career military or pacifists, jar-heads or tree-huggers, military special ops or anti-war protestors.[293]

Yes, the impact of war on combatants and civilians always is unforgettable, no matter how noble and right or base or misguided the motives behind it; no matter "how necessary" or not the war is; no matter how heroic or denigrating the behaviors engaged in; no matter how life-sustaining or life-depriving the consequences of our individual and collective actions ultimately are.

And what can be done about the pain and preoccupation that go on, despite all medications and therapy, venting and bearing witness, and in spite of having been provided solace and support, compassion and honor?

The path to optimal post-war healing is a path whose essential elements remain the same whether the context is Vietnam, Iraq, Afghanistan, 9/11 or even Katrina.

To go beyond merely surviving war and moving on to enhancing the post-war lives of veterans of all eras, their families, and our country, Americans must be willing to expand our comfort zones. There must be a willingness to look outside the confines of each of our small circles of personal familiarity and haven, to venture along avenues and by-ways that one simply has not considered or tried.

---

293. "Jar-head" is a widely-used term to describe a US Marine, deriving from the haircut that Marines are required to have. "Tree-huggers" refers to environmentalists and conservationists who are very strong adherents of their causes. "Special ops" refers to Special Operations forces who are highly trained warfare specialists, such as the Army Rangers and Navy Seals.

Several significant decision-making points are discussed in this chapter. These are choice-points that far too few veterans have actualized. Each of these choice-points has the potential to expand our personal circles of healing and promote further recovery from the seemingly permanent effects of war. On the other hand, these choices may not be easy to appreciate, and certainly are not easy for many veterans to make.

Vietnam veterans who returned to a peacetime Vietnam in 1989 and 2000 were stunned by their intensely positive experiences in meeting the Vietnamese people and former enemy veterans. Similarly, a number of us who met with Soviet veterans of Afghanistan in the 1980's and early 90's found we had more in common, and a greater sense of brotherhood, than we had to set us apart. All such connections, as well as those made by three veterans and sixteen history students who traveled together to Vietnam in 2000, illustrate the core element of the crucial remaining steps in the healing post-war journeys that many war veterans have yet to actualize:

to allow and promote an ever-widening inclusion of people, relationships and positives that heretofore have remained largely outside the healing circle of many veterans. Otherwise, the healing circle is arrested.

Of course, a large number of veterans *have* been able to move on with their lives. Many are very successful and contented, becoming outstanding members of their communities. Others have become influential leaders at the local, state, national and even international levels. However, even among those who have become quite successful and "don't have PTSD," there can still be painful and unresolved elements related to their war or post-war readjustment.

Additionally, there are many who have learned to chronically tolerate an existence that has retained the ever present poison of unresolved war and post-war pain. Along with carrying this toxic burden, too many veterans have continued, to varying degrees, to exist, to act, to feel, to perceive and to believe, that they will remain troubled and on the fringes of society.

By most reputable estimates 26% to 40% or more of the 3.14 million Vietnam theater veterans, or more than 800,000 in all, have been negatively impacted by the war and post-war readjustment. Many of them have never seen a mental health professional for war-related symptoms.[294] And even among those who have, many have obtained just a portion of the healing they could enjoy. And the surveys of Iraq war veterans reveal percentages of up to 30% with war-related mental health concerns.

---

294. Kulka et al, 1990.

MANUAL-BASED TREATMENT: AVOIDANCE OF THE CORE ASPECTS OF WAR AND READJUSTMENT

The trauma-focus treatment intervention technologies that have developed over the past 10 to 20 years have as a whole have been very impressive in terms of offering substantial relief from the anguish of PTSD symptoms, such as the pain and vividness of recurring war-trauma memories of war-traumatic events.[295] However, focusing primarily on what are considered to be the core PTSD symptoms can only get you so far (these are defined by the *DSM-IV-TR* as: re-experiencing the original trauma in some way, numbing/isolating/detachment/avoidance concerning reminders of the original trauma, and physiological arousal).[296]

There are other areas that require healing, too. And these areas are contained within the expanding healing circle that will be described. Core post-traumatic stress symptoms that are missing from the *DSM-IV-TR* definition of PTSD include: (1) damaged self—denigrated, disordered and fragmented identity, self-hatred; (2) existential malaise—the "broken connection", a sense that one's life is out of orbit; (3 disconnections between cognitions, affect, physiological responses and environmental cues; (4) preoccupation with blame—externally or internally directed; (5) pre-occupation with or actual loss of control over affect and behaviors; and (6) the central role of rage, grief and terror/fear.

Trauma-focus and cognitive-behavioral manual-based treatment approaches provided in individual treatment sessions are the vogue these days. And the manual-based treatment approaches have much to offer: the ability to target specific symptoms, consistency of application across different providers, relatively easy to learn, and easily replicable and testable in standard outcome

---

295. Trauma-focus treatment technologies include Thought Field Therapy, Eye Movement Desensitization and Reprocessing Therapy, Traumatic Incident Reduction, and the Counting Method. Established psychological treatment strategies have been adapted to trauma-focus therapy, such as memory enhancement, exposure therapy and peer group treatment. A range of such technologies is described in a self-help oriented book, Glenn R. Schiraldi, *The Post-Traumatic Stress Disorder Sourcebook. A Guide to Healing, Recovery and Growth* (Los Angles: Lowell House, 2000).

See also: R.M. Scurfield, "Treatment of posttraumatic stress disorder among Vietnam veterans," in J.P. Wilson & B. Raphael (Eds.), *International Handbook of Traumatic Stress Syndromes* (879-888) (New York: Plenum Press; R.M. Scurfield, 1994); and R.M. Scurfield. "War-related trauma: An integrative experiential, cognitive and spiritual approach," in M.B. Williams and J. F. Sommer (Eds.), *Handbook of Post-Traumatic Therapy* (181-203) (Westport, CN: Greenwood Press, 1993).

296. See American Psychiatric Association, The Diagnostic and Statistical Manual of Mental Disorders, IV, Text Revision (Washington, DC: American Psychiatric Association, 2000).

research protocols. Furthermore, such manual-based approaches have been adapted both to trauma-specific symptoms and to such important broader areas of functioning as living and coping skills, eating disorders, and management of sleep disturbance, anxiety and other troubling symptoms.

Unfortunately, there is a critical downside. The VA, the DOD and other providers have the strong tendency to promote such cognitively-based manualized protocols as *the* reputable way to offer clinical services to trauma survivors. This has the laudable goal of endorsing replicable empirically-based treatment protocols. Conversely, this can result in a chilling effect that stifles creativity and innovations in treatment, restricts funding to these favored cognitive approaches and promotes a few select manualized treatment approaches that are almost entirely cognitive-behavioral in nature — a "one size fits all" approach.

Additionally, there has been a growing emphasis in sectors of the VA and in the DOD to move towards a "strength and resilience" model and away from a trauma-focus model. This seems to have been accompanied by a tendency to substantially downplay focusing on underlying trauma-related issues and dynamics. Rather, the motto seems to be: let's forget about directly addressing the trauma experiences themselves to an appreciable degree; instead, let us emphasize current living issues, skills-building, strengths and resilience. As Yogi Berra said, "*déjà vu* all over again." This is where many mental health providers were before the diagnosis of PTSD was established in 1980 — avoiding meaningful attention on the trauma experience.

Clearly, such non-trauma-specific areas indeed should be an important area of treatment emphasis. However, the combination of almost exclusively emphasizing narrowly-defined, easily replicable manually-driven trauma-focus intervention strategies and strength and resilience models, and to offer such almost entirely in individual treatment sessions, has serious limitations. These limitations seem to be moving many VA, DOD and other providers towards a treatment modality that continues *to ignore* critical aspects that are distinctive to the longer-term legacy of the psychological and social impact of war and post-war readjustment.

These critical aspects distinctive to war-related trauma and its aftermath are at the heart of the expanded model of healing strategies that are described in this chapter. Unless each of the following is seriously considered in a meaningful way as part of the post-war healing process for veterans and their families, many veterans of all eras are literally condemned to continue to be shackled to demons of war and post-war readjustment.

FOUR INTERPERSONAL ASPECTS OF HEALING THAT ARE DISTINCTIVE AND CRITICAL FOR WAR VETERANS

Several aspects of the war experience must be considered in determining what an optimal healing experience requires. First, war trauma by definition is embedded within the context of the veteran's military peer group, the small operational military unit. The intensity of the relationships that develop, such as within a fire-team, squad, platoon, two-person sniper team, gun or armored vehicle or ship or air crew, is extraordinary as well as necessary to survival in the unpredictable and hostile milieu of war. This includes both one's peers and immediate military authorities who are trusted to lead the unit successfully.[297] Veterans almost never have a solitary experience of war-trauma; rather, war-traumas are *inextricably enmeshed* within the remarkably powerful interpersonal influences and interactions among military comrades.

And so, their healing also will be lacking if they only receive trauma-focus interventions that ignore or downplay this critical interpersonal factor. Individual interventions, by definition, do not directly address the issues of how the war trauma has impacted the veteran's identity; and that is inherently based on relationships with peers and small unit commanders. Such issues may include the loss of a buddy, "shameful" behavior, "mistakes" that had catastrophic results, possible resultant peer rejection or severe problems with military authorities.

Such trauma-intertwined-with-relationships dynamics and issues must be addressed; soldiers almost always are preoccupied with how their attitudes and behaviors are perceived and accepted, or rejected, by their peer group.[298] This includes what has been described as the primary concern and fear of combat soldiers that can even transcend the fear of being killed — letting down their comrades-in-arms and being seen as a failure or coward in their eyes.[299]

Four issues are often overlooked by mental health providers, the veterans themselves and their families.

- Racism
- Sexism and gender-based trauma
- Homophobia
- Medical evacuation trauma

---

297. Scurfield, 1994.
298. Ibid.
299. B. Shalit, *The Psychology of conflict and combat* (New York: Praeger, 1988).

Racism, Sexism and Gender-Based Trauma and Homophobia

One can never assume that veterans' post-war state of mind and social or psychiatric troubles are only, or even primarily, related to classic combat stressors (i.e., exposure to death and dying) or to the stressors related to deployment in a war zone (i.e., physical deprivation, isolation and distance from home). Three special populations of war veterans are at risk from additional stress: racial minorities, women, and gays and lesbians.

Unfortunately, many clinicians, family members and the public are largely oblivious to the problems these groups within the veteran population face. And at times even the veterans themselves may not realize or admit to themselves the salience of race-, gender- and/or sexual orientation related experiences.

Attention to such special population-related stressors and traumas require specific inquiry as to the veteran's possible exposure to race-, gender- and/or homophobic-related stressors and trauma.

Racism, sexism and sexual trauma, and homophobic attitudes and behaviors are quite prevalent in society at large. It is foolish to assume that those attitudes and behaviors were not carried into and exaggerated in the military context, both in basic training and while deployed in a war zone.

Military service stressors include a lack of privacy, forced intimacy in working, playing, eating and sleeping conditions, deprivation of normal living comforts, exhaustion, constant vigilance, frayed tempers and nerves, accumulation of tension, anxiety and rage, constant pressure and, in a war zone, the constant threat of serious injury and loss of life, all coupled with repeated experiences in isolated, volatile, unsupervised and dangerous situations.

It is inevitable that prejudices, personality flaws and pathological attitudes and behaviors will become activated. And it is inevitable that such attitudes and behaviors will include racism, sexism and sexual assault, and homophobia. Such negative and prejudicial attitudes and personality types and behaviors are deeply entrenched in American society.

Racism Trauma

Many combat soldiers have said:

There wasn't racism out in the bush, but that there sure was back in base camp.[300]

Indeed, I was co-investigator of a precedent-setting research study of exposure to race related experiences by Asian-American and Pacific Islander Vietnam veterans while on active duty, during basic training and while in the Vietnam Theater. This was the first study ever to specifically and systematically

---

300. I discuss this in detail in R.M. Scurfield, *Healing Journeys*, 2006.

investigate the presence and role of overt and more covert race-related behaviors and attitudes in a war zone. The bottom line finding was startling:

> Exposure to race-related experiences was the single strongest predictor of the subsequent development of PTSD, even more so than exposure to combat stressors.[301]

As discussed in detail in Volume 2 of *A Vietnam Trilogy*, serious race-related events were reported among US military personnel both directed towards each other, and towards Vietnamese civilians and enemy combatants. The relevance of race-related stressors is not confined to the Vietnam War and Asian Pacific Islander veterans. Indeed, racism is inherently infused in the prevalent conditioning that military personnel are subjected to in training: dehumanization of the enemy. Racist bias and stereotypes of the enemy unfortunately can then become generalized by some combatants towards the civilian population as well. This was rampant in the Vietnam War, quite prevalent in the Persian Gulf War and has been reported among some US military personnel in Iraq.

Issues of exposure to racism and a bicultural identity conflict may well be a particularly significant stressor among American military personnel who are racial minorities; especially for those who are of the same or similar racial or ethnic heritage as the people the US is fighting against. From my perspective as a third-generation Syrian-American, I have briefly discussed the ramifications of such for American military personnel of Arab heritage, who look Arab or are Moslem, in terms of both the Persian Gulf War and the Iraq War.[302]

---

301. C. Loo, J. Fairbank, R. Scurfield & D. King, Asian American Vietnam Veteran Race-Related Study. Honolulu, HI: VA Merit Review, Department of Veterans Affairs, 1966-69. For a complete discussion of race-related trauma, see R.M. Scurfield & D. Mackey, "Racism, trauma and positive aspects of exposure to race-related experiences: Assessment and treatment implications," *Journal of Ethnic & Cultural Diversity in Social Work*, 10 (2) (2002), 232-47. Regarding the race-related study in Honolulu and among Asian-Pacific Islanders, see: C. Loo, J. Fairbank, R. Scurfield, L. Rusch, D. King, L. Adams & Y.C. Chemtob. "Measuring exposure to racism: Development and validation of a Race-Related Stressor Scale (RRSS) for Asian American Vietnam Veterans," Psychological Assessment, Vol. 13 (4) (2001), 503-520; C. Loo, K. Singh, R. Scurfield &: B. Kilauano, "Race-related stress among Asian-American veterans: A model to enhance diagnosis and treatment," Cultural Diversity and Mental Health, 4 (1998), 75-90; C. Loo, "Race-related trauma and PTSD: The Asian-American Vietnam veteran," Journal of Traumatic Stress, 7 (1994), 1—12; C. Loo , "Race-related posttraumatic stress disorder," in a Report on Asian Pacific Islander Veterans by the Vet Center Asian Pacific Islander Veterans Working Group. Washington, DC: Readjustment Counseling Service, Department of Veterans Affairs, 1998), 40-50.
302. I mention this regarding the Persian Gulf War in R.M. Scurfield, *Healing Journeys*, 2006, and about 9/11 in an earlier chapter of this book.

Gender-Based Trauma

In addition to racism, many of the women veterans who have been treated in various VA PTSD programs have described a litany of sexual harassment, demeaning attitudes and behaviors, sexual assaults and/or gender-based violence towards them while on active duty and in the war zone. Many male military personnel still believe strongly that no women should be in a war zone. Indeed, many of the early Vietnam veteran combat rap groups would not allow women veterans in — they were relegated to groups for wives and partners of combat veterans!

Military personnel are not exempt from their fair share, and indeed the military combat culture may attract more than their fair share, of the many males in US society who espouse a sexist, gender-specific domination and even a violent attitude toward women. Indeed, too many male military personnel have a particularly demeaning attitude towards women in the military, as a woman Vietnam veteran described to me:

> Many .... considered all of us women who were in the military to be either promiscuous whores or lesbians. "Why else would a woman want to be in the military?!"

(And this attitude clearly has not been confined to Vietnam.)

Available statistics concerning the prevalence of sexual assault trauma among veterans shows that: 38% of former servicemen receiving VA health care reported having been sexually harassed; 23.3% of women and 3.5% of men serving between 1970 and 2000 report having been sexually assaulted; and 11.1% of women and 1.2% of men report having been raped while in the military.[303] Pentagon authorities report that sexual assault incidents in reservists called to active duty increased 40% from 2004 to 2005; the increase is possibly at least partly related to a new program encouraging victims to report sexual assaults.[304] The National Center for PTSD suggests[305] two screening questions for sexual trauma:

> While in the military, did you experience any unwanted sexual attention, like verbal remarks, touching, or pressure for favors?

---

303. T.W. Lineberry, S.J.Ramaswamy, M.Bostwick and J.R. Rundell "Military sexual trauma. How to identify and treat a unique form of PTSD." *Current Psychiatry*, 5 (6) (2006, May), 53-54.

304. Department of Veterans Affairs, Report to Congress on the Study of Sexual Trauma among Reservists on Active Duty for Training. According to documents provided March 301, 2006, by the Subcommittee on Health, Committee of Veterans' Affairs, US House of Representatives. See also: Lineberry et al, 2006.

305. A. Street and J. Stafford, "Military sexual trauma: Issues in caring for veterans." National Center for Posttraumatic Stress Disorder 2006): Available at: *http://www.ncptsd.org/war/military_sexual_trauma.html*.

Did anyone ever use force or the threat of force to have sex with you against your will?

Ramaswamy asserts that exposure to sexual trauma is so prevalent among veterans that screening for sexual trauma is important for all veterans, male and female [306] — and, I would add, for all active duty personnel as well.

Homophobic Trauma

Third, there is the awkward accommodation that the military has adopted concerning gays or lesbians in the military: "Don't ask and don't tell." The pejorative attitude and ignorance of the DOD concerning homosexuality is further illustrated by the recent uncovering of a memorandum in which the DOD erroneously classifies homosexuality as a psychiatric disorder. This is remarkable in that homosexuality was removed by the American Psychiatric Association as an official classification of psychiatric disorder as far back as 1980 in the publication of the *Diagnostic and Statistical Manual III*. [307] And, of course, there is no empirical evidence whatsoever to support the military's insistence that having homosexuals in the military is detrimental to the military mission.

Problems of and against gays and lesbians in the military have received very minimal attention, in contrast to race relations. However, I have personally observed that virulent homophobic attitudes and behaviors were very prevalent; when there was a draft, these were directed against male military personnel who came across as effeminate, who tended to be unmercifully harassed by their peers.[308] And this applied to men who may or may not have been gay, only that they did not come across as "masculine" enough.

This brief discussion of race-, gender- and homophobic-related stressor and traumas may serve as a caution to ensure that such potential issues are specifically explored as possible traumatic experiences. The chances are that, if no one asks, most veterans will not volunteer such information. Such unaddressed and unresolved issues may severely inhibit the ability of veterans to move ahead with the circle of healing that is necessary for optimal post-war recovery.

---

306. S. Ramaswamy et al, "A primary care perspective of posttraumatic stress disorder for the Department of Veterans Affairs," *Journal of Clinical Psychiatry*, 7 (4) (2006), 180-187.

307. American Psychiatric Association, *Diagnostic and Statistical Manual of Mental Disorders III* (Washington, D.C.: APA, 1980)

308. R.W. Eisenhart, "You can't hack it, little girl: A discussion of the covert psychological agenda of modern combat training." *Journal of Social Issues*, 31 (4) (1974), 12-23.

MEDICAL EVACUATIONS BOTH WITHIN AND FROM A WAR ZONE

If you don't ask, you won't be told — that holds true in a fourth area as well. That is the series of terrible stressors that characterize medical evacuation. Any military personnel (or civilian contractor, Red Cross worker, etc.) who were medically evacuated from one location to another within a war zone, or out of a war zone, have suffered an extraordinary sequence of events above and beyond the initial trauma. First, an entire series of events unfolds that is always stressful and frequently traumatizing. Second, there almost always is a vortex of avoidance, denial and silence about it.

The result is that health care providers, both military and civilian, family members and not infrequently the medically evacuated casualties themselves, fail to address this extraordinarily stressful series of experiences.

> The whole evac process — people just don't know how traumatic the whole med-evac process was. Each time we were transported somewhere else was a trauma in itself.[309]

The resulting silence can trigger short-term consequences that include a severe impact on the veteran's mood and ability to be cooperative and complementary to the efforts of health care and mental health providers. Longer-term consequences include enduring imprints on personality traits, identity, mental health, and attitude and behaviors regarding both physical and emotional recovery and towards the military, health care providers (military, VA and civilian) and other issues that ultimately impact on one's physical, emotional and spiritual readjustment and recovery.

The ability to engage in an expanded circle of healing requires that the medical evacuee has been able to identify and process the series of stressful if not traumatic experiences that characterize what happens from the time one has been wounded and through the post-medical evacuee stabilization and early recovery stages. This exploration is necessary to be to identify, explore and address any significant issues.[310]

Following is an outline of the events and experiences that are characteristic of medical evacuation and that are rarely later discussed. It would be quite self-limiting if not self-defeating to attempt to embark on the various steps of an expanded circle of healing without addressing possible issues related to these steps:

- Experiences and treatment at the scene of the wounding
- The evacuation from the scene to the first acute receiving and stabilization medical station.

---

309. R.M. Scurfield, *Healing Journeys*, 2006, Chapter 2.
310. Ibid.

• Experiences and events at the first acute receiving and stabilization medical resource.

• Subsequent transfers, if any, in-country.

• The medical evacuation flight out of the war zone.

• Experiences and events at the initial receiving hospital outside of the war zone, such as in Germany (Iraq casualties), Japan (Vietnam casualties) or stateside.

• Experiences during transfer from the initial receiving hospital outside of the war zone to one or more additional medical facilities.

• Initial and early communications by health care providers with family members and the initial communication and meetings between family members and the wounded evacuee.

• The initial stages of the longer-term treatment, rehabilitation and recovery process that still require hospitalization.

• Subsequent transfer to or stages of the medium- and/or longer-term treatment, rehabilitation and recovery process that still requires considerable medical services.

This is a series of stressful it not traumatic experiences for the evacuee who is literally a captive medical or psychiatric patient. And days, weeks, months, years or decades later any or all of this may require sensitive and specific inquiry, understanding, tactful confrontation and challenges to be able to get the evacuee to look at, admit, express and discuss, and resolve to the extent possible.

Many of these issues affect the medical evacuee's relationship with health care providers, both military and then VA and other civilian providers.

From An Intra To An Inter-Personal Journey Of Healing

> We are part of the earth's destiny. Life is a sacred way, songs were sung, paint given, words spoken. We are honored, all of us standing in the sacred circle made complete. We are all people. We need power to live, give to each other power, to heal, to complete our sacred work in healing veterans, warriors.
>
> — George Amiotte[311]

Most war veterans (and survivors of other types of human-induced trauma, such as sexual assault, kidnapping, torture, abusive relationships) who

---

311. From the 1992 video (spoken by George Amiotte, Lakota Sioux and Vietnam veteran): *Camp Chaparral: A Healing Circle.* Portland, Oregon: Northwest Video Networks. See also the description of the "circle of power," in Patrick J. Twohy, *Finding A Way Home. Indian and Catholic Spritual Paths of the Plateau Tribes* (Spokane, WA, University Press, 1987).

require substantial healing take their initial steps in a way that is quite intra-personal, deeply private in focus. Even this path oftentimes, although not always, requires the guidance and/or support of a trusted companion such as a counselor, clergy or spiritual guide, a family member or very special friend. Through this process, the veteran is assisted to eventually reach a level of self-acceptance and understanding, of self-management and self-protection, of healing from the psychological and social wounds of war.

Inherent in this process is the willingness and ability to prudently re-enter into closer meaningful relationships with some other people.[312] Putting this into the framework of the healing circle, in addition to that trusted companion who may have become part of the veteran's journey of healing: the veteran needs to be facilitated to expand his or her healing circle to include existing significant others in his or her current life — if any such relationships are still active at all — such as a partner, parent, child or other relatives and close friend.[313]

The most likely persons the veteran will allow initially into his or her healing circle are not so much family members but rather a select number of other veterans. This is because the identity of being a veteran is one of if not the most pronounced aspects of identity for many veterans. Indeed, often one's identity as a war veteran transcends or overshadows identity based on gender, age, race, ethnicity, religion, and socio-economic status.

The strong initial tendency for war veterans is to mingle with other veterans of the same era, generation and war — World War II veterans with other World War II veterans, Korean War Veterans with other Korean War veterans, and so forth.

Typically, veterans who are in clinical treatment are seen individually, or in a therapy or support group comprised of other veterans of the same era who they become close to. Or a small number of veterans may be included in one's inner circle who has been met in the course of daily life. Or there is vet-to-vet

---

312. Again, see Glasser, *Choice Theory*, 94-106. Also, for specific implications of the impact of trauma on the family and working with family members of trauma survivors, see, for example, Don Catherall, "Family as Group Treatment for PTSD," in B.H. Young & D.D. Blake, *Group Treatments for Post-Traumatic Stress Disorder (15-24)* (Philadelphia: Brunner/Mazel, 1999)); C.R. Figley, *Burnout in Families: The Systematic Costs of Caring* (St. Lucie Press Innovations in Psychology Book Series, 1998); Patience H.C. Mason, *Recovering From the War: A Woman's Guide to Helping Your Vietnam Vet, Your Family and Your-self* (New York: Viking, 1990); and various writings of Aphrodite Matsakis, to include *Vietnam Wives* (Kensington, MD: Woodbine House, 1988).

313. The reader is reminded of the important work of Ron Murphy and associates. See Ron Murphy et al, 2003, that was referenced earlier concerning the resistance or unwillingness of a number of veterans with chronic PTSD to let go of long-standing symptoms of PTSD. The same dynamics apply to a willingness to expand those who will be admitted to one's circle of healing.

interaction at a veteran's service organization or perhaps in activities that support various veterans' issues such as raising funds for a memorial.

However, for too many veterans who continue to have long-standing war- and/or post-war related issues, allowing one or a few fellow or sister veterans into the veteran's inner circle typically is where the expansion of the healing circle stops.

Fractured, Alienated and Voided Relationships

There is one thing that can never be believed: if a veteran ever says that "combat had no impact on me."[314] The unmitigated reality is that *combat always has an indelible impact on all of its participants.*

This impact of combat in those who have a troubled post-war read-justment is often a legacy of, to varying degrees, hatred, bitterness, anguish, resentment, loss, grief and/or alienation. These powerful negative emotional states may linger like a cancer, eating a person away from within.[315] Fur-thermore, inevitably veterans who are living such a conflicted existence continue to be in varying degrees of restricted and unsatisfying levels of relationships with others, with community and even with country.

We can and must do much better than that. There is much more to recovery than individual treatment to excise war-related negatives. A common thread describes all veterans who have some significant continuing or exacer-bated disturbance related to their war, deployment and/or post-war read-justment. This includes those who have remained conflicted to some or to a

---

314. Sarah Haley, "When the Patient Reports Atrocities. Specific Treatment Consider-ations of the Vietnam Veteran." *Archives of General Psychiatry*, 30 (1974, February), 196.

315. I am indebted to Gestalt Therapy writers for descriptions of such concepts as toxic elements that people introject, the power of psychological "unfinished business" from prior life experiences that demands expression and attention, and the range of powerful and effective therapy strategies and techniques that I have found to be very effective in my therapy interventions with war-veterans of all eras. For one of the clearest and easiest books on Gestalt Therapy to read, see Joel Latner, *The Gestalt Therapy Book* (New York: Bantam Books, Inc, 1973), and *The Gestalt Therapy Book* (High-land, NY: Center for Gestalt Development, 1986). See also: Erving & Miriam Polster, *Gestalt Therapy Integrated: Contours of Theory and Practice* (New York: Vintage Books, 1973) and Edward W.L. Smith (ed.), *The Growing Edge of Gestalt Therapy* (Secaucus, NJ: The Citadel Press, 1976); B. Feder & R. Ronall (Eds.), *Beyond the Hot Seat: Gestalt Approaches to Group* (Highland, New York: The Gestalt Journal Press, 1994); G.M. Yontef, *Aware-ness, Dialogue & Process: Essays on Gestalt Therapy* (Highland, NY: Gestalt Journal Press, 1993); J. Zinker, *In search of good form: Gestalt Therapy With Couples and Families* (San Fran-cisco: Jossey-Bass, 1994); Gerald Corey, "Gestalt Therapy in Groups, " in *Theory and Practice of Group Counseling 5th Edition* (304-307) (Belmont, CA: Brooks/Cole, Wadsworth/Thompson Learning, 2000); and *The Gestalt Journal*.

considerable degree, those who have been unable to co-exist reasonably peace-fully with at least some aspects of their war experiences and issues, and those who have remained strangers in their own country, on the margins of com-munity, and society, and perhaps even of their families.

Such veterans have not sufficiently, if at all, expanded their healing circles to positively and increasingly include relationships that have been fractured, alienated or voided.[316]

Can and Should the Veterans' Circle of Healing be Expanded?

Not necessarily — for those veterans who, along with their immediate family, are both content to live within a relatively constricted and isolated circle of relationships. Or for those veterans who have been able to attain a modest sta-bilization and relief from their war and post-war demons, and want to leave it alone. On the other hand, it is my contention that once a veteran who has been sorely impacted by war attains a certain level of accommodation and post-war recovery, and the veteran seems to be "stuck" or has reached a plateau and appears unable to progress further, then that is probably where the veteran will almost certainly remain. Unless, that is, the veteran's circle of healing is expanded.

It is incumbent upon each of us, upon each veteran and each trusted com-panion, to ferret out exactly who else the veteran most needs to allow to enter into his circle of healing, in order to attain a more peaceful existence.

---

316. My thinking about the veteran's healing circle is indebted to important sources. One is my American Indian (Seneca Tribe) heritage that perhaps has made me particularly receptive to the traditional American Indian healing circle ceremonies, in which the power of giving testimony and bearing witness as warriors share their war experi-ences in a supportive circle. Of course, the circle has even more ancient roots as both a physical and symbolic unity. See J.P. Wilson, *Trauma, Transformation & Healing* (New York: Brunner/Mazel., 1989). Also, there is the very insightful and more recent writing of William Glasser that I have become familiar with in using his work as a text in my graduate social work advanced interventions course. Glasser's viewpoint is that satis-fying relationships are the essence of a healthy and fulfilling life. Also, readers will note my adaptation of Glasser's "the solving circle" in my discussion of the circle of healing. My thinking about the healing circle obviously has parallels to Glasser's solving circle and relationships constructs. See W. Glasser, *Choice Theory. A New Psychology of Personal Freedom* (New York: HarperCollins Publishers, Inc., 1998), 94-106.

Let's be frank: the veteran may not want to take this next step.[317] Of course, in the end, it is left to each of us to decide what relationships are to be allowed into our personal circles of healing, what relationships require repair or fortification, and what new relationships need to be added to further our post-war healing.

What are the relationships that are required to help us to make sense of the seemingly nonsensical? Sometimes it is those fractured or toxic relationships that are intrinsically infused within the veteran's war and post-war life-experiences that need to be addressed.

However, many veterans continue to deny or have been unable to recognize and appreciate the paradoxical relationship that they have. There will remain forever a powerful bond with certain relationships — with the bad and with the good.

Along with recognizing this, there must be some degree of willingness and movement to allow all elements, the bad and the good, of at least some such additional relationships to be incorporated into the veteran's inner circle of healing. Otherwise the issues related to these relationships will remain unfinished and toxic, and the veteran will continue to remain bonded to them.[318]

It is incumbent for veterans to face honestly the question of who or what relationships he or she is still distant from, alienated from, fractured from, feel a toxicity about, that are related to the war and post-war issues?

EXPANDING THE CIRCLE OF HEALING

The Circle Restored
> Today there is a new feeling of strength
> And self-direction among the People.
> It would be good if the Circle of Powers
> Were made whole again.
> It would be good to see again
> Men and women, Elders, priests, deacons and Sisters
> All equal in sharing in the circle of gifts
> For helping the people.

---

317. Of course, for these three veterans this chasm was initially bridged when each agreed to be guest speakers at a Vietnam History course, and in John's case, by becoming a regular guest lecturer at the classes. And this is another way to open the circle of healing that does not require a return to Vietnam: being a speaker at college and high school forums or otherwise engaging with students and younger generations.

318. For a wonderful description of the process of healing for trauma survivors, see Judith Herman, *Trauma and Recovery. The Aftermath of Violence — From Domestic Abuse to Political Terror* (New York: Basic Books 1992/1997).

It would be good to sit down together,
To listen to the Elders,
To listen to each other's hearts,
To consider, to choose, to pray
For a way of traveling together
Best for the whole People. [319]

What does it take for veterans to have a flowering of their healing circles? What is it that is not whole? Which relationships are fractured, and what is the exact nature of the toxic elements?

There is a fundamental truth that applies to almost all Vietnam and other war veterans. In our culture there is one set of relationships that may not be fractured but rather separated by age and generational issues, and at least five fractured or toxic relationships exist for many veterans that transcend any particular era of war.

And yet sufficient attention to such areas is sorely lacking from the most commonly provided interventions, especially those that exclusively or primarily target specific PTSD symptoms related to specific traumatic incidents per *DSM-IV-TR* criteria.

These include veterans' in many cases damaged or broken relationships with:

- Veterans of different eras, theaters and generations.
- Non-veterans and the community.
- The veterans' own government and society, due to possible issues of betrayal.
- The people of the country the veteran fought in.
- God, a higher power, or any set of principles and belief concerning an inherent goodness and interconnectedness of humankind.

Veterans of other Generations, Eras and Theaters

The first people a veteran is likely to let into the inner circle of healing, if any, are veterans who share their war and post-war experience. World War II veterans relate primarily to selected other World War II veterans, Korean War veterans with selected other Korean War veterans, and so forth. This is an understandable tendency.

It was accentuated in the early years during and following the Vietnam War because of initial hostility and lack of support by many traditional veterans' service organizations towards Vietnam veterans and the generation gap that provided dramatically different viewpoints. It took many years for this nega-

---

319. Twohy, 245.

tivity to dissipate. And there is a further reinforcement of this tendency when a new war comes along.

First there are inherent tensions between funding to support programs and services for the older veterans of previous eras versus the funding needed for the current era of veterans. Second, oftentimes veterans of previous eras feel a bittersweet reaction to the attention and recognition paid to more recent veterans.

These dynamics reinforce the strong tendency to associate with nobody, or only with those who served where and when the veteran did.

However, when veterans are open to expanding their relationships to include veterans from different eras, they may learn to see beyond the belief that only a small group of people on this planet — veterans who served in war where and when you did — could possibly understand what they went through and could possibly care about them and their experiences. Meaningful interactions with veterans of different eras and wars helps to promote solidarity as well as the awareness that, beyond the uniqueness of each era and theater of war, there also is a universality of the experience of war and its social and psychological impact.

This may be the first and most accessible step to expand a veteran's inner circle of healing; it can offer substantial dividends in breaking isolative and exclusivity tendencies. The connectedness and healing that such association can bring was reflected in a 20-session trauma-focus outpatient trauma-focus therapy group that I co-facilitated with veterans of World War II, Vietnam and the Persian Gulf Wars. It was an amazing experience to watch as communications, understanding and, yes, brotherhood, evolved among these three eras of veterans.[320]

---

320. Unfortunately, the VA National Center for PTSD did little to let people know of the availability of these dramatic professionally edited educational video-tapes of these 20 treatment sessions and an accompanying 66 page companion monograph. The three-set videos and companion monograph provide a rare video and written resource and have proven quite helpful to sensitizing people to the dynamics of war-related issues across three eras of veterans. In addition, these tapes have proven invaluable in offering talking points and discussion of alternative interventions through illustrating some of the therapeutic strategies and interventions provided. Clinicians and others can observe first-hand live clinical sessions in which amazing communication and healing processes were achieved, as well as less-than-desired outcomes, with several of the group participants through a Gestalt/Existential trauma-focus approach applied in a peer group modality across three generations of combat veterans. See: R.M. Scurfield and I. Powch, *Journey of Healing,* and A. Perkal (Department of Veterans Affairs: National Center for PTSD, Honolulu, HI. 1997). Copies of this three-tape video series can be obtained free of charge as long as copies are available through Allan Perkal, former Media Coordinator, at Perkman@hawaii.rr.com or 808.383-7877.

Of course, a therapy group isn't the only way to experience the discoveries and relationships that can develop. It takes the right attitude and willingness to be receptive to and seek out such contacts. One way to do this is to become involved as a mentor to help the Iraq and Afghanistan veterans of today who are facing many of the very same kinds of post-war challenges and issues that veterans have faced before. An association as a mentor with the current era of veterans allows the older veterans to "give back" by sharing their perspectives of having been there and faced that, and to make sure that the new era of veteran knows that they are not alone. And no one knows better how terrible such feelings of utter aloneness can be than other veterans. And no one knows better what the families of new veterans have been facing than families of other veterans.

Of course, the very process and act of giving of one's self, one's time, and one's experiences, information and perspective repays the mentor immeasurably. It is an amazing opportunity to focus on the concerns of others for whom you have something invaluable to offer — yourself as a war veteran or family peer with your unique experiences and world view. There is a mutually enriching affirmation and validation of each other, a solidarity of brother- and sister-hood, a stimulation of aliveness and reenergizing of a vitality of purpose in living. As a bonus, new friendships may evolve that are bonded not in the crucible of blood but in the crucible of human connecting and transformation.

Non-Veterans and Communities

Another of the fractured and toxic relationships for many veterans is with non-veterans. The importance of how one performs and is accepted by war comrades is so powerful that it inevitably spills over onto the soldier's relationships with persons who are not veterans and indeed, with their communities. Often there is a conviction that non-veterans and home-town communities cannot possibly understand what war was all about. Consequently there is a discomfort, if not an unwillingness, to share deeply about one's war experiences with non-veterans and the community.

The reluctance or even the inability to relate intimately to non-veterans can extend to the veteran's primary family relationships. A wife of an Iraq War veteran described how difficult her adjustment has been to "what the war did to her husband." She couldn't help feeling left out since her husband seemed to prefer being with other soldiers than with her, and she is very aware of the distance between them that she cannot seem to bridge:

> I know there's a lot of things that he can talk to his [soldier] friends about . . . But I'm sitting here thinking, "Why can't he talk to me?"[321]

---

321. Corbett, 2004, 60.

Sometimes the exclusion of non-veterans is due to distasteful experiences that the veteran has had:

> One of the hardest things when I came back [from Iraq] was people who were slapping me on the back, saying "Great job." Everyone wants this to be a good war so they can sleep at night. But guys like me know it's not a good war. There's no such thing as a good war. [322]

And what could be more inclusive for a war veteran than to allow non-veterans to be participants in one of the most emotional and challenging war-related life-experiences: a return to the scene of battle?

We tried it in May of 2000 with a combined study group that is described in Volume 2. The implications of this shared experience between veteran and non-veteran are enormous (and there are significant parallel ramifications for veteran's children, spouses and extended family members who typically are not systematically and meaningfully incorporated into the veteran's healing).[323]
The breakthrough to understanding was especially touching, given that universities were at the heart of the anti-war movement protesting what was portrayed as an immoral and unjustified war, and which many historians now characterize as an intrusion into a civil war in a third-world country (and that may also ultimately be what historians describe as happening in the Iraq War).

Many US soldiers who fought heroically in Vietnam and then came home only to be made to feel unwelcome felt quite uncomfortable with university students and faculty. There was a barrage of scapegoating, and blame, and moral condemnation in both directions.

And this only widened the chasm between many returning veterans and their communities. This phenomenon continues to be played out over peace protests and demonstrations against more recent wars. There is a tension between America's cherished constitutional right of free speech and the question of what protest behaviors are appropriate while a war is in progress.

By visiting Vietnam in the company of students, the veterans in question allowed a major expansion of their circle of healing — and that provided untold benefits to a mutual trans-generational relationship of understanding, acceptance and trust.[324]

Another example of expansion of the veterans' circle of healing to include non-veterans is veterans' involvement in community support groups such as Alcoholics Anonymous and Narcotics Anonymous.[325]

---

322. Goodman, 2004, 50.

323. My thanks to Sherrill Valdes, Miami VA social worker, for reminding me of this important parallel. Personal communication, July 3, 2006.

324. Wiest, A., L. Root & R.M. Scurfield, "Post-Traumatic Stress Disorder. The Legacy of War," In G. Jensen & A. Wiest (Eds.), War in the Age of Technology. Myriad Faces of Modern Armed Conflict (295-332). (New York & London: New York University Press, 2001).

Sadly, other than referrals to community AA or NA, almost no veteran treatment programs never move the veteran much, if at all, beyond the veteran-to-veteran circle. (After all, the VA's productivity standards give little or no "credit" or reimbursement for VA staff time spent with non-veterans, even in mixed groups.) Hence, the prevailing treatment programs cannot and do not meaningfully address the relationship between veterans and people who are not veterans — including their families.

UNIQUE COMMUNITY-BASED PROJECT FOR MILITARY VETERANS

Unfortunately, American society offers little in the way of meaningful activities that involve recognition, reception and ongoing support at the local community (or at the national) level for welcoming, accepting and integrating military personnel back. And there are few established community rituals to assist in the necessary transition from warrior to peacetime citizen. Conse-quently, many military personnel and veterans never attain a satisfactory post-war healing from their psychological, social and moral injuries. This is because, as eloquently described by Jonathan Shay, such healing and recovery can only occur fully in community — not in one-to-one clinical interactions.[326]

One exception is found among the American Indian nations who have a warrior tradition. Such nations understand that warriors (community members who served on active duty and were deployed to war zones) need the reception and acceptance of their communities in helping to make the warrior-to-peacetime transition.[327] I was privileged to participate in just such a ceremony in the Northwest that was extremely powerful and affirming.[328]

Sherrill Valdes and Janice Postlewaite have developed an impressive and progressive outreach, community networking and collaboration effort at the Oakland Park VA Outpatient Clinic (which is part of the Miami Veterans

---

325. Sherrill Valdes, personal communication, July 5, 2006.
326. Jonathan Shay provides an arresting analogy of the Odyssey and the post-war adven-tures and healing of Odysseus; a basic message is that post-war readjustment can only happen in the context of the community. J. Shay, *Odysseus in America: Combat trauma and the trials of homecoming* (New York: Scribner, 2002).
327. R.M. Scurfield, "Healing the warrior: Admission of two American Indian war-veteran cohort groups to a specialized in-patient PTSD unit." *American Indian and Alaska Native Mental Health Research: The Journal of the National Center,* 6 (3) (1995), 1-22.. See also J.P. Wilson, "Culture and trauma: The sacred pipe revisited." In J.P. Wilson (Ed.), *Trauma, Transformation and Healing. An Integrative Approach to Theory, Research and Post-traumatic Therapy* (New York: Brunner/Mazel, 1989)
328. R.M. Scurfield, *A Vietnam Trilogy,* 2004., See also John Wilson, *Trauma, Transformation and Healing,* 1989.

Healthcare System). The Miami Veterans Healthcare System leadership has been an advocate for seamless care and has encouraged the OEF/OIF Committee to be advocates and be progressive in meeting the needs of returning veterans. This was the first VA health care facility in the country to hire a full-time OEF/OIF Coordinator (Janice Postlewaite). These efforts have enhanced broad-based community coordination, organization and implementation of services to military families in the greater Miami/South Florida area. This approach includes outreach to and a broad range of community-based services involving active duty medical patients, military units, families, and a range of community providers. (The model is described in more detail in Appendix III, "Facilitating a Broad-based Community Involvement in Services for Reservist Military Personnel and Their Families.")

Sherrill also described a marvelously creative project that provided acceptance, validation and recognition by the community.[329] This project involved returned Iraq veterans, family members, Vietnam veterans and the community represented by quilts that had been lovingly stitched for Iraq veterans returned from deployment.[330]

In the words of Sherrill Valdes:[331]

> [I]f the family could be engaged along with the community in sincere support of the veteran, this may relax defense mechanisms, survival behaviors and have a positive effect on the soldier's journey of reintegration and readjustment into civilian life. To facilitate this process, I learned about a group that was coordinating and creating a network of quilt-makers throughout the United States to give to wounded returning soldiers and received permission to create a ceremony of appreciation in which the quilts could symbolize community support. The quilts took approximately 3 months to make. . .

> The importance of receiving appreciation, compassion and acceptance from others, including fellow combat veterans [of other wars], and the symbolic role of the quilts was evident in a recent holiday activity . . . that would be shared with their families and the community. Additionally, the goal supports and validates the returning soldiers' experience. Returning soldiers were invited to the party.

> When the party began, the former Vietnam combat soldiers listened to returning soldiers and showed empathy. Some important thoughts of wisdom passed on from the Vietnam PTSD group to the returning veterans were: "Even though you are home, don't be surprised if it feels different. You have changed, you just haven't had the time to truly reflect within yourself ... You're still looking over your shoulder. . ."

---

329. Sherrill Valdes and Janice Postlewaite, "To serve those who served," Florida Chapter of NASW Annual Social Work Conference 2006, Ft. Lauderdale, FL
330. The contact person regarding quilts for our military is Catherine Roberts; 302.629.5398 or cc.roberts@comcast.net
331. Sherrill Valdes, "Torn to Pieces/Stitched Together: Gifts of Love for OEF/OIF Returning Soldiers Journey Home from Combat." Handout distributed at the June, 2006 Annual Conference of the Florida chapter of the National Association of Social Workers, Ft. Lauderdale, Fl., June, 2006.

After an informal ceremony where the Vietnam and Iraq soldiers thanked each other for their service and sacrifice, an informal ceremony for the presentation of the quilts began. The returning soldiers were informed of the emotional investment and commitment needed to complete each quilt, and of the fact that the quilt makers wanted them to use the quilts as a reminder that they are loved and know that each stitch was made with prayers for their safety. . . The Iraq returning soldiers felt acceptance and appreciation. They have told me that the quilts are on their beds and that they have been very meaningful to them. One soldier commented: "While we were over there being torn to pieces, these people have been stitching the pieces together and want us to cover ourselves and begin the healing."

The clinical intervention was beneficial for the Vietnam and Iraq combat soldiers, and the quilters were appreciative to have their quilts provide special meaning to the soldiers. Thus, the healing continues with the community, combat soldiers from a former war and begins with the new returning combat soldiers.

This project beautifully illustrates the expansion of the healing circle beyond Iraq veterans only with veterans of their own war to include family members, veterans of a previous war (Vietnam) and ordinary citizens who were the quilters. Sherrill Valdes, not a veteran, and Janice Postlewaite, a veteran, are examples of the best employees in the VA system — veterans and non-veterans who can see that the whole vision of comprehensive healing involves the veteran, family, military, civilians and communities.

US GOVERNMENT AND AMERICAN SOCIETY

The government sends us to war.
The military uses us in war.
And society forgets us after war.

A natural extension of allowing non-veterans into one's healing circle is related to the distinct and powerful relationship between active duty military personnel and veterans on the one hand, and government and political leaders and society on the other. The government, the military leaders and society delegate the Armed Forces to do that which is otherwise both forbidden and severely punished:

Members of our Armed Forces are agents of death who are sanctioned by our government and American society to do whatever is necessary to protect our country, to include killing and maiming others and if necessary to sacrifice their own lives and those of their comrades.

This assignment is undertaken on the basis of a dual understanding. Firstly, that the members of the Armed Forces are willing to go, repeatedly, into harm's way, and at great risk to their personal physical and mental health, in the interests of national security. In return, the government and society make a lifelong commitment to honor, support and assist active duty military and veterans in recognition and various forms of benefits for the extraordinary risks that have been undertaken.

Even in the context of this official and societal sanction, as has been described, it can be quite difficult for soldiers to live with themselves afterward. (If this were not the case, there would not a single World War II veteran who would have ever been troubled by his or her war experiences, since they had an entire nation united in support of them during the war and who enthusiastically welcomed them home afterwards.)

How is it possible for combat veterans to make this readjustment from war to peacetime civilian life? Many take solace and pride in the reward that comes from within, from the satisfaction of having carried out a duty and responsibility and having made a sacrifice for their country. As President John F. Kennedy said, "Ask not what your country can do for you; ask what you can do for your country." And as so eloquently stated in a letter to the editor of a local newspaper:

> The brave men and women of our Armed Forces are making sacrifices for the security of our country and the survival and growth of liberty and freedom around the world. Why? Because no one else in the world has the means, the will, the character of courage to do so. No one![332]

However, this internally derived reward requires a fundamental trust and conviction that the government and society know what they are doing in deploying troops to a given region, and will fully honor the promises that were made at the time of recruitment. Such promises are the core of this transcendent trust relationship.

And so, it is promised that they will be honored and they will be provided with appropriate sustenance in the form of monetary compensation, educational, health care and other benefits. However, as described in an earlier chapter, many have had experiences that suggest that this was an empty promise, that this trust has been voided by the government, and by society.

The sense of betrayal this engenders gives rise to rage or despair. It is particularly problematic when soldiers feel that the reasons given for going to war were less than truthful or that the war turns out to be unjust, immoral or just not right or necessary.

> I'm very proud of my military service... But I am disheartened and personally hurt, after seeing [fellow and sister American military personnel] two people lose their limbs, and a 19-year-old girl die, and three guys lose their vision, to learn that the reason I went to Iraq never existed . . . [333]

---

332. M. Fullilove, "Bush appreciates that this is our time in history." Letter to the Editor. www.*SunHerald.com*, Biloxi, MS (2005, January 30), B-2.

333. Goodman, 2004, 55.

Another Iraq veteran stated:

> I'm really a patriotic soldier . . . I was really upset about what happened on 9/11, and I really wanted to serve. I lost a buddy of mine in the World Trade Center. I believe what we did in Afghanistan was right.

But what he experienced in Iraq told him that this was not right.

> We were fighting all the time. The only peace is what we kept with guns. A lot of stuff we heard on the news . . . wasn't true. When I arrested people on raids, many of them were poor people. They weren't in with the Ba'ath Party. The people of Iraq were attacking us as a reaction to what the majority of them felt — that they were being occupied. [334]

The impact is particularly severe when military personnel witness first-hand that the government is not doing all that it can to provide them with the means to effectively carry out their missions, such as making sure that their equipment is adequate for the job. There were dramatic failures on this score for months, as troops were provided unarmored Humvees that were vulnerable not only to improvised explosive devices but to small-arms fire as well.

And then, two days after Secretary of Defense Rumsfeld suggested that "it was beyond the Pentagon's control" to increase production of armored Humvees, the Army reworked its contract and gave the green light for the sole contractor to boost production of armored Humvees by 20%. The contractor had stated months before that it had unused capacity and could readily boost production, if asked to do so. [335]

A distressingly similar foot-dragging continued concerning the inadequate ceramic plates in vests or body armor worn by most personnel that cannot withstand certain munitions used by the enemy. [336] Indeed:

> . . . more than a year after military officials initiated an effort to replace the armor with thicker, more resistant plates, tens of thousands of soldiers are still without the stronger protection because of a string of delays in the Pentagon's procurement system. [337]

It would only cost an estimated $160,000 to provide improved body armor to all US forces in Iraq! Is it any wonder the disastrous impact on military retirees and other veterans who may feel lied to and betrayed by their government? Such behavior by the military, and permitted by society, wounds veterans further still.

---

334. Ibid.
335. Tom Squitieri, "Army late with orders for armored Humvees." USA Today, Cover Story (2005, March 27), A1, A2.
336. Moon, C.A. "For lack of body armor, troops die. Why the delay?" *USA Today* (2006, January 13), 10A.
337. Moss, Michael, "US Struggling to Get Soldiers Updated Armor." New York Times (2005, August 14). Accessed on-line.

Promises were broken yet again when military retirees noticed that Chief Justice Rehnquist was admitted for treatment to a flagship military hospital when military retirees had been turned away. A number of military retirees voiced that this was repudiation of the transcendent trust relationship with government and society.

One final example that has led veterans to distrust the veracity and intentions of the government in regards to veterans occurred earlier in 2006. The VA started a "second signature required" (SSR) policy for many "high-dollar" disabilities; the VA required that such claims be re-approved by another VA staffer. In and of itself, such a review could be justified as a prudent analysis to insure that compensation awards were awarded only on valid claims. However, it turned out that the VA did not provide a second review for claims that were *denied* by the first VA staffer.[338] If the VA were truly concerned to ensure veterans were getting a fair and just disposition on compensation claims, as well as to ensure that VA benefits were not being abused, then of course a sampling of all initial decisions would have been planned — not just those that were approved, but also those that were denied. No wonder that veteran's advocates decried this plan by the VA and labeled it as a way to contain costs — not a way to insure the highest quality of decision-making concerning whether veterans deserved to be awarded compensation for a service-connected condition.

This is, after all, the governmental agency established to serve veterans; how could veterans not see this as a betrayal of the transcendent trust relationship between the government/society and veterans?

What to Do About The Betrayal?

There is no easy way to address this fundamental betrayal. In the spirit of expanding the circle of healing, it would seem evident that any fractured relationship between veterans and government or society needs serious attention.

Remaining stuck in the anger or rage, the resentment or bitterness, the mistrust or paranoia, the social discomfort or alienation that can be an outgrowth of this betrayal, is rationalized by many disillusioned veterans as justified and warranted considering the nature of this betrayal. And too many therapists and manualized treatment approaches simply ignore this critical issue. But optimally the disenfranchised veteran needs to be assisted to deal with and not ignore this issue and persist in wallowing in rage, mistrust and alienation. The rage may have served a useful purpose over the years, fueling an inner drive and determination to influence, if not fight against, "the system." Maybe

---

338. Larry Scot, "VA launches PTSD review." Accessed August 4, 2006, at VAwatchdog.com. See also Steve Robinson, "VA's PTSD review continues at the Institute of Medicine." Accessed August 3, 2006, at www.veteransforamerica.org.

that is why my personal favorite bumper sticker reads: "Always challenge the dominant paradigm."

But what is the veteran willing to do now, in order to open a door that allows him or her to move ahead? Perhaps the veteran has become or can be active in a veterans service organization, a non-profit organization or a self-help group, or a local, state or national election battle to support veterans' issues; or choosing to not remain silent and disenchanted on the sidelines when this fundamental trust violation repeats itself again with a new generation of active duty military personnel and veterans; perhaps choosing to become an activist about both veteran and non-veteran issues that are personally important, be they environmental, economic, social, religious or spiritual.

And so, the negative fallout on veterans and their families when our country's leadership and society break that fundamental trust relationship can be minimized if not overcome by a willingness to look at expanding one's healing circle. This expansion would involve engaging with key relationships at the local, state, national or even international governmental or societal levels that have not previously been allowed into the veteran's healing circle. Unfortunately:

> Such consciousness-raising and action-oriented activation at a more macro level rarely is a therapeutic objective of almost any mental health interventions.[339]

However, perhaps especially for veterans it very much has to be, in order to make the transition from disgruntled or apathetic veteran to very active citizen-soldier. The relatively recent formation of a national Veteran's (Political) Party is an interesting example of how such a focus can be channeled.

There is one other very important way for veterans to consider reconnecting with society, a way that is mutually beneficial. People who have suffered can be the very best suited to help others, "and a person crosses the final barrier of helplessness when he or she learns to use the experience of suffering itself as a means of reaching out to others."[340] A woman in Wisconsin is described who lost her son in the crash of a Marine Corp helicopter:

> For the first time, she began noticing how frequently helicopter crashes were reported in the news. Now, whenever a military helicopter crashes, she sends a

---

339. Radical social work and radical psychology movements in the 60s and 70s are a notable exception and offer a strategy and perspective for social-issue and social reform conscious therapists to consider incorporating elements of into their practice. See, for example: R. Bailey & M. Brake (Eds.). *Radical Social Work* (New York: Pantheon Books, 1975); P Brown (Ed.), *Radical Psychology* (Harper Colophon Books, 1973); and The Rough Times Staff, *Rough Times* (New York: Ballantine Books, 1973). I also wrote a controversial journal article on incorporating social reform into direct practice. R. Scurfield, "An integrated approach to case services and social reform." Social *Casework: The Journal of Contemporary Social Work* (1980, December), 610-618.

340. Yancey, 192-193.

packet of letters and helpful materials to an officer in the Defense Department, who forwards the packet on to the affected families. About half of the families strike up a regular correspondence, and in her retirement this Wisconsin woman leads her own "community of suffering." The activity has not solved the grief over her son, of course, but it has given her a sense of place, and she no longer feels helpless against that grief.[341]

And this is a gift, suffering and surviving, that veterans have to offer, not only to the current era of veterans as described earlier in this chapter, but also to non-veterans who need a caring, sensitized human being to connect with. Some veterans may not necessarily do well with trying to help other veterans because it hits too close to their own issues. For such veterans, they may well find it easier to reach out and connect to non-veterans who are in need, i.e., with youth, a disabled population. Vets helping vets, vets helping non-vets, and vice-versa. And so, veterans who are not interested in political activities can seek out a similar person-to-person humanitarian activity to allow society back into the circle of healing. The choices and the opportunities are limitless.

And for the helping veteran there is a wonderful bonus:

> There is no more effective healer than a wounded healer, and in the process the wounded healer's own scars may fade away.[342]

I can personally attest that in this process of care-giving to another, the giver is rewarded at least tenfold. Is there any better antidote to preoccupation with one's own woes, anger, disillusionment and isolation?

The People and Land of the Country of Deployment

Two return trips to a peace-time Vietnam have taught me and both the veteran and non-veteran participants an invaluable lesson. This is the unique and precious opportunity to both witness and experience how an entire land and people have survived and regenerated, a land and people once ravaged by war. The people and land of Vietnam have been excluded by many Vietnam veterans from their circle of healing. This exclusion typically is based on the veterans' continuing to associate the Vietnamese people and land with negative and horrific experiences from the war — and so they remain fixated on hatred, bitterness, or discomfort towards the Vietnamese people and Vietnam.

The veterans' choice to exclude the people and land of Vietnam from their circles of healing has been exacerbated and reinforced by two powerful dynamics. Firstly, there are the still present effects of conditioning through military training and day-to-day exposure to combat and stress while deployed that encouraged them to dehumanize the enemy, and usually the citizens.[343] Secondly, there was the nation's long-standing diplomatic and economic isolation of

---

341. Ibid., 193.
342. Ibid.

Vietnam. The preoccupation with the people and land of Vietnam is further exacerbated by a denial on the part of many Vietnam veterans of a reality that must be faced sooner or later. And it is a reality that Iraq and Afghanistan veterans will have to face sooner or later, too; or it will forever remain a toxin eating away at their insides. Many veterans (and other Americans) still refuse to admit that there is a bond between America and American veterans and the country and people of Vietnam. We are *inextricably* bound together through the experiences of the war.

For veterans who deny the reality of this permanent bond, or who recoil from the thought of it, there are two simple tests. (For veterans of other eras, such as Iraq, just substitute "Iraqis" or "Iraq" for Vietnamese and Vietnam.) The first would be to relate to Vietnamese-Americans living here in America. How do you feel about such an idea? Are you willing to do it? Have you done it? When you see, or hear, or are around Vietnamese, do you usually feel or are reminded of something positive or negative? Just by trying on this idea you can see if you are still held to some degree by the toxic elements of the extraordinary bond that you have with the Vietnamese people. This is not at all healthy for you — and it is very unfair to the Vietnamese people as well.

There is a second test: consider going back to peacetime Vietnam. Allow yourself to simply observe or become immersed in the Vietnam of today, a peacetime Vietnam that simultaneously propels us back to the war tapestry, and presents positive images to juxtapose alongside the decades-old war-memories.

Many veterans try very hard to not accept the fact that "enemies" like "friends" share an iron bond. This is especially true given the way trauma sears memories into our minds and into our bodies. Sometimes, the harder we try to forget, the more ingrained it all becomes.

Certainly, establishing some kind of dialogue with Vietnamese Americans, and/or returning to Vietnam, is neither a cure-all nor the only avenue toward healing. However, these are two ways a veteran might consider that can make it possible to finally come face-to-face with the enduring relationship he or she has with the Vietnamese people and land — and allow the passion and pain to be defused, attaining a more peaceful co-existence with this relationship. As one veteran said, the return visit brought home to him:

> That my fellow and sister veterans, and our country, are, indeed, veterans of both "The Vietnam War" and "The American War" [as the Vietnamese call it]. And so are the Vietnamese people and country.

This realization is necessary if one is to be able to integrate and synthesize within the formation of a more complete gestalt, to help make each of us more

---

343. See the discussion of dehumanization as a survival strategy while in the war zone in *A Vietnam Trilogy*, 2004, and the parallels to the aftermath of 9/11 described in *Healing Journeys*, 2006.

whole.[344] And a similar struggle faces many veterans who have fought in other countries, to include Iraq and Afghanistan veterans and their families — to both recognize and shift their permanent relationship with the country they have fought in to include Iraqi and Afghani people and ultimately (after enough time has passed) even the enemy combatants.

BOTH THE NEGATIVE AND THE POSITIVE POLARITIES OF WAR

Veterans must also consider allowing into their circle of healing certain relationships not only with persons or with institutions, but their relationships with the hurt, the losses, and the horrors of war that they have been fixated on.

And this is typically the focus of therapeutic interventions — to sensitively uncover, re-explore, reflect and express troubling and painful aspects of trauma so that they can be "exorcised." However, it is essential to also give appropriate attention to the positive side of those hurts and losses — which many veterans would be very loathe to acknowledge.[345]

> Joy and woe are woven fine,
> A clothing for the soul divine,
> Under every grief and pine
> Runs a joy with silken twine.
> It is right, it should be so;
> Man was made for joy and woe;
> And when this we rightly know,
> Through the world we safely go
>
> —William Blake [346]

Some veterans (and other trauma survivors) describe severe psychological pain but also report positive impacts on their overall post-trauma life as a result of their experiences in surviving the original trauma and attempting to make some positive meaning of their post-trauma life. Indeed, there are survivors who describe a transcendent highly positive post-trauma life course and perspective on life.

All trauma experiences contain the combination of both troubling and potentially positive aspects in terms of the possible impact on one's post-trauma

---

344. Joel Latner, *The Gestalt Therapy Book*, 225-227.
345. See related readings on "post-traumatic growth", a term coined by C.G. Calhoun and R.G. Tadeschi in the 1990s. Calhoun, C.G. & Tadeschi, R.G., "Beyond recovery from trauma: Implications for clinical practice and research." *Journal of Social Issues*, 59 (1980), 357-371; R.G. Tedeschi & L.G. Calhoun, *Trauma and Transformation. Growth in the Aftermath of Suffering* (Thousand Oaks, CA: SAGE Publications, 1995).
346. Malcolm Muggeridge, *A Third Testament*, 65-66.

life. Hence, a central therapeutic strategy, especially in the middle and later stages of stress recovery, should be to facilitate the discovery and appreciation by the trauma survivor of such positives.

The positives of having served in the military and in a war zone are relatively easy to identify and fully acknowledge.

> Many times I have said that I gained much more than I lost from being in Vietnam. The taste is sweeter. The flavors are more beautiful. The delights of this earth are more fully appreciated and enjoyed. — Vietnam veteran

However for a substantial number of veterans (and survivors of other human-induced traumas), the potential or actual positives are not so readily identified or acknowledged. The challenge is to allow into their healing circles or accept that there are extraordinary positive corollaries or polarities of the very same deeply troubling issues and negative memories that have been haunting the veterans for decades.

Typically, these positives have been embedded beneath negative preoccupations and are largely if not completely overlooked or minimized by the survivor — unless a re-framing is facilitated to enable self-acknowledgment that the positive aspect also is true and has relevance to them — and to their families. This can be a most challenging task for the veteran and the family, yet it is essential if the veteran is to move beyond simply attempting to eliminate negative memories and symptoms.

Following is a listing of some of the common negative preoccupations of military combat veterans who have survived war trauma, and the accompanying potentially valid positive aspects. Facilitating the veteran's ability and willingness to be able to recognize, and then to accept, these polarities is a dramatic expansion of the veteran's circle of healing.[347]

Negative aspect:Nothing means anything anymore." Feelings of confusion, despair, not being clear about what is valued in life, or where I am going with my life.

Positive aspect: Priorities."What is really important now?"[348] Development of very healthy questioning and/or a reaffirmation of values, priorities, what is and is not important and meaningful.

---

347. G. Schiraldi, *The PTSD SourceBook*, 2000, took my original explication of these trauma polarities (Scurfield (1994) and composed them into this tabular format that this section is adapted and elaborated from.

348. Such is described by Bob & Penny Lord as the one positive that can be grasped when one's physical body has been ravaged by disease. *Saints and Other Powerful Women in the Church* (Westlake Village, CA: Journeys of Faith, 1989), 387-88. I would add that this potential positive applies equally to the aftermath of exposure to human-induced trauma.

In addition, there are a number of other polemic issues and struggles which need to be faced if they are present.

Negative aspect:All-pervading sense of loss, grief, and preoccupation with hurt.

Positive aspect:Comradeship may have occurred at an extraordinary level, indeed to a degree that has never been attained before or since the trauma. The fact that such comradeship occurred at one time means not only that I have the potential, but that I have actualized such a bonding at least once in my life — and have demonstrated the ability to achieve it again.

Negative aspect: Difficulties arise in dealing with "everyday" stresses.

Positive aspect: Knowing that I have and can remain committed and effective under the most trying of circumstances.

Negative aspect:Very low self-esteem, shame and/or guilt at the fact that I was "imperfect" during the war as part of surviving, and there has been continuing difficulty to adjust to post-war life.

Positive aspect:Appreciation of the strength and courage that it took for me to survive both the war and the difficulties since the war.

Negative aspect:Disturbing loss of trust and loss of faith in our country's institutions (military, legal, law enforcement, government).

Positive aspect:Development of a very healthy questioning of the motivations and behaviors of those institutions, realizing that when such institutions become immoral, everyone suffers, and that they need to be held accountable.

Negative aspect:Having little tolerance or acting out when confronted by depersonalized and insensitive behaviors of authority and institutions.

Positive aspect:The development of very strong convictions that I am "not just a number" and am entitled to be treated with dignity and respect.

Negative aspect:Becoming isolated and alienated, feeling that others can not possibly understand my trauma experience and neither what I have gone through or what I am going through.

195

Positive aspect:Rediscovery of the shared bonding with others who have survived war, a specialness that would not be possible without having had the war experience to begin with ["For those who have fought for it, freedom has a taste that the protected will never know"] — and also discovering that there are others who have not been through the experience of war who somehow have a very special understanding and bonding with me.

Negative aspect:Morbid dwelling on the fact that I should have died, or should not have survived, or am deeply resentful of the physical and emotional pain and loss I have had to suffer and endure and remember all these years.

Positive aspect:Every moment, every breath since surviving the trauma has truly been "bonus time." It is extraordinary that I did survive, that I am even here and have the opportunity to appreciate, indeed cherish and take advantage of this remarkable opportunity to make the most out of this "second-chance" and the limited time I have here on this planet.[349]

Negative aspect:It is terrifying to take risks or be exposed to dangers, or I am an "adrenaline junkie" who is constantly exposing myself to dangerous, unhealthy or unnecessary risks.

Positive aspect:I appreciate the thrilling and peak experiences that did occur in the war, and I am willing to promote "healthy and safe" stimulations to enhance my life today.

Negative aspect:I continually bemoan and resent my post-war difficulties and deprivations and how "life isn't fair".

Positive aspect:I have a deep appreciation of the value of freedom and my abilities to persevere in the face of extraordinary and unrelenting pain and obstacles.

---

349. The concept, "bonus time," is something that my very dear friend and veteran colleague, Steve Tice, a severely physically disabled Vietnam veteran, has described to me on several occasions. Having survived a near-death experience at Hamburger Hill when hit by a rocket-propelled grenade, over the years Steve came to be able to appreciate that his time on this planet since then is all bonus time — he should have died but he did not — and thus it is to be savored. Steve can elucidate this concept much more powerfully than mere words on a piece of paper can.

Negative aspect:I am in deep and unrelenting pain, and believe that I am weak or sick because I repeatedly remember the troubling and horrible aspect:s of what happened (to me and/or to others).

Positive aspect:I understand and appreciate that it can be a sign of health and virtue not to forget what happened. Those experiences and the lessons of war that should have been learned must not be for-gotten by anybody or by our country — or we will be doomed to have them repeated, again and again. After all, if my fellow and sister survivors and I do not remember, who will?

Negative aspect:Accepting total or exaggerated degree of responsibility for the trauma that occurred in the war zone.

Positive aspect:I now realize and appreciate that when a nation goes to war, *everyone* in that nation bears some responsibility for all that happens in that war.

In helping the veteran (and family) to strongly consider and be willing to not only accept but to embrace the presence of the potentially positive aspects of the trauma experience, a crucial therapeutic discovery is made: aspects of both negative preoccupation and the accompanying positive dialectic are valid, and even the most horrid traumatic experiences also can and do contain extraor-dinary lessons about life and extraordinary growth possibilities.

And when this discovery is made, the veteran and family finally will be able to fully comprehend the true answer to the question, "Is the glass half empty or half full?" The answer? "It is both half empty *and* half full."

ONE MORE RELATIONSHIP TO CONSIDER: FORMATION OF THE LAST GESTALTEN

I cannot promise you happiness in this world, but in the next.[350]

One more pairing of trauma negative and positive is related to a belief in an afterlife.

Negative aspect:Experiences in the war zone can lead to loss of one's belief in God or religion and of one's faith in humanity.

---

350. The Blessed Virgin Mary speaking to Saint Bernadette of Lourdes. In: B&P Lord, *Saints and Other Powerful Women in the Church*, 1989, 213.

Hey, God, talk to me. No bullshit with me. Talk to me. People tell me, "Oh, God's going to help you." Yeah. He cheated me. I try as much as I do to talk to God; I feel I've been cheated. He's not going to talk to me [when] . . . when I'm dead? If he's a forgiving person, why do I have to live like this [in such moral pain over having "enjoyed" killing in Vietnam]? I want peace, whether dead or alive, I want peace.[351]

Positive aspect:Positive changes in outlook, expansiveness of world view, and insights, perceptions, and quasi-religious or religious/spiritual insights, a potential for religious/spiritual rebirth and/or renewed optimism for humanity.

I certainly have prayed to God and I think it helped me when I prayed. In fact, I know it has or I wouldn't be here today. Faith is one of the ways people pull themselves through seemingly impossible times.

Why was I allowed to live? It's luck . . . we all traded bullets with the enemy for a heck of a lot of times, and we've seen a lot of buddies go down and I think God was with me . . . That's why I'm here today.[352]

That is one more possible expansion of the healing circle for veterans having a spiritual or religious belief in a higher power or God. Veterans who do not have such a faith would find the expansion of their healing circle complete at the previous level, which includes accepting the dialectic polarities of both the positive and negative aspects of the trauma and its aftermath. Indeed, many "non-believers" consider adherence to religious beliefs and practices to be similar to the placebo phenomenon in medicine and mental health; that it is *believing* there is a higher power that explains any improvements in one's functioning, not that there is an actual existence of such a power that explains change.

Congruent with this viewpoint is the conviction that putting one's faith or reliance on religion or belief in a higher power is merely a retreat from the realities of this world. Indeed, that reliance on prayer and rituals and faith can be used as an escape and an excuse to not engage in choices and actions over which one has control and that could actually influence and make a difference about the underlying causes — in this case, the degrading inhumanity of war and the lack of post-war supports.

Regardless of whether one believes or not in a higher power or God, all war veterans do come to their own conclusions as to why they survived and others did not. Some believe that their survival was totally a matter of luck, of random chance:

Your time didn't come. My time didn't come. Their time didn't come.[353]

---

351. *Journey of Healing* video, 1997. Clinical excerpt with Mario, a Vietnam veteran helicopter door gunner.
352. Ibid., clinical excerpt with Chuck, a World War II veteran infantryman.

Further, ancient beliefs included recognition of war gods that were instrumentally interconnected with chance:

> I'm just glad you're here instead of being [blown to] smithereens. Things like this [why you survived and others didn't] are why the ancient cultures had war gods and worshipped them the way they did. Because they were the gods of chance. These were the things that people recognized. It was either you, or them . . . [354]

Homer's Greek soldiers clearly attributed good and bad luck in combat to the gods:

> "Damn this day," he said. "A fool would know that Zeus had thrown his weight behind the Trojans . . . As for ourselves, no luck at all, our shots are spent against the ground." [355]

For those whose beliefs include a higher power or God, those who struggle with the question of whether such exists, and/or those who believe that there is an interconnectedness and life force among humans that transcends cities, countries, cultures and continents, this is yet another relationship that beckons to be accepted into the veterans' circles of healing.[356] However, many war veterans have had the opposite experience: the trauma of war has led to a crisis of faith and for some, alienation, a fracturing, a rending asunder, a feeling of having lost any belief in and relationship with God. "Why God? Why Me?" "This is God's will? How could you let this happen, God?"[357]

There is a paucity of empirical studies that address the impact of war and post-war readjustment on spiritual or religious beliefs and practices. However, clinicians do describe various ramifications of such among war veterans. Tick

---

353. Ibid., clinical excerpt with Fred, a Vietnam veteran truck driver. See also an excellent discussion about war, luck and gods in J. Shay, *Achilles in Vietnam. Combat Trauma and the Undoing of Character* (New York: Atheneum, 1994).

354. R.M. Scurfield and I. Powch, *Journey of Healing* video. Clinical excerpt by Bill Kilauano, peer counselor.

355. Quote from the *Iliad* in J. Shay, *Achilles in Vietnam*, 139-140.

356. I write this commentary from my own personal familiarity as a practicing Roman Catholic and the fact that a large majority of the many veterans I have worked with clinically have had some issues related to God or a higher power.

357. For some excellent writings that describe various war-related spiritual, religious and moral issues, se: W. Capps, The unfinished war: Vietnam and the American conscience (Boston: Beacon, 1988); R.J. Lifton, The broken connection: On death and the continuity of life (New York: Simon & Shuster, 1979); W. Mahedy, Out of the night: The spiritual journey of Vietnam vets. (New York: Ballantine, 1986); and W. Mahedy "Some theological perspectives on PTSD." NCP (National Center for PTSD) Clinical Quarterly, 5 (1) (1995), 6-7. Also, Steve Tice highly recommends Joseph Campbell, Hero with a Thousand Faces (Princeton, NJ: Princeton University Press, 1990); see also Phil Coustineau (Ed), The Hero's Journey. Joseph Campbell. On his life and work (New York: P Brown/Stuart, 2003).

contends that war-related PTSD is best understood not as a stress disorder but as an identity disorder and "soul wound" that affects the personality at the deepest levels.[358] Nelson-Pechoa studied 154 Vietnam combat veterans and found that alienation from God and difficulty reconciling one's faith with Vietnam experiences were associated with higher levels of both guilt and PTSD symptoms. Conversely, three factors, (1) church worship in which God is used as a coping resource, 2) a global spiritual orientation, and 3) forgiveness were associated with better adjustment and lesser severity of PTSD symptoms and guilt.[359]

Numerous authors report from their experiences with war veterans that significant if not central therapeutic attention to spiritual development should be incorporated into helping veterans with their post-war adjustment. For example, Claude Ashin Thomas, a Vietnam veteran who is a Buddhist monk and peace activist, describes strategies for transforming the seeds of violence in ourselves in order to be able to live with less judgment and more well-being, tolerance and peace.[360] Kearney et al. describe the need for spiritual support as part of maintaining a sense of purpose, motivation, dignity and self-esteem.[361] Other authors contend that addressing spiritual aspects should be at the heart of attempting to help war veterans with their post-war traumatic stress issues.[362] Chaplain Major John Morris describes how the experience of war "bruises a soldier's spirit." Indeed, he estimates that about one-third of the military per-

358. Edward Tick, War and the soul: Healing our nation's veterans from post-traumatic stress disorder (Wheaton, IL: Quest Books, 2005)

359. Margaret Nelson-Pechota, Spirituality in support-seeking Vietnam veterans: guilt, forgiveness, and other correlates of long term adjustment to combat-related trauma. Dissertation (Illinois Institute of Technology, 2003).

360. Claude Anshin Thomas, At Hell's Gate: A Soldier's Journey from War to Peace. (Shambhala Publications, 2004)

361. K. George E. Kearney, Mark C. Creamer, Richard P. Marshall and Anne Goyne, Military stress and performance: the Australian Defence Force experience. (Melbourne, Australia: Melbourne University Press, 2003);

362. Just a few such writings: Gail M. Barton and Lawrence La Pierre, "The spiritual sequelae of combat as reflected by Vietnam veterans suffering from PTSD." American Journal of Pastoral Counseling, 2 (3), 1999, 3-12; Larry Dewey, War and redemption: treatment and recovery in combat-related posttraumatic stress disorder. (Aldershot, England: Ashgate, vi, 2004); Manual Jiminez, "The spiritual healing of post-traumatic stress disorder at the Menlo Park veteran's hospital." Studies in Formative Spirituality, 14 (2) (May, 1993), 175-187; Edward Tick, War and the soul: Healing our nation's veterans from post-traumatic stress disorder (Wheaton, IL: Quest Books, 2005); and Karen M Clark, Bosnian Muslim refugee adjustment to life in the United States: the moderating role of spirituality and social support. Dissertation. (Washington, D.C. Catholic University of America, 2004) describes how religious and spiritual beliefs act as resiliency factors for Bosnian refugees and how refugees turn to their religious and spiritual beliefs as a way to make sense out of their displacement from their homeland.

sonnel he has encountered have lost any faith that they once might have had. A further complexity related to religious beliefs is that many military personnel over the past several years have come to the conclusion that not only is religious belief not relevant to their healing but that religious passions indeed fuel the wars of the world — such as in the Middle East, Iraq and Afghanistan. Certainly, religion can be used in a cynical way to urge on the fighting forces and as a rationale to justify any actions against anyone who is a "non-believer."

US military personnel represent a wide variety of religious beliefs and spiritual searching. As men and women confront life and death and survival in the war zone, they are increasingly finding ways to make some meaning out of that and out of the moral issues that are inherent in wars.[363] Interestingly, those veterans and survivors of other trauma who remain obsessed with the question about "why" or the cause of their problem ("What did I do to deserve this?" "What is God trying to tell me?" "Am I being punished?") often turn against God.[364]

Conversely, some veterans focus not on the cause but on their response to the trauma — their individual responsibility for their own responses. This requires moving from "why" to "how should I react now that this terrible thing has happened?" "Suffering produces something besides the pain and anguish. It has value. It changes us."[365]

> Quite simply, qualities like perseverance will only develop in the midst of trying circumstances . . . We rejoice not with the fact that we are suffering, but in our confidence that the pain can be transformed . . . what we make out of it . . . [366]

Of course, it is possible to have confidence that the pain suffered during war and/or afterwards can be transformed through meaningful contemplation and actions without having any belief in a higher power. On the other hand, even when there is such a belief, anyone who has gone through a life-threatening or physically or emotionally disabling experience might not necessarily have a strengthened belief in and relationship with God or a supreme higher power.

In either case, survivors can still be helped immeasurably by understanding the negativity, entrenchment, self-defeating attitude and behaviors that result from focusing on the "cause" of pain rather than on one's response to it, i.e., what the survivor is doing about it.

One's relationship with God or a higher power, or a belief in humanity, is paramount for many people. For them, that relationship is pivotal and must be included in the relationships addressed in the healing process.

---

363. Krista Tippett, "The soul of war," Speaking of Faith from American Public Media, May 25, 2006.
364. Yancey, 106.
365. Ibid., 106-108.
366. Ibid., 108.

A Christian interpretation of the American Indian healing tradition, the Circle of Power, includes both men and women, and the Creator, as essential to healing:

> This would be a Circle of men and women
>
> Who feel they are sons and daughters of their Creator,
>
> Brothers and sisters in Christ,
>
> Full of reverence for the Holy
>
> Present in all Creation.
>
> This would be a People full of trust
>
> In each other and in their Maker,
>
> Together facing and choosing a path
>
> From the past into the future and the totally unknown.[367]

What is the distinctive combination of relationships necessary for each veteran to be able to progress along a path that will maximize healing from the inhumanities of war and its aftermath? For some it will include their relationship with a God or higher power; for others, it is one's important relationships here with people; and for some it is both. In any case, for optimal healing all veterans, their families and their communities must be able to complete the formation of wholes where war too often has brought pain, separation, division, alienation and isolation for far too many.

> Making gestalts is making wholes. It is the process of unifying disparate elements in one's being, in one's life.[368]

Each person has his or her unique constellation of relationships that we connect with on our individual and collective journeys of healing that will make it possible to further develop, to grow, to actualize, to facilitate the formation of seemingly disparate or unconnected parts into ever-increasing and fulfilling gestalts or wholes. May all of you, my brother and sister veterans, your families and friends, your communities and all of the civilians here and world-wide who have been so sorely impacted by the horrors of war, of all wars, be able to continue our growth and continually enrich and expand our circles of healing.

For me and for you, I am sure that our journeys have moved along, to some or to considerable degrees, through stagnation, regression, and advancement, in spurts and lulls, in conflict and angst and some degree of peace, and perhaps even joy, over the months, years and even decades. For me, the journey has been a remarkable one, finally arriving at the realization that "Peace begins with me — and you."

---

367. Twohy, 246.

368. Joel Latner, *The Gestalt Therapy Book*, 225..

As our journeys continue, perhaps one day each of us will be able to increasingly expand our circles of healing towards the last gestalten. Growth towards true healing and peace, be it individual, familial, communal, national or global in nature:

> . . . consists of being able to form gestalts of greater and greater complexity . . . enlarging our possibilities, we constantly create solutions that are more encompassing and more complex . . . Making gestalts is making wholes. It is the process of unifying disparate elements. As we grow, we become capable of organizing more and more of the field into wholes. Functioning freely, we do not stand apart from this process. The wholes we make include ourselves. We are part of the unity of the field.

> The farther reaches of this process are traditionally matters for philosophy and religion . . . this direction is toward the last gestalt . . . In the more advanced stages of this process, we are embracing ourselves and the cosmos. The gestalt is: I and the universe are one . . .

> The last gestalt is beginning to know the immensity of the extent of our interaction with everything else. As we read, we move our eyes — and the whole interconnected universe moves. The last gestalt is apprehending this viscerally, body, mind, and soul, to the depths of our being, leaving nothing out.[369]

---

369. Ibid., 225-227

AFTERWORD

On the day that I finished the manuscript for the second and third volumes of *A Vietnam Trilogy* series, I received my first written communiqué from someone who had read Volume 1.

> I just finished reading your book, *A Vietnam Trilogy*. I read it all in less than two days. I could not put it down once I started reading it. My husband is a Vietnam veteran ...
>
> We had been married for [X] years when our marriage dissolved. Some years later we remarried. In reading your book, it seemed as if a light bulb went on. I can now better understand the issues in our marriage and our relationship. I kept telling my children that "ignorance is bliss." If I only had known [before now] what my husband went through in Vietnam, it would have saved us all much heartache and pain for so many years.
>
> Nevertheless, quite by accident we discovered the Vet Center, about a year ago. Just within the last two months, my husband has actually sought counseling.
>
> Thank you! Thank you! For all of your work in this area.

And my hope was buoyed that the *Vietnam Trilogy* series might make at least a little difference in our understanding the impact of war. If so, then my labor of love has, indeed, been a blessing.

A COMMENT ON KATRINA AND OTHER DISASTERS

In the summer of 2005 I was just finishing writing this book, when Hurricane Katrina slammed head-on into the Mississippi Gulf Coast, devastating the community where I work and live — Long Beach. And over the nine months since August 29, I discovered that there were remarkable parallels post-Katrina and post-war.

The University of Southern Mississippi — Gulf Coast (USM-GC) campus sits directly on the usually placid Mississippi Gulf Coast, about 100 yards from the water. Fully 30% of the university's 350 staff and faculty were displaced due to destruction or heavy damage to their residences and personal belongings.[370]

The destruction to the surrounding southern Mississippi communities was massive:

• Over 235 confirmed deaths and 68 still missing as of December 7, 2005.[371]

• 68,700 homes and businesses were destroyed, 65,000 sustained major damage, and 60% of the forests in the coastal communities were destroyed along with much of the shipping and fishing industry. [372]

• The neighboring community of Pass Christian had 80% of its homes destroyed as well as four out of the five primary and secondary schools, and the town lost 100% of its sales tax revenue as no gas stations or shops were re-opened. [373]

Hundreds of thousands of Katrina survivors in Mississippi have been experiencing an overwhelming sense of loss, grief and malaise over the destruction of places of employment, small and large businesses, churches, schools, neighborhoods, recreational facilities, historic sites and even entire communities — the loss of so much about life that was familiar and cherished along the entire Mississippi Gulf Coast.[374]

Unlike many of my colleagues and community residents, I was fortunate to still have a home that was habitable. And the ongoing battles with the insurance companies as to what damage was caused by wind and rain versus storm-surge water are extremely contentious; many homeowners have been left feeling that they are being ripped off by their insurance companies — with disastrous financial consequences.

My greatest personal loss was that my university office was totally destroyed. Thirty years of data collected over several years, 1,000+ books, hun-

---

370. R.M. Scurfield, "Social work interventions at a Mississippi university devastated by Hurricane Katrina." Social Work Today Online January 2006 E-Newsletter.

371. G. Pender, "The first 100 days after Katrina: Progress seen in small things, but frustrations abound." *www.SunHerald.com*, Gulfport, MS, C-1.

372. Editor's Notebook, "The first 100 days after Katrina: What is the enduring image of Katrina?"*www.sunsherald.com*. Gulfport, MS, December 7, 2005, C-4.

373. Editor's Notebook, "The first 200 days after Katrina: A city-by-city update on recovery."*www. Sunherald.com*, Gulfport, MS, December 7, 2005, C-8.

374. R.M. Scurfield, "Post-Katrina aftermath and helpful interventions on the Mississippi Gulf Coast," *Traumatology, Vol. 12* (2), in press, Summer, 2006.

dreds of videos and journals, artwork, etc. — all were swept away. And it appears that neither personal nor university insurance will cover any of the loss. Even more profoundly, many residents suffered the losses of *both* their homes and offices or businesses.

I became very involved in volunteering to provide post-Katrina counseling and emergency housing assistance to university faculty, staff and students, as well as making numerous professional and community presentations about post-traumatic stress and coping in the aftermath of Katrina.

Thousands of volunteers from throughout the country have come to southern Mississippi to help with debris removal and recovery efforts, assistance that has not been adequately provided by governmental organizations. The positive side of this cannot be overstated.

As a Vietnam War veteran, I am acutely aware that there are some parallel experiences and reactions post-Katrina and post-Vietnam. The extent of the destruction itself is, indeed, reminiscent of what one sees in a war zone. Then there was the very visible presence of National Guard and Reservists standing guard duty for months, mile after mile along the railroad tracks that run parallel to the gulf and separate much of the worst hit areas closest to the beaches from less devastated areas further inland. Military humvees, deuce and a half military trucks full of soldiers, helicopters — *everywhere.* Concertina (razor) wire stretched in double rows alongside the railroad tracks, mile after mile after mile, interspersed by checkpoints manned by uniformed and armed military personnel. Meals Ready to Eat (MREs) and water trucks, the gasoline smells and ever-present noise of generators, the terrible stench from the debris, storm surge muck and rotting organic materials strewn over miles; this included more than *three million* chickens and contents of shipping containers of pork bellies scattered from the port of Gulfport.[375] And then there were the inescapable heat and humidity — oppressive and omni-present.

And, as there is for soldiers returning from deployment, there was a strong sense of disorientation when coming home; coming home to a world that was now unfamiliar.

> Eleven months after Katrina, whenever I go down Highway 90 (next to the Gulf of Mexico), I must pay extremely careful attention so as not to miss a turn. The obliteration of almost all that was familiar, mile after mile after mile is mind-numbing. It begins to blend together in a desolate landscape, shattered, of seemingly never-ending palates of grey and grime and ruin. It is devoid of what used to be grand and colorful ante bellum homes, restaurants, piers and marinas.

> And, eleven months post-Katrina, I still find myself driving by "unfamiliar" roads that I had known intimately from years of commuting and pleasure-driving. No wonder many people still are walking around and functioning while in a daze. And

---

375. B. Walsh, 2006.

how could immersion in such wide-spread destruction not propel many war veterans back to their own personal war zones?[376]

Another painful parallel between post-war life and post-Katrina life is the powerful sense of being forgotten. In addition, there is resentment over the government's broken promises and failed commitments to veterans and their families and to the victims of this natural disaster, and resentment towards the rest of society who seem to have forgotten what we all went through.[377]

Furthermore, the Gulf Coast is home to major Navy and Air Force bases, with regular deployment of many personnel overseas while the affected families remain back in the midst of Katrina-ravaged destruction. Imagine the anguish of military personnel being deployed at the same time that their own families and communities were suffering terribly from Katrina.

> Is anyone aware that Naval Construction Battalion 133 is starting to deploy this weekend? How can we send homeless soldiers to Iraq to help build someone else's' world when their own is destroyed? It is an absolute disgrace and something needs to be done about it.
>
> Some of these men and women have lost their homes completely; most have significant damage. Loved ones are being left behind to clean up after the largest natural disaster our nation has seen. This is so wrong on so many levels. We need our men and women here at home to stand together with us, not with foreigners. Christine Kelley, Gulfport. [378]
>
> *Bring the Guard Home*
>
> The "noble" cause of this illegal, immoral war in Iraq is bankrupting and destroying us here at home. Our National Guard is all over in Iraq with the equipment, generators and water trucks we so badly need on the Mississippi Gulf Coast, and will continue to be needed for weeks and months to come. Bring our Guard home *now*. [379]
>
> *Mississippi needs its National Guard at Home.*
>
> I am a soldier stationed in Iraq. I belong to the Mississippi Army National Guard out of Poplarville. The National Guard's stated mission is to be of help to Mississippi communities in times of crisis, such as hurricanes and other national disasters . . . Mississippi is our state and we are not able to help our own people. Instead we are stuck in a country where the consensus is that we are an occupational force instead of a liberating one.
>
> So, why are the powers that be mobilizing full-time Army units to do our job [in the US] for us? Yes, we have been called to duty here in Iraq, but a crisis has arisen in our own land and in our own backyard.... We have several more months before we go state side. During that time, our families and loved ones and neighbors must

---

376. Scurfield, in press, Summer, 2006.
377. Ibid.
378. C.L. Kelley, "Our nation is shipping homeless soldiers to Iraq." *www.sunherald.com*, September 11, 2005, B-2.
379. Sound Off, "Bring the Guard Home," *www.sunherald.com*, September 24, 2005, A-2.

struggle all by themselves with the disaster left in the wake of Katrina. How can we expect the people of Iraq to view us as heroes when they know that our families in our own country have been left to fend for themselves?

We here in Bravo Company of the 155th are left feeling totally helpless. I say: send us home and bring the full-time units in to relieve us so that we can do what we have been trained to do. SPC H (Eddie) Perez, Iskanderyah Iraq. [380]

A substantial number of war veterans, including me, have found ourselves to be in a painfully familiar situation. We want to support our troops overseas but we believe that the US is once again engaged in an unnecessary, unjust and tragic war that should not be happening. Conversely, there is the generally accepted realization that a precipitous pull-out now might well have catastrophic consequences — and that such consequences might be inevitable no matter what the US does at this point. At the same time there is the continuing contrary argument that this war is right and just, and that the country must support the troops.

Yes, here is a segment of US society once again caught in the excruciating dilemma — the duty to protest what it sees as wrong, the obligation to avoid undermining our troops, the desire to support our leaders and the responsibility to question them when their decisions appear to be misguided.[381]

Now there is a new Hurricane Katrina-induced dilemma. Is not the enormous cost and manpower required to sustain both our very large military presence overseas and the rebuilding of an entire nation (Iraq) detrimental to our ability to do right by our own people? How can the US possibly wage such a war and rebuild an entire nation overseas while leaving Louisiana and Mississippi bereft? In the words of one protestor, "Make levees, not war."

There is another parallel between being a veteran and a Katrina survivor — the troubled legacy of the Department of Veterans Affairs (the VA) and the post-Katrina FEMA response. While there are many wonderful individual VA providers, the VA as a system continues to have many programs and services that are under-funded, inefficient, error-prone, and certainly not enough medical and regional office sites that could be called anything approaching a state-of-the art medical and benefits system for our veterans and their families. And now there has been the saga post-Katrina of an inexcusable and incredibly inept disaster response by the federal government — that in turn was obfuscated by denial and buck-passing at high agency and governmental levels. Once again veterans are seeing how politics and policies proclaim that the nation must fully fund and provide for the current massive war effort — at the expense of programs for the sick, the elderly, children — and veterans. Furthermore, an adequate budget to address the massive destruction and rebuilding required on the Gulf Coast has

---

380.   E. Perez, "Mississippi needs its National Guard at home." *www.sunherald.com*, September 12, 2005, C-2.

381.   R.M. Scurfield: 1992, 2004, in-press, 2006.

been pitted by a number of politicians against the massive budget for the continuing "war on terror." Mississippi US Congressman Gene Taylor stated:

> In this instance [Mississippi's request for federal disaster assistance], the president
> of the United States is treating Iraqis better than he's treating South Mississippians
> . . . When we faced funding for the war and rebuilding Iraq, the president said he
> didn't want that at the expense of anyone else's funding. But when it comes to help-
> ing South Mississippi, anything there has to be offset somewhere else, taken from
> some other Americans' funding . . . After running up $2.4 trillion in debt the last five
> years, all of a sudden they're going to be fiscally responsible? [382]

On the Mississippi Gulf Coast there is a very strong pro-military presence,
not only several military bases but also many retired military personnel and their
families who live in the area. Mississippians have a very strong and proud history
of military service and support. To see families in distress from Katrina while the
heads of their families are deployed overseas is heartbreaking, as is the sight of
troops returning from deployment to find families and communities decimated
by Hurricane Katrina.

Still, South Mississippians have witnessed the incredible generosity of the
national (and international) community in responding in the aftermath of
Katrina. The following letter beautifully expresses the essence of the good that
can come shining through in the aftermath of disasters such as Katrina.

> Five days after the storm . . . I decided to venture out and see who I could help. I
> have a young lady friend who lost everything and she decided to join me . . . We then
> proceeded to a low-income neighborhood in D'Iberville that was hit hard. Almost
> every family we went to said they didn't need anything, but the people down the
> street did. In this little community, they were looking out for each other. They were
> doing the best they could to spread the resources out amongst all of them.

> And my young friend was shaking hands, giving out meals, smiling and laughing. I
> watched her as she interacted with everyone and I realized that even through her
> loss, she found a way to give. She gave hope and joy and love. That is the greatest
> lesson I learned: through it all, our spirit and lives are what live on. Thank you, my
> young friend, for the lesson. I will always remember it. [383]

The resilient people of the Mississippi Gulf Coast have not only survived,
they have been enriched — and continue to enrich others. Personally, I am
blessed to have a renewal and enhanced appreciation of the importance of my
relationship with my wife and daughter (we experienced together the harrowing
onslaught of Katrina) and with our sons in California and our extended family.
And so many friends and relatives cared and reached out across the miles. And

---

382. G. Pender, "Time is slipping away. Hopes for federal aid face do-or-die week."
www.sunherald.com, Gulfport, MS, A1, A20.

383. L. Hafford, "One who lost everything still had much to give." *www.sunherald.com*,
September 22, 2005, B-4.

that kind of outreach is a potent antidote to even the devastation of a Katrina —
or of war.

More Headlines

I had vowed to stop reading the newspapers because it seemed as if every
day there was a new story about the Iraq War. At that rate, I would never be able
to finish this book.

Mental disorders are on the rise among Afghanistan, Iraq veterans

Over 26% of eligible soldiers who came to VA hospitals seeking medical treatment
between October 2003 and February 2005 were diagnosed with mental disorders.[384]

VA budget won't meet needs of returning troops

The President's budget request for VA Health Care Services for FY06 barely covers
annual cost increases — let alone the substantial increase in the number of new veterans from Iraq and Afghanistan.[385]

Help Mississippi military families

More frontline troops in Iraq and Afghanistan are National Guard members and
reservists now than ever . . . Sadly, many families of citizen soldiers face declining
household incomes since the breadwinner's military pay is often less than their
civilian salary . . . families face unexpected financial hardships in addition to worry
about their loved one's safety. [386]

It's not up to Congress to define a veteran

The Veteran's Health Care Eligibility Reform Act, passed by Congress in 1996,
allowed *all* veterans access to VA health care services. By the year 2003, veterans
had been divided into eight priority groups for VA eligibility . . . The 2006 budget
proposal would restrict VA health care to groups 1 through 4. As stated, groups 5
through 8 will cease.

---

384. Marilyn Elias, "Mental Disorders are on the rise among Afghanistan, Iraq veterans.
   Funding cuts could overburden system." *USA Today* (2005, March 31), A1. Lt. Gen.
   Kevin Kiley, US Army Surgeon General, reported that a full 30% of US troops
   returning from Iraq have developed stress-related mental health problems some three
   to four months after returning home. See "More troops developing latent mental
   disorders. Symptoms appear several months after returning from Iraq, military says."
   Associated Press. Accessed on-line on MSNBC, July 28, 2005.
385. Roger D. Clark, Executive Director, Bayou-Gulf States Chapter, Paralyzed Veterans
   of America, Letters to the Editor, *SunHerald*, Biloxi, MS (2005, April 1), D2.
386. Pat Quinn, Lt. Gov, State of IL. Letters to the Editor, *SunHerald*, Biloxi, MS (2005,
   April 1), D2.

Guess who gets the blame? That's right, the veterans will be blamed for over-using their VA health care benefits in the past. [387]

And then I broke my vow again, as I was going through my manuscript "yet another time." Three more headlines jumped off the newspapers:

Army general: US troops may be needed in Iraq through '09

The Army is planning for the possibility of keeping the current number of soldiers in Iraq — well over 100,000 — for four more years, the Army's top general said Saturday. [388]

Senator: War crippling Mideast. Hagel, R-Neb, says Iraq resembles Vietnam.

A leading Republican senator and prospective presidential candidate said Sunday that the war in Iraq has destabilized the Middle East and is looking more like the Vietnam conflict from a generation ago . . . Sen. Chuck Hagel, who received two Purple Hearts and other military honors for his service in Vietnam . . . "By any standard, when you analyze 2 ½ years in Iraq . . . we're not winning," he said. [389]

And then, the *coup de grace:*

Emotional wounds don't end their war. Troubled troops are back in battle.

A growing number of troop [are being] recycled back into combat after being diagnosed with PTSD, depression or other combat-related disorders — a new phenomenon that has their families worried and some mental health experts alarmed. The practice, which a top military mental-health official concedes is driven partly by pressure to maintain troop levels and runs counter to accepted medical doctrine and research that shows re-exposure to trauma increases the risk of serious psychiatric problems.[390]

Has our government and military learned *anything* about the human impact of war, the long-term consequences of exposure to high levels of combat stressors that have been public knowledge for several decades and what to do about it that is humane and ethically responsive? I fear that back (Vietnam) to the future (Iraq and Afghanistan) is already upon us. I hope and exhort that enough US citizens vow to do all that one can do to not ever again allow the government and US society to downplay the full human cost of war and our moral obligations to address not only the short-term but also the longer-term impact.

387. Jim Ferencak, Gautier. Letters to the Editor, *SunHerald*, Biloxi, MS (2005, August 21), D2.
388. Robert Burns, "Army general: US troops may be needed in Iraq through '09." The Associated Press. www.sunherald.com, (2005, August 21), C-1.
389. Douglass K. Daniel, "Senator: War crippling Mideast. Hagel, R-Neb., says Iraq resembles Vietnam." The Association Press. www.sunherald.com (2005, August 22), B-1.
390. Chedekel, L & Kauffman, M., "Emotional wounds don't end their war; troubled troops are back in battle." *www.sunherald.com,* (2006, May 18), B4.

This applies to the physical and emotional casualties who are combatants, their families and other citizens of the US and other countries that also are disadvantaged by the gross expenditures of human and monetary capital that this country pours into war.

In the words of Dwight David Eisenhower, upon his return from serving as Commander of the Allied Forces in Europe during World War II:

> Every gun that is made, every warship launched, every rocket fired, signifies in the final sense a theft from those who hunger and are not fed, those who are cold and not clothed. This world in arms is not spending money alone; it is spending the sweat of its laborers, the genius of its scientists, the hopes of its children.[391]

Pax mentis and *Semper fi.*

---

391. *ThinkExist.com.* Accessed April 2, 2006.

Appendix I. Cognitive Reframing Technique: Determining the Percentages of Responsibility

For readers who may wish to apply this technique to survivors of trauma other than war, the steps of the Percentages of Responsibility technique are described herein in wording that is generically applicable.

First Step: Facilitate a clear explication/description of the event and the survivor's perception and rationale for the degree of self-responsibility assumed. Give prompts to help the survivor verbalize the details, preferably in the first-person present tense, as if it were happening now.

And so you are feeling totally (or almost totally, or mostly, or . . .) responsible . . . Let's give a percentage to it. If we can assume that there is a total of 100% responsibility for . . . what percentage have you given to yourself, what percentage have you blamed yourself for? You don't have to be exact — just give an approximation — what you feel is the percentage of responsibility that is on you.

Are you sure that your responsibility is about __? Is it maybe more than that, or less than that?

Then, the survivor must verbalize exactly how much of the responsibility he/she has assumed. *It is essential not* to attempt to rescue or change the person's opinion at this time, no matter how unrealistic his/her assigned percentage of responsibility might seem.

Then, the survivor is challenged to convince the clinician/group how it was that he/she deserves to be held x% responsible. The survivor must indicate how and what he has been remembering and saying to him/herself to remain convinced of his/her (exaggerated) sense of responsibility.

Second Step: Challenge the survivor's exclusion or minimization (or inflation) of the role of others who were at the immediate scene of the trauma. This includes such persons as the perpetrator(s), and other observers/ witnesses: who kept silent, didn't step up and do something, or did too little too late . . .

Use the following prompts as you go through the roles of each of the people identified at the scene:

Really? Are you sure that is a fair percentage to assign to him/her? Should he get more or less than __to __ percent?

By the way, did you have any responsibility for that person being there that night?

(And, if he/she did have any responsibility for any other persons being there, he/she then is challenged to convince the clinician/group that the person himself had absolutely no responsibility for being there, and how the veteran had totally "forced" the other person to be there.)

The above strategy is then systematically applied *to all other persons* who were present at the actual scene of the trauma.

Once convinced that the survivor has considered all others who were there, he/she is again challenged (without worrying if the numbers add up to 100%) to make sure that he has applied the proper (in his own mind) amount of responsibility to each of them for what happened and didn't happen there involving that event.

Now, let's add up the percentages of responsibility for each person present (typically, it will be discovered that the total is well over 100%). The survivor is then confronted with this impossibility, since the total can only equal 100 percent.

Do you think that you need to reevaluate some or all of the percentages you have assigned? Is yours still x %, which means that all of these other people split up the remaining __ percent, yes?

Third Step: Challenge the survivor's exclusion or minimization of the indirect responsibility of others were not at the immediate scene of the trauma

Are there any other people who deserve some share of the responsibility for what happened that day? Are there others who directly or indirectly had something, anything, to do that influenced the event ever occurring in the first place, or who had some influence on what happened that day?

Do any of the following have any degree of responsibility whatsoever for what happened to you that day—or who have any degree of responsibility such as for supporting or ignoring, the war . . .

What about the public news media_(television, radio, newspapers, magazines) that oftentimes pays much more attention to what news that "sells" the best and attracts the most viewers—at the expense of really critical moral and social issues about what is really going on.

What about the entertainment industry that tends to glorify and glamorize war, and downplay the horrific nature of it?

What about our country, our society, John Q citizen: who go along with spending billions of dollars on new military weapons and maintaining a defense industry that dwarfs the military threat of any other country in the world — and who cut social programs first and threaten to rescind on our nation's long-term promise to our retired military?

Fourth Step: Re-challenge the survivor's sense of his/her own percentage of responsibility for behaviors and consequences regarding the trauma.

Now, let us return to you and what you did and did not do, and how much responsibility you had for being in the military in the first place, for being there that day, for what you did and did not do there that day? Because you were there, you did ___ and did ___ and did ___.

And so, we are not here to try and explain away any of whatever percentage of responsibility you truly believe and feel that you deserve for what happened that night — once you have fully considered all the others who deserve some responsibility, too.

And so, considering all the other factors and people both there and not there, what piece of the responsibility for ___ do you now believe is yours?

Fifth Step: Challenge the survivor to consider if he/she has been "punished" enough for his/her personal share of the responsibility for what happened

Now, tell me (us) how much you have suffered and punished yourself all these years over the ___ percent or so of the responsibility that you had blamed on yourself for what had happened.

In other words, take into account all the times you have suffered pain from remembering and agonizing over what happened, criticizing yourself, feeling guilty, screwing up your relationships, etc., because you were feeling so bad or so unable to forget? How much?

The clinician/group then discusses the degree of responsibility the person has now assigned internally, and how this percentage compares with the self-punishment suffered (which has been based on a much higher assumption of responsibility).

217

The survivor must now make a very clear, forceful statement to the clinician/group about if he has concluded whether he has engaged in (self-punishment, or been punished) "enough," "not enough," or "more than enough"—in comparison to his/her newly assigned percentage of responsibility. (It is often helpful to have the survivor repeat this statement to several individual group members.)

Sixth Step: Explicates a non-self-destructive plan to provide additional "payback" for one's share of the responsibility

The survivor is now challenged, again, to conclude if he/she "has been punished enough" or "has suffered enough" or "his/her family has suffered enough" for his/her percentage of the responsibility. If he/she has the slightest indication that he is not absolutely convinced that he/she has been punished or suffered enough, the client is facilitated to develop a non-self-destructive, "healthy" pay-back plan.

This is a plan that provides additional payback through its positive, quality of life sustaining, proactive stance, rather than through a self-destructive, reactive stance.

This significant reframing process will require considerable readjusting of cognitions, feelings and memories.

Seventh Step: Conceptualize and commit to a homework assignment

It is recognized that the survivor has just gone through a relatively quick process in which he/she almost surely has come to a substantially different perspective of his/her guilt regarding the trauma that has been bothering the survivor for months, years or decades. Naturally, the survivor will be full of an array of thoughts and feelings and memories, and will need some time to review, revise and consolidate his/her thinking and conclusions.

To this end, the survivor is now facilitated to:

Think about taking time at home to reflect on what has been discussed today, and truly take into account the full circle of persons and circumstances involved: was anyone missed who should be included, or anyone included who should be excluded from having any responsibility?

Review and re-calculate (if that seems appropriate) the set of percentages he has assigned to various people to ensure that they add up to 100%, and

Begin to develop an initial longer-range plan to provide additional pay-back, if any, that he/she feels and believes he must still provide—to include any specific steps and a time-table needed to undertake the positive, life-promoting payback plan.

Eighth Step: End the session in a way that recognizes and confirms:

1. What important things happened today
2. The strength and courage of the survivor to have been willing to go through this process and how this may have impacted on you the clinician and group members (if conducted in a group).

Appendix II. Rationale and Recommendations to Test New Trauma Treatment Protocols in the War Zone and Their Longer-Term Impact

An ethical trauma therapist in the civilian world typically does not do "exposure" or "uncovering" therapy with people who are currently in dangerous/ traumatizing environments — because the person needs to be in a "survival mode" to cope with existing, pending or potentially new traumatic situations. For example, the first line of counseling strategy with someone in a violent domestic relationship is to insure and promote their personal safety, which means an immediate cessation of all violence in the home — or leaving that violent relationship at least for the time being.[392]

It must be recognized that any interventions demonstrated to be effective in civilian environs have no corresponding evidence to affirm their effectiveness that if they are used in a war zone there will be a positive impact on short-term *and* longer-term post war zone functioning. Such studies have never been conducted.

Let me give an example. Someone is injured when a commuter helicopter crashes shortly after take-off from an airport in Los Angeles. He is traumatized by the crash and his injuries to the extent that he/she has recurring nightmares and disturbing memories of the event, finds it difficult to even think about helicopters, see pictures of helicopters or be in the vicinity of the sight or sound of them — let alone get close to one or attempt to ride in one again.

One accepted cognitive-behavioral treatment strategy would be to offer some form of gradual exposure or desensitization regarding the traumatic experience of being injured in a helicopter crash and to address the accompanying

---

392. Scurfield, 1994.

traumatizing memories, feelings and reactions. The client is then taken through a series of therapeutic steps, such as being exposed systematically to a series of thoughts about the event, perhaps leading to exposure to pictures or movies, and ultimately to the point where there is some direct exposure to a helicopter or subsequently perhaps eventually sitting in one or going up on a flight again in one. Such an intervention strategy must be planned, implemented and evaluated with the rigor and knowledge of available mental health research and program evaluation expertise.

Now, while a treatment protocol similar to that briefly described has been documented to be effective in treating PTSD related to such traumatic experiences in civilian life, the author is not aware of any empirical evaluation of the effectiveness of conducting such a treatment protocol *in a war zone*. For example, a soldier could have been riding in that very helicopter on a combat support mission in an occupied city in Iraq and suffered injuries in an ensuing crash caused by enemy fire. And subsequently that soldier has recurring nightmares, memories and disturbing fears about the event, can't stand the thought of getting back into a helicopter and is referred by his unit commander to a military mental health provider.

Would it be in this soldier's best mental health interests, both short and longer-term, to engage in an identical series of desensitization steps to get back into a helicopter and be "forced" to return to duty in a war zone where he will once again be a target and very possibly a repeat victim of another traumatic incident in a helicopter? Or, would it be appropriate to make significant modifications in the treatment protocol to account for the fact that that soldier is being desensitized to return to almost certain exposure to further trauma? Certainly, this strategy could be justified as a way to "conserve the fighting strength" and get the soldier back to duty ASAP.

However, would exposure to a subsequent additional violent traumatic experience in a helicopter exacerbate the original traumatic incident and not only trigger but promote even greater psychological trauma as a result of cumulative damage from the two helicopter traumatic events? And what would be better for the longer-term mental health of this soldier — to have been medically evacuated out of country after the first traumatic incident because he/she did not respond to 10 days of mental health interventions — or to have been "forced" to return to duty and then suffered this second similar traumatic incident?

Does the military chain of command, or military mental health providers for that matter, *care* — or should they — about which tactic would be more beneficial to the longer-term mental health of that individual soldier?

Military medical care providers will be in a double bind in terms of the understandable pressure from military authorities to focus on interventions to achieve short-term or acute benefits and to avoid, or give substantially less consideration to, the possibly competing benefits in the longer term, post-war. Also, there is the problem that many active duty personnel refuse or are very reluctant to utilize mental health mental health resources due to the risk to their military careers and the likely negative reactions from their peers.

In addition, there is a serious problem of confidentiality of medical records in the military.[393] Finally, frankly, there is a widespread perception that there are government and military officials who are not to be trusted in terms of the objectivity and completeness of their presentation and/or interpretation of data and analyses that might shed a critical or negative light on current military policies and procedures and on the actual and complete human cost of waging war.

Because of these factors, for the military alone to oversee, design, implement, analyze, interpret and publish the results of any such studies would be suspect to many outside observers. In this regard, the model that the Department of Veterans Affairs engaged in, concerning the National Vietnam Veterans Readjust Study[394] or a variation of thereof is worth considering. That would be to recruit an impeccable and diverse cohort of leading traumatologist researchers and thinkers (who do not have current active-duty, Guard or Reserve status) to develop the parameters and content of a national request for proposals (RFP). This RFP would lead to a contract to a civilian research group or consortium for just such an outcome research study of both the short and longer-term outcome of applying and comparing alternative trauma-focus treatment protocols to Armed Forces personnel pre-deployment, while deployed, post-deployment and post-military discharge—both shorter and longer-term. There also must be an over-sampling strategy to ensure that higher-risk categories of military personnel are included in the study in sufficient numbers to generate meaningful outcome data. This would include those exposed to high levels of combat, death and injured (front-line combat units, combat support units and medical personnel); racial minorities, women and those wounded in action.

It is remarkable to me that such a study has never been proposed, let alone implemented. Do we not care enough about the longer-term impact of military medical interventions on war zone veterans?

---

393. For an interesting discussion of the problems related to confidentiality of mental health information in the Army, in which a commander's "need to now" can supersede an Army mental health professional's right to maintain confidentiality of such records, see: J.F. Leso, "Confidentiality and the Psychological Treatment of US Army Aircrew Members." *Military Medicine*, 165 (4) (2000), 261-262.
394. See *A Vietnam Trilogy*, 2004.

APPENDIX III. BROAD-BASED COMMUNITY INVOLVEMENT IN SERVICES FOR RESERVISTS AND THEIR FAMILIES

In the fall of 2003, the Miami VA Healthcare System began to prepare for active duty reserve troops returning home.[395] Returning reservist soldiers are eager to come home to their families, readjust and rebuild their lives. They expect everything to be the same and believe they will be normal, but all soldiers come home changed and they learn again what normal means. Challenges include medical and/or psychological effects, family relationships, the specter of further deployment and for some reservists in Florida [and in Mississippi and Louisiana] deployment with hurricane disaster duty. Also, the reservists' families do not have the protections offered by the formal and informal support provided by military bases.

Concerns identified included: 1) providing a Seamless Care Transition Program for wounded soldiers transferring from a military hospital to a VA Medical Center, inpatient care; 2) applying the seamless care approach in an ambulatory care setting; and 3) conducting comprehensive psychosocial assessments by a social worker on each soldier registered for ambulatory care. The scope of the assessments was to a) increase the awareness of the soldier's medical and psychiatric needs, b) see that these needs were addressed in a timely continuum of care manner and c) understand each soldier's goals, strengths, support system, and internal and external stressors as he/she returns to the family and interfaces with the community.

---

395. The content of this appendix was provided on July 22, 2006, by Sherrill Valdes, social work supervisor, Miami VA Healthcare System. I have modified and rearranged the wording for formatting purposes.

Outreach activities to the military units were made to identify psycho-social stressors by speaking with soldiers, spouses and facilitating focus groups; identified issues addressed included employment, education, healthcare, family relationships, financial needs and spiritual concerns. The VA social workers explored community resources for this population, but discovered little or no awareness of the soldiers' family needs in the community, no communication regarding military families among existing services and a lack of resources or unmet needs for the family.

A proactive and advocate role was taken to increase community and civilian awareness of the soldiers and families, establish networking and provide appropriate services. In Sherrill Valdes' words:

> Community involvement means more than flag waving; the community must pro-vide a comprehensive "safety net" for our service men and women to help in their healing journey. The most essential truth about war and the citizens of a country in war is, "we are all in it together." "We have the troops who are directly in harms way, their families and significant others who support them. As citizens we vote, pay taxes, which are used for the war effort and support each soldier in country. Our responsibility as citizen's increases when military families live in our neighbor-hood and communities, to support families who have a member deployed and assist them with readjustment issues upon their return. The community bares the respon-sibility to provide a "safety net" which is present on the military bases for military families. How to identify, address and then provide such a plan may cause difficulty within the community. However, its efforts contribute to community well being as the returning soldiers are in all segments of the community.

> This is the model we employed. After identifying the needs with the help of the psy-chosocial assessment and outreach, our first task was to stabilize the family. We contacted the school system and helped them to establish ways to identify the chil-dren who had loved ones serving, had peer counselors work with them and if they needed additional help, a mental health agency agreed to work with the children on a sliding scale basis. We suggested support groups for the children, thus providing services that the family could utilize without much trouble for them. The agency also stated they would provide treatment for the spouses who were not deployed, thus, helping families who were not eligible for care at the VA and increasing treat-ment options for them. We identified an agency which would host the project on networking among agencies and focus on meeting the soldier's needs. After 2 ½ years, the school system has made a position for a social worker to identify the chil-dren and military families, assess their needs and treat them. The social worker is responsible to implement the program in all county schools.

> The community task force that was formed has been meeting for 2 ½ years. It has increased awareness in the community. For example, task force members empha-sized the need for availability of local resources provided in a timely manner. VA Social Work Service has developed a resource book (*Resources for returning Operation Iraqi freedom and Operation Enduring Freedom Veterans*), and two State agencies have required all their districts to comply with the model that was developed. Social Work Services [at the VA] continues to have an advocate role in the development of

a long term "safety net" plan to assist in the transition process. In addition, the community networking plan outreached to faith based agencies, businesses, volunteers and other agencies that could secure long term provision of services and support; they continue to identify needs and advocate for securing and maintaining services.

Recommended Readings

Archibald, H.C & Tuddenham, R.D, "Persistent stress reactions after combat. A 20-year follow-up." *Archives of General Psychiatry*, 12 (1965), 475-481.

Corbett, Sara, "The permanent scars of Iraq," *NY Times Magazine* (2004, February 15) 34-35.

Cozza, S.J., "Combat exposure and PTSD," *PTSD Research Quarterly*, 16 (1) (Winter, 2005), 1-7.

Eisenhart, R.W., "You can't hack it, little girl. A discussion of the covert psychological agenda of modern combat training." *Journal of Social Issues*, 31 (4), 13-23.

Frankl, Viktor, *Man's Search for Meaning: An Introduction to Logotherapy* (Boston Beacon Press, 1959).

Herman, Judith, *Trauma and Recovery: The Aftermath of Violence. From Domestic Abuse to Political Terror* (New York: Basic Books, 1997).

Hyer, L., Scurfield, R.M., Boyd, S., Smith, D. & Burke, J., "Effects of Outward Bound experience as an adjunct to in-patient PTSD treatment of war veterans." *The Journal of Clinical Psychology* 52 (3), (1996), 263-278.

Kulka, R.A., Schlenger, W.E., Fairbank, J.A., Hough, R.L., Jordan, K., Marmar, C.R. & Weiss, D.S. *Trauma and the Vietnam War Generation. Report of Findings From the National Vietnam Veterans Readjustment Study* (New York: Brunner/Mazel, 1990).

Kushner, Harold S. *When Bad Things Happen To Good People* (New York: Schocken Books, 1981).

Kutchins, H. and Kirk, S.A., "Bringing the war back to DSM" (101-125), *Making Us Crazy. DSM: The Psychiatric Bible and the Creation of Mental Disorders* (New York: The Free Press, 1997).

Lofton, R.J., "Advocacy and corruption in the healing professions." In C.R. Figley (Ed.) *Stress Disorders Among Vietnam Veterans: Theory, Research and Treatment* (209-230) (New York: Brunner/Mazel, 1978)

Lyke, M.L. "The unseen cost of war: American minds." *Seattle Post-Intelligencer* (2004, August 28).

Ninh, Bao, *The Sorrow of War*. (London: Minerva, 1994).

Scurfield, R.M., "Post-Katrina aftermath and helpful interventions on the Mississippi Gulf Coast, *Traumatology, Vol. 12* (2), (in-press, summer, 2006).

Scurfield, R.M. *Healing Journeys: Study Abroad with Vietnam Veterans. Vol. 2 of A Vietnam Trilogy* (New York: Algora Publishing, 2006).

Scurfield, R.M. *A Vietnam Trilogy. Veterans and Post Traumatic Stress: 1968, 1989 & 2000* (New York: Algora Publishing, 2004).

Scurfield, R.M., "The collusion of silence and sanitization about war: One aftermath of Operation Desert Storm," *Journal of Traumatic Stress*, 5 (3), (1992), 505-512.

Scurfield, R.M. & Mackey, David W., "Racism, trauma and positive aspects of exposure to race-related experiences: Assessment and treatment implications." *Journal of Ethnic & Cultural Diversity in Social Work, Vol. 10* (1), (2001), 23-47.

Scurfield, R.M., "Healing the Warrior: Admission of Two American Indian War-Veteran Cohort Groups to a Specialized In-patient PTSD Unit." *American Indian and Alaska Native Mental Health Research: The Journal of the National Center*, 6 (3), (1995), 1-22.

Scurfield, R.M., Wong, I.E., & Zeerocah, E.B., "Helicopter ride therapy for inpatient Vietnam veterans with PTSD," *Military Medicine*, 157 (1992), 67-73.

Schiraldi, G.R., *The Post-Traumatic Stress Disorder Sourcebook. A Guide to Healing, Recovery and Growth* (Los Angeles: Lowell House, 2000).

Terry, Wallace. *Bloods: An Oral History of The Vietnam War By Black Veterans*. (New York: Ballantine Books, 1984).

Van Devanter, Linda. *Home Before Morning. The True Story of an Army Nurse in Vietnam* (New York: Warner Books, 1983).

Wiest, Andrew, Root, Leslie and Scurfield, Raymond, "Post-traumatic stress disorder: The legacy of war." In A. Wiest & G. Jensen (Eds.), *War in the Age of Technology. Myriad Faces of Modern Armed Conflict* (New York & London: New York University Press, 2001), 295-332.

Wilson, John P. (Ed.), *Trauma Transformation and Healing: An Integrative Approach to Theory, Research and Post-Traumatic Therapy* (New York: Brunner/Mazel, 1989).

Yancey, Philip. *Where is God When It Hurts? A Comforting Healing Guide for Coping With Hard Times* (Grand Rapids, MI Zondevan, 1990).

ACKNOWLEDGMENTS

First and foremost are the hundreds of veterans of so many wars, peace-keeping operations and covert operations who have allowed us, the care providers, to bear witness as they laid bare their hearts and souls, nightmares, anguish, courage, strivings, redemption and perhaps above all, their worthiness; it has been a privilege and an honor, both breath-taking and humbling.

A very special acknowledgment is due to my wife, Margaret, Director, Fleet & Family Support Center, US Naval Construction Battalion, Gulfport, MS, for her content input and for insuring that I fully considered the realities of active duty military service in the world today; I have especially become very aware of the "can do" attitude, sacrifices and contributions of Navy Seabees and their families.

I cannot express enough my gratitude to LTC Kathy Platoni, clinical psychologist and Army reservist called to active duty. At the time I was writing this book and sending pre-publication excerpts to Kathy in Iraq, she was serving as the Deputy Commander for Clinical Services, of the 55th Medical Company (Combat Stress Control unit) in Iraq. We compared many notes and communications before, during and after she was serving our troops in Iraq. Kathy's contributions in this book, and to the US military, are priceless. Thank you, Kathy, and all of your military mental health and other medical colleagues.

Special acknowledgement goes to four long-time friends, colleagues and brother sojourners, all of whose support made this book possible: Vietnam veterans Steve Tice and Angelo Romeo, Vietnam Era Veteran John Wilson, and John Fulton, my inspirational and first VA Chief of Social Work. And while I have never met or communicated with him, through reading The Sorrow of War, North Vietnam Army veteran and author Bao Ninh has been an inspirational influence to always consider and honor the perspectives of the enemy and the civilian populations of the countries in which we have fought wars.

A very special acknowledgment is due the staff of programs serving veterans that I directed or collaborated with: the Vietnam Veteran's Liaison Unit in Los Angeles (Shad Meshad, Bruce Pentland, Jim Dwyer et al); the VA Vet Center Program at over 200 store-front locations nationwide; the Post-Traumatic Stress Treatment Program at American Lake VA, Tacoma, WA (Steve Tice, Ann Gregory, Tom Olson, Casey Wegner et al); the

Pacific Center for PTSD in Honolulu, HI (Jim Cordeiro, Lori Daniels, Allan Perkal, Winona Kay et al); the PTSD Residential Rehabilitation Program in Hilo (Bridget Souza Malama, Jim Cariaso, Emmet Finn et al); and the Biloxi VA, Gulfport Division — since destroyed by Hurricane Katrina (Leslie Root et al.) and Biloxi Vet Center (Harry Becnel et al.). And I am indebted to Sherrill Valdes at the Miami Healthcare system for her contributions to the expanding circle of healing chapter and for her decades of dedicated service to veterans and their families — and to many other unnamed VA staff throughout the country.

My knowledge and perspective reflected in this volume has been enriched by my collegial relationships with many, to include: Charles Figley, whose writings and leadership continue to enlighten the field of traumatology; Bruce Lackie (who has very generously kept me abreast of important materials relevant for this book after Hurricane Katrina destroyed my university office and who provided me with many boxes of books to help me start to replenish my library); Glen Schiraldi whose book, *The Post-Traumatic Stress Disorder Sourcebook*, is a great compendium about trauma particularly suited as a self-help resource); "sister" Janet Viola; the VA National Center for PTSD, especially the leadership of Matt Friedman, Fred Gusman, Bruce Hiley-Young, Joe Ruzek, Terry Keane and associates; Frank Walker, Jerry Melnyk, Rose Sandecki, Nelson Korbs, Chuck Causey and Jonathan Shay; and the late Chaim Shatan, Erwin Parson, Sarah Haley, Bob Laufer, Raoul Espinosa, Raymond Clark and Al Trujillo.

As a faculty member at the School of Social Work, University of Southern Mississippi since 1998, my appreciation for Director Mike Forster and his support of my writings; and for our previous social work secretaries (Tammy Moss and Angela Benvenutti) and their invaluable support, beautiful personalities and professional assistance with my many manuscripts. University of Southern Mississippi History Professor Andy Wiest has been outstanding in teaching military history and in leadership of study-abroad and veteran-related projects; indeed, there would have been no Vietnam Study Abroad course 2000 if not for Andy's vision and leadership. My thanks to LTC David D. Rabb for sharing information about the Kuhlmann Group Debriefing Model used in Iraq; to Chris Mapp for his editing input and to Algora Publishing for supporting publication of a three-volume series that was necessary to more fully explicate the impact of war and what to do about it.

In closing, this book would not have been possible without the support, inspiration and manuscript input of my wife Margaret and my sister Tomi; our wonderful young adult children Helani, Armand and Nicolas; and my extended Scurfield, Monsour, Yaghmai, Niolet, MacDonald and Lytle families. All have been invaluable to my post-war readjustment and hence to making this book possible. Truly, I am blessed to have such a wealth of relationships.

Printed in the United States
60764LVS00005B/292-336

9 780875 864853